VESTIGE OF EDEN, IMAGE OF ETERNITY

Daniel Toma

VESTIGE OF EDEN, IMAGE OF ETERNITY

Common Experience, the Hierarchy of Being, and Modern Science

Franciscan University Press

Franciscan University Press
1235 University Boulevard
Steubenville, OH 43952
740-283-3771

Distributed by:
The Catholic University of America Press
c/o HFS
P.O. Box 50370
Baltimore, MD 21211
800-537-5487

Cataloging-in-Publication Data available from the Library of Congress.

Casebound ISBN: 978-0-9995134-7-7
Paperback ISBN: 978-0-9995134-8-4

Cover and text design: Kachergis Book Design
Cover photograph by Dr. Henry Oakeley, courtesy of the Wellcome Collection

Printed in the United States of America.

To Margaret, Anastasia, Paul, and Jack: my purpose in life

To St. Thérèse of Lisieux

The consideration of creatures is also necessary to set aside errors, not only for the building up of truth, but also for the destruction of errors. For errors about creatures sometimes lead one astray from the truth of faith, so far as errors are inconsistent with true knowledge of God. . . . Through ignorance of the nature of things, and consequently, of his own place in the order of the universe, this rational creature, man, who by faith is led to God as his last end, believes that he is subject to other creatures to which he is in fact superior. Such is evidently the case with those who subject human wills to the stars. . . . It is therefore evident that the opinion is false of those who asserted that it made no difference to the truth of faith what anyone holds about creatures, so long as we think rightly about God. For an error concerning creatures, by subjecting them to causes other than God, spills over into false opinion about God, and takes men's mind away from Him, to whom faith seeks to lead them.

–St. Thomas Aquinas, *Summa contra Gentiles*

One thing have I asked of the Lord, that will I seek after:
That I may dwell in the house of the Lord all the days of my life,
to behold the beauty of the Lord and to inquire in his temple.

–Psalm 27:4

CONTENTS

Preface ix
Acknowledgments xiii

Introduction: Fascinated by Nature and Science 1

PART I. ROADBLOCKS TO REALITY

1. The Common Experience of Nature 19
2. Science and Common Experience 40
3. The Immateriality of the Intellect 57
4. Interlude on Reason and Faith 83

PART II. THE VESTIGE OF EDEN

5. Life: Flat or Full? 105
6. The Perfection of the Cosmos 123
7. Science in a New Cosmology 142
8. The Truth of Two Tales 176

PART III. THE IMAGE OF ETERNITY

9. The End of Human Life: The Holy Trinity 205
10. Attaining Our End through Deification 225
11. The Church and Her Liturgy 242
12. The Cosmos as a Ladder of Liturgical Perfection 262

PART IV. CONCLUSION

13. Anaphysics: Understanding from the Height of Reality 293
14. Back to the Woods and Beyond 304

Bibliography 317
Index 327

PREFACE

Three great cosmological worldviews arose from the development and union of ancient and medieval thought. These were the natural law/natural sciences worldview of the Latin West, the hierarchical philosophical worldview of Greece, and liturgical worldview of the Hebrew/Syriac world, all in their own manner attempting to express a similar truth. Each had origins in the ancient world and reached a synthesis under scholastic medieval thinkers, such as Albert the Great and Thomas Aquinas. As the synthesis of these three worldviews developed, it was enriched by and incorporated into Catholic tradition and became identified as a cosmological worldview of the Catholic Church. *Vestige of Eden, Image of Eternity* (*VEIE*) offers this worldview, updated with modern science, for consideration in modern discussions regarding science, philosophy, and religion. Little known today, this worldview is completely novel to most modern ears, including academic philosophers and theologians, and even more so to scientists. This volume is not primarily intended for academic specialists, though I trust many of them will profit from it. *VEIE* is intended to be a generalist work appealing to a broad audience.

This worldview maintains a correspondence and connection between the structure of the universe and the divine plan of creation. The hierarchical structure of creation, known by our reason, is a reflection of and participation in the liturgy of the Church, a "blueprint" for reality. The primary purpose of this creation, as stated by Irenaeus of Lyons, is that the world was a "divinely appointed milieu" for "producing mature persons to reflect the life of God."[1] Creation is made for deification, for drawing creatures with intellects into a *participation in the very life of the three persons of the Trinitarian God.*[2] Everything in creation from the highest angel to the lowest amoeba and subatomic particle somehow aids in this purpose to a greater or lesser degree.

Therefore this worldview necessarily draws on a wide range of disciplines – theology, philosophy, and various sciences – to paint a sweeping portrait of the whole, a cosmic panorama that ranges from the minutest to the most grandiose of creatures. With such a scope, it is not possible to achieve academic rigor at every point of argumentation, but the evidence adduced here is sufficient to demonstrate the *reasonableness* of this worldview. Because of this broad sweep, it is necessary and possible to rely on more general sources. For instance, for theological sources regarding general Catholic teaching, support is noted in the *Catechism of the Catholic Church* and then embellished in particular with St. Thomas Aquinas, Matthias Scheeben, Dionysius the Areopagite, and St. John of the Cross. I use other sources as needed for less known topics, such as the liturgical structure of reality. Philosophically, I rely heavily on Thomas Aquinas and Aristotle. Instead of comparing various thinkers and academic opinions, I spend time trying to explain more difficult concepts and form a narrative appealing to a general audience. Here again, the focus is to limit academic disputation and minutiae in order to appeal to and keep the attention of the intended reader.

To further facilitate this narrative, I have taken the liberty of lumping together two groups of thinkers, those I call "ancients and medievals," and those I call "moderns." This is admittedly an abstraction, but a necessary one

1. Nichols, *Catholic Theology*, 69–70.

2. Levering, *Doctrine of Creation*, 52: "Creation is thereby linked with deification; it is a matter of the cooperative response of creatures to the divine ideas." In particular, as noted in the above quote and explained on other pages (52–53, 71, 85, 88, 97, and 271), at the center of the divine plan for creation is deification. This book by Levering, a theologian, has overlaps with mine, but with different emphases.

to streamline a comparison and contrasting of what I think are two roughly distinct forms of approach to reality; the former is in general more open to immaterial reality, the latter more concerned with the material aspect of things. I would like to stress here that this by no means is an intent to completely separate the two. There are good and bad aspects of both groups, as well as areas of overlap.

Some time ago, I had a discussion with a colleague, a professional biologist, regarding the nature of this book. When I stated that my book examined theology, philosophy, and science, I was immediately stopped short: "I know science, I have a little idea of what theology concerns (something about God), but I have no idea and have never understood what philosophy is about." For such people this book is written: the modern person of all stripes who is not acquainted with premodern thought, as well as the educated nonspecialist who is interested in a broad range of topics. After decades of discussing these matters with college and graduate students, I am sure that they too will find the themes and evidence of this volume engaging.

ACKNOWLEDGMENTS

Many people contributed to the ideas and reading of this book over the past serval years. I explicitly mention several below, but this list is by no means exhaustive. I am indebted and grateful to all.

Funding for the writing of *VEIE* came from two sources. First, I would like to thank the Hektoen Institute of Chicago and Dr. Patrick Guinan. Dr. Guinan approached me in 2011, after a talk I gave in Chicago on subject matter that became part of the basis of *VEIE*, with the idea of putting it in writing. Dr. Guinan and the Hektoen Institute funded my work during the summers of 2012, 2013, and 2014, and for 20 percent of my sabbatical year during academic year 2013–14; the Hektoen Institute funded my sabbatical and one of the summers, and Dr. Guinan funded the other two summers. Dr. Guinan also funded the first edit. Second, I would like to thank Minnesota State University, Mankato, for funding 80 percent of my sabbatical year, when I wrote the majority of the text.

I extend my deep appreciation to the library staff at Bethany Lutheran College of Mankato, Minnesota. The library at the college generously provided me with a small room – desk, chair, and bookshelves – in which to write during the whole of my sabbatical.

Special thanks needs to be given as well to Kenneth Howell, PhD, who read and reread the manuscript, edited it, helped with reviewer critiques, did translations from Latin, consulted for the first (historical) half of chapter 4, and spent untold hours on the phone discussing it. I cannot express sufficient appreciation to him.

Likewise, I would like to thank Richard Cross, PhD, for years of discussion leading up to *VEIE*, for reading it, helping with reviewer critiques, consulting on parts of chapter 7 dealing with psychology and Isaac Newton, and for the many suggestions while I wrote. Dr. David Pence and I spent many lunches together discussing, arguing (to the scandal of those eating at tables near us), and hashing out the placement of science in a Catholic setting. Pat Harrington read the manuscript and contributed many corrections. Several other people contributed corrections as well. Thank you for all of them.

Thank you to Matthew Tsakanikas, PhD, of the Theology Department at Christendom College for helping with the theology of *VEIE* by participating in many discussions, contributing several sources, and helping to answer some of the reviewer critiques. He also was the first "publicist," having taught several of the ideas contained in *VEIE* in one of his theology classes at Christendom, beginning a few years before publication.

I cannot leave out Fr. Hugh Barbour, O. Praem., of St. Michaels Abbey in Silverado, California, who, among many things, introduced me to the wisdom of the Christian East by having me read St. Dionysius the Aeropagite and by being a "tutor" of sorts over the seven years I lived in California regarding St. Thomas Aquinas and St. Dionysius. Thank you.

Thanks are extended to Msgr. Stuart Swetland, president of Donnelly College in Kansas City, Kansas, for the help and encouragement he gave me.

Thanks to Fr. Tim Biren, all the students, and Fellowship of Catholic Undergraduate Students (FOCUS) team members at St. Thomas More Newman Center in Mankato, Minnesota, from roughly 2010 to 2014, for feedback from talks I gave there and discussion groups that contained material upon which *VEIE* is based, as well as for being great students and people with whom to interact.

Last, but by no means least, I have to say thank you and extend my love to my wife Margaret, for being who she is and putting up with me, and to my three children Anastasia, Paul, and Jack, for being themselves.

INTRODUCTION

Fascinated by Nature and Science

As a boy of eleven, moving suddenly from a sitting to a standing position one evening, I no longer believed in God. Maybe God did exist, but I just couldn't assent to belief at that moment. It scared me to death. All at once, I was faced with a world independent of what my parents told me. What occurred to me was a question: Why should I believe? In retrospect, one of the reasons for this question was all that I had read of modern science. All the science books I had read kicked the pedestal out from under me, and I had no way to ascend to anything higher than the world around me. They broke any connection between the world of faith and the world of science. I was a product of the modern tension between science and religion that had permeated our culture and educational system. This event has driven my life ever since. I have wanted to know: What is the nature of Reality?

Growing up, I was always fascinated by nature and science. As I roved the hills and hardwood forests of rural southern Indiana with my ever-faithful Airedale Terrier Bliss, I observed and experienced the natural world in the unfolding of the seasons. From the steamy, shimmering landscape of summer, to the brilliant maples, tulip poplars, and beeches of autumn, to the quiet brown countryside and slate skies of winter that yielded to the diverse hues of green in spring, I reveled in the beauty around me. Performing many outdoor labors on a small farm with the comings and goings of the denizens of the woods and creeks, I pondered the origin and cause of things. Questions of truth, ultimate origins, and purpose have been my life's passion, my only real concern.

Since those days some thirty to forty years ago, I have thought almost continuously about science, the universe, ultimate causes, and truth. While majoring in biology at Indiana University, I also embraced the Catholic faith of my ancestors as my own. After studying for the priesthood as a seminarian for a couple of years, I began teaching both religion and science classes in Catholic high schools. When I decided to pursue a doctorate in behavioral genetics at the University of Illinois at Urbana-Champaign, I knew I was following a course prepared for me by those early encounters with nature in the hills of southern Indiana. Later, as a research scientist at the Neurosciences Institute in La Jolla, California, I studied the effects of gene expression in the brain on behavior. Now, as a professor of biology at a midwestern university, those same questions are with me today. For nearly forty years, I have not ceased to wonder about ultimate questions.

My yearnings for knowledge have not been unique to me. Christof Koch, a leading researcher on the biological basis of consciousness, states in his book *Consciousness: Confessions of a Romantic Reductionist*:

> Religion and science are two modes of understanding the world, its origin, and its meaning. Historically, they have opposed each other. Ever since the beginning of the age of Enlightenment, religion and the West have been in retreat, losing one battle after another. One setback was the Copernican revolution, which removed earth from the center of the universe to the distant reaches of the galaxy containing a hundred billion stars. But the worst blow was delivered by Darwin's theory of evolution by natural selection. It removed humans from their God-given dominion over earth and replaced the epic story of Genesis with a tale stretching across the eons, full of sound and fury, signifying nothing. Evolution dethroned humans from their exalted position; we are but one species among innumerable others. In the molecular signature of our genes we can trace our descent from the primate lineage and, in the remoteness of deep time, from pond scum.
>
> As a consequence, much religious doctrine is incompatible with the modern worldview. This mismatch should not be surprising, as the myths and doc-

> trines that underpin the great monotheistic religions were formed at a time when little was known about the size, age, and evolution of Earth or the organisms populating it.[1]

Koch encapsulates the dominant academic opinion on the relationship of religion and science when he states that religion has been losing the battle to science over the nature of the universe ever since the Enlightenment, and that Copernicus destroyed the idea that the earth was at the center of everything. Then, according to this view, Darwin destroyed the creation account in Genesis, replacing it with the theory of evolution, which ultimately tells us that we are products of pond scum. The result is that religion and science are incompatible because people before the modern era were ignorant of the findings of modern science.

Koch's historical and philosophical opinion is an archetype of modern scientific opinion. A 1998 survey in *Nature*, one of the most prestigious scientific journals, found that only 7 percent of scientists in the National Academy of Sciences believe in a personal God, and 7.9 percent in human immortality.[2] Another study from 2009 showed that 51.5 percent of all professors in twenty disciplines (not just scientists) at institutions from community colleges to elite universities believed in a personal God, much lower than the national average of 95 percent.[3] A 2010 study of natural and social scientists at twenty-one elite American research universities found 36 percent believing in a personal God.[4] Among those academics who do believe, it is my experience that many would likely still agree with Christof Koch, that religious doctrine and the modern worldview are incompatible. They, in practice, wall off their professional life from their faith. I have found as a university professor that many students also hold to the incompatibility between religious doctrine and science, even those that are serious about their faith. They simply relinquish the argument about nature and the universe to the dominant scientific opinion.

For several years after my crisis of faith at age eleven, I pondered these questions, sometimes believing more, sometimes less. Before my college years, I reflected on them in view of my experience of the natural world in

1. Koch, *Consciousness*, 15.

2. Gregory, *Unintended Reformation*, 35n2.

3. Gregory, *Unintended Reformation*; Pew Research, *Scientists and Belief*, 3.

4. Gregory, *Unintended Reformation*, 35n2.

the hills of southern Indiana. In my studies as a microbiology major, the questions persisted and became more sophisticated. I spent many hours in the Indiana University library, pouring over philosophical and theological works from the Greek and medieval thinkers. Nestled among those learned tomes was a detailed two-volume work by the twentieth-century Thomistic philosopher and theologian Reginald Garrigou-Lagrange, *God: His Existence and Nature*. For a year and a half, I lived and breathed this work and persisted in getting others to explain to me the Aristotelian concepts that Garrigou-Lagrange used. I went to the root of the question of whether it was reasonable to believe in God. I found it was and in so doing rediscovered my Catholic faith. After years of reflection, I am now convinced that my experiences of nature in the rolling hills of southern Indiana were a necessary preparation to accept what I have written in this book. Nor was I alone, for the greatest minds of natural philosophy and theology confirmed it. A correct schooling by nature frees the intellect to grasp the Cause of nature.

Scientist to the Core

Science has captivated my imagination as much as nature itself. The universe is around fourteen billion years old. Nonliving and living things developed over this period, governed by the laws of physical matter. There is a sequence of simple to more complex life forms in the fossil record, and I believe that atoms and molecules and other theoretical entities do exist. By and large, I accept the findings of the modern sciences; I do not yearn for a return to a prescientific age. Only an irrational person would do that. Science and technology have given us many things and released our lives from much toil, hardship, and misery that our ancestors faced. I would not be alive were it not for modern medicine—I was a sickly child prior to about age six—and none of my own children would be here either, as they were all born prematurely. Thanks to modern science, my children and I are in good health and no worse for wear. Additional billions would not be here if it weren't for modern agriculture and the green revolution, both products of modern science.[5]

5. Easterbrook, "Forgotten Benefactor of Humanity." Easterbrook was the first to make the claim of a billion humans saved from starvation by Norman Borlaug, father of the Green Revolution and Nobel Peace Prize winner in 1970. Many others seem to agree with this estimate.

Beyond its utilitarian role, I find science fascinating for itself. Besides experiencing the outdoors as a child, two things fired my desire for scientific knowledge. The first was fossils and dinosaurs. Before moving to southern Indiana in my early teens, I grew up on the other side of the Ohio River in northern Kentucky. My father, a mechanical engineer, had some land south of Louisville. The Ohio River and its adjacent tributaries in that area of the country are prime Devonian fossil territory.[6] The creek beds where I walked were covered with beautiful fossils. I collected grocery bags full before I was twelve. Studying these fossils and reading about prehistoric animals constantly occupied my imagination.

I am also a child of the Apollo program of the late 1960s and early 1970s. The 1969 Apollo 11 moonwalk by Neil Armstrong and Edwin Aldrin was my second clear recollection of a public event, next to the 1968 World Series. I sat captivated in front of the television, taking in every moment of the next six Apollo moon shots, which culminated in the successful Apollo 17 landing in the Taurus-Littrow Valley, and the three days on the moon by Harrison Schmitt and Eugene Cernan, the last man to walk on the moon. The explorations of the lunar rover across the foreboding alien moonscapes fired my imagination and left me awestruck by the power and capabilities of modern science. Few things created by human ingenuity are more awe-inspiring than the liftoff of the Saturn V launch vehicle, arguably the most impressive machine ever made, with its nearly eight million pounds of thrust generated by fifteen tons of propellant per second, equal to that of a nuclear weapon. Its slow release over a few minutes of flight time arched the Saturn V into the blue sky on a pillar of liquid fire. I can still sit captivated while repeatedly watching videos of these launches after a hard day's work.

I have never lost interest in science. In my late thirties, I checked the Mars Odyssey and Spirit Rover website *every day* for the first year they were on Mars. I am probably the biggest fan of the effort to clone a woolly mammoth; I search the website for news on its progress on a regular basis. I fancy myself something of an amateur expert on elephant evolution in this con-

6. The Ohio River area near Louisville, Kentucky, is one of the best places in the world to find Devonian era (400 million years ago) fossils, such as crinoids, brachiopods, corals, and mollusks (see the Falls of the Ohio website, accessed November 2, 2018, http://www.fallsoftheohio.org/visitor_info.html).

text. Today, in my fifties, I retain a childlike wonder that modern science has given us many things that hold out great promise.

By the time I began my PhD work around the age of thirty, the questions I had regarding belief in God were long settled. These questions had passed on to devouring as much as I could about my faith, reading in theology, philosophy, and spirituality and working out in detail the basis of classical philosophical ideas for demonstrating immaterial existence. My research topic concerned the molecular genetic basis of social behavior in honeybees. Here as well, the power of modern science was evident. One could manipulate the demographics of a colony of bees and change individual bee behavior. Further, science revealed a highly complex system of organisms in bees[7] – thus a detailed highly ordered system in nature was opened up to me. And yet many of my colleagues used this information to undergird ideas opposed to faith. As a result, I found in my work an interesting dichotomy. I sat for many hours watching and collecting bees in front of colonies. Their behavior was fascinating in ways that were an extension of my experiences in Indiana. But many of the people I encountered had left their faith, or at least thought religion was opposed to reason. Two fundamentally different insights into the same science presented themselves. Why? Sitting at the bench for hours putting together scientific experiments, it was at this point that I began to home in on the nature of scientific knowledge. What were the assumptions undergirding a scientific experiment that in the end yielded this presumed protest to faith?

With my PhD in hand, I moved on to the Neurosciences Institute in California in the late 1990s. At the time, it was a wonderful enclave of scientists, headed by Nobel Laureate Gerald Edelman and devoted to one mission: the study of the biological basis of consciousness and the functioning of the brain. Here again, the power of science was more than evident. I worked on gene expression in the brain of a model genetic organism, the fruit fly, and was able to alter its behavior by introducing doses of a given gene.[8] One really can precisely engineer life. But here the dichotomy between my beliefs and those of the other scientists was even more extreme. Except for one tech-

7. Winston, *Biology of the Honey Bee*, 72–213. See also two excellent books by Dr. Tom Seeley, *Honeybee Democracy* and the *Wisdom of the Hive.*

8. Toma et al., "Identification of Genes," 349–53.

nician, to the best of my knowledge, I was the only one with any religious beliefs.

It was there that I became acquainted with Christof Koch's scientific work.[9] His work, in my opinion, counts among the more profound efforts in the noble enterprise of science. I agree with Koch that, as a matter of historical fact, religion has been losing the battle to science concerning the nature and meaning of the universe, in both academia and in public opinion, but I agree with little else in his philosophizing about science or its significance. That is one of the key points in this book, namely, the difference between scientific data on the one hand and philosophizing about science on the other. That difference is what accounts for the divergent views on the implications of science.

The facts of science are just that: facts. As I sit here writing, my glass of water is more or less half filled. Or is it half empty? The fact is that there is half in the cup. That is the fact. The interpretation of whether the glass is half full or half empty depends on something beyond the fact: in this case, one's state of mind. Am I more optimistic or pessimistic at present? Regarding the fact of the amount of water in the glass, either statement is equally true. While in this case both statements are equally true, is it possible that we could have differing frameworks, which are truly better or worse, to discuss facts? Scientific research, as science, collects facts; that is all. Science needs a broader framework or philosophy, a worldview if you will, to understand them. Different worldviews differ profoundly in their assumptions.

The promise and success of modern science are also two of its biggest problems. Science *captivates* our imagination, giving it an aura beyond its capacity. Moon landings, space stations, black holes, quasars, dinosaurs, nuclear reactors, genetic engineering – in short, all the things discovered by science – are fascinating. We learn how nature works to such a degree that

9. Christof Koch was, until 2013, the Lois and Victor Troendle Professor of Cognitive and Behavioral Biology in the Division of Biology and the Division of Engineering and Applied Science at the California Institute of Technology in Pasadena. Presently, he is president and chief scientific officer of the Allen Institute for Brain Science in Seattle, Washington (see "Christof Koch, Ph.D.," Allen Institute for Brain Science, accessed March 1, 2019, https://alleninstitute.org/what-we-do/brain-science/about/team/staff-profiles/christof-koch/). He is among the leading authorities in the world regarding the biological basis of consciousness. While I am critical and disagree with much of his philosophical thought, I have the utmost regard for him as a scientist, and for his scientific work.

we can effectively control powerful forces. For this reason, science has a captivating power that is incontestable. It is in the appeal to the imagination – evidenced by the wild success of science fiction books and movies – that it perhaps exerts its greatest public influence.

This is driven home to me when I teach introductory genetics. Students do not seem to like classical genetics in the first part of the class – many claim it is boring – and are much more interested in modern molecular genetics. Yet classical genetics established the principles of the field, and learning it requires much more pure intellectual exercise than imagination. Modern molecular genetics, while glitzy, is simply an extension of the old. This glitziness, manifested in the power to alter living systems, holds interest in the subject much more because it stimulates the imagination. Who wouldn't rather learn the basis for cloning a mammoth than understand the basis for Mendel's ratios of peas? Classical genetics and traditional philosophy and theology are primarily intellectual efforts that take disciplined imaginations to understand them properly. Aristotle said that undisciplined emotions interfere with intellectual thought.[10] A wild imagination pulled this way and that by emotions severely distracts the mind.

Does that mean that parts of the scientific enterprise are bad because of their attraction to our imagination? Absolutely not! Our imaginations are an essential part of our human nature. We use the imagination in all our thoughts. Yet we must not overestimate the limits of our scientific imaginations, as is often done. Everything has limits and so does science. It is not the fault of science but a fault in our thinking, in our worldview. And it is a serious fault. Small mistakes in understanding the world and the limits to our knowledge cause great errors in the end.

Are we simply products of material forces, or are we also products of something beyond matter? And can the natural world lead us to true knowledge of this something beyond? Must the findings of modern science and the beliefs of religion be in such radical opposition? The answer to these questions radically alters how we approach life. The religious believer can't

10. One of the general thrusts of Aristotle's ethics, echoed as well in his *De Anima*, is that proper knowledge occurs when one holds oneself ready for it. This occurs either through the cultivation of virtue (and hence ordered emotions) or when nature orders a person internally through time or circumstances (Aquinas, *Aristotle's Physics* VII, lec. 6).

wall off his faith from nature because he is part of it. Unfortunately, many (if not most) Christians in the modern era have done precisely that. They have abandoned all the cosmological representations by which faith has been expressed. These are acts of desperation and are completely unnecessary. Cosmological representations are our first scriptural presentations, the very forms in which God chose to speak about himself.[11] But if we disregard these representations, what remains of our faith? The Christian philosopher Pope John Paul II, in his encyclical letter on Faith and Reason (*Fides et Ratio*), reminds us that the same God who reveals himself as Father is also the One who creates and sustains nature.[12] We cannot be intellectual schizophrenics. We live our life in the material world; faith cannot be lived with our head in the clouds. It does matter what we think of our universe; it matters greatly.

Understanding the Playing Field

In addition to roving about the countryside with my Airedale Bliss, I watched and played baseball. Perhaps my first memory of a public event was the 1968 World Series between Mickey Lolich and Denny McClain of the Detroit Tigers and Lou Brock of the St. Louis Cardinals.[13] Lolich won Most Valuable Player because he set a series record in winning all three games he pitched, one that stands to this day. The Tigers were down three games to one but came back to win three in a row. The 1968 World Series was also interesting in that both teams won several games in the other team's ballpark. Anyone who has followed sports knows this is an exception to the rule. Any set of statistics will show that most teams win more home games than away games. Why is this? It is because they know their own park, its feel, the

11. Smith, *Wisdom of Ancient Cosmology*, 5–6. The citation is of material in the foreword by Jean Borella, who presents a good discussion of the impact on Christian thought that occurs by abandoning the frameworks more proper or compatible to Christianity. Regarding the book as a whole, I have mixed feelings about it. There are parts that I think are extremely insightful and well argued, while I approach other parts, such as chapters arguing for a young earth on the basis of science, with skepticism. Smith argues for a young earth based on some cutting-edge physics, such as white hole theory, which I am not competent to judge. As I discuss in this book, however, I hold to an old earth and think this perfectly compatible with the Faith.

12. John Paul II, *Fides et Ratio*, 34.

13. "1968 World Series," Baseball Almanac, accessed March 1, 2019, http://www.baseball-almanac.com/ws/yr1968ws.shtml.

fans—it is *home*. You always get more done at home than on the road because it is the focal point of organization for your life. You know home best and are most comfortable there.

This is precisely the problem for religious people, particularly Christians. Christians have no home ballpark in which to think about and integrate modern knowledge into their religious beliefs. They only play away games. Most do not even know what their ballpark, or framework, is when thinking about reality. They believe in God as a Trinity of Persons and that he sent his Son Jesus Christ, but they have no idea how a proper view of the universe and its structure relates to these truths. In other words, how did God create the ballpark in which his creatures order and organize their lives? Most Christians don't even know they have a ballpark of their own.

They assume that a secular worldview is true without really examining it because of the way they have been educated. That is one of the major reasons Christians fail to integrate their science with their religious beliefs; they only think about and debate modern knowledge in the ballpark (framework) formulated by secularists. Worse than that, they assume that the other team's ballpark is the right place to think and debate. If you play according to the other team's rules, you will get burned more often than not. Christians have lost their framework, their story as it were, for explaining the things of the world; that is why they lose so often. They reflexively assume the general philosophical outlook of secular materialism in many areas of thought and public policy. They have lost before ever beginning. The problem is that there are fundamental differences in assumptions between their view and that of a materialist worldview concerning reality. It is in these assumptions that the real heat of the debates lies. Christof Koch's statements about the universe, about religion, and about the ignorance of premodern people crucially depend on a few critical assumptions. Foundations are critical.

After decades of conversing with scientists, sitting at laboratory benches, and thinking about exactly what I was doing in experiments, these differences have surfaced. First, can science say anything about the possibility of beings beyond matter (God, angels, souls)? Koch probably says yes[14] (science

14. Koch, *Consciousness*, 165–84. I say "probably," in that there is a logical inconsistency in what he says. Koch states that "the only certain answers come from science" (184). He argues against all traditional notions of an immaterial soul and ideas of God (deism, theism, the God of the Old and New Testaments).

can say they don't exist), and I would say no! But if science can't say anything about the immaterial world, does that mean we can have no rational knowledge of it? In other words, are things not consisting of matter per se irrational and unknowable? Koch would say yes,[15] and I would say no. At the heart of these two questions is an even deeper one. What is the basis for our claims to know reality? Reviewing history shows that there *really* is a difference between pre- and post-Enlightenment thought; there has been a fundamental shift in what it means to know reality.[16] Therein lies the biggest problem. This shift in thinking has removed our access to meaning and purpose in reality. Our modern world is faced with a crisis of meaning.[17]

Those differences bear on a crucial question. Is there anything about us humans that is immaterial? If so, can we know it? Koch says no,[18] and I say yes. The human intellect is an immaterial thing. This is one of the lynchpins that makes a world of difference. The answer to the question of the intellect naturally leads to another. In addition to human reason, is faith itself reason-

---

He argues strongly against the account of Jesus's turning water into wine as violating the laws of the physical universe (173–75), in a fashion suggesting that he misunderstands, as I argue in chapter 3 regarding his idea of the soul, the possibility of transcendent reality and what it implies. And if a God is truly transcendent (beyond matter and its laws), how can science, which is limited to the empirical (matter), as I argue in chapter 2, say anything about reality that is truly transcendent? Koch states, "I do believe that some deep and elemental organizing principle created the universe and set it in motion for a purpose I cannot comprehend" (183) and then identifies this "principle" as something close to the idea of Spinoza's God, which is not much help because there is widespread debate regarding exactly what Spinoza's God was. Many think it an abstract type of pantheism. Based on Koch's own arguments in his chapter 10, devoted to issues of religion, God, and transcendence, where he claims science and empirical research as the only certain knowledge and implies that a belief in reality beyond matter is irrational ("we search in vain for direct empirical evidence for such an eternal being above and beyond natural forces"), one would have to think of the idea Koch has in mind as some type of "principle" that depends on matter, which it in turn somehow organizes. This idea is consistent with his idea of a "soul" as "conscious phenomenal experience" (168) distinct from but dependent on the underlying physical substrate and not immortal: "once the underlying physical system disintegrates [it] is extinguished" (168). This lack of true transcendence and rational discourse regarding transcendent being places Koch far from any Christian or ancient Greek notion of transcendent reality: God, angels, or souls. Likewise, Koch certainly argues that science, as that which provides empirical knowledge, is the only reasonable approach to reality.

15. Koch, *Consciousness*, 165–84.

16. Kohak, *Ember and the Stars*, 14–15. Kohak notes this was a central thesis of the Czech philosopher Emmanuel Radl, with which he agrees.

17. This, I think, is the essential thesis of Kohak's book: it is one long argument to recover meaning in nature and reality against the dominant Western trend for the past few centuries to the contrary.

18. Koch, *Consciousness*, 165–84.

able? Koch would certainly say no,[19] and this is the natural consequence of reductionistic materialism. Koch's answers position him as an agnostic, holding that if there is anything beyond matter, it is unknowable. Understanding the often unstated assumptions of such a worldview demands a different playing field from which to view the modern world.

The Argument in a Nutshell

My goal in this book is to paint an alternative picture to the modern materialistic worldview. It is a worldview that includes all that is true and good in modern science while rejecting the scientistic assumptions of materialism. This different worldview is fully capable of incorporating the data of modern science and scholarship untouched and unaltered, but it is broader in scope and more powerful than what is presently used in modern academia. It has deep roots in ancient Greek and medieval thinkers;[20] in my mind, it has never been successfully challenged, only dismissed as irrelevant.

19. Koch, *Consciousness*, esp. 173: "What remains is neither empirical knowledge nor logical certainty, but faith."

20. There are a wide range of philosophers in ancient Greek and medieval thought. Exactly when ancient thought ended and medieval thought had its beginnings is open to dispute, although it was certainly sometime in the early Christian era. In general, when I speak of ancient Greek thought, I am referring to the corpus of thought that began in ancient Greece itself and by Roman times had spread throughout the empire and the Near East. This thought I hold had its apogee in the writings of Plato and Aristotle. In a given area of thought I may hold one to be better than the other. But considering the arguments of my book, Aristotle is the primary, but not exclusive, thinker I have in mind when referring to ancient Greek thought. Some may argue that this is a limited view, and it may well be. But in addition to being what I consider among the greatest refinement of ancient Greek thought, many developments among prior thinkers gradually led to his positions. As such, I also think he is a representative of the best of Greek thought that went before him. Other significant Greek thinkers I have in mind are Plato, as mentioned, and certain later ones, such as Plotinus, deriving from him.

Medieval thought in this book concerns thinkers of Christian tradition developing out of this Greek context to greater and lesser degrees. I include those in three Christian traditions – Latin, Greek, and Syriac. Of particular note are Pseudo-Dionysius the Areopagite, St. Thomas Aquinas, St. Augustine, St. Maximos the Confessor, St. John Damascene, and St. Ephraim the Syrian. Furthermore, I draw on movements of thought stemming from these thinkers into the modern era up to the present age. In particular, I refer often to the Carmelite St. John of the Cross.

In sum, I have drawn on a wide range of thinkers in presenting my analysis in this book, with particular emphasis on those listed, all of whom are luminaries in the history of thought and seem to me to have a common thread running through them.

In Part I, I argue for two key truths underlying the present reason-faith debacle. The first is how we know reality. I claim that the modern materialistic worldview dismisses much of the basic human contact with reality, which I refer to as "common human experience."[21] Many years of doing biological experiments have shown me, however, that even our most sophisticated experimental designs depend on such common experience. Then I proceed to argue that it is possible to know that the human intellect is immaterial. The skepticism of the modern materialist about human consciousness is unjustified. In this first part, I do not use arguments based on faith or religion, not because I think faith is weak, but because most people assume that one is speaking religiously whenever God, angels, and the soul are mentioned. That opinion is one of the general and unspoken but false assumptions of the modern materialist mind. Before the modern era, this was simply not the

21. The phrase "common human experience" might be somewhat curious to the professional philosopher. I am using this phase in a manner similar to Archbishop Fulton Sheen's "common sense" (*God and Intelligence*, 172) when writing of the first principles, while at the same time I make a nod to Kohak (*Embers and the Stars*; see my chapter 1 for an analysis of this idea). Sheen writes that "The natural, spontaneous, primitive and infallible judgements of the human reason constitute 'common sense.'" (*God and Intelligence*, 171). He notes that Boethius calls them "common conceptions." He goes on to state (*God and Intelligence*, 171) that these conceptions, or first principles, are never learned, taught, or forgotten and are "apprehended by the light of intelligence from the most simple and evident facts about us" (*God and Intelligence*, 175). They are "found among all men, that is, they are common to all men. This is why it is said that they arise out of common appreciation, or consent, or instinct, or the common sense of humanity" (*God and Intelligence*, 171–72). The emphasis on "common appreciation, consent, or instinct" leads me to the term "common experience," which I hope will help the reader, who may not be acquainted with this idea, to see *why* these principles are so basic. Following somewhat closer to the sense in which Kohak writes, I am asking the reader to look at the meaning of the human experience of reality (the natural world unencumbered by modern human artificiality, according to Kohak). What have all humans understood everywhere – not in terms of a general consent, but what do all humans rely upon at the most basic level despite their differences? The common human experience of reality results from the examination of the experience of all peoples, seeing what they know and what they have needed intellectually and practically, everywhere and at all times. What one finds are the first principles of speculative and practical reasoning. These principles exist prior to our contact with reality, and it is in the immediate first contact with reality that we know them. This is what it means to be a *knowing being.* This is a type of "experience," in a loose sense, that of the connatural knowledge of reality, which our knowing faculties immediately grasp. The use of this phrase may help those unfamiliar with these principles to see that all our speculative and practical reasoning are based on them. Everyone, everywhere, uses them. So the phrase "common human experience" is a term I am using to "justify" first principles, and in so doing convey them as well. To argue for them, one cannot use a proof, because upon these all proofs are based.

case, and for good reasons. I am not so arrogant as to think that I can answer every problem or objection that can be raised against my view, but I believe that debate functions best when the problem is rightly formulated.

In Part II, I reach back to ancient and medieval thinkers to show that their understanding of nature, science, and human knowledge is as relevant to us today as it was then. The modern materialist dismissal of them is sheer arrogance often mired in ignorance of what they really thought. They built a powerful framework for understanding all human experience without prejudice against the material side of it. Although some of their factual knowledge was deficient, this in no way invalidates their fundamental insights about reality, as I will explain in due course. Their understanding of reality as a hierarchy of beings subsumes the best of modern science. If the proper distinctions are made, scientific data become fully compatible with classical philosophy.

I have titled Part II "The Vestige of Eden," as it outlines a cosmological ballpark from a rational standpoint, one that is fully compatible with Christian doctrine. From the standpoint of Christian doctrine, the framework accessible to the rational powers of the mind as presented constitutes the ordered creation remaining after the Fall of Adam. As such, it is a vestige of what once was.

In the last part, Part III, I provide a fuller framework for all modern disciplines and their ultimate relationship to faith. This way of viewing reality is a *fundamentally* different one from the modern assumptions, but it is an old way at the same time. It was shared by the Fathers of Christianity, those foundational thinkers living in the early centuries of the Roman Empire. This view of reality finds deep resonance in certain Doctors (learned teachers) of the Church as well, those key thinkers who developed the Christian faith in dialogue with the disciplines inherited from the ancient Greeks (e.g., mathematics, astronomy). Lest you think you have heard it, you most likely have not.

This framework – what I hold to be the true Christian answer – has not been adequately brought forward and discussed in modern debates.[22] It is

22. The idea of creation as a liturgical structure is certainly present in certain modern theologians, such as Benedict XVI (Joseph Ratzinger) in his *Spirit of the Liturgy*. But the actual structure (various parts) of the liturgy as the very form of creation is rarely if ever (at least I have not yet found it) pre-

not the standard religious or scientific answer given; it is not creationism, evolution, or intelligent design. It disappeared rapidly with the onset of the Enlightenment because of fundamental misunderstandings of it, certain antireligious sentiment after the Enlightenment, and the fascination with the power that scientific progress offered the human race. This framework raises the debate to a much higher plane, one that is fundamental to our understanding of ourselves and the world around us. It is more powerful precisely because it can encompass a greater range of the human experience. Therefore it is fully compatible with both reason and faith.

This framework is the liturgical structure of the Church. The Church's liturgy – the form of public worship commonly called the "Mass" – thus constitutes the deepest insight into the present order of reality and that of eternity, or heaven. It is a "blueprint" for all of creation. Therefore Part III is titled "The Image of Eternity." Reflecting on Part II, it is this very liturgical pattern that we dimly perceive in the rational order of reality accessible to our mind in our deeper insights into nature. The Church, whose structure is liturgical, was preexistent in the mind of God for eternity; it was instantiated in heaven with the creation of the angels, and in the material universe with the creation of Eden.[23] As such, it constitutes our greatest understanding of the nature and purpose of reality.

---

sented in an explicit manner as I argue was done earlier in Christian history. One could possibly argue it implicitly in such works as the *Spirit of the Liturgy*.

23. Puhalo, *Creation and the Fall*, 12. That the Church was first in the mind of God is stated by John Chrysostom, *Homily 3 on Ephesians*, no. 12. The angels and Eden are referenced in the *Shepard of Hermas, Visions 2:4*, no. 13. This is the first of several references I cite later when discussing these topics. St. Thomas Aquinas and St. Ephrem the Syrian, both Doctors of the Church, one from the heart of the Latin West and the other from the easternmost tradition of the Church in Syria, held these positions. Also, Flannery, "*Lumen Gentium*," I.2, states, "Already present in figure at the beginning of the world, this Church was prepared in marvelous fashion in the history of the people of Israel and in the old Alliance."

Part I

ROADBLOCKS TO REALITY

1 THE COMMON EXPERIENCE OF NATURE

Human beings have observed the cycles of nature and derived meaning from them for millennia. This common experience of nature has provided solace for troubled souls and stimulated rational thought. In human history, religion, philosophy, and science have all been connected to the natural order and our human experience of it. But is there any meaning or sense to nature, or is it simply a collection of brute facts waiting for humans to impose meaning on it? Different answers to the meaning of nature lead in radically different directions. Scientism is the epistemological or knowledge claim that the only kind of reliable knowledge is what can be garnered from modern science. It is usually linked to materialism, the ontological or reality claim that the only reality that exists is the material world.[1] Quite to the contrary, pre-Enlightenment thought held that our common contact with reality was the key to unlocking a much vaster universe than simply that indicated by our senses.

1. Throughout this book, I am not disputing any valid scientific knowledge (facts). I am only disputing the interpretation of these facts through the lens of materialism. This is a key point and one that I mention several times in this work. I maintain that the facts of science do not lead to the conclusions of materialism.

Time It Was, and What a Time It Was

The rhythms of nature became clear to me growing up in southern Indiana, but those rhythms were more than external observations. From them I culled a sense of my own being. It seemed as if they were a part of me and I of them. Nature and human life were intertwined. Known as the "Crossroads of America," Indiana occupies the heart of the country. Many highways crisscross the state, east to west, north to south. The old National Road, which took pioneers from the Appalachians to the Midwest, crossed through Indiana. Culturally, the state is nearly bifurcated into a northern and southern half. While the northern half is essentially characterized by northern midwestern culture, the crossroads phenomenon is never more apparent than in the southern half of the state, which sociologically is a blend of northern and southern culture, producing what is considered the northernmost extension of the Upland South. This region is bordered on the north by Indianapolis, the cosmopolitan gateway to the northern part of the state, and on the south by Louisville, Kentucky, whose motto is "Gateway to the South."[2] These crossroads carry into religious beliefs as well. There are nearly homogeneous swaths tens of miles wide, north to south, of various denominations extending east to west across the state. One of these bands that goes through the middle of southern Indiana is nearly entirely Catholic, with towns like St. Martin's, St. Henry's, St. Meinrad's, and St. Mary's clustered together. Some of these towns were traditionally 98 percent Catholic. Twenty miles to the north or south are swaths that are nearly 100 percent Protestant, typically Southern Baptist, Pentecostal, or Church of Christ.

Toward the east, this middle swath of Catholicism outpaces Protestantism immediately to its south as it nears Louisville, arcing south to encompass the Knobstone escarpment, called by the locals simply "the Knobs." The Knobs are geologically the most rugged part of the state of Indiana, rising sharply from the Ohio River Valley just north of Louisville. It is an old land with some of the first settlements in the Midwest. Piercing through the region was the Buffalo Trace, a trail the bison used to travel to the falls of the Ohio as they crossed the river to the salt licks of Kentucky. In the early

2. Although not an official motto as far as I can discern, it was prevalent enough that I would see it here and there in Louisville and hear it on the news as I was growing up.

1970s, Interstate 64 was blasted through the Knobs, connecting Louisville with St. Louis and replacing the old Louisville–St. Louis Road. This opened the region to an influx of people from the Louisville area, to the point that much of what were once rural regions north of Louisville are now bedroom communities. At that time, in my early teens, I moved to the area onto 30 acres that my father bought, to the place I called home. It remained largely rural through my high school and college years, bracketed on the west by a 200-acre farm, on the northwest by a 1,200-acre spread, to the northeast by a 420-acre farm once owned by President Zachary Taylor, and on the east by several homes.

Extensive hardwood forests covering two-thirds of the region are the dominant flora. If memory serves me, southern Indiana was at one time the third-largest supplier of hardwood timber in the nation. Driving down the back roads afforded frequent encounters with logging trucks and sawmills. Climatologically, the region is near the boundary of a "humid continental" climate to the north and a "humid subtropical" climate to the south, with long, hot, and humid summers, long falls and springs, and shorter cool to cold winters with moderate rainfall.

The Rhythms of Nature

Summer is the prescient season of the year, which is marked by its presence or absence. The abundant green forests emit vast amounts of water, increasing an already humid climate. At summer's height, the air hung with a heavy haze, and the familiar hard blue sky softened somewhat into a powder blue. The fields shimmered with heat reflected at the high sun. Summer days stretched long, with the lengthening shadow of evening. The predominant noise was annual locusts humming in the heavy growth. Bees, wasps, butterflies, dragonflies, grasshoppers, katydids, and praying mantises were all there. My personal favorite was the robber flies as they darted to and fro in pursuit of their prey, punctuating the humid air. There was an oppressive heaviness to the land in the summer, but it was not a malevolent oppressiveness. Any type of inconvenience or oppressiveness in our technology-filled world is considered bad. But I learned that is not so. The heaviness of summer weighed on the imagination and mind in a good sense. It was the long hand of nature pressing and holding the mind, forcing it to see that which it couldn't if too distracted by modern conveniences. It held and quieted the imagination. It was a type of asceticism that Aristotle and the Greeks thought necessary for the mind to function properly. Away from the sights and sounds of the city, surrounded by timber and fields under a high sun and thick air, one began to see, to see the meaning hidden in nature. After a long day's work mowing fields or clearing brush, one could walk out in the early evening to hear the locusts' song and know that what one accomplished was good; the land itself was good and had a meaning. The place we owned was one of the original houses in the area, and there was a feeling that others had come and gone, done the same, and passed away. What they did was good, too.

There was a common purpose between me, the previous inhabitants, and the land; I learned that I was a natural part of the world. While I would eventually leave, the natural world would remain. It spoke of a purpose stretching beyond me. The other beings there – deer, turkeys, raccoons, coyotes, fox, rabbits, squirrels, fish, and the occasional cougar seen by locals – came and went as I did during the summer, some by day, some by night. There was a purpose to them, not mine, but a purpose nonetheless. And they reminded me of things past. The bison of the Buffalo Trace, just a few miles away, are gone, along with the bears, wolves, and elk. They are all gone. Unlike my prior fantasizing about dinosaurs, I could use my imagination in a judicious manner to realize that they, too, had a purpose. If things with purpose come and go, from where does the purpose come, and what lasts after they are gone? Despite the contingency of these creatures, something greater lasts.

Summers gave way to drawn-out falls, at first almost as hot and oppressive as summers. Eventually, the land cools and the humidity disappears. The abundant oaks, maples, hickories, beeches, tulip poplars, butternuts, and walnuts would be aflame with reds, oranges, burnt oranges, and yellows, entire walls of color stretching for hundreds of yards along a field's edge. Persimmons, hickories, and walnuts would drop abundant fruit on the ground. A relief came over the land and you. It was a time of cutting wood. My father didn't let me use a chainsaw until I was fifteen; before that, I did all the woodcutting with a buck saw and axe. Cutting wood by hand must have been one of the more dogged jobs of humans before modern technology.

Wrestling with such a tough, hard substance lets one see a passive resistance in things. Things *are something* with which to be reckoned.

Fall terminated in winter during slate-gray Novembers with temperatures in the 40s, brisk winds, and brown landscapes. The dominance of summer had ended, and things were silent. Another type of asceticism presented itself, one that heralded winter. Both Novembers and winters with their silence, sometimes with snow, tuned the mind to the potency of nature. Things were there but waiting. Life was underfoot but silent. This time of the year was more brutal to the imagination, stripping it of its fancies and wanderings. Silence and solitude beget pure thought. The tracks of the few active denizens of winter had no effect; they could not break the potency so evident to the mind. They were punctuated instances of the release of potential life, a few raindrops that heralded the potential thunderstorm, short manifestations of something greater.

Eventually, winter always yielded to spring and the lengthening of the day. The grass would green and fish would reappear in the stream. Spring in the hardwoods with its sequence of florals is just as glorious as fall. Smoky redbuds, white plums, dogwoods, locusts, dandelions, clovers, honeysuckles, and wild roses all signaled inherent beauty. The air yielded to one thick scent after another; first the plums, then the locusts, honeysuckle, and roses. The landscape seemed transformed by the life reshaping it. A great power was released that manifested itself in beauty. I could never accept that beauty was in the eye the beholder. Many have written of the snows of Kilimanjaro for a reason: they are beautiful. Beauty is the delight of the good.[3] If the land was good, it was beautiful. This beauty transcends personal opinion.

Late February and March constituted my favorite time of the year. At the base of my father's property was a spring that arose from a cave system on the

3. Aquinas, *Summa Theologica* (*ST*) I, q. 5, a. 4, ad 1. The good is the desire for being or, in other words, the desire for something that exists. Thus good is the same thing as being, when we consider that it is desired (*ST* I, q. 5, a. 1, c.). Many ancient and medieval thinkers held that the good is the desire for being and beauty is the delight of the good. With these and similar topics regarding general philosophical principles at issue throughout this book, I frequently cite what I consider to be among the highest development of these ideas, namely, the works of Aristotle and St. Thomas. Because each of these thinkers could be cited many times for these ideas, I simply cite one or two places in their more prominent works. In the articulation of such general philosophical principles, others have arguably equaled Aristotle and St. Thomas, but none have exceeded them.

hill jutting up on the south side of the property. It ran underground on the east side of the property, and on a quiet day you could place your ear to the ground and hear it flow. Not quite at the middle of the base of the property, it came out of the ground in a depression that was lined with old creek stones. People who knew the history of the area said it was once a common spring for many people; on the north side of our property was an old overgrown road that ran toward it. If I dug near the spring, I could find pottery, first glazed and then unglazed. I therefore assume Native Americans used it as well; they are gone, having also lived their lives on the land. This spring never ran dry, even during the occasional extended drought. It was the source of a stream that was an endless object of fascination for me. The stream ran through the hardwoods and was a microcosm of a wider and deeper meaning. Each season, it provided a wealth of insights into the natural world. Late February and March were particularly nice because life was exploding in the stream and all along it: new fish, plants, water striders, and birds. In early spring, there was an absence of ticks and chiggers that would arrive by late April. Still, I could find the remains of winter. Deer bones and those of other animals remained along with piles of crayfish exoskeletons from the raccoons eating them. I noticed that the claws of the crayfish were turned slightly upward as a last act of defiance, hanging on to life. The claws had purpose as well.

The flow of natural time and the cycling of the seasons point to meaning and purpose in nature. Reflective human observers can sense that nature is more than brute fact. Time flows in nature with meaning.

Time: Natural versus Artificial

In *The Embers and the Stars*, which surely counts as one of the most beautiful books of philosophy ever written, the Czech philosopher Erazim Kohak says that this cycling of the seasons gives us an awareness that things have meaning.[4] Only if things have meaning are they intelligible. Intelligibility—the ability to be known and understood—is interchangeable with meaning and the nature of a thing.[5] If things have meaning, one is faced with a choice

4. Kohak, *Embers and the Stars*, 73–78, 82–85, 97–103.

5. Kohak, *Embers and the Stars*. See esp. 8–9, 47–50, 68–69, 71–74, 78–79. This is one of the basic points of the entire book, however.

either to accept or reject that meaning at some level. The subtitle of Kohak's book—*A Philosophical Inquiry into the Moral Sense of Nature*—must strike the modern secular mind as an absurdity. Yet Kohak persuasively argues that nature has a moral sense because it displays purpose and is intelligible to the human mind. This is the basis for morality.[6]

The experience of the seasons taught me that there is a meaningful sense to time, a right time. There was a right time on that 30 acres in southern Indiana for me, the same right time for the deer, turkey, and raccoon when I was there. Before that, there was once a right time for the Native Americans, the bear, and the bison. There was and is a natural temporality in all these things. As a scientist who has studied biological rhythms, I know that the natural temporality of life is cued into that of physical events. The sun and the moon are both timekeepers for our bodily rhythms. So the temporality of our human life is linked to that of the greater world; there is meaning in both. But humans are not deer, nor turkey, nor bison, nor bears. They know that something always remains beyond their time. As all things have a time, so something remains. Something is behind and beyond the time of nature.

Erazim Kohak notes another idea of time, that of the clocks on our walls. We have clocks to manage our environment. Because we tire at different rates, and darkness comes sooner or later depending on cloud cover, the temporality of nature isn't sufficiently precise to govern our comings and goings in a busy, urbanized world. Kohak captures the difference: "The idea of 1800 hrs on the six of June 1981 is pure artifact, a construct imposed upon nature's rhythm, subordinating and ordering it. Still, for the specified purpose for which it was designed – and on the assumption that we know the purpose independently of it – it is a powerful tool. The usefulness of such a construct, however, remains inevitably contingent on the prior purpose which brought it into being. The construct becomes problematic already when we seek to apply it beyond the scope of its original intent."[7]

The idea of clock time, the time used by scientists in experiments, becomes a problem when we take this artifact, whose only legitimate basis is derived from meaningful temporality, and apply it to our lived experience.

6. Kohak, *Embers and the Stars*. See esp. 8–9 and 67–85. This is another fundamental point of the book.

7. Kohak, *Embers and the Stars*, 16.

Such is the case with nanoseconds or billions of years — they are useful clock time constructs in physics, chemistry, geology, and biology but virtually unintelligible at the level of human experience. It is a human construct to treat clock time as if it were the only way to think of time and all other ideas of time as purely subjective. If we believe that our habitual use of artificial time means that there is no real meaning to time, we have made a grave error. This is one of the key mistakes of the modern world. We surround ourselves with gadgets made with parts. We convenience ourselves with technology made possible by scientific progress in controlling the interaction of parts and their forces.[8] Matter in motion is the idea of clock time. Simple matter in motion affords precise control, all good if kept in perspective. It can be a powerful tool, but it also fires our imagination, and we reify it into something real, which it is not. We educate our children to perform, to accomplish, and to get good jobs simply because we can do such powerful things. But it is all at a cost. We put layer after layer between us and the experience of reality as lived, shielding ourselves from meaning.[9] Kohak continues,

> The technical reason which produces the machine cannot teach us its human use. We can only speak of a *right* time only in the matrix of natural time, the rhythm of human life and the cycle of the seasons. On an infinite line of uniform number moments, however, the very notion of a "right" time becomes wholly unintelligible. Here the time cannot be "right." There can only be Tn . . . T∞. The decision to disconnect the machine at T3 rather than at T6 or Tn becomes arbitrary. To make it, we would need to have recourse to the recognition of the rhythm of natural time, the rhythm of a human life. Having, however, convinced ourselves that our linear time construct alone is real while all else, including our awareness of natural time, is "merely subjective," we have effectively foreclosed such a recourse. Instead, we stand helplessly over the machine and the agony, hoping that a committee will reduce the anonymity of the decision which we can no longer make responsibly as moral subjects.[10]

Which is more real, natural or artificial time? What exactly is a given point at 2:00 p.m. on October 9, 2013? We experience that denser objects fall through less dense mediums (Newton's apple falling from the tree),

8. Kohak, *Embers and the Stars*, 15–19, 22–26.

9. Kohak, *Embers and the Stars*, 11–12, 22–26.

10. Kohak, *Embers and the Stars*, 17.

but scientifically we measure it as the force of gravity causing acceleration in meters per second squared. Both meters and seconds are artifacts; any other unit could do as well. We can assay an animal's behavioral reflex as the amount per second. This is measurement by artifact. It yields great power and control, but isolating an instant of time, a snapshot of an animal, or a fossil found at this layer at so many meters is not reality. Facts result from a bracketing of things in reality, a kind of isolation of facts from their natural context.[11] By themselves, they have no meaning.

Part of the alienation modern people feel in today's world is due to technological triumph. Having interposed numerous gadgets between themselves and reality, they view the universe as cold matter in motion but intuitively understand themselves as something greater. Nature becomes something alien to them.[12] And it plays into every side of the political landscape. The communist divorces individual human life from natural reality and views it simply as a cog in the wheel of the party, a pure producer. The secular capitalist sees nature as a giant resource pit to be used and tamed at will. The extreme environmentalist decides humans are a plague and must be done away with so that nature can "recover" some fancied "pristine" state, again a product of the imagination. The truth of the matter is that humans are a critical part of nature, from which they derive meaning; in turn, humans give another type of meaning to nature. Nature needs humanity as much as humanity needs nature.[13] We are intellectual creatures, and ideas mean things. If we misunderstand nature, we misunderstand ourselves.

Scientism, so prevalent in our culture, is directly opposed to the idea of common experience, such as the natural experience of time. Anyone who is familiar with the tenets of scientism will know there are few things more detested in its ideology than the everyday experience of the common person. The ordinary person is thought to be ignorant. The true understanding of reality comes from the laboratory. Facts such as clock time, collected in experiments, not from experience, are the final arbiters of truth. Scientism is a type of Gnosticism. Gnosticism is an old philosophy from the ancient world that held that the secrets of reality are only known by and available to

11. Kohak, *Embers and the Stars*, 22–26.

12. Kohak, *Embers and the Stars*, 13, 22–26, 38–40.

13. Kohak, *Embers and the Stars*, 89–109.

a privileged few. Instead of drawing from common experience, one should understand reality from experiments. An ivory tower is constructed, elevating scientists over everyone else. Academics espousing scientism insulate and isolate themselves from the common experience of the world. To them, the world from which facts come has no meaning in and of itself. Perhaps that explains why there are fewer believers among academics and scientists. They have exorcised the source of meaning from their thinking and replaced it with constructs of the imagination. Nor is this effort restricted to the ivory halls of higher academics. The 2007 Harvard Task Force on General Education stated that the "aim of a liberal education [is] to unsettle presumptions, to defamiliarize the familiar . . . to disorient young people and help them find ways to re-orient themselves."[14] The common experience of human life must be corrected.

Learning from Common Experience

Perhaps this preference for knowledge from the laboratory over and opposed to knowledge based on common human experience explains why those who adopt scientism generally have a disdain for ancient philosophy, a disdain that often blocks their ability to understand it. The ancient Greek and medieval philosophers viewed the task of philosophy as homing in on and drawing out the common human experience of reality. They saw an intimate connection between human life, moral judgments, and the nature of things, or, as they called it, *de natura rerum*. This insight into the natural temporality and its meaning are old indeed. The hard fact remains, however, that we moderns were not the first ones to see this natural temporality or its meaning. The ancient Hebrew poet Qoheleth proclaimed:

> For everything there is a season,
> and a time for every matter under heaven:
> A time to be born, and a time to die;
> A time to plant, and a time to pluck up what was planted;
> A time to kill, and a time to heal;

14. Faculty of Arts and Sciences, *Task Force on General Education*, 1–2. Although there are statements in the context of this quotation with which I agree regarding liberal education, I find the general idea that a liberal education must defamiliarize and disorient to be objectionable.

A time to break down, and a time to build up;
A time to weep, and a time to laugh;
A time to mourn, and a time to dance;
A time to cast away stones, a time to gather stones together;
A time to embrace, and a time to refrain from embracing.
A time to seek, and a time to lose;
A time to keep, and a time to cast away;
A time to rend, and a time to sew;
A time to be silent, and a time to speak;
A time to love; and a time to hate;
A time for war, and a time for peace.[15]

This fittingness or comportment between selected moments and appropriate human actions of which the poet speaks signals a keen awareness that time and life have some kind of meaning. His is not the culturally determined perspective of ancient Hebrew culture alone. It reflects something wider and greater, the common experience of humanity that intuited meaning in things and possessed a sense of right and wrong. The experience of the average human being was the foundation of understanding upon which classical philosophy was built; it was the application of the rules of reason to this body of experience. Common human experience contained the truth in a hazy manner, and philosophy's purpose was to clarify it by the search for principles and causes. Philosophy refines and hones; it does not contradict common human insights. The ivory tower of modern academics was absent then. Collectively, the man at work in his field or shop was the indispensable source of knowledge about reality, to which philosophy applied distinctions and employed reason to refine causality and morality. The common person and academic were of one mind and were reciprocally dependent on each other; the philosopher needed common experience as the basis of thought, and the common man needed philosophy for the refinement and clarification of his thinking.[16]

15. Eccl 3:1–8. Unless otherwise stated, all biblical citations are from the Revised Standard Version.

16. I am writing in generalizations, and as I previously stated, my tendency is to emphasize philosophically Aristotelian/Thomistic thought, where this point is certainly the case. Once can point out thinkers, both ancient and medieval, who disagreed with this. As a general idea toward which pre-Enlightenment thought tended, however, I believe this to be correct. See also notes 18 and 19 below with corresponding text.

One of the most remarkable human abilities often escapes our notice: the ability to generalize and visualize abstract objects and ideas. Experience tells us that things exist. There are plants, but they are not animals. So life is not limited to plants. There are people, but they are not purely animals. So life is not limited to plants or animals. And these things are not stars or the moon. Existing things are not limited to living or nonliving things. There is such a thing as existence itself, not limited by any one thing. My faithful Airedale, Bliss, was my teacher. As I wandered the hills, streams, and fields with my canine companion during my teen years, I became aware that she could perceive things I could not, such as odors and high-pitched sounds. Her prancing to and fro with head held high, sniffing the air, drove home to me that my senses were limited on the lower side of reality. If so, what reason could I give for denying that they were limited on the higher side?

Why must the general idea of beings be limited to matter? Why must existence, considered in itself, be confined to material things? Reading the experience of ancient authors reveals that the common person had a general awareness of something greater beyond the immediate experience of reality. People had a hazy idea of transcendent being, a being beyond matter.[17] In the general notion of existence, they saw no logical reason to be limited by mere observation.

Existence was for the ancient observers more than the bare fact of things out there. Like us, they found themselves attracted to things and saw that attraction as good. So any being, insofar as it exists, is good. The appreciation of being as good is also an experience of the beautiful. Springtime in southern Indiana is good and beautiful, not just a brute fact. The locust trees in spring have a heady, beautiful scent. Likewise, the honeysuckles along the lane exude a sweet scent in the warm sunlight of spring, complemented by yellow, white, and red flowers. These are beautiful because they are good, and they are good because they are beautiful. Robber flies darting to and fro have a beautiful flight. Water striders in March skimming swiftly on the

17. The actual proof for God is somewhat more complicated than I present. God is utterly and infinitely beyond the being of the universe, and as such is no "Great Being" among the beings of creation. He is, again, infinitely beyond all other being and as such is completely "Other" (Transcendent). Thus nothing in creation, or correspondingly in our concepts, is anything like him. My point here contains, once again, a nod to Kohak. The experience of creation gives us, as I (and he) state, a hazy insight into the transcendent, but not a formal proof. The formal proof is beyond this book.

stream above the new fish are captivating. The water itself from the spring gurgling over the old springhouse stones makes a pleasant sound. The taste of apples from the old tree in the fall and the potential of life under a winter snow are good. The feel of hardwood bark while sliding your hand over a cold winter tree and the pungent smell of fresh split oak are good as well. So is the glimpse of an owl flying in the tops of the lone stand of pines among the hardwoods on a gray November day.

These things are real; they are good; they are beautiful. The person who senses that these things are objectively meaningful is on to something real, not simply something he has constructed in his mind. Apprehending the natural world as desirable and good forces a choice on the observer. The mind must first learn a kind of humility to receive reality as it presents itself. Only after learning to receive reality with the intellect can one ignore the ravings of a wild imagination hungry for the next enticing installment of technology. Only then can one begin to truly *see*, in the classic philosophical sense of theory. Theory, deriving from the Greek *theoria*, really means *seeing*.[18] This seeing, this *theoria*, was considered the foundation of contemplative knowing prior to the Enlightenment. It was around this point in history and thereafter that the general trend in philosophical thought attempted to reduce this variegated wonder to matter in motion and meaningless physicality.[19]

The seamless garment with humanity woven into the tapestry of nature led these contemplatives to ask about the purpose of nature. For what is nature? For whom is nature? Why does nature exist? Why do I, as a human being, find it so beautiful, so good? Such contemplatives sensed at a visceral level that human choices, actions, and thoughts were not unrelated to the natural wonders around them. The symphony of nature echoed in the hu-

18. Kohak, *Embers and the Stars*, 3–26.

19. Kohak, *Embers and the Stars*, 14–15. I completely agree with the analysis of Kohak (and Emanuel Radl, the biologist/philosopher whom he cites) regarding this point on these pages. Historically, Kohak and Radl held that this change occurred in the Renaissance. Others think it occurred more around the time of the Enlightenment (Kenneth Howell, personal communication, July 2018). So I generally keep to the usage of the Enlightenment. While one may correctly point out there were plenty of thinkers in the Renaissance and Enlightenment who were devout scholars, the philosophical basis of their ideas in general had made a fundamental shift that had not worked its way throughout their thinking and particularly their religious convictions. This shift regarded the nature of the intellect, and I discuss this in chapter 3.

man consciousness, which led the emperor-philosopher Marcus Aurelius to ask, "He who does not know what the world is does not know where he is. And he who does not know for what purpose the world exists, does not know who he is, nor what the world is. But he who has failed in any one of these things could not even say for what purpose he exists himself. What then dost thou think of him who [avoids or] seeks the praise of those who applaud, of men who know not where they are or who they are."[20] For the second-century emperor, as for Stoics before him, human morality implied and was implied by the natural world. It provided the objective basis of morality. There was a higher law that requires a choice to be made. All the natural realities call for an assent to their being, to their goodness, and to their beauty. One chooses to accept reality or ignore it. This general notion of meaning in things based on common experience gives us a real basis for the transcendentals: being, the one, the good, the true, and related ideas such as existence, the beautiful, and the moral.[21] That is why most people throughout history have believed in something greater, and why so many cultures assent to a higher being. People are not ignorant or stupid because they believe; they do so because the experience of reality carries with it meaning. Things are knowable insofar as they have meaning. Why are so many educated people today unable to see that meaning? Is it because they have thrown off the shackles of primitive thinking, or is it because they have erected so many barriers, or artifacts, between themselves and reality through their education?

Oaks and Raccoons Teach Philosophy

Ancient thinkers were not content with general impressions and experiences of nature. They sought to give a rational account of these observations in a manner that endures in modern science. Contrary to popular perception, science did not begin in modern times but in antiquity. Roaming the woods

20. Aurelius, *Meditations*, 221–22.

21. Aquinas, *Truth*, vol. I, q. 1, a. 1. The transcendentals are those concepts that are related to the idea of being and add nothing to it. For instance, the good is the idea of being as desirable, or from the standpoint of the will. The true is being as it exists in the intellect. None of these things by themselves is limited to matter, nor is existence only in matter implied in any way in them; hence the word *transcendental* or "transcendent" to matter. Here again, many other citations could be made to works of St. Thomas and other thinkers.

and fields of southern Indiana, lollygagging beside the stream, I often carried with me various field guides of insects, leaves, fish, and mammals. Such books are nothing but applied cause and effect. Why is it that the tree in the field is the same tree from year to year? It is because the tree has an intrinsic nature that makes it a specific causal locus.[22] Specific causes have specific effects.[23] The field guides contain drawings of the oak leaves, bark, and acorns that an oak tree reliably produces from year to year. Things in nature for the most part have reliable causal powers.[24] The average person can look in the field guide and correctly identify a swamp white oak. All swamp white oaks are of the same nature and so produce the same effects from year to year.

This idea is particularly driven home in distinguishing certain closely related organisms, such as different types of oak trees. Oaks are broadly categorized into red and white oaks. In each of these classes, numerous species are found. In the eastern United States, red oaks can be classed as scarlet, northern, eastern black, southern red, bear, and blackjack oak, while white oaks can be broken into eastern white, post, overcup, burr, English, durand, chapman, chinkapin, basket, swamp, chestnut, and nine others.[25] To distinguish them, these guides include detailed drawings with arrows or circles pointing to small, almost unnoticeable, differences to the untrained eye, such as subtle ridge differences on the edges of leaves, differences in the cup on the acorn, or placement of leaf buds. Because these differences are reliable for a given species, it leads to the conclusion that the given species of tree is a real locus of causality year after year. The same is true for fish, dragonflies, beetles, and other insects. If these minutiae are so reliable, there must be a cause of their reliability, given the vicissitudes to which the organisms are subject in the natural world. Just as it requires a trained eye and skilled hands to carve details in wood, or to make an elaborate quilt — these are highly specified arts, and a precise cause is needed to produce them — the same is true with nature, because highly specified differences need a specific cause.

Raccoon tracks teach the same truth. Animals have a nature that causes

22. Harre and Madden, *Causal Powers*, 5–7. The idea of a "powerful particular" or the individual existing thing as a center of causality (causal locus) is the theme of the whole book.

23. *ST* I, q. 2, a. 2, c.

24. Harre and Madden, *Causal Powers*, 5–7.

25. Petrides and Wehr, *Eastern Trees*, 88–94.

their bodies to develop certain forms, such as feet that leave prints. When I first started exploring the creek with my Airedale Bliss, I noticed abundant tracks in the mud along the creek edge, particularly near rock ledges hanging out over the creek. These were often accompanied by crayfish remains. I looked them up in my field guide and found them to be raccoon tracks. I then saw raccoons along the creek and observed where they walked. Low and behold, the same tracks. I could always be confident that whenever I saw those types of tracks, I knew raccoons had been there. Raccoon tracks are always made by raccoons, as deer tracks are made by deer, coyote tracks by coyotes, and opossum tracks by opossums. And the reason I could be confident is that things in nature are causal beings. Effects proceed from causes. And not just any cause. Effects are proportionate to their causes – specified differences need specific causes.

What could be more certain than the fact that nature produces specific, observable effects? And why? The simple explanation – which modern science loves – is that those causes are in the nature of things, in the *natura rerum*, and not in our heads. The Roman poet Virgil, writing a long poem about agriculture called *Georgics*, reflected this realist perspective when he declared *felix qui potuit rerum cognoscere causas* ("happy is he who could know the causes of things").[26] Virgil knew, as did every farmer, that the knowledge of causes was crucial to success in planting and harvesting. The natural philosophers of the Renaissance took Virgil's maxim to a whole new level, seeing in it the essence of everyday knowledge and the height of scientific inquiry. For them, as for Aristotle, true science was an investigation into causes. Yet the modern skeptical mind does not rest content with the simplest explanation. David Hume, the eighteenth-century Enlightenment philosopher, was a relentless critic of causality.[27] One billiard ball hitting another on the pool table was not justification for believing in causality, Hume argued. For him, there was no causality, just a succession of events. If that were the case, then just about any animal could make raccoon tracks. I can tell you they are not. Raccoon tracks are caused by raccoons.

26. Virgil, *Georgics*, book 2, l. 490. Translated by Kenneth Howell, personal communication.

27. For a good summary of Hume's position on causality, including the degree to which scholars think he held a strictly noncausal position, along with references to his works, see Lorkowski, "David Hume."

Ancient philosophers, as precursors of modern scientists, were not Humean. They accepted the evident causality in the world and sought to understand it even further because their task was simply a refinement of what we all experience. Aristotle, possibly the most brilliant natural philosopher of all time, posited four types of causes: material, efficient, formal, and final.[28] A glass triangle displays them all. The material cause is the glass, the efficient cause is the person who made the glass triangle, the formal cause is the shape of the triangle, and the final cause is the purpose for which it was made (perhaps decoration?).

Aristotle also saw that the best *theoria* – the best vision of reality – was one that invoked these causes to explain not only nonhuman nature but even human actions. And he could not have been more on target. Everything we do presupposes these four. When we cook a meal, we determine the food to be prepared (material cause), the type of dish to be made (formal cause), how it is to be put together (efficient cause), and the purpose (final cause). In common experience, we haven't fully accounted for something unless we give an account of these causes. And we rank them in importance. Nothing gets done unless there is a reason for doing it, and the manner in which it gets done is determined by the purpose as well. So the purpose or final cause is the cause of causes, according to the ancient and medieval thinkers. In cooking a formal dinner (final cause), we select good food (material cause) and prepare fancy dishes (formal cause) in a careful manner (efficient cause). If a quick dinner is needed on a rainy night, maybe hot dogs and cheese on a piece of bread (pig in a blanket) will suffice.

Even highly intellectual activities, the kind no animal can perform, submit to this causal analysis. My son comes to me with an assignment to write a paper:

> "What is it?" I ask.
>
> "Paper and pencil." (He thus answers with a material cause. This makes little sense.)
>
> I ask again, and he says, "I am writing with paper and a pencil." (He answers with an efficient cause. Still not much sense.)

28. Aristotle, *Physics*, vol. 1, 329–42; idem, *Metaphysics*, vol. 2, 1600–1601; Aquinas, *Commentary on Aristotle's Metaphysics* V, les. 2–3.

Again, "What is it?"

"I am writing a paper on the difference between substance in Plato and Aristotle." (He answers with the formal cause. Understandable.)

"Why are you writing it?"

"To get a job?" (He answers with a utilitarian final cause.)

"To get a job? Really? Is that all?"

"To gain insights into reality to understand myself and the truth of the world better." (He answers with final causality.)

The why and what of a thing are always the guiding causes behind anything. We see these realities in nature as well, as evidenced by our basic questions about things:

What is it made of (material)?
What is it (formal)?
Where did it come from, or how is it made (efficient)?
Why is it here, or to what end is it ordered (final)?

Whether cooking food or writing a paper on philosophy, we employ all these causes to function in our daily experience. Further, the importance assigned to these causes in general experience is an argument itself against scientism. One would think the student as odd who responds, "Pencil and paper" (the material) to a question asking him what he is writing. An account of reality based purely on parts and their interaction is similarly flawed. Why do we settle for pure mechanism to explain nature when we would not tolerate it in our everyday work?[29]

Everything we do, think, and say presupposes these causes and the general awareness of truth, goodness, and beauty. These are among the first philosophical refinements of the general experience of humanity. Their reality cannot be denied without denying reality itself. Someone might claim that causality isn't necessary, but anyone who claims that effects don't need

29. Specifically, by what intellectual right do we disregard formal and final cause in nature if our most basic day-to-day actions presuppose these as the most important? Anyone who claims to give a full account of a car by merely describing its parts, or a research paper by describing the pencil and paper, or a football game by describing the football and stadium and protective gear would be laughed at. So why in modern materialism do we do away with formal and final cause in describing nature?

causes still looks both ways before crossing a street. If not, reality will impinge itself violently upon that person.

Or someone may deny the importance of common human experience, relegating it to an inferior status. In chapter 2, I show that this is impossible because science itself depends on the general experience of humanity. Ancient philosophy says that truth is found in our basic sense of reality and can be seen from the experience of all humans across all cultures and all times, not local urban legends. How do we know the difference? Common experience is *not* my mother's blueberry cream pie. In her heyday, my mother could bake an excellent blueberry cream pie, consisting of a vanilla pudding base with fresh blueberries and whipped cream on the top, all refrigerated before eating. As the vanilla pudding was cooking, the house was filled with a great aroma that made me want to lick the bowl. If it was still being cooked, my mother would draft me into stirring the pudding. She always stirred clockwise, and if I stirred counterclockwise, she would strongly object, claiming that the pudding would come "un-stirred." She apparently learned this from her mother, handed down from generation to generation. Apart from the possibility that Irish mothers have a window on reality that no one else has – something that crosses my mind now and then – it is safe to assume that this is not common knowledge to all cultures and times. It is not our basic human understanding of reality. Nor is any other knowledge of this kind.

Within common human experience there is found the knowledge presupposed by all cultures across all times in history. This understanding is known immediately upon contact with reality, refined and codified into formal principles by philosophical thought.[30] There are not many of these self-evident truths. Among them are cause and effect, broken into the four types of causes discussed above, as well as the understanding that a real world exists, that this reality possesses an intrinsic order (or hierarchy), the principle of non-contradiction, the principle of identity, and the principle that a whole is greater than the sum of its parts. We have discussed cause and effect, and the next two truths are self-defining.[31] The principle of

30. *ST* I-II, q. 51, a. 1; *Truth*, vol. I, q. 8, a. 15, c.

31. *ST* I-II, q. 94, a. 2; *Truth*, vol., I, q. 1.

non-contradiction[32] follows our perception of reality: a thing cannot both exist and not exist at the same time and circumstance, or a thing cannot be both alive and dead at the same time and circumstance, or a thing cannot be both affirmed and denied at the same time and circumstance. In the moral sphere, it is defined as "do good" (that which enhances your being and life) and "avoid evil" (that which moves you to nonexistence). The principle of identity[33] holds simply that a thing is what it is and not something else. I am a human and not a dog. It is this principle that allows me to use the personal pronoun "I." I intuitively understand myself as a knowing subject. That a whole is greater than the sum of its parts is self-explanatory as well.[34] These principles are the basis of our conversations and thoughts. All our knowledge presupposes these causes and perceptions of reality. If one wishes to deny them, he would have to prove their nonexistence or nonimportance, because such denials are not self-evident. Even the denial of them presupposes their use. The proposition "cause and effect is *not* true" presupposes non-contradiction in the use of "not." What is self-evident is that our experience tells us we do know things, or else we couldn't function in the real world.

These are the foundational truths we use to function in the everyday world. If these were just conveniences of the human mind, why do they allow us to function so well? If they did not truly inform us of the world, we would fail just as much as succeed in using them. So there must be a real connection with these ideas and reality, simply because we use them successfully in all facets of life: in practical daily use, in our thoughts, our morality, and our investigation of the world around us. We do not assume them; rather, our minds simply *know* them immediately upon a correct experience of reality. This is what it means for a human to be a *knowing* being. Our minds do not labor to learn them. Likewise, science does not prove them or discover them. Either we are correctly perceiving and knowing reality, or we must suppose that humans are an aberration of the natural world, since we are coming up with these ideas and they do not offer a true knowledge of reality. If that is the case, how did we become so independent of nature?

32. *ST* I-II, q. 94, a. 2; *Commentary on Aristotle's Metaphysics* IV, les. 6.

33. *ST* I-II, q. 94, a. 2; *Commentary on Aristotle's Metaphysics* IV, les. 6.

34. *ST* I-II, q. 51, a. 1; I-II, q. 94, a. 2.

So which is correct? Classical philosophy that claims the basic human experience – or contact – with reality is the basis for our knowledge, or materialism/scientism claiming the experience of the laboratory? No one should underestimate the importance of this question. I believe one of the two most important mental blocks to accepting the ancient quest of pre-Enlightenment thinking is that science has the final word on all matters cosmological and epistemological. In other words, it is thought to be superior to common experience. But if modern science ultimately relies on the self-evident principles outlined above, which in turn are refinements of our common experience of reality, then modern science relies in the end on common experience to interpret its data.

Moreover, these self-evident principles are the basis on which classical philosophies prove the existence of immaterial realities such as God and the immateriality of the intellect. So if modern science relies on common experience, it can in no way reject the foundations of classical philosophy or deny that common human experience has meaning and purpose. The claim of scientism, which asserts that no such things can exist, is groundless and not derived from science but from a materialist framework devoid of scientific validity. In chapter 2, I explain that science is based on common human experience, which was the foundation for proofs of the existence of God and of other immaterial realities in pre-Enlightenment times. In chapter 3, I discuss the nature of the other critically important mental block to accepting common experience: the immateriality of the intellect.

2 SCIENCE AND COMMON EXPERIENCE

Many people outside the practice of science imagine it to be uniform and monolithic, but scientists know that this is not the case. The procedures of chemistry and biology, for example, are different, even though both are sciences. When we expand the scientific horizons to physics and mathematics, the differences loom even larger. All the empirical sciences do share the goal of testing hypotheses against nature, but using the natural world as a standard did not begin with modern science. The common experience discussed in chapter 1 used basic contact with reality as the origin of its principles. The difference lies in how that basic contact is used. In this context, modern science is only a refinement of this human use of the natural world.

Medieval philosophers reflected much on the different sciences and sought to construct an encyclopedia of the sciences. For them, philosophy was the science of the sciences because it both plumbed the depths of the scientific foundations and ultimately led to higher things. But their definition of science differed in meaning from the same word used in modern times. The Latin *scientia* is a translation of the Greek *episteme*, which is the word Aristotle used to denote true knowledge, as opposed to opinion. A science, then, was to yield true knowledge within a limited range of reality (e.g., the science of motion or kinematics). In the estimation of medieval thinkers, true knowledge, or a science, was not limited to material reality. For them, metaphysics and natural theology were sciences that could yield true knowledge even though they exceeded the material world. Science in the modern sense would be much more akin to opinion to them.

What the ancients and medievals realized – and the main point of this chapter – is that all the empirical sciences rest on the foundation of self-evident principles, known by our contact with reality.[1] This truth has not been restricted to the ancient world, however. Niels Bohr, a father of atomic theory, recognized this truth after many years of reflection upon his own practice: "All account of physical experience is, of course, ultimately based on common language, adapted to orientation in our surroundings and tracing of relationships between cause and effect."[2]

Kinds of Science

The sciences can be classified according to different criteria. Two of the most important are what a science depends on for its truth and its degree of certainty. The most certain of all sciences, at least of those practiced today, is mathematics. Geometry proves that every triangle has 180° as the sum of all its angles. How do we know that there are 180° in triangle *ABC*? Mathematically speaking, it is a simple demonstration.[3]

Any circle, such as the dashed one on the following page, contains 360°. Cut it in half to make two hemispheres, such as the hemisphere below line *a*, to give 360 ÷ 2 = 180°. Then cross two lines, *c* and *d*, at point *x* on *a*. This divides the hemisphere below line *a* into angles *D*, *A*, and *E*, which are equal to 180° because they contain all the degrees in the hemisphere. Now all one has to do is show that angles *ABC* are equal to *DAE*. The first is easy, as *A* = *A*. Next, a geometric law states that when any line, such as *c* or *d*, cuts two parallel lines, such as *a* and *b*, then the opposing angles generated (*D* and *B* with line *d*, or E and *C* with line *c*) are equal. Thus *D* = *B* and *E* = *C*. Again, *A* = *A*. Therefore *ABC* is equal to *DAE*, and *DAE* = 180°, and so *ABC* = 180°. Now

1. Sheen, *Philosophy of Science*, 163–78.
2. Bohr, "Quantum Physics and Biology," 1–5.
3. Euclid, *First Three Books of Euclid's Elements*, I, prop. 32.

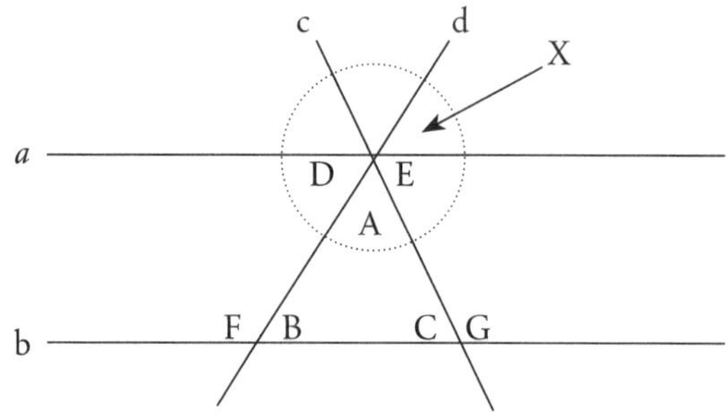

one could make any possible infinite number of triangles by altering the slants of lines *c* and *d* and the conditions would still be the same. The proof above therefore shows for certain that all possible triangles (in Euclidean space) ideally have 180°. And the reason we understand there are 180° is because the mathematical proof follows from an ideal understanding of the nature of a triangle, a geometrical figure bounded on three sides. Given this understanding, to contain 180° follows naturally from it, as shown in the proof.

This kind of geometric proof is not the kind used in the empirical sciences. Mathematics is a distinct body of knowledge from empirical science.[4] The natural sciences use mathematics, but they are not the same; mathematics is a rational science of abstract objects, such as the ideal triangle. It only in part depends on things in the material world. Could you prove that all triangles have 180° by the methods of the empirical sciences? No! Empirical science fails to grasp the nature of the triangle; it simply measures instances of triangularity. The empirical approach is to go out with a protractor, measure many instances of triangularity in the world, sum these, and divide by the number of triangles measured. Because all triangles that exist in our world of matter are imperfect, one could never arrive at the kind of certainty characteristic of a geometric proof.

Another reason that one could never come to the knowledge that triangles contain precisely 180° by the method of the empirical sciences is that there is no such thing as a perfect protractor. One may therefore find some close approximations to 180° when measuring triangles. For instance, one

4. Aquinas, *Trinity and Unicity of the Intellect*, q. 5, a. 3.

may arrive at a measurement of 179.5°. But the next twenty instances that one measures might all be somewhat greater than 180°, so that you might end up with 180.2°. If you never knew mathematics, your certainty as to the degrees in a triangle would be questionable. You would have precise calculations, however; 180.2° is a precise number.

This is a hallmark of empirical science: great precision, but low certainty.[5] Remember the half-full or half-empty glass of water? How much water does it contain? Say the glass was a half-liter glass (500 ml), and you found it to contain 249.3 ml of water. Is your eyesight good enough to ascertain the precise water level? What if you measured it again and got 249.4 ml (this happens a lot in science)? You might average them to 249.35 ml. Are you certain? What if the next measurement gave 249.43 ml? It is not uncommon in science to get several different measurements with the same instruments. Those are precise but uncertain amounts.

We see this same phenomenon in a more common scientific fact. All organisms contain deoxyribonucleic acid (DNA) to store protein information.[6] DNA, the molecule inside cells that contains code for proteins,[7] was the false basis for such movies as *Jurassic Park* and the true basis for such television shows as *Crime Scene Investigators*. How do we know that all organisms contain DNA? Simply because all organisms we have analyzed contain DNA. Does this mean that all organisms contain DNA as the information molecule? All we know is that all organisms tested so far do contain it, but that is no guarantee that all organisms do. Unlike mathematics, in which every possible triangle has the same 180°, empirical science is always open to refutation and therefore uncertain.

Several decades ago, in fact, certain viruses were found to have ribonucleic acid (RNA) instead of DNA in this role as an information-bearing molecule.[8] But scientific opinion is divided on whether viruses should be considered living organisms.[9] If they are not living, then we can still say

5. Sheen, *Philosophy of Science*, 179–90.

6. Raven et al., *Biology*, 256–59. For this and subsequent references to more common and broadly acknowledged biological and scientific facts, I cite textbooks. Original references can be traced from these.

7. Raven et al., *Biology*, 41, 278–301.

8. Raven et al., *Biology*, 524, 527.

9. Among many articles, see, e.g., Rice, "Are Viruses Alive?," 100–105.

only that DNA is the information-bearing molecule in living things, but if they are living, then we would have to modify our claim to say that nucleic acids are the information-bearing molecules. As a matter of fact, some labs have synthesized additional nucleic acid-like molecules other than DNA or RNA that can function in organisms to store information.[10] Before they knew that DNA was used, some noteworthy scientists thought proteins could do the job, and there is no intrinsic reason that they can't.[11] So it is theoretically possible for organisms to use other molecules besides DNA. In other words, there is no *intrinsic* reason for the information storage in a cell to occur through DNA – it is not *necessary* for it to be so. That is simply the only molecule that has been found. Just like measuring triangles scientifically with a protractor, one could find others that don't match the present known organisms.

Why is empirical science like this? Because it analyzes *individuals*, and individuals vary. Mathematically, one can understand exactly what a triangle is, and so logically deduce certain knowledge from this starting point. So long as the correct procedures of reasoning and logic are followed, subsequent knowledge is certain. Not so for empirical science. Because individuals vary, all subsequent discoveries are to a greater or lesser degree uncertain.

The precise but uncertain knowledge of empirical science is sufficient for sending rockets to the moon, or for cloning a mammoth, or for making nuclear reactors. So long as scientists consistently get a range of measures within a certain tolerance, they can do remarkable things with nature. For example, if the measure of the temperature tolerance of concrete used to construct a nuclear reactor vessel is found repeatedly, through many measurements, to be far above the temperature tolerance needed for controlled nuclear fission reactions, that concrete will be sufficient. Scientist or engineers may not really understand the exact nature of the thing, but if they can reliably get what they want from it, this is all that is needed. All science proceeds by measuring individuals: repeated measures of the energy expelled by a rocket fuel, repeated observations of an animal in a tree, repeated observations of distant galaxies, or repeated measures of insect resistance owing to cloning a gene into a corn plant. The repeated measurement of individual

10. Pinheiro et al., "Synthetic Genetic Polymers," 307–8.

11. Klug et al., *Concepts of Genetics*, 232–33.

instances is the *sine qua non* (that without which not) of science. One of the first things taught in a lab is that the more repetitions, the better the understanding. Science proceeds by measurement taken in the broad sense of multiple observations. The only things that are measurable and observable are material things, things extended in space and time. Science is bound by its methods to the study of material entities. But what if there exist beings that are not amenable to measurement, things like human minds, souls, angels, or God? If such beings or entities exist, science can say nothing about them because it is limited to the empirical and the measurable.

There is another, deeper sense in which the experimental procedures of science are limited; or, rather, they rest on foundations not provided by the science itself. I want to ask whether empirical science is dependent on self-evident principles. If so, then it is dependent on the common human experience of reality, because it is from this experience of reality that one comes to know these principles. And while we come to know self-evident principles from material being, they are not per se limited by material being. Nothing inherent in any self-evident principle is subject to the limits of space and time. For instance, why should cause and effect, considered *in itself*, be limited to only material things? These are transcendent principles of knowing and can yield proofs for immaterial entities. In a sense, they stand to nature in general as mathematics does to the triangle. They give certain knowledge of being from which further certain knowledge can be had through proper logic and reason. Therefore if science is subject to common experience, not only can it say nothing about immaterial being, but also it has to be consonant with the understanding of reality based on common experience and self-evident knowledge. This becomes clearer when we examine scientific experiments.

A Classic Scientific Experiment

William Beaumont's work[12] provides a clean example of experimental science. Beaumont was born in Lebanon, Connecticut, in 1785. He left home in 1806 and became a schoolmaster in Champlain, New York. While there,

12. The account of Beaumont's life and the experiment are taken from Harre, *Great Scientific Experiments*, 39–47.

he educated himself in medicine and related sciences, finally obtaining a degree in medicine. Under the tutelage of a certain Dr. Chandler in Vermont, Beaumont learned the practical, clinical aspect of the profession. Joining the US Army in 1812, he afterward practiced medicine and then rejoined the Army, having been assigned in 1820 to Ft. Mackinac in Michigan.

It was in the Army that he met Alex St. Martin, a French-Canadian who was accidentally wounded in the abdomen by a discharged musket. The musket ball pierced the abdominal wall and passed into the stomach, leaving a gaping hole. St. Martin recovered because, as Beaumont noted, he was a remarkably fit individual of outstanding physique. But while St. Martin was convalescing, the food he ate would pour out of the hole in his stomach. When "fully healed," a moveable flap of skin had grown over the hole, allowing Dr. Beaumont direct access to the stomach. He took the opportunity to inquire into the nature of digestion, which was little understood at the time.

Beaumont devised an experiment by withdrawing gastric juices from St. Martin's stomach and placing them into a vial. He then placed the vial in a water bath so that he could vary the temperature several degrees above or below that of the natural body. Beaumont would put various food in the vials, such as bread, sausage, coffee, or fish, and by varying the temperature, he could measure the time it took for complete digestion. At the same time, he would tie a piece of the same food that was in the vial on a piece of string, pull back the flap of skin, and lower the food into St. Martin's stomach. When he would observe digestion taking place in the vial, he would simultaneously remove the food in St. Martin's stomach and compare natural digestion with that occurring in the vial. If the food in the vial was in the same condition as the stomach, Beaumont concluded that digestion was occurring in the same manner in both the vial and in the stomach.

Now the primary question that Beaumont had in mind concerned whether digestion was of a purely chemical nature or was due to some mysterious, unknown force of life. By removing the gastric juices from the stomach, he was effectively able to replicate digestion outside of a living organism. Through many repetitions, Beaumont concluded that digestion in the vial was the same as it was in the stomach, the natural place for the process. Beaumont concluded that digestion in the stomach was of a purely chemical nature. Thus Beaumont learned some details about digestion by performing the experiment with the vials. But Beaumont could never have reached that conclusion if he had not been able to compare the natural digestion in the stomach with the results in the vial. Thus the stomach acted as the natural control (standard) for his experiment.

Now reflect on how this experiment brings to light some of the principles outlined previously. It illustrates these principles at several levels. At the most general level, all Beaumont did was set up a series of causal conditions – the vial at various temperatures, the gastric juices, and the food – and observe the effects over time. This simple fact can be generalized: all experimental science consists of setting up a series of causes to elicit effects. All conclusions are based upon these effects because all empirical research presupposes these general cause-and-effect situations. The specific nature of the causes (e.g., chemical reactions) is learned through the experiment, but the notions of cause and effect in general are known prior to the experiment.

At a more refined level, the conceptual structure of Beaumont's work relies upon four causes: efficient, material, formal, and final.

Material causes: vials, gastric juices, food, temperature
Formal cause: the experiment design of external digestion
Efficient cause: Beaumont's construction of the experiment
Final cause: to study digestion

Careful thought shows that all scientific experiments follow this general structure by using or presupposing these four causes. In the case here, all Dr. Beaumont did was to take a situation (natural digestion), which is not observable to the unaided senses, and create a set of conditions to bring digestion up to the level of our common observation. By observing digestion in a vial and comparing it to the food removed from the stomach, Beaumont could effectively see what is occurring in the stomach. Now that he had brought the unseen of the stomach into the range of our common experience, he could then judge this question in the same manner that he would judge any other experience – by the use of other self-evident principles. For instance, in the question "Is the food digested or not in the vial?" the word "not" is a practical application of the principle of non-contradiction. Again, if Beaumont saw in a particular case that the food was still undigested and concluded the food was the same as it was before being placed in the vial, he would be applying the principle of identity: the food was still food and not something else.

Recall that the natural digestion in the stomach functioned as the control in Beaumont's experiment. Why did Beaumont need a control? Why does any scientist need a control? Broadly speaking, empirical science can be classified into observational and experimental sciences. Observational science consists principally in just that – observation. Much of early science consisted of this. Astronomy is a good example. One observes through telescopes what is going on in the solar system or other galaxies. No control of the place is possible because of the distance. A control is needed in experimental science, however, the type of science most people think of when they think of science. Experimental science occurs when one sets up a more or less controlled environment to isolate and study the nature of one aspect of the subject under study. For instance, if one wanted to determine whether a diet is good for losing weight, one might collect twenty people and place them on the diet in question. At the same time, one would have twenty other people in similar conditions of the twenty on the diet eat a normal diet. The similar conditions of, say, the home, workplace, and physical health are necessary to ensure that none of these are the reason for losing weight. For example, if five of the dieters had the stomach flu, their resultant loss of appetite would muddle the results. The normal diet is the control group (the standard), because one is comparing the effects of one set of food against another.

Such was the case with Beaumont. Beaumont could not know whether digestion occurred in the vial unless he had a natural, untampered instance of it in St. Martin's stomach. Digestion was only known to be digestion in the vial because it had the same effects as that in the stomach. In other words, digestion was known *before* the scientific experiment took place. The thing studied scientifically (digestion in the vial) was less known than that in the stomach, which was less scientifically studied.

The same pattern is obtained in all scientific experiments: the thing less analyzed is more understood in a certain sense, or else it could not be used as a standard. Let's take Cro-Magnon man (the technical term for humans as they existed about twenty thousand years ago). Did they know what the color red was? Twenty thousand years ago, these cave dwellers painted exquisite drawings of animals on the cave walls of France using a variety of brilliant colors, including red.[13] They did not know that red light emits light around 760 nm.[14] The only way to know that was to test the wavelength of *red* light. But the Cro-Magnons knew red without having to know that it emitted at 760 nm. They truly knew *red* when they saw it. So too, we knew red light before we understood that it emitted at 760-nm wavelength, that is, before we understood it through science.

Similarly, Beaumont – as well as the Cro-Magnons before him – knew certain truths from common experience before Beaumont had any thought of a scientific experiment. Though the Cro-Magnons, as far as we know, did not dream up any experiments, their cave paintings suggest a human desire to understand the world around them – the same desire underlying Beaumont's experiments on digestion. And both the nineteenth-century physician and the prehistoric cave dwellers depended on a common experience of cause and effect. They both knew that specific causes produced specific effects.

Recall that the ultimate reason for Beaumont conducting his experiment was the question of whether digestion is purely a chemical process, as opposed to some unknown life force. Beaumont answered this in the affirmative, and here we find yet another application of cause and effect. How? By his reasoning process. If the food is digested in the vial outside the stomach under purely nonliving chemical conditions in the same manner as the food is found digested when withdrawn from the stomach, then one can conclude that the causes of digestion in the vial are the same as the cause of digestion in the stomach. Because we are knowing beings and can be confident of our perceptions of reality – we can really know things as true – we can in confidence extrapolate our knowledge to regions unknown. In the case that follows in the next section, this intellectual effort can be validly extended even to places physically unattainable by us as well.

Sir Isaac Newton and Causality

The same rationale underlies the whole of modern astronomy. Sir Isaac Newton, arguably the greatest scientist of all time, used the same method

13. Tattersall, *Masters of the Planet*, 11–13.

14. Sears et al., *College Physics*, 642.

of reasoning in his famous work, the *Principia Mathematica*. Drawing on a panoply of observations made by Tycho Brahe and Johannes Kepler at the beginning of the seventeenth century, Newton several decades later was able to do precise enough calculations of planetary movements to show that they obeyed the laws of gravity.[15] The law of inertia was formulated by performing experiments with objects on earth. Galileo and others had already done so. Newton's achievement was to combine terrestrial and celestial mechanics into a unified theory. He concluded that if the effects (gravitational) observed in objects distant from the earth were the same as those on earth, then the causes must be the same.[16] In other words, because distant celestial objects produce the same effects observable on earth, the same causal factors that are operational in our solar system must also apply to distant galaxies. Thus the general conclusion that the laws of nature in distant reaches of space are the same as those we find here on earth is based on the assumption of the universality of cause and effect.

The encyclopedia of science since Newton's day has expanded exponentially, but the same assumption of effects being proportionate to their causes reigns. Since the advent of the twentieth century, modern astronomy has expanded its observational base into much more sophisticated theories of galactic origins, the Big Bang, the expanding universe, and so on. But all these still presuppose the same underlying assumptions. None of these objects are near enough to actually visit, so all our information is based on observations of their movements (as was the case for Newton) or how light is emitted from them. Some of this light is not visible, such as x-rays or microwaves, so we use devices that can detect them and then transform them into digital readouts or into light spectra that we can observe. Once done, we can judge them by the way we judge anything else that we see. For instance, we can use visible light to infer chemical composition. Certain elements and molecules emit only certain specific wavelengths of light, just like oaks or raccoons have specific features to them.[17] This information about the light spectra of elements and molecules was determined by experiments on earth.

15. For an explanation of how Newton incorporated Kepler's three laws of planetary motion and derived them from the principles of dynamics, see Westfall, *Never at Rest*, 402*ff*.

16. Koyré, *Newtonian Studies*, 255.

17. Shaw, *Astrochemistry*, 41–83.

By observing the same light spectra from objects in outer space, we infer that they are composed of the same chemicals that we find here on earth, which emit the same specific light spectra: the same effect, the same cause.[18] An effect is proportionate to its cause.

Distant galaxies and human digestion are different, but both are instances of modern science. They each constitute specific examples of bringing the unobservable into the observable to understand reality better by the use of cause and effect. Beaumont used the vial outside of the stomach to bring phenomena that are unobservable to the unaided senses (digestion) up to the level of common sight. Once accomplished, he judged these phenomena in the same way he judged anything else. These are the same questions and observations everyone uses in common human experience. And our answers to these questions all presuppose the same basic self-evident principles.

Otto Stern and Subatomic Particles

Otto Stern investigated whether subatomic particles moved in discrete quanta, or packets of energy.[19] One prediction of quantum theory stated that electrons orbited an atom much as planets orbited the sun, but that they moved between orbits in essentially instantaneous jumps when a discreet amount of energy had been absorbed. It would be similar if one planet could only move into the orbit of another planet by having the precise amount of energy to instantaneously pop into the new orbit, as opposed to smoothly going from one orbit to the other.

Stern had to be able to observe whether electrons existed in these discrete states, or packets, as opposed to a whole series of intermediate states between each orbit in the atom. How is that possible given the trillions of atoms moving at nearly the speed of light? He began by heating samples of lithium to high temperatures in a small container called a crucible. The vaporized atoms were immediately fed into a vacuum tube and traveled at high energies because of the heat of vaporization. The problem was that there are many electrons on these trillions of atoms with many energies, but he needed a beam of atoms of only one energy, or one state of electrons, so to speak. Here Stern

18. Shaw, *Astrochemistry*, 41–83.

19. Harre, *Great Scientific Experiments*, 212–20.

came up with an ingenious idea. He focused the vaporized atoms through the narrow slits between the teeth of two gears spinning at high speeds and in opposite directions. When the fine teeth of the two gears aligned, a gap resulted that allowed only the atoms with the same precise amount of energy to pass through the gap in the teeth between the two gears. This arrangement gave him his desired beam of atoms of the same energy.

A second problem was that atoms can have different orientations. One could be pointing up and the other down, a situation that could distort any interpretation of a discrete state. To solve this problem, he passed the beam of atoms through a slit in a long, powerful magnet to align all the atoms in the same orientation, similar to the way atoms in iron filings can be aligned by magnets. He then focused this beam on a photographic plate. If there were no discrete packets of energy, he should have expected to see a whole series of images of graded sets of states corresponding to the orbits. If there were discrete states, then he should expect to see only two orientations for any before-and-after energy corresponding to the different discrete states of electron configurations in the atoms (the up or down, so to speak). The latter is exactly what he saw, showing discrete quantum states.

Stern's experiment shows the same structure as Beaumont's. A distinct set of causes produces a discrete effect. Further, the whole design of the experiment revolves around the four causes discussed previously:

Material causes: lithium, the crucible, the gears, the magnet, and the photographic plate
Formal cause: the order of the experimental machine
Efficient cause: Stern's construction of the apparatus
Final cause: to determine whether subatomic particles had discrete quantum states

The whole experiment was one complex process of getting a sufficient number of atoms at the correct state of energy in the correct orientation to be able to concentrate on a photographic plate so that the cumulative effect could be observed. Were the atoms in two discrete states or a series of states? Stern reasoned that the answer had to be one or the other, an application of the principle of non-contradiction. This experiment was a fundamental verification of the predictions of Niels Bohr regarding quantum physics. As previously quoted, Niels Bohr also said that all science uses the same self-evident principles based on common experience to arrive at understanding. Ironically, it is the same field of quantum physics that is often invoked under the sway of scientism to claim that common experience has no validity.

From Darwin to DNA

No one doubts that Charles Darwin was a brilliant observational scientist who collected enormous amounts of data from fossils and living organisms to formulate his theory of natural selection. Darwin discovered that there was tremendous variation of organisms through deep time and concluded that this variation was the material upon which the natural environment would favor or disfavor the survivability of an organism.[20] He came to this conclusion by observing pigeons and other agricultural animals in the hands of their keepers. These keepers favored certain traits in populations of organisms, such as feathered feet in pigeons, and would breed animals with those traits to produce elaborate types of animals for show.[21] From this, Darwin made an inference of causality similar to that of Newton and Beaumont, that is, that there was a selecting force at work on the variations.[22] The artificial breeding displays the four types of causes:

Material cause: the observable traits in the animals
Formal cause: the final condition of the organism
Efficient cause: the breeder manipulating the process
Final cause: the purpose for which the breeder acts

Darwin extrapolated from artificial breeding to nature itself:

Material cause: the natural variation of traits
Formal cause: the final condition of the organism
Efficient cause: the forces of the environment
Final cause: survival (reproduction of the next generation)

20. Darwin, *Origin of Species*, 88–132.
21. Darwin, *Origin of Species*, 31–58.
22. Darwin, *Origin of Species*, 31–132.

In the Victorian world of Darwin's science, there was as yet no knowledge of genetics. Gregor Mendel and his famous peas came not long after, but the discovery of the structure of DNA had to wait until the mid-twentieth century.[23] Modern molecular biology began as a recognized subdiscipline in biology in the middle part of the twentieth century. The discovery that heralded this field was the elucidation of the double-helical structure of the DNA molecule by Francis Crick, James Watson, and Maurice Wilkins, for which they won the Nobel Prize in 1963.[24] Watson and Crick were modelers and looked at data (effects) from experiments on DNA from which they built a model to account for this data. The model was an artificial representation of the structure of DNA, whose real counterpart was the cause of these results. When the model they produced fit all the data, they concluded that they had found the cause behind the known results of experiments with DNA.

We see, then, in these instances of scientific work – whether experimental, such as Beaumont or Stern, observational, such as Newton and Darwin, or even model-based, such as Watson and Crick – that all presuppose the same rational inferences of cause and effect and other self-evident principles. Beaumont and Stern used this in both their experimental design and their final interpretations of the results. Beaumont also used these results to infer the unseen inner workings of the stomach. Newton based his whole astronomy upon this same inference: what was good for earth was good for deep space. Darwin did the same; he inferred an analogous causal mechanism in nature, based upon what he saw breeders doing with artificial systems and his own observations of nature. Applying this to the past, he in part did for time what Newton did for space. What was true in the present was true in the past. Watson and Crick used cause and effect to back-extrapolate, so to speak, from effects (data) to cause (model). This multilayer causality has not escaped cutting-edge modern science. Alwyn Scott, a founder of nonlinear biology, in the *Encyclopedia of Non-Linear Science* (a nascent discipline) states, "Twenty-four centuries ago, Aristotle described four types of causes (material, efficient, formal, and final), which overlap and intermingle in ways that were often overlooked in 20th century thought, but are now under scrutiny."[25]

23. Klug et al., *Concepts of Genetics*, 3.

24. Klug et al., *Concepts of Genetics*, 249

25. Scott, *Encyclopedia of Non-Linear Science*, vii.

While I have focused on cause and effect, one could go over all these experiments in detail with the other self-evident principles I mentioned – the existence of a real external world, reality as ordered, the principles of non-contradiction and of identity – and show the same consistency and assumptions.

Science and Self-Evident Knowledge

These scientific experiments are but the tip of the iceberg. Many others, like Mendel's work with peas, could be cited, and all are beautiful examples of reliance on common experience. If one critically examines the underlying assumption of any scientific work, one will see that it relies on the same self-evident knowledge derived from common experience, the same experience that everyone uses every day. Far from superseding common experience, or making it irrelevant, the scientific enterprise is simply another example of it. Science examines reality in such a manner as to allow much greater precision, which can enrich the ancient understanding of reality but not contradict it.

One philosopher of a previous generation recognized this fact. Fulton Sheen, whose book *The Philosophy of Science* addressed the relation of modern science to ancient philosophy, would go on to become a priest and a bishop. Summing up the discontinuity and continuity between modern science and ancient philosophy, Sheen wrote,

> Facts in our day are not the same as facts in the time of Aristotle or Thomas Aquinas. But the principles by which these facts are interpreted have not changed, for common sense remains essentially the same throughout the ages. Facts of chemistry revealed in the days of St. Thomas are not the same as the chemical facts revealed to us today. In his day it was generally believed that the earth was made up of four elements: air, earth, fire, and water – a heritage of the early Grecian sciences. Today we know that there are not four elements but 92 elements. But while the science of chemistry has changed its outlook, it is not true to say that philosophy has changed its principles. The principle of identity, the principle of contradiction, the principle of finality, the principle of the ordered harmony of the universe remain just as true today as they did thousands of years ago. There is no reason in the world, therefore, why these immutable principles should not be applied to the new facts of our

> day just as they were applied to the facts of ancient days. There is very likely to be an unwarranted prejudice on the part of modern scientists to the fact that simply because the scientific facts have changed, therefore philosophical principles are inapplicable to them, and that our knowledge is quite superior to the knowledge of the ancients and the middle ages. It is to be granted that our facts are better, but it is not quite certain their interpretation is better … Our instruments are far better than the instruments of the ancients, but there is nothing to indicate that our reasoning about the facts discovered by these better instruments is superior to that of the ancients. After all, if we concern ourselves with facts alone, what is the difference between the facts revealed by new science and the facts in the days of Aristotle? It is principally a difference in measurement. In simple terms, the ancients measured in terms of yards; we measure in terms of inches. We speak of protons and electrons, they spoke of atoms; we speak in terms of light years; they spoke in terms of solar years. Today's facts are more minute but the theoretical reasoning about facts is essentially the same.[26]

Sheen's insights into the history of thought bring to light an important truth: our knowledge of particular changes can alter our empirical theories of material reality, but the process of reasoning about those particulars remains essentially the same as it was thousands of years ago. This accounts for the difference between mathematics and philosophy on the one hand and the empirical sciences on the other. After all, the truth of the proposition that every triangle has 180° is as true today as it was when it was proved in antiquity. The philosophical principles sketched in this chapter (e.g., cause and effect, the four types of causes, etc.) have not changed, either. The challenge is to develop a worldview that honors the advances of the empirical sciences while simultaneously building on the timeless wisdom of ancient philosophy.

26. Sheen, *Philosophy of Science*, 165–66.

3 THE IMMATERIALITY OF THE INTELLECT

Back Home in Indiana

From earliest memory, I was interested in trees and had mastered the identification of many hardwoods by my early teens. I found myself fascinated with giant old trees that jutted into the sky. Across the creek at the base of our property and down a ways from the spring was a huge old white oak, by far the largest tree in the area. I once took the circumference and calculated the diameter as close to 6 feet; it was probably several hundred years old. Its trunk is no more than 15 feet high and hollow somewhere in the middle, a fact I discovered when, on more than one occasion, I stared into the tree and a raccoon in the hollow on the top of the trunk stared back at me. The branches of the old tree spread out in a broad crown above the trunk. When we first moved there, I found the tree was entangled in two huge grapevines, each 3–4 inches thick, intertwined among the branches. Soon afterward, I took an old corn knife and cut the grapevines at their base. A feeling of satisfaction at having freed the venerable old giant from its predicament came over me.

This first section of this chapter bears similarity to Kohak's *Embers and the Stars* (89–130). I feel a great kinship with and indebtedness to Kohak's work. My experiences growing up in rural southern Indiana have a great deal of commonality with his time spent in New Hampshire.

Why would one feel a sense of satisfaction toward a tree? A tree is not venerable in the way a saint is thought to be, or any other human being for that matter, but it is venerable in its own right. It forces a type of respect on you when you lay your hand on such a large creature, sensing its immense bulk, or when you run your hand up against its rough gray bark and step away to gaze at the immensity of the thing. It had been there for centuries weathering heat and cold, floods from the creek, deer and elk. When it was young, it endured lightning and somehow survived the cutting of the old-growth forests when pioneers arrived. It fought the good fight through the centuries and survived. Above all, it stood simply as an object of beauty in its own right; it deserved a kind of respect, veneration in the loose sense.[1]

"Respect" is also the word to describe a similar experience of splitting the wood of such oaks in the fall. It is the same experience of anyone who has had a maul wedged tightly in hardwood while trying to free it for twenty minutes. A piece of wood being cut for fire is not the same as a living tree, but it nevertheless commands respect. And different types of wood – oak, maple, elm, black cherry – all command a slightly different type of respect. Oak with a heady smell of tannin, maple with a sharp smell not quite fruity, and cherry with its full fruity odor all split different but cleanly, whereas elm is tough and stringy. Respect is engendered by both the lived experience of nature and grappling with nature to have her yield her secrets.

The large slabs of fossilized limestone by the creek side command a type of respect as well.[2] The simple presence of their ageless being engenders respect. It is just there. It exists. Overturning creek rocks, I could observe the young fish writhing in their glistening eggs in March. Here, life was different from the oaks but still engendered respect. Veneration for the natural world is even more pronounced when encountering animal life. While lacking the age and bulk of the oak, animals have a dynamism and an intensity of life and beauty that no plant has. The whole creek system in March elicits a profound veneration as well: new fish, water striders, diving beetles, clams, frogs, raccoons, crayfish, opossums, new flowers along the stream's edge. They all evoke respect and even belonging. Somehow, I knew that the

1. Kohak, *Embers and the Stars*, 122–29.

2. Kohak, *Embers and the Stars*, 95, 128.

complexity and dynamism of life, so evident in the creek and its inhabitants, were linked to who I am.

The same sense of meaning occurred while walking along the lane on a clear night and seeing the deluge of stars in the Milky Way. The immensity of the heavens with its innumerable points of light elicits a feeling of awe, humility, and veneration. Still, despite its size, a sense of my belonging to this universe suggests that something personal is behind it. I never felt alone even though at times I would spend hours by myself. Standing still in the middle of the woods after a fresh snow, I could not escape the realization that there is something personal about reality – not exactly personal in the sense of being human, but in the sense of engendering respect, awe, and veneration. Most of all, I had a sense of belonging.

This perception of meaning – more than passing feelings – was greatest in the presence of human evidence. The creek stones stacked around the sides of the spring, the Model A fender buried in the old roadbed, the roadbed itself, the pottery just beneath the ground by the spring, the old barn, and the old tools in it left by the previous owners were all personal things used by personal beings. These things evoked a sense of relatedness or belonging to these former residents, even though I am not closely related to them by blood.

The evidence of humans like myself indicated personhood, persons who planned, hoped, dreamed, loved, and raised families. They worked the same land, viewing it with a similar respect as I did. They were persons in the truest sense. All the rest – animals, plants, and rocks – also had a sense of being personal about them, but in a qualitatively different manner from humans. They were personal in that that they elicited awe, respect, and a sense of belonging in human beings, but they were not sufficient for being a true person. It is one of the greater insights that the common unreflective experience of reality can give a human being: reality in a certain sense is personal, or at least there is a person behind it.

It forces the question of whether reality – all reality – is personal or impersonal. Erazim Kohak provides us the insight that the only fitting cosmological background to our human personhood is that the universe itself partakes of personhood.[3] Being a person is a given in the common experi-

3. Kohak, *Embers and the Stars*, 122–29, 209.

ence of humanity. This personal experience of reality coupled with the idea that there is an Ultimate Cause constitutes *the* experience with which to be reckoned: reality is ultimately a Personal Cause.[4] This experience of reality as personal yields an answer as to what it means to be a person.

In the experience of belonging to a greater whole – be it the heavens, the creek, or membership in a family – to be personal means to be *in relationship with*.[5] Being in relation with others distinguishes the personal from the private. I used to take walks for miles on the back roads near our place. A few miles away was an old gravel driveway leading into some woods. At the base of the driveway, an old board nailed on a tree warned, "privut property, keep out!" I never ventured up that road, as I did not think the *persons* who lived there were too *personal*. They didn't seem interested in being related to other people. Yet to be a person means precisely to be able to enter into a relationship with another person. How can one be *personal* without being *related to* someone? Nonhuman reality around us is somewhat personal in the sense of evoking an experience of belonging. I am related to it at some level. I too was a member of the creek community.

Yet personhood is more, too. The reality of personhood seems to be beyond the grasp of science. It seems to require something more or, maybe better said, something more fundamental. What differs in a human that allows one to be a *true person*? What precisely is it about a person that allows one to be truly *personal*, to be truly related, and not by blood, to other humans? What engenders true friendship in humans? In my long walks with Bliss, I asked myself what made me a person in the true sense, and her not. What was not going on inside of her that was going on inside me? She sensed, interacted with her surroundings, and was happy to see me every day, but there was a radical difference. As far as anyone knows, she never asked the same questions about me. The answer is explicitly and implicitly contained in one word: intellect or intelligence.[6] Yet the matter is not so simple, because ancient and medieval thinkers meant something vastly different by the term "intelligence" from what post-Enlightenment thinkers meant. For many modern thinkers, intelligence has nothing to do with love;

4. Kohak, *Embers and the Stars*, 122–29, 209.

5. *ST* I, q. 28, a. 2, arg. 3.

6. *ST* I, q. 39, a. 1, c.

to put intelligence and love in proximity astounds people today who have been steeped in post-Enlightenment thought. For ancient and the medieval thinkers, however, intelligence and love were intimately related.

What Is Intelligence?

For most moderns, both academic and nonacademic, intelligence is a problem-solving faculty or a calculating machine, which is the reason why animals are thought to be sentient and intelligent. Defined in this manner, animals certainly do have intelligence, and human beings differ only in degree, not in kind. This provides the basis for the modern contention that humans are simply animals with nothing in particular to *really* distinguish them.

Ancient and medieval thinkers would have found this modern notion of intelligence impoverished and paltry, wholly lacking in explanatory power. For the ancients, modern science can investigate certain effects of the intellect in material things, but not the intellect itself. Their much richer conception of intelligence has been so eclipsed in modern thought that it has virtually vanished from any possibility of being seriously entertained. Yet, as I show, science is not equipped to understand intelligence because science is bound purely to material things. This limitation, coupled with the philosophical ideology of materialism, effectively destroyed the ancient idea of intelligence.

The ancient and medieval idea of the intellect is that of an acquisitive faculty of being (reality), both that of material and immaterial being.[7] It does not *sense* things; it *understands* them. In the act of knowing, the intellect becomes one with the nonsensible, or intelligible, aspect of its object.[8] It grasps meaning in things, focusing on what something is at its deeper level. A good material analogue is the hand. The hand grasps a material, sensible object; it possesses it.

Consider also how the sense of taste and smell works. Aristotle appealed to the senses to explain this property of the intellect, but he used the sense of sight.[9] An understating elucidated by modern science of how taste and smell

7. Aquinas, *Commentary on Aristotle's De Anima* III, lec. 3–8.

8. Aquinas, *Truth*, vol. I, q. 2, a. 2.

9. Aquinas, *Truth*, vol. I, q. 2, a. 2.

work might better appeal to the modern mechanistic mind than would Aristotle's explanation of sight. Tasting and smelling both work in essentially the same way.[10] An organism has three-dimensional pockets called taste or odorant receptors on the tongue or in the nasal lining, respectively. Taste and smell occur if a molecule released by the object that is being tasted or smelled can bind and fit into, or have the same shape as, the receptor. When this occurs, a signal travels through neurons to the brain, and taste or smell is perceived. Here we have a situation where part of the object sensed (that which is tasted or smelled, i.e., molecules released from the object) binds to and unites with the perceiver. The perceiver is thus aware (knows the sensible object) by uniting with part of it. Why not the same analogously for nonmaterial things?

As opposed to holding on to a material object, or part of it, the intellect grasps the being of things. In this sense, it is the terminus of love. How so? Consider the hand again. If I desire a sensible object, my hand reaches out to grab it. My holding it with my hand is the end of desire, or affection for a thing. My hand possesses it. Ancient and medieval thinkers thought similarly about the intellect. The desire for a good, or the being of a thing, and the delight of that good, is called love. The intellect is that thing that possesses the object of love. Love is the desire of the intellect for its object and the delight therein.[11] As the affection for a sensible object ends in physical possession, so love for a thing ends in its possession by the intellect and the consequent resting in its possession. Love ends in union.[12] As far as we know, only human beings are capable of such a love.

The most extreme physical attraction (erotic love) ends in the physical union of sex. True love, or intellectual love – *philia* (love of friendship) or *agape* (love of another purely for his own sake and not for oneself) – ends in intellectual, immaterial, or spiritual union.[13] As physical union finds its fulfillment in the production of offspring (fruition), so – as I develop later in

10. Raven et al., *Biology*, 925–26.

11. *ST* I, q. 19, a. 1; I, q. 20, a. 1.

12. Among many excellent sources in Christian literature, see de Sales, *Treatise on the Love of God*, 37–39.

13. These three types of love can be found throughout the history of human thought and were clearly distinguished by the ancient Greeks.

this book — does intellectual union find its fulfillment ultimately in a third, a type of internal fruition. Thus love was ultimately not an emotion for the ancients and medievals, because emotions originate in the senses. Animals have emotions like humans. *But humans are the only beings in the material universe that have intelligence.*[14] It is this idea of the intellect that allows anyone who has it — humans and angels — to be *personal* in the truest sense. It allows them to be *related to*, in the most radical sense where one literally is the other in the intellect. Oneness in the intellect — true personal union — is the terminus of love.[15] In the Bible, this notion of intelligence is called "the heart of man," the very core of his being, the part of the human being that only God can directly access.[16] And remember, this idea has nothing to do with intelligence quotient, or IQ. Just because the person next to you is "smarter" in this sense, according to a modern idea of calculating ability, this does not mean that he or she is able to love or be a person more than you. On the contrary, this ancient idea of the intellect, assumed in ancient Hebrew culture and articulated by the greatest of Greek philosophers, contends that the intellect is immaterial. It grasps a thing at its deepest level, the level beyond sense. If a thing is not sensible, it is immaterial, so the intellect must

14. There is no valid scientific evidence for any other intelligent life form in the material universe. There is only scant indirect evidence that *any* life, including bacteria, might possibly exist outside of our planet. This evidence basically consists of the presence of water, organic molecules, minerals that could (but not necessarily) be deposited by organisms, isotope patterns and atmospheric constituents possibly (but not necessarily) indicative of life, positions of planets in stellar zones favorable to conditions living things need, and types of life found here on earth that are able to survive extreme conditions (Ward and Brownlee, *Rare Earth,* 1–33; Shaw, *Astrochemistry*, 274–82). The crux of the argument for intelligent life on other planets at present is the size and complexity of the material universe. The argument is that in such a vast universe, life and intelligent life *must* have arisen elsewhere. As G. K. Chesterton put it with regard to a proponent of this argument in his time, Herbert Spencer, "He popularized this contemptible notion that the size of the solar system ought to over-awe the spiritual dogma of man. Why should a man surrender his dignity to the solar system any more than to a whale? If mere size proves that man is not the image of God, then a whale may be the image of God; a somewhat formless image; what one might call an impressionist portrait" (*Orthodoxy*, 53).

15. *ST* I, q. 19, a. 1; I, q. 20, a. 1.

16. See, e.g., the *Philokalia*, a large collection of texts by Eastern Christian Fathers and mystics. The *Philokalia* is a highly revered source in the Christian East. It has been described as the lens that allows one to properly interpret Scripture. It contains among the best commentaries on the Eastern "Jesus Prayer," or Prayer of the Heart. The idea that the intellect, as I have described, is at the core of man is highly prevalent throughout. See Nikodimos of the Holy Mountain and Makarios of Corinth, *Philokalia.*

be immaterial.[17] This notion of the intellect is so foreign to modern people, whether highly educated or not, that it is likely to be rejected prima facie.

Is it reasonable that the human intellect must be immaterial?[18] Consider again the triangle.[19] We discussed how a triangle can be proven mathematically to have 180°. The proof is clear and absolutely certain. But how do we *understand* this? How can we understand that it has *exactly* 180°? How can we understand *perfection*, a *perfect* 180°? No experience of actual, existing triangles in our material world would be sufficient, because no existing triangle is perfect. Why is no existing triangle perfect? Imagine a triangle built out of three 1-meter sticks. Anyone who has ever cut wood will know that no matter how even the ends of two pieces of wood are, upon close examination, the ends have tiny jagged edges. I have seen pictures of the surfaces of such objects taken under electron microscopes, objects that were made from different materials and supposedly cut as smoothly as possible. Under such powerful magnification, these supposedly flawless surfaces are simply microscopically jagged edges. So, no matter how perfectly cut our sticks are, they are far from even.

Why is a perfectly smooth edge impossible in the material world? Physics provides the answer.[20] Each of these sticks is made up of an unimaginable number of atoms. Even the very ends of these sticks would contain trillions upon trillions of atoms. Now, each atom is composed of a center, called a nucleus, made up of subatomic particles called protons and neutrons. Protons are positively charged, and therefore so is the nucleus. Around the nucle-

17. Aquinas, *Summa contra Gentiles* (*SCG*) I.44.

18. I must again emphasize that I am not attempting to *demonstrate* the immateriality of the intellect, as it is beyond the scope of this book (but is certainly possible). I am attempting to show that it is *reasonable* to assert that it is immaterial.

19. There exists more than one means of showing the immateriality of the intellect. I have chosen, based on my experience with scientists and students of science, what I think might be one that perhaps makes the most sense to them. This is the idea of the intellect's ability to know something that, strictly speaking, is not found in material things: a perfect thing. The intellect must abstract the idea of perfection by removing the limitations of matter found in materially existing things. Then, as stated by Aquinas, "The operation of anything follows the mode of its being" (*ST* I, q. 75, a. 3, c). Or, as stated previously, an effect is proportionate to its cause. As I argue, if one can conceive of something not found in matter, one must have a cause proportionate to that. Hence, if one can conceive of something immaterial, something exists in the conceiver that is immaterial. This we call the intellect. See also Adler, *Intellect*, 41–53. Adler mentions triangles but gives other arguments as well.

20. Calle, *Superstrings*, 109–31.

us move electrons, one for each proton, as electrons are negatively charged (positive and negative attract). These electrons move at near–light speed in a cloud of differing orbits, their position constantly changing. The likelihood that each electron of the trillions of atoms at the ends of all three sticks is simultaneously in the same position to give equal lengths on all three sticks is impossibly remote. Further, electrons are shared by atoms near each other, thus linking them together. These electrons can switch to differing orbits in an atom or to different atoms at times. So a given electron may not even be in the same orbit at any given moment. Modern physics claims that protons are made up of yet smaller particles called quarks.[21] Here is the same problem at a yet finer level. Even deeper, modern string theory postulates that these particles in turn are strings of energy billions and billions of times smaller than the particles themselves.[22] How does one measure distance in energy?

Even if, for the sake of argument, we granted the possibility of perfectly existing triangles in the material world, the problem would still be how we could know it. Quantum mechanics, a science that studies subatomic particles and their behavior, states that one can only know the probable position of a particle.[23] But probability is not perfection. Magnify that by the incredible number of electrons that are present, and it becomes evident that with a perfect hypothetical triangle, it would still be impossible to know it as really perfect. Consider another argument. How could we measure the sticks composing the triangle? To know them as perfect, one would have to have gradations on another meter stick as small as the electrons (or quarks) to perfectly measure the sticks of the triangle. We are faced with all the same problems in the measuring device itself.

So truly quantifiable perfection does not exist in a material object. Nor could it be even knowable from the properties of matter. And yet we *can* know that a *perfect* triangle would indeed be *perfectly* 180°. We can extend this argument to other geometrical shapes as well – a perfect square (four *exact* sides), a perfect circle (all points *exactly* equidistant from a central point in two dimensions), a perfect sphere (all points *exactly* equidistant from a

21. Calle, *Superstrings*, 448–53.

22. Greene, *Fabric of the Cosmos*, 330–47.

23. Greene, *Fabric of the Cosmos*, 280.

central point in three dimensions), and so on. Therefore, if such ideas are knowable, there must be a nonmaterial basis to the idea of perfection because the sensory (material) world does not contain perfection. Experience shows that we really can know what it means to be perfect. This could only be the case if we have some power or capability inside of us that makes this knowledge possible. Just as oaks and raccoons need specific causes to produce specific effects, so do we need a cause that has the capacity to know immaterial ideas. An effect is proportionate to its cause. This power or capability is what the ancients called the intellect.

Reflect for a moment on the unique character of the idea of a perfect triangle. It is precisely that it is the *ideal or perfection* of what exists. It is a universal (archetypal) triangle. It is what all triangles ideally should be, but it does not exist in material things. Why? Because material things are individual, not universal. They are extended in space and time. So universality cannot actually exist in matter by itself. It is always *this* thing, *this* triangle with its defects, which exists individually. The same could be said of a dog. We can have a universal idea of dog in our mind, but not in reality. We never say that such-and-such dog is "dogness," just as we never say this or that human being is "humanity," that is, the ideal human. We have never experienced dogness, humanity, or triangularity as such, only *this* dog, *this* human, or *this* triangle. Perfection does not exist as such in the external world, but it does exist in our intellect. Perfection is something that transcends individual material things, which is precisely what is meant by the ideal thing. So our intellect must be a capacity to transcend the limitations of individuality and materiality. It must be immaterial.

The Art in Caves and the Art of Intelligence

The power of human intelligence is on full display in cave art that is more than twenty thousand years old. Ian Tattersall, one of the leading experts on human evolution, discusses this power in his book *Masters of the Planet*. He argues that the uniqueness of humans is evidenced in their art on the cave walls of France because they show their creators to be capable of abstract and symbolic reasoning. Tattersall argues that while comparisons with apes may be a helpful starting point in the study of human evolution, the results are unexpected.[24] Human beings are more than just improved versions of the apes. Alluding to the resistance found in certain academic circles, Tattersall asserts, "it turns out that we modern human beings are not simply an improved version of them."[25] The art on the cave walls in Spain and France clearly demonstrates that they "not only thought as we do but ... left an overwhelmingly convincing body of evidence to prove it:"

> Best exemplified by the famous animal images on the ceilings and walls of caves such as Spain's Altamira and France's Lascaux and Chauvet, the power and sophistication of this ancient art is somehow magnified by the knowledge that its painters lived in an unthinkably remote epic of modern human history ... The antiquity of this art is astonishing; exposure to it nonetheless makes you fully understand Picasso's alleged remark that the Ice Age painters had left him little to accomplish. Certainly, it's impossible to imagine better evidence that the wonderful and unprecedented human creative spirit was already fully formed at that distant point in modern prehistory.[26]

What kind of art did the cave dwellers produce that left such an impression of their full humanity on Tattersall and other observers? The walls of Lascaux, so full of animal images, are "drawn with the deftness, observation, and clever stylization that place their creators among the greatest artists ever."[27]

> Among and upon these instantly recognizable animal figures are placed geometric motifs – grids, lines and lines of dots, dartlike signs – that clearly had very specific meaning to their creators. Sadly, today we have no way of knowing just what it was the artist had intended to express; but if you consider the clear specificity of the images together with the complex ways in which they are juxtaposed, you rapidly begin to realize that this art was not simply representational. It was symbolic. Every image in this cave and others, realistic or geometric, is drenched with meaning that goes far beyond its mere form.[28]

Here, Tattersall immediately recognizes one of the telltale signs of human intelligence: symbolization. The horses drawn by the cave inhabitants, dated to around thirty-four thousand years ago, exceed the individual

24. Tattersall, *Masters of the Planet*, 10.
25. Tattersall, *Masters of the Planet*, 10.
26. Tattersall, *Masters of the Planet*, 12.
27. Tattersall, *Masters of the Planet*, 13
28. Tattersall, *Masters of the Planet*, 13.

material horse: it "is a supremely symbolic object: in its flowing lines it is not merely a representation of the chunky horses that roamed the Ice Age steppes of Europe, but an abstraction of the graceful essence of the horse."[29] The relevance to the process of human knowing today does not escape Tattersall's notice. "If there is one single thing that above all else unites all human beings today, it is our symbolic capacity: our common ability to organize the world around us into a vocabulary of mental representations that we can recombine in our minds in an endless variety of new ways."[30]

It is this human capacity for idealization and meaning that stands at the center of the ancient and medieval idea of intelligence. The painted horse is an idealization, or attempt at perfection, of the individual horse that Ice Age people observed. The geometric motifs found with these paintings, says Tattersall, clearly had specific meaning to their creators. We have no way of knowing just what that meaning was, but how is it that he is able to infer that there was a meaning? The individual grid lines and dots do not in and of themselves contain meaning. If meaning were totally encapsulated in the material itself, we would know what it was. There would be only one possible interpretation.

No reasonable person would deny meaning to cave art and the artists that created it. The meaning transcends the individual fact of dots or grid lines, or, as Tattersall states, "it is drenched with meaning that goes beyond its mere form."[31] To understand this meaning, as well as the essence of the horse, we must have some capacity that transcends individual material conditions. Meaning and the essence of things are known in the intellect; the intellect is immaterial. This is what gives humans their dominance over the world. We can understand the principles – idealizations – of things and attempt to apply them to our material conditions. Thus as Thomas Aquinas put it, a swallow only builds a house in one manner.[32] It is bound to the individual material circumstance. Because humans understand the universal beneath the particular, they can build houses in many different ways; they transcend the individual material conditions.

29. Tattersall, *Masters of the Planet*, 187.
30. Tattersall, *Masters of the Planet*, 14.
31. Tattersall, *Masters of the Planet*, 13.
32. *SCG* II.66

Among the most celebrated challenges levied by science to the uniqueness of human symbolic expression is the dance language of the honeybee, made famous by Karl von Frisch, for which he won the Nobel Prize in Physiology or Medicine in 1973.[33] Honeybees conduct a unique dance in a figure-eight pattern, through which they communicate the directions and richness of distant food sources (over 100 meters away).[34] It is a complex behavior with several components conducted in the dark of the colony on a vertical comb. It is thus a gravity- and auditory-based form of communication (the observing bees listen to it). The listeners then go to the entrance of the colony and transform the gravity-based vertical and auditory cues into cues about the external world of visual and horizontal features so as to locate the food source. As a result, researchers claim that their juxtaposition of cues is tantamount to human comparisons of things in their own symbolic thought.

The dance of the honeybee is certainly striking, but we need to think more carefully about it for a moment. Recall that Thomas Aquinas said that animals only do things one way. This is far different from the normal use of human language. Human symbolic communication has multiple juxtapositions. Consider the following sentences:

1. The boy gave the book to the girl.
2. The boy gave the girl the book.
3. The book was given by the boy to the girl.
4. It was to the girl that the book was given by the boy.

These four sentences all have roughly the same meaning: a boy who gives, a girl who receives, a book that is given, the act of giving. These syntactic variations on one basic meaning are all possible because of the regular rules of English grammar. The dance of the honeybee simply doesn't possess this rich syntax.

Metaphor is yet another example of multiple meanings in a set of words. In the sentence "The man achieved the heights of spelunking," height is certainly not used in its literal meaning. Caves are below ground. Height

33. Raven et al., *Biology*, 1146.

34. Von Frisch, *Dance Language*, 28–328.

here means "greatest achievement possible," not a physical direction vertically upward. Yet in the bee dance, each component has only one possible signification. For example, dancing upward on the comb can only mean "fly toward the sun," while dancing down can only mean the opposite. That is it.

The comparison of animal communication – the dance of the honeybee being one of the most complex – with human language gives us the grounding for what Ian Tattersall discovered in the art of prehistoric cave dwellers. All human art and culture depend on humans possessing a symbolic communication system, one that abstracts from the material particulars and universalizes individual experiences, while bees, like all animals, are bound to the particular or individual experience. This in turn raises the more particular question: if the intellect can accomplish such a remarkable feat, just what does it understand in existing material things? To answer this, let's return to the triangle and explore it from the standpoint of the causes.

Material and Formal Causes

Suppose I had a glass triangle. This is an artificial example based on human art. It is not, therefore, a perfect example of a natural thing. But we will begin with human art, as it is better known to us than the things of nature. It is composed of glass and the shape of a triangle. If not glass, it would not be glass; if not the shape of a triangle, it would not be a triangle. Neither of these two causes (glass and triangularity) are reducible to the other. Many things are made of glass and are not triangular. If the glass was all one needed to be triangular, all things of glass would be triangular. Likewise, many things are triangular and not glass. In this case, the glass is the material cause—the material the figure is made of—and the triangular shape is the formal (it is the shape—form—of triangularity) cause. It is a triangular shape and not a circular one. The shape and not the glass organizes the glass into a triangle; it is its ordering principle, the cause of its triangularity.

What the intellect knows primarily in this case is the shape of the triangle – its organizing principle or cause. From this cause, one can understand many facets of its geometry. Less well do we understand glass. One would have to be chemist to delve into its properties. Extending this to natural objects, we say that what one understands directly by the intellect is the essence, or nature, of a thing. In part, the essence of a thing is composed of the formal cause, the principle of order, as existing in a material manner. The sensible properties of the individual are grasped by the senses, which are known indirectly by the intellect. So in natural material objects, we know them by a combination of intellect and the senses.

In natural material things, matter by itself is unknowable, as it is not organized by a formal cause. Think of it as an amorphous blob. The actual individual is less known in a certain sense than the formal cause because it is composed of both formal and material causes. Why matter by itself is unknowable can be seen in thinking a bit again about the glass triangle. The glass can be any number of types of shapes – triangle, circle, square, rhomboid, horse, or man. It has the potential to be any of these. Likewise, so does iron have the potential to be these, as does clay, ceramic, silver, wood, plastic, or any other "material." What is common to them is the property (capacity or potential) to be any shape. Abstracting from these types of materials, which we use to make things in art, matter in its raw essence is simply the potential to be material, or shapeable in three dimensions. It, by itself, is not anything at all, just a potential to be material. This is how the ancient and medieval mind understood it. And if matter is not actually anything, it is not by itself knowable. To know something, it must exist or be ordered, because one cannot know a purely amorphous thing. One might respond that we do in fact know what glass or iron or any of the above materials are. Correct. That is because the material used in art is already a thing: glass, iron, clay, and so on. They are composed of both material and formal cause. If it was simply true matter – potential – we could not use it. Art is not nature, just a representation of it.

Physical theory gives us examples of this idea of matter. Subatomic particles are close to the level of the material cause. They generally only exist in union with other things. Electrons typically exist only with protons and neutrons to form atoms. Below these, quarks typically only exist together to form protons (and other hadrons). For any of these to exist by themselves, one must deliver large amounts of energy to the systems to allow them to exist independently. Hence the electrons in the old television tubes had to have large amounts of electrical energy. Physicists hypothesize that the first fractions of a second of the early universe were dominated by independent quarks, electrons, protons, and other subatomic particles, as the universe was hot and energetic, allowing these to exist.[35] They must be pumped full of energy to exist independently. String theory claims that at the most basic level these particles are simply bits of energy that can be tuned one way or another to form a given particle.[36] They have a capacity to be any number of different particles. Werner Heisenberg, one of the founders of quantum mechanics, reached roughly the same conclusion that Aristotle did, namely, that matter was simply a raw potential to exist materially.[37]

Natural things of the material universe are composed of two things: a formal cause and the material cause, or the potential to be material. Individual things, extended in space and time, are a composite of both types of causes. The actual existing thing is the form (dogness) existing as *this* material object, or *this* individual dog. One only knows the formal and material causes as existing in a real thing, *this* dog. The intellect comes to know by removing or abstracting the form as understood to exist in matter, from the dog. The formal cause of dogness then exists as immaterial in our intellect since our intellect is immaterial. So our intellect becomes the other, not materially – or else it would be an actual natural dog – but immaterially in the intellect. The form of the dog molds our intellect as an artist puts a shape in clay or glass. This is precisely how true knowledge is possible, and only possible in this manner. We possess the same formal cause immaterially in our intellect as that which exists materially in the real dog. We truly are one with the formal principle. True knowledge is therefore impossible for the materialist, as all they can claim to know are neurochemical impulses stimulated by an exterior object. There is *nothing* truly common between the knower and the known. An object truly material as understood in scientism cannot be known. If I know a thing and another knows it as well, it is because we both possess the same formal aspect in the same manner. Material things cannot be shared or possessed in this manner. No two people can take the same bite out of an apple, as it is individual or material. But we both can understand

35. Perlov and Vilenkin, *Cosmology for the Curious*, 155–62.

36. Greene, *Fabric of the Cosmos*, 330–47.

37. Herbert, *Quantum Reality*, 26–27. See also the analysis of Edward Feser, "Heisenberg on Act and Potency," September 17, 2009, http://edwardfeser.blogspot.com/2009/09/heisenberg-on-act-and-potency.html.

the formal principle of appleness, which is above individuality — this is what to be immaterial means. It is this same thing that allows us to know meaning and metaphor in words; in a world consisting only of matter, I could not write one word communicable to another.

Therefore the human intellect knows the essence of things, but not the object completely as existing in its individual manner. This is why intellectual discourse can often be dry. When we talk about a rose, the intellect does not know all the things that make a real rose attractive — its color, smell, and feel. The poet tries to capture the whole thing. This is why poetry is more appealing to many than simple intellectual discourse. Further, this is the basis for human culture — art, theater, dance, history, music, and the like. These are all forms of grasping the material object in its totality, owing to the limitations of our intellect and the material component of things.

Medieval thinkers thought of the act of the intellect as grasping the essence hidden inside things as a kind of union. Picking up on Aristotle's famous dictum that "all human beings desire to know," they viewed that desire as terminating in a union between knower and known. As discussed, the formal principle is possessed by both, albeit in a different manner. This ability to be one with another in some way gives the possessor of intelligence the property of being a true person, one who can relate to another in the most radical sense of entering into union. This is why beings lower than humans (animals, plants, and nonliving things) are not, properly speaking, persons. While they may have certain personal characteristics in the limited sense of commanding respect simply because they are, or are alive, they are not persons in the fullest sense in that humans cannot have a true personal relationship with them.

Being a person is thus the standard for reality. The ability to enter into a true relationship or become one with the other — that is, to exist in a fruitful communion and union with the other — is what gives reality its greatest meaning. Beings lower than humans are judged meaningful in their approximation to this capacity. Herein lies the true value of humans from the point of view of the material universe. By knowing reality lower than us, we can elevate it in our intellects to immateriality, conferring on it, in us, the capacity to be intellectual (or "personal" in a sense), ultimately to enter into union with our Creator, who is immateriality in its highest manner. We elevate such creatures to the capacity for love. Far from being an anomaly in nature, we are the completion of the physical and chemical laws of the history of the universe, enabling it to achieve its end – the stability of intellect that allows it to be truly personal in human beings. We truly belong to nature and nature to us. Contrary to the claims of radical environmentalism, nature needs us to complete it. As such, we must respect it as well. Nature is not ultimately reducible to property or resources at our disposal.

Intelligence and Psyche

As with every other material thing, human beings are composed of a formal and material cause. The material cause seems easy enough to understand, but what could possibly be the formal cause in a human being? The traditional answer, derived from the Greeks, is that the formal cause in any living thing is simply termed a *psyche* (in Greek) or an *anima* (in Latin). These words were translated into English as "soul," but the original meaning is far from what most moderns think of as a soul. Recall our triangle for a moment. As the idea of the triangle is the organizing principle or cause of a triangle, so the psyche is the organizing or ordering principle of every living thing.

I refrain from overusing the word "soul," as it carries connotations for moderns that are far from the meaning I wish to explain. How are we to think of the psyche? Consider again the glass triangle. The actual triangular shape (idea) exists as the cause or ordering principle shaping the matter to be an individual triangle. In an actual human being, it is the psyche or anima that causes the matter to be ordered in the shape, or form, of a human body. The product of this union is the actual individual being. *The reality of an intellectual psyche united with matter is called a human person, or the actually existing individual human being. In the natural order, the psyche does not exist as separated from bodies.* In humans, this organizing principle of matter also has a power that can do an immaterial act – thinking – and as such is immaterial. To the modern materialist, the notion that an immaterial thing could act or affect matter is absurd and excluded from the outset. But what is inherently irrational in the claim that our psyche (or soul) is an organizing cause with an immaterial power (intellect) that orders matter to be an actually existing human body? It certainly wasn't irrational to Plato or Aristotle, and one could certainly not accuse either of irrationality. And consider that in the same way that all the properties of triangularity in glass arise from the form of triangularity, so all our organic and biochemical functions issue from our formal cause, or psyche, organizing matter. When we understand a material thing with our intellect, the intellect separates the formal cause of the object perceived and unites with it immaterially. The psyche or soul does not exist as something apart from matter, but it can be separated in our thought.

Some historical understanding further elucidates this idea and explains the errors of scientism. The early Church Fathers lived and thought in a Platonic milieu; they compared the idea of the psyche in Platonic authors and in the New Testament. Contrary to popular misunderstanding, the early Christians did not reject Greek philosophy or science at all; they adopted, modified, and employed it in their proclamation of the Christian Gospel. The Platonic notion of the psyche was used but was never accepted outright as correct. It formed the basis for a rational discussion of the psyche, but the Platonic idea of a soul imprisoned in the body was largely rejected because in Christianity, as in Judaism, the body was something good because it was created by God. The body could therefore not be a prison for the soul. These early Christian thinkers also held that that the soul and body did not preexist the living human being, contrary to Plato's doctrine. In other words, the body and the psyche existed only as a unified being, the composite, a real human being. These ideas were refined under the later recovery of the Aristotelian corpus with its theory of the relationship of the four causes, which many medieval thinkers found more in line with the fundamental impulses of Christian thought. It was much closer to the Christian idea that the soul organized matter as a cause but did not preexist the body. In the modern era, however, there was something of a return to the Platonic notion of a soul existing in a body, which was then falsely attributed to Christianity.

The Inadequacy of Scientism

A common mistake made by many people is to think of the soul as existing in a body. Nothing could be further from the truth. This is the Platonic idea that was commonly accepted among certain Christians and non-Christians alike, probably because it was easier to understand and seemed to fit with

Christian ideas. Most books on science make this critical mistake. But the truly Christian notion of the soul (psyche or anima) entails that the formal and material causes exist only as united in an actual living thing. The soul does not have preexistence, running around, as it were, like a ghost trying to inhabit a body. Recall, too, that matter is simply the potential to be a material thing, so the body does not have preexistence either. Any real body can actually exist only as an ordered or organized thing if it has the formal (organizing) cause. This confusion of the Platonic and Christian ideas of the soul is evident in the following sentences written by the neuroscientist Christof Koch: "Plato ... conceived of the individual as an immaterial and immortal soul imprisoned in a material and mortal body. This concept is the very embodiment of dualism, the belief that reality consists of two radically different sorts of things—the mental or spiritual, and the physical.... These Platonic views were subsequently absorbed in the New Testament. They form the basis of the Christian doctrine of the soul."[38]

Koch then explains the problem with dualism in connection with the early modern philosopher René Descartes:

> The dualism they advocate, in which the mind forces the brain to do its bidding, is unsatisfactory for the reason that the 25-year-old Princess Elizabeth of Bohemia had already pointed out to Descartes three centuries earlier – by what means does the immaterial soul direct the physical brain to accomplish its aim? If the soul is ineffable, how can it manipulate actual stuff such as synapses? It is easy to see causality flowing from the brain to the mind but the reverse is difficult. Any mind to brain communication has to be compatible with natural laws, in particular with the principle of energy conservation. Making the brain do things like messing with synapses takes work that the soul would have to perform and that has to be accounted for.[39]

Koch makes both historical and conceptual errors here, leading to a false posing of questions. The writers of the New Testament never incorporated the Platonic idea of the soul into their theology. Only Christians reading the New Testament have incorporated the Platonic idea into their reading. But this historical mistake became the basis for the dualism that Koch finds so

38. Koch, *Consciousness*, 165–66.

39. Koch, *Consciousness*, 167.

untenable. It was not so much Plato but a Cartesian dualism that Koch criticizes. During the 1500s and 1600s, the Aristotelian idea of matter as a potential to be material changed into matter by itself as a *real existing thing* – the extended body and the soul inhabiting it (this was never the Christian position). This was a fundamental misunderstanding regarding Christian and ancient Greek thought. Many scientists (and people in general) like Koch assume this is the Christian position. They have never seriously examined and engaged the actual Christian doctrine and so are criticizing a straw man.[40]

On the false assumption of a dualistic Christianity, Koch asks, "by what means does the immaterial soul direct the physical brain to accomplish its aim? If the soul is ineffable, how can it manipulate actual stuff such as synapses?" These questions are predicated on a misunderstanding. The actually existing human is this body as it exists. There is no ghost inhabiting a body, as a captain inhabits the ship. In the same way that the triangular idea accounts for all the triangular properties in the actually existing triangle – whether it be glass, iron, clay, or what have you – the soul accounts for all the properties of the body as formed, except for extension in space and time, or what we can call individuality (from the material cause). Is it a reasonable question to dispute, then, why there are three sides to a glass triangle? It is because it is a triangle. Such is the case with the human directing himself, having a heart beat without his conscious effort or using synapses in his brain.

In short, a human is: (1) a psyche or anima with an immaterial power (intellect) organizing (2) a material cause or potential to be material. The actual human is a being (individual human person) that exists as *this* actual body. Living human bodies make use of cells, molecules, biochemistry, neurons, synapses, organs, and all that goes with them. The real human body is a body with all its accoutrements. So when Koch asks how the soul remembers anything, and what logic it follows, we respond that it remembers by means of material instrumentality and follows the logic derived from the laws of the physical universe. Why? Because it does these as an actually ex-

40. Stating succinctly the relation of soul and body, I quote the Catholic Catechism: "The unity of soul and body is so profound that one has to consider the soul to be the 'form' of the body; i.e., it is because of its spiritual soul that the body made of matter becomes a living, human body; *spirit and matter, in man, are not two natures united, but rather their union forms a single nature*" (emphasis added). Catholic Church, *Catechism of the Catholic Church*, 365.

isting human individual, not a disembodied soul. Koch's question is simply misplaced. It is the actually existing human person doing these things, not a soul floating in a body. In a similar vein, who reasonably asks how a cup's shape is expected to hold coffee, apart from the ceramic of which it is composed? If Koch were to follow his thinking to its logical end, he would have to question how the shape of a cup can hold coffee and conclude that the ceramic does it without being in the shape of a cup. But, of course, the cup *is* the organizing shape of a ceramic cup – it forms ceramic to be a cup.

It is far from unreasonable or irrational to believe that a human being has an immaterial power owing to its ability to understand such things. In fact, it is only rational, given our reasoning about the perfect triangle and nature of causes. When Koch asks how an immaterial soul – with somewhat muddled distinctions – can do anything without the laws of energy conservation, he is again operating on an erroneous assumption. He assumes that immateriality is in some way dependent on matter, or, more generally, that everything that exists is contained in some definition of matter, even if matter is only energy. This is a completely gratuitous assumption.

That is precisely why the term "*im*materiality" (im- = not) is used when defining being beyond matter. It is transcendent to matter in all its forms and is known only intellectually, not by sense experience or imagination. There is nothing irrational in this idea at all. Take a walk with your dog, as I did and discussed previously. Certain things are not plants. Others are not animals. Some things are living, others not. If existence is not limited to this or that thing, or living or nonliving, why must it be limited to matter? The idea of existing, or being, does not contain a limitation to materiality. Why must everything a priori ultimately depend on matter? Why is the only rational, non-naive, and mature explanation that there is nothing above matter?[41] Koch's science, which is also my science, cannot tell us this, as it is limited to the analysis of material things. Science is dependent on common experience, by which one can reason to immaterial being, but science has no power to say anything about nonmaterial existence. Koch can only come to these ideas extra-scientifically.

Koch's opposition to dualism is really aimed against what philosophers

41. Koch, *Consciousness*, 167–68, 184.

sometimes call radical realism. Radical realism states that both soul (formal cause) and body exist before their union, and it is this false assumption that is the core of his misunderstandings. The position espoused by Aristotle and later by the Church was a position of moderate realism. Moderate realism claims that matter and the formal cause exist together only as *this* individual thing.[42] In moderate realism, a real distinction must be maintained between the causes but not in the actual existing thing. *Both* glass and the triangular shape are needed to produce an *individual* glass triangle.

Moderate Realism

What is the relationship between our immaterial intellect and matter based on moderate realism?[43] Moderate realism says that because the actual existing thing is the individual, the intellect needs material reality (the senses) in order to function properly. The senses provide humans with the stuff of thinking, or, as the medieval philosophers were fond of saying, "There is nothing in the intellect, which is not first in the senses" ("Nihil est in intellectu quod non prius in sensu"). From this, we can deduce that any intellectual action needs a material representation of the object to think about it. Even if the object being considered has no matter (such as God), we think of God by way of some metaphor such as a glowing light. The actual understanding is itself immaterial, however. Such is the role of the brain to present with precision a sensory (material) image to the intellect; it is the organ of "common sense."[44] The brain then integrates all the sensory inputs and forms them into a unified sensory representation (the common sensible). The senses do not think; only the intellect does that. The more powerful the thinker (human vs. insect), the more complex the brain needs to be to support a sophisticated sensory image. As Thomas Aquinas states in his *Summa contra Gentiles*, "Now the body is the instrument of the soul, and an instrument is for the use of the principle agent: therefore, the disposition of the instrument necessarily must be such as becomes the principle agent."[45]

42. See Adler, *Intellect*, 41–53, for an analysis of the various forms of realism in the context of an argument for the immateriality of the intellect.

43. Adler, *Intellect*, 41–53.

44. Aquinas, *Commentary on Aristotle's De Anima*, III, lec. 1–3.

45. *SCG* IV.73.

In other words, our brains are so complex because we have a truly immaterial intellect with which to think. Modern neuroscientific research supports this idea of complexity. Our brain is arguably the most complex thing in the known universe. There are 2×10^{11} (200 billion) neurons, 1.25×10^{14} (125 trillion) connections, and $10^{1,000,000}$ possible connections (compare this to an estimated 10^{79} particles in the universe).[46] This exceedingly complex organ processes all the sensory information coming in from all the senses and forms them into a complete sensory representation of the object perceived. It functions in a similar manner to a hammer for a carpenter. Although the hammer is separate from the carpenter, the brain is a real part of an individual human being. No exhaustive understanding of the properties of a hammer can lead one to argue that the carpenter does not exist; so, too, no exhaustive scientific analysis of the properties of a brain leads one to conclude the immaterial intellect does not exist. It is simply not in the capacity of science to be able to make such conclusions.

One of the more fascinating aspects of Koch's work has been the attempt to locate specific regions of the brain, down to the cellular level, that contain these integrated sensory images.[47] Koch made use of patients with epilepsy so severe that direct surgical intervention was needed to remove the brain tissue that caused the epileptic seizures. This intervention required identifying the exact location of the offending tissue. After the insertion of a dozen or so electrodes of hair-thin wire into the soft tissue of the brain, patients were attached to a monitor recording the neural activity of the brain. The patients lived in the hospital for a week or so, until they had another seizure. When a seizure occurred, it was then possible to triangulate the position of the tissue causing the problem before performing an operation.

The patients were shown pictures of animals, words, famous people, landscapes, and the like, and the consequent neural activity could then be triangulated and recorded. While not all images elicited a response, some yielded interesting results. Certain neurons would respond to categories of objects, such as animals, but a few neurons were much more specific. They would respond to familiar faces, such as that of President Bill Clinton, to cartoons of

46. Edelman and Tononi, *Universe of Consciousness*, 37.

47. See Koch, *Consciousness*, 75–79, for the account of Koch's work with epilepsy patients and the localization of "concept" neurons.

Bart and Homer Simpson, and to photos of the actresses Jennifer Aniston or Halle Berry. The neuron responding to Jennifer Aniston was so specific that it would not respond to other actresses or to pictures of other blonde women. The Halle Berry neuron would also respond to a cartoon of her and to her name spelled out. Other neurons responded to images of Mother Theresa, cute little animals, Saddam Hussein, or the Pythagorean theorem. Koch and colleagues think that these neurons, dubbed concept neurons, belong to a larger group in the hundreds or thousands responding to a familiar object. They are generated initially, upon seeing an object, by patterns of neural spiking in higher-order cortical regions. Repetitions of these experiences result in specific neurons being dedicated to them; they are the cellular substrate of a given familiar image. It is thought that even more abstract but familiar ideas are represented here as well, such as the value of π or the idea of God.

This research fits perfectly well with the ancient and medieval ideas of body and soul. The soul is the organizer of living matter by forming the material potency into a body, and neither soul nor body preexists, but exists only as *this* individual human being. All the functions of the individual are a union of both causes, material and formal, in a real existing human being. The individual human is the union of the formal (immaterial) and material (matter). It is precisely because of this union that we must use an image to begin our thought, even if the thing thought of is not sensible per se, such as the Pythagorean theorem, π, or God. Everything a human learns is gained through the senses, resulting in a sensible image put together by the brain. All of this is held by ancient and medieval thought. Modern neuroscience, à la Koch and colleagues, has shown that specific groups of neurons are the substrates of these images. The only difference between modern and ancient science, as Fulton Sheen noted in the quotation at the end of chapter 2, is a difference in measurement because our instruments are better. Instead of saying "the brain," we can now refer to a specific group of neurons. The image in these neurons is used by the immaterial intellect as a hammer is used by a carpenter. It uses a tool in the process of arriving at an understanding of the nature of a thing. No amount of specificity of neurons found by modern science can claim a contradictory position to this, as science by its nature cannot claim knowledge of what is beyond the senses.

Conclusion: Nature, Intelligence, and Science

In chapter 2, I cited the philosophical work of Fulton Sheen, showing that modern science has allowed a greater precision in our knowledge that can effect a greater control of reality by man.[48] Christof Koch's work perfectly exemplifies this idea: his science has offered much greater control of the human brain, but his philosophical inferences contradict his assumptions, undermining his conclusions and the effectiveness of his arguments. Science cannot contradict our common experience, as it itself presupposes this experience. By triangulating neurons in the brain, Koch hopes to find the *cause* of electrical firing upon seeing the images. In effect, he has merely stated more precisely pre-Enlightenment thought rather than contradicting it, as he thought. Koch presupposes cause and effect, one of the self-evident principles derived from common experience. And this experience again is one of the bases for the ascent of our thought to immaterial being, such as the intellect. It is the arena of the intellect that is the focal point of tension between pre- and post-Enlightenment thought. Taking the position of pre-Enlightenment thinkers, the intellect is not a calculating machine but a power to unite with being, all being.

In our intellect, we become in an immaterial manner what is outside of us in material reality. We take on that which we don't have – the other. The human intellect can within itself raise beings without intellects (e.g., animals, plants, and inanimate things) to immateriality, allowing them, in humans, to become that which they cannot be by themselves. This process allows the whole of the material universe to return in human beings to its Creator, that One who is analogously Being, Intellect, and Love itself in the highest possible manner. To the creatures possessing intelligence, the intellect in turn perfects them by allowing them to expand to what they are not, and to overcome the limitations of their individuality. Between two or more intellectual creatures, the intellect allows them to enter into meaningful relationships and to be *persons* in the most radical sense: beings who can commune with, become one with, and mutually perfect each other. Ultimately, possessors of intelligence can enter into union with their Creator, completing the action of love that draws us toward the Personal Source of all things.

48. Sheen, *Philosophy of Science*, 165–66.

4 INTERLUDE ON REASON AND FAITH

Most of what has been said so far can be known by the normal use of human reason; Greek thinkers (e.g., Plato, Aristotle) formulated many of these truths apart from the Jewish Scriptures and before Christianity. Knowledge attainable by reason constitutes our natural knowledge, truths known by the use of our own natural powers. For many modern readers, the approach I have been outlining seems foreign only because it differs from what they have imbibed from modern culture, both everyday and scientific.

Most Westerners have been taught to think about reality only from a materialistic standpoint that assumes no other possible way of rationally approaching the nature of things. This assumption is perhaps the dominant factor in the bifurcation of reality into religious and nonreligious: many people have divided the world in their minds into religious things (going to Church, God, angels, the soul, morality) and nonreligious things (the universe, science, politics, economics, psychology). This division contributes to

For the first, historical, part of this chapter ending at the section titled "Reason and Faith," I wish to express my great thanks to Kenneth J. Howell for advice, guidance, and consultation. For general references for this part of the chapter, see Howell's *God's Two Books*, "Copernicanism and the Bible in Early Modern Science," and "Galileo and the History of Hermeneutics."

the nearly complete breakdown of any use of the intellect in matters deemed religious. Christians sometimes make the same assumptions as materialist people because their minds have been shaped by materialist categories.

Materialists think religion and science are in conflict. Where did this idea of conflict come from? Most importantly, is it true? Most materialists, atheists, and secularists tend to think that someone introducing claims like the ones I made in previous chapters is unnecessarily injecting religion into science. Nothing could be further from the truth. So why would they think this? Part of the answer lies in the time they were educated. In the last quarter of the nineteenth century, a narrative of conflict with regard to the history of science came from leading cultural figures, such as John Henry Draper, Thomas Henry Huxley, and Andrew Dickson White.[1]

Clarifying Key Terms

Discussions of science and religion are often marred by imprecise language and inadequate definitions of "science," "religion," "theology," "faith," and "philosophy." I indicated in chapter 3 that the definition of intelligence differs radically in its usage in modern science from the way the medieval thinkers understood it. The same can be said for other terms. Representatives of scientism often do not distinguish between religion and theology, a distinction well known to all who have studied theology. The term "religion" derives from the Latin *religio*, cognate of the verb *religare*, "to bind back or again," and so signifies devotion and piety. One may be very religious with little knowledge of theology. In some worldviews, such as Buddhism, it may not make much sense to distinguish the two, because Buddhism has little theology in the Western, Christian sense. In Christianity, religion must be distinguished from theology because the latter is "faith seeking understanding" (*fides quaerens intellectum*), a phrase that appears in the eleventh-century thinker Anselm, though it has clear antecedents in earlier writers (e.g., Augustine). Traditional Christian theology, then, is the application of human reason to the data of revelation.[2] Philosophy is

1. See, e.g., Draper, *History of the Conflict*, and White, *History of the Warfare*.

2. Among the many medieval expressions of theology as the application of reason to the data of faith, Thomas Aquinas gave one of the most influential in *ST* I, q. 1.

the pursuit of truth and wisdom that Christians adopted from the ancient Greeks, because they perceived it as a help or handmaiden (*ancilla*) to understanding the revelation given by God in nature and in Scripture. In the Middle Ages, philosophy, including natural philosophy, was considered an essential prerequisite to the study of theology. All medieval theologians had immersed themselves in logic, rhetoric, geometry, and astronomy before pursuing theology. Yet the Western medieval thinkers I discuss in this book understood the goal of philosophy to be the discovery of truths that human reason could attain apart from any special act of divine revelation. Many modern people tend to confuse philosophy and theology; for these medieval thinkers, they were distinct.

Theology is related to faith in several ways. Faith has a double meaning in theology. Many moderns think of it only in one of these ways, understandably so because they have unconsciously adopted the assumption that faith is only subjective. This meaning is technically called *fides qua creditur* (the faith by which it is believed) and indicates the subjective faith of an individual. The other meaning important for our purposes is *fides quae creditur* (the faith that is believed) and indicates the objective content of the Christian faith. This content is objective in the sense that it has a meaning and significance apart from what individuals may think or believe. The importance of this distinction between faith as subjective belief and the faith as objective content will become apparent later.

Historically, Christian theology has never imagined that true knowledge comes only through faith. Reason, in its broadest sense, has always held an honored place among the best of Christian thinkers. This confidence in reason is why Christians have been deeply involved in science, sometimes at the forefront of research (e.g., Galileo, Kepler, LeJeune, LeMaitre, Mendel, and Pasteur). These historic figures believed that there were rational foundations for the traditional Christian view of creation, foundations that allowed for all types of bona fide knowledge to be easily grafted into Christian thought. Early Christian thinkers and the medievals who built upon them looked about and found in Greek philosophy (Aristotle, Plato, the Stoics) views compatible with their own. They then developed and perfected those ideas with Christian revelation.

Reason and Faith: A Historical Sketch

From the earliest Christian centuries, many thinkers were confronted with the claims of reason against Christian claims. While some Christians, usually those less educated, rejected reasonable claims out of hand because they perceived them as contradictions to their new faith, moderate and careful thinkers distinguished between bogus and genuine knowledge claims. In the second century, Tertullian of Carthage, in defending the Trinity against Praxeas, spoke of God as a rational being.[3] Origen of Alexandria, the foremost biblical scholar of the Greek-speaking Church, valued knowledge from outside the Scriptures. In a letter to Gregory Thaumaturgus, he asked his friend to extract from Greek philosophy what may serve the purposes of Christianity. In that list, he included subjects traditional in Greek education: geometry, music, rhetoric, and astronomy. Origen then introduced a literary theme that would guide Christian thought for centuries to come. He invoked the story of the Exodus (Ex 12) as justification for incorporating pagan knowledge into Christianity: in the same way that the Israelites took the Egyptians' gold and silver when they left Egypt, so Christians should use the gold and silver of their pagan world. While avoiding the trap of pagan idolatry, Christians should not be afraid of knowledge drawn from the culture around them.[4]

The most important Christian thinker in the West by far with regard to reason and faith hailed from north Africa: Aurelius Augustine. Augustine has left us with a legacy that exceeds any other ancient writer. Born in 354, Augustine recounts his first thirty or so years in his famous *Confessions*, a life as varied and mixed as one might imagine that of any ancient scholar. Once ordained the bishop of Hippo Regius, he worked tirelessly in multiple capac-

3. Tertullian, *Against Praxeas* 5, trans. Kenneth Howell, personal communication, 2017. "Rationalis enim deus, et ratio in ipso prius, et ita ab ipso omnia: quae ratio sensus ipsius est" ("For God is rational and reason is first of all in him and thus everything from him [is rational]: his consciousness is reason").

4. Origen, *Letter to Gregory*: "But I am anxious that you should devote all the strength of your natural good parts to Christianity for your end; and in order to this, I wish to ask you to extract from the philosophy of the Greeks what may serve as a course of study or a preparation for Christianity, and from geometry and astronomy what will serve to explain the sacred Scriptures, in order that all that the sons of the philosophers are wont to say about geometry and music, grammar, rhetoric, and astronomy, as fellow-helpers to philosophy, we may say about philosophy itself, in relation to Christianity."

ities as pastor, teacher, polemicist, and peacemaker. Somehow during such a busy life, Augustine still found time to dictate and write over five million words that survive to this day. His importance for the intellectual history of the West can hardly be exaggerated; no Church Father from the first five centuries of Christianity shaped the Western world as much as Augustine. And it was Augustine who would use the same theme as Origen to establish a positive view of all knowledge for subsequent Christian thinkers.

Augustine drew upon and reinforced two crucial ideas: God is the source of all truth, and therefore no two truths can contradict one another. God created the world and the natural laws that govern it. What God placed in creation would not contradict what he revealed in the Scriptures. There are many passages in his writings that reiterate these two important principles, but perhaps the most famous comes from *De Doctrina Christiana* (*On Christian Teaching*):

> If those who are called philosophers, especially the Platonists, have said things which are indeed true and are well accommodated to our faith, they should not be feared; rather, what they have said should be taken from them as from unjust possessors and converted to our use. Just as the Egyptians had not only idols and grave burdens which the people of Israel detested and avoided, so also they had vases and ornaments of gold and silver and clothing which the Israelites took with them secretly when they fled, as if to put them to a better use. They did not do this on their own authority, but at God's commandment, while the Egyptians unwittingly supplied them with things which they themselves did not use well. In the same way, all the teachings of the pagans contain not only simulated and superstitious imaginings and grave burdens of unnecessary labor, which each one of us leaving the society of pagans under the leadership of Christ ought to abominate and avoid, but also liberal disciplines more suited to the uses of truth, and some most useful precepts concerning morals. Even some truths concerning the worship of one God are discovered among them. These are, as it were, their gold and silver, which they did not institute themselves but dug up from certain mines of divine providence . . . he [the Christian] should take this treasure with him for the just use of teaching the gospel. And their clothing, which is made up of those human institutions which are accommodated to human society and necessary to the conduct of life, should be seized and held to be converted to Christian uses.[5]

5. Augustine, *On Christian Doctrine*, 75.

When Augustine speaks of "the liberal disciplines," he is thinking of some of the same fields of knowledge that Origen had listed (geometry, music, rhetoric). The study of these subjects had been integral to Augustine's own education as a rhetorician. His writings reveal a man who was a subtle and careful thinker, who never precipitously or too quickly locked on to a solution to a deep problem. He often asked more questions than he answered.

Augustine was intrigued by the creation account in Genesis and tried on at least five occasions to write a definitive commentary on it.[6] To compare these different accounts makes for fascinating reading as one follows Augustine's thinking through a problem. Three salient points emerge from Augustine's wrestlings. (1) His absolute confidence in the Scriptures as the authoritative word of God. He is sure that the biblical authors teach truth. (2) The fallibility of human interpretation of the Bible. When does one interpret Scripture literally? When metaphorically? How does the Bible convey truth in language we might today call mythological? Why does the Bible use so much anthropomorphic language in describing God and his actions? Augustine poses these questions and hundreds more, of which most people in most ages have never thought. His purpose was to distinguish between true and faulty interpretation of the Bible. (3) Truth in the Scriptures and truth from outside Scripture are compatible. If there seems to be a conflict – as there seemed to be in the matter of the motion of the earth centuries later – Augustine is certain that there is some mistake in either the interpretation of the Bible or in the interpretation of nature. At times, he counsels changing one's interpretation of Scripture in the light of bona fide knowledge of the natural world (i.e., science). Because all truths originate in God, there can be no real contradiction between natural and revealed truths.[7]

Thus Augustine, as the most influential Church Father in the Latin-speaking West, left a twofold legacy of the compatibility of all truth and the value of the liberal arts. Yet, because of his many duties as a bishop, Augustine was never able to work out a curriculum the way that Boethius did. In

6. For an explanation of Augustine's long engagement with the text of Genesis, see Howell, "Natural Knowledge," 117–45.

7. Two historical works that expand on this theme are Harrison, *Bible, Protestantism, and the Rise of Natural Science*, and Howell, *God's Two Books*.

Boethius, we discover the systematic foundations of the medieval curriculum, which honored the seven liberal arts (trivium and quadrivium).

Boethius, born in 480, would become a learned and prominent Roman statesman. He is best known for his *Consolation of Philosophy*, a work written in prison during the last year of his life, before his execution in 524 or 525. This work became immensely popular in the Middle Ages and passed through hundreds of editions after the advent of printing. Speaking fluent Greek, Boethius intended to translate all of Plato's and Aristotle's works into Latin but was thwarted in his efforts, even though he did write numerous works on the seven liberal arts. Many scholars think that it was because of his influence that the liberal arts became so prominent and widespread in medieval education. The trivium (grammar, rhetoric, logic) provided the linguistic foundation for the more advanced quadrivium (arithmetic, geometry, astronomy, music). Each of the latter four subjects was treated in a mathematical and quantitative manner. Thus what we today call science was an integral part of medieval education. The crowning work of these disciplines was natural philosophy, the general study of nature, which served as the foundation for the sciences. All who had become masters in theology, medicine, and law (the three "graduate" disciplines) had the same background in their bachelor of arts degrees: trivium, quadrivium, natural philosophy.

By the high Middle Ages, European intellectuals had understood and adopted the curriculum of the liberal arts (disciplines) that Boethius had articulated. Later, the liberal arts were safely ensconced in the foundations of medieval universities. The founders of these institutions of higher learning believed in a profound, underlying unity to all knowledge. And the idea of a university where all serious fields of knowledge were studied was in turn based on the Christian conviction that all knowledge had its origin in God, who is the supreme truth.

One example of such a study of knowledge is in the early days of the founding of the University of Paris, in the twelfth century. One of the most significant players in this drama was the Victorines, the Canons Regular of St. Augustine at the Abbey of St. Victor in Paris. Among their luminaries was a canon named Hugh, whose famous *Didascalion* showed how all natural knowledge led ultimately to knowledge of God because the universe was like a book in which God's power could be seen. Hugh of St. Victor wrote, "For the whole sensible world is like a book, as it were, written by the hand of God, that is to say, created by divine power, and each of its creatures are like forms, devised not by human effort, but rather established by the divine will in order to make manifest the wisdom of the invisible things of God."[8] Hugh's metaphor of nature as a divine book was not his invention. By this time, it was commonly accepted and appealed to by learned men everywhere. This metaphor underlay the work of astronomers in the scientific revolution and served as a powerful motivation for the investigation of the natural world, from Nicholas Copernicus of Frombork and Andreas Vesalius of Brussels to Isaac Newton of Cambridge and John Ray of the soft English countryside. The preceding centuries of Christian involvement with the pursuit of knowledge were not unknown to these men, nor were they simply an isolated fact.

The scientific revolution of the sixteenth and seventeenth centuries proved to be as momentous for the Western world as the voyages of exploration and the Protestant Reformation. Nothing in the modern world today would be what it is had not these three cultural movements shaped our history. In the historiography of these two centuries, one finds inconsistent accounts. The nineteenth-century antagonists of religion set the backward and benighted dogmas of Christianity against the enlightened scientists of the new order. The likes of John Henry Draper and Andrew Dickson White offered a narrative of conflict between dogmatic religion and innovative science. This version of history was enormously influential in the first part of the twentieth century, so much so that one no less than Bertrand Russell adopted the warfare metaphor in his lectures on science and religion.[9] Highly learned and unusually analytical, Russell naively swallowed the story. There was only one problem: the picture of the warfare of science and religion was overdrawn and distorted. It simply did not fit the facts.

Since the Second World War, research into the scientific revolution has opened up wider and deeper perspectives on this foundational period in the

8. Hugh of St. Victor, *Didascalion*, book 7, chap. 4. The translation comes from Howell, *God's Two Books*, 209.

9. Russell, *Religion and Science*.

history of science. With regard to religion, there were at times questions and potential conflicts between the claims of traditional Christianity and the emerging sciences, but almost all of the greatest thinkers worked within a context established by the medieval framework discussed previously. Not only were the brick-and-mortar structures of the universities the backdrop of research, but also the tradition of disputation within natural philosophy provided the conceptual background for further investigation. We must pass many intricate details of this history to note only some of the more important ideas relevant to our concern.

Religion in general and theology in particular played a motivational role in many of the leading figures of science and its promotion. Two who stand out are the astronomer Johannes Kepler and the statesman Francis Bacon. Bacon's *Great Instauration* included a lengthy prayer for the advancement of knowledge. Part of that prayer is "Wherefore if we labor in Thy works with the sweat of our brows, Thou wilt make us partakers of Thy vision and Thy Sabbath. Humbly we pray that this mind may be steadfast in us, and that through these our hands, and the hands of others to whom Thou shalt give the same spirit, Thou wilt vouchsafe to endow the human family with new mercies."[10]

In the same vein, the greatest astronomer of the scientific revolution, Johannes Kepler, paused to offer a prayer for the advancement of the church. In his *Harmony of the World*, Kepler expressed his hope for harmony in the human world as a reflection of the celestial harmonies his science had revealed: "Holy Father, keep us safe in the concord of our love for one another, that we may be one, just as Thou art one with thy Son, our Lord, and with the Holy Spirit, and just as through the sweetest bonds of harmonies Thou hast made all Thy works one; and that from the bringing of Thy people into concord the body of Thy church may be built up in the Earth, as Thou didst erect the heavens themselves out of harmonies."[11]

These are clear expressions of the religious motivations of early modern scientists, inasmuch as they unhesitatingly voice their sense of the unity of truth in both the natural and the revealed realms. Being motivated by religious faith does not reflect an absence of conflict, but conflicts that did arise

10. Bacon, "Great Instauration," 23.

11. Kepler, *Harmonies of the World*, 58.

did not usually lead to an abandonment of faith or of religion. Johannes Kepler faced serious opposition from his Lutheran coreligionists at times, but his goal of revealing the Trinitarian God in the cosmos remained with him his whole life.[12]

Because conflict and warfare are most clearly seen in the case of Galileo Galilei according to the historiography of the late nineteenth century, some understanding of the historical facts is necessary, because Galileo's encounter with the Roman Catholic hierarchy seems to be an ever fertile ground for those who wish to deliver on their own conceptions of the proper relation between science and religion. Despite the enormous historical literature that one finds on Galileo, there are still many highly educated people who do not know about the basic facts of the case, and few who know how to navigate among varying interpretations. We must distinguish between two separate historical events and, in both cases, labor to understand them from the point of view of the participants, not from the perspective of later history. Many myths have grown up around the Galileo Affair, making it difficult to distinguish between historical reality and later mythical interpolations. What are the facts?

The first event is the condemnation of March 5, 1616, by the Congregation of the Index. Scholars differ over who precipitated this condemnation, but one thing is certain. Galileo's famous *Letter to the Grand Duchess Christina*, written in early 1615, was a central impetus in bringing about the condemnation. None of Galileo's works were mentioned in the text of the condemnation itself, but the official declaration condemned the belief in the motion of the earth as contrary to good philosophical reasoning and to Scripture. The decree condemned a book by a Carmelite named Paolo Foscarini, whose *Letter on the Copernican Opinion* argued that Holy Scripture did not teach anything about the motion of the earth and that therefore the idea of terrestrial motion could not be heretical in theology. It also prohibited Copernicus's *De Revolutionibus* "until corrected."[13]

Galileo's *Letter to the Grand Duchess Christina* has been subject to vari-

12. Howell, *God's Two Books*, 109–35.

13. Among the voluminous scholarship on the Galileo Affair, it is crucial to read the original documents that have been nicely translated in Finocchiaro, *Galileo Affair.* The *Decree of the Index* is found on 148*ff*. Foscarini's letter has been translated in Blackwell, *Galileo, Bellarmine, and the Bible*, 217*ff*.

ous interpretations. One of the best is Maurice Finocchiaro's argument that Galileo was not trying to argue for Copernicanism against Scripture or the Church. Rather, Galileo simply wanted the Church to refrain from making any judgment at all on the matter of earth's motion. Galileo's arguments are based on the historical precedent of Augustine and on the long-accepted belief that knowledge of nature and divine revelation could not contradict one another. His reasoning in this *Letter* is a model of clear but subtle argument. It was for this reason that the Church eventually accepted Galileo's approach as well founded. For example, Pope Leo XIII issued an encyclical, *Providentissimus Deus* (November 18 1893), in which he basically endorsed Galileo's approach to the reconciliation of apparent conflicts between the Catholic faith and science. I say "apparent conflicts" because neither Galileo nor the official Church ever believed that there could be true conflicts between the Christian faith and science. Galileo says as much in the *Letter to Christina*. As spelled out above, the prevailing Christian tradition had long before accepted Augustine's guidelines outlined in his *Literal Commentary on Genesis* (*De Genesi ad Litteram*).

In any case, we possess Cardinal Bellarmine's certificate of May 26, 1616, in which he says he informed Galileo of the congregation's decision, endorsed by the pope, and said that the Copernican opinion cannot be "defended or held."[14] All knowledgeable parties of that day, including Galileo, acknowledged that there was no proof for the Copernican system by the standards of proof generally accepted in that day. Galileo willingly followed the cardinal's injunction. He continued to work on arguments for and against the theory, but he did not advocate it, even though he still believed that it was true and that good arguments would be forthcoming.

As Galileo developed arguments for the Copernican system after the condemnation by the Congregation of the Index in 1616, he was greatly encouraged when an old friend of his was elected to the papacy in 1623. Maffeo Barbarini mounted the papal chair on August 6, 1623, as Urban VIII. The new pope invited Galileo to visit him, and the two talked as they walked in the Vatican gardens. Supposedly, Urban told Galileo that the 1616 decision was an unfortunate one but that it could not be revoked, or at least that it

14. *Cardinal Bellarmine's Certificate*, dated May 26, 1616, is found in Finocchiaro, *Galileo Affair*, 153.

was not prudent to do so. Urban encouraged Galileo to write a new book on the Copernican system, but he warned him to be careful not to advocate the new theory, only to offer arguments for and against it.

During the next seven or eight years, Galileo wrote the famous *Dialogue on the Two Great World Systems,* which was published in 1632.[15] This book was approved by the censor of Florence (where Galileo lived), but other clerics condemned the book. This is where historical opinion divides. Some thought that Galileo was *not* advocating Copernicanism, only discussing it. Others thought that the book clearly did advocate the new theory. The censors in Rome had enough evidence in their minds to justify calling him before the Inquisition so that he might defend himself against charges of heresy. The proceedings took place in the spring of 1633. The inquisitors asked three evaluators to review the book. The most detailed report was tendered by a learned Jesuit, Melchior Inchofer, who cited many passages from Galileo's *Dialogue* that demonstrated that he taught, defended, and possibly held the Copernican theory as true.[16] Galileo was asked on four separate occasions if he had ever or now held the theory to be true. In these four depositions, he denied holding to the theory after he was ordered not to do so.

In essence, the question at the trial of 1633 was whether Galileo had in fact disobeyed the injunction of 1616. In the end, Galileo was found guilty for disobeying the earlier order. He was eventually placed under house arrest in his villa in Arcetri, just across the river from Florence, for the remainder of his life. He died in 1642 at seventy-eight years of age. He was not hindered in his scientific work, since he published his greatest work of science in 1638, *The Discourse on the Two New Sciences,* and no Church authorities saw this book as a violation of his sentence, showing that they were not against scientific research per se.

The question that most people ask today is whether the Church was right to condemn a scientific theory, and of course we assume without much argument that religious bodies should not interfere with science. But in the seventeenth century, things were not so clearly delineated as today. Furthermore, we must remember that no one, not even Galileo, had any real proof

15. Among the many editions of the Dialogue that have been printed, Maurice Finocchiaro has provided one of the best, with commentary: Finocchiaro, *Galileo on the World Systems.*

16. See Inchofer's assessment in Finocchiaro, *Galileo Affair,* 262–70.

for the motion of the earth in 1632. The first experimental confirmation of stellar parallax, the needed proof agreed upon by both sides, did not come until the nineteenth century with Bessel's observations. Thus believing that the earth was motionless was not absurd in the seventeenth century.

Still, there is the question as to whether the Church should have made any determination of this matter at all, no matter whether there was proof or not. Here it is important to see that it was probably Galileo who forced the issue. Some clerics, circa 1613–14, urged Galileo not to enter into scriptural interpretation or the theology of the matter. They said that there would be no problem if he just stuck to the astronomy and the physics. This advice was based on the relative separation of natural philosophy and theology that had existed since the Middle Ages. Galileo's actions seemed to violate this relative separation. Still, many (both Catholics and Protestants) in that day believed that Scripture taught that the earth could not move. Although this was never official Church interpretation, it was a pervasive belief.

The later recognition of the Church's error in this matter is based on two ideas central to Catholic theology. One is that the Church should pronounce on matters of faith and morals (*de fide and moribus*), not on scientific theories. This belief is not new and was not new in Galileo's day. Second, Catholic theology operates on the assumption that no two truths can ever really contradict one another.[17] If something can be shown to be true in science – and for something to be true in science is not a simple matter – the Church says that it is proper to interpret Scripture in a way that accords with that truth. This is essentially what St. Augustine said in the fifth century, and what Cardinal Bellarmine reaffirmed in his famous *Letter to Fr. Paolo Foscarini* in Galileo's day.

In sum, the Galileo case involved a division over a complex question about the motion of the earth, but one that was answerable in principle. Figures like Cardinal Bellarmine and Christopher Clavius believed there was not sufficient proof (physical or astronomical) to conclude that the claim was true. Galileo believed it was at least provable. What all these figures held in common was at least as important as what divided them. They all believed in the Augustinian principle of the compatibility of truth from different sourc-

17. See the section "Reason and Faith" below.

es, specifically from nature and Scripture. While there might be, and indeed was, conflict over specific truth claims, there was no sense of the incompatibility of science and religion.

The first overt claims of incompatibility arose later in the seventeenth century and flourished in the eighteenth century, under the pens of Enlightenment figures such as Diderot, Voltaire, and the Encyclopedists. Even a superficial reading of Enlightenment advocates displays their animus against formal religion. Some of them identified superstition and religious practice, an equivalence never officially countenanced by any major Christian body. With regard to science and its implications for religion, the Enlightenment had little real impact, but it did sow the seeds for attacks of atheists and agnostics in the nineteenth century. Throughout that century, there was a growing belief that matters of religion and creed were subjective, and separate from the objective truths of science. The narrative of conflict and the growth of philosophical materialism tilled the ground for views commonly accepted today. This brief account of the history of reason and faith gives some insight into how we lost the ancient Christian idea of the unity of knowledge and the ultimate compatibility of natural and supernatural knowledge. Nevertheless, in the writings of Thomas Aquinas lies a clear and articulate understanding of how faith and reason complement one another to give a fuller picture of reality.

Reason and Faith

In his *Summa contra Gentiles*, Thomas Aquinas reiterates the teaching of Augustine on the compatibility of reason and faith: "Now the knowledge of the principles that are known to us naturally has been implanted in us by God; for God is the author of our nature. These principles, therefore, are also contained by the divine Wisdom. Hence, whatever is opposed to them is opposed to the divine Wisdom, and cannot come from God. That which we hold by faith as divinely revealed, therefore, cannot be contrary to our natural knowledge."[18] The principles (reasons) of everything are contained in God. God is like giant blueprint for all that is. This blueprint includes

18. *SCG* I.7.

that which is known by the natural human powers of reason reflecting on the natural world (natural knowledge) and those things above reason that are given in the tradition of the Church (faith as divinely revealed). Because both come from God, who is the standard for all reality, it is impossible that one could be in conflict with the other, if properly understood. If something is reasonable, it is so because it first comes from God. Proper understanding is the key. Many matters of knowledge can be in apparent conflict because of human error in reason and judgment. This, I maintain, is the real problem between science and faith in our present world: all the legitimate findings of science are interpreted and taught according to the faulty philosophy of materialism, which fundamentally contradicts Christianity.

Thomas teaches three types of knowledge: (1) that which is found through the natural powers of reason (rational knowledge),[19] (2) that which is understood by being given to us (revealed) by a higher power (the prophets, angels, or God),[20] and (3) the space where the two overlap, the interpenetration between rational and revealed knowledge.[21] The light spectrum provides a good analogy to the relation between rational and revealed knowledge. Our eyes can see only a small range of actual light, that is, visible ranges. Below that threshold are the infrared and microwave, and above it are the ultraviolet, x-ray, and gamma ray. Either of these two extremes, such as microwave on the lower end and all on the upper end, is harmful to human eyes because they can bear only a natural range of light intensity. Even a more intense light, such as that of the sun, which is in our visible range but too bright, can damage our eyes. So our sense of sight is hurt not only by extremes beyond its visible range, but also by extremes of intensity within the visible range. The visible range of light is within our natural powers. Other ranges can only be observed by such means as special glasses, visors, telescopes, or indirect inference using such things as autoradiograph film.

Knowledge is much like the light spectrum. Human beings have natural powers of their intellect just as there are natural powers of sight. The natural powers of the intellect can grasp the things of this world made of matter – rocks, minerals, mountains, stars, plants, animals, and humans –

19. *SCG*, I.3.
20. *SCG*, I.5
21. *SCG*, I.4.

as our eyes can perceive the visible range of the light spectrum. These are the direct objects of our mind, and the knowledge of them is called rational. This knowledge comes to us through our sense experience of these objects and our intellects consequently understanding them. Just as our sight needs help to grasp light beyond its natural powers, there are things beyond our mind's power. Everything we experience has its limits, including our own powers of knowing. It stands to reason, then, that there are things beyond our power to know. To know such things, God must reveal them to us, either directly by himself, or through angels, or the prophets. Such knowledge is called revealed knowledge, or revelation. For the Christian, doctrines such as the Trinity, the Incarnation (Jesus Christ is God), and the sacraments fall into this category. The entire corpus of revealed knowledge is the deposit of faith (*depositum fidei*) professed by Christians. This knowledge is not irrational; it is simply above our natural ability to know by ourselves. If revealed knowledge is above reason, it is because it is more intellectual, and hence truer, because God himself is infinite Intellect. And given the Christian and rational idea that God is infinite, or unlimited, why shouldn't there be such knowledge?

Aquinas contends that there are things that are knowable by reason but that are also revealed.[22] Such knowable things include that God exists and has certain attributes: that he is Intelligence, Will, Power, and so on ("Ever since the creation of the world, his invisible nature, namely, his eternal power and deity, has been clearly perceived in the things that have been made," Rm 1:20). The possibility of the existence of angels and knowledge of certain of their attributes is another example of this knowledge. Why would some aspects of knowledge be both natural and revealed? Some of these types of knowledge are so lofty, so difficult to attain that many people do not have the time to study and understand them. Therefore God has also revealed them.

Revealed knowledge comes to us in two forms from God though the authority of the Church,[23] first in the written tradition of the Church through Scripture (the "Bible") and second in the oral tradition (popes, councils, and

22. Many of the questions regarding God and his creatures in the first two books of the *Summa contra Gentiles* fall into this category. These two books deal with rational demonstrations.

23. *Catechism of the Catholic Church*, 80–83.

saints) of the Church ("hold to the traditions which you were taught by us, either by word of mouth [oral] or by letter [written]," 2 Thes 2:15). Once revealed, this knowledge can be passed on through our natural learning powers (reading theology or hearing the truths of faith taught), but it can also be directly infused into our intellects by God (a mystical experience).

What, then, is the relationship between reason and faith? Reason provides a preparation for faith. It makes faith reasonable to have.[24] Because both material and immaterial beings are created by the same God, some of the principles in material things overlap with those in immaterial things. These are some of the self-evident truths discussed in chapter 2. For example, cause and effect are known by our natural knowing powers in experiencing the natural world, but there is nothing in cause and effect that limits them to material reality. Similar types of knowledge – the true, the good, the one – are called the Transcendentals and allow the mind to pass from material to immaterial reality. These truths perceived in the natural world give us a pedestal to higher things. St. Thomas notes in his *Commentary on Job* that Job disputed with God.[25] How can a mere man dispute with God? Thomas notes that Job says, "I know things according to your knowledge." In other words, Job understands that all truth comes from God. In a sense, he is using the truth of God himself to "debate" with God. Because God is the "teacher of all truth," this is in no way disrespectful of God. Thus Thomas states, "the gifts of grace [God's help] are added to nature in such a manner that they do not remove it, but perfect it. So it is with the light of faith that is infused in us gratuitously; it does not destroy the light of natural knowledge with which we are by nature endowed."[26] It is by natural knowledge that we come to know the world around us and we learn to think. Revealed knowledge perfects this, teaches us the ultimate Truth, and aids us through grace. Perhaps the best example of this interplay is from the First Letter to John:

> That which was from the beginning, which we have heard, which we have looked upon and touched with our hands, concerning the word of life – the life was made manifest, and we saw it, and testify to it, and proclaim to you the eternal life which was with the Father and was made manifest to us – that

24. *SCG*, I.6–8.

25. Aquinas, *Literal Exposition on Job*, 213–14.

26. Aquinas, *Trinity and the Unicity*, q. II, a. 3.

> which we have seen and heard we proclaim also to you, so that you may have fellowship with us; and our fellowship is with the Father and with his Son Jesus Christ. (1 Jn 1:1–3)

The correct use of our natural knowing powers—understanding with our senses and intellect that a man of extraordinary power (Jesus Christ) is present—leads to the acceptance of revealed knowledge that this extraordinary person is God. Natural knowledge, with God's help, properly formed, prepares for an acceptance of the Revealing Authority: God. Faith is not ultimately dependent on reason for its validity, but it is reasonable to have. And the knowledge of faith is not unreasonable, either. Once known, we can apply reason to revelation in the study of theology, as faith seeking understanding (*fides quaerens intellectum*).

All this underscores why it is so important to think correctly about the natural world. This interplay of reason and faith is of paramount importance in learning about our natural world. God has ordered our world and made us humans such that to rise to him, we must use our natural knowledge, aided by God's help, as well as that of grace through faith given by God. The soul or psyche is the seat of the immaterial intellect, and so the correct perception of the natural world is critical. Because we are intellectual beings, a fundamental disjunction occurs if we view faith as irrational. We are not split personalities; we cannot have a life of faith and another of reason that contradicts the former. When faith and reason are viewed as conflicting, one or the other must be relinquished. A false religion would be one that contradicts reason. Or, as a Jewish philosopher once put it, "No one can serve two masters; for either he will either hate the one and love the other, or he will be devoted to the one and despise the other. You cannot serve God and mammon [the world]" (Mt 6:24).

Misunderstandings of the natural world have devastating consequences and are one of the principal grounds for the crises of faith that students experience in the transition to the young adult years. Those conceptions of nature underlie the whole dichotomy of reason and faith in the modern world. Such generic misunderstandings gleaned from how the science books were written and how I was educated, even at grade school levels, underpinned the problems I had when I was younger. Certainly, there were no overt attacks on faith in the books I was reading nor in the classroom at that age, but the framework presented, how it was presented, and implicit assumptions in the educational system based upon a materialist philosophy were all that was needed to do damage. Small errors in the beginning lead to great ones at the end. Early Christian thinkers, such as Augustine and Boethius, understood such problems along with their effects, and they worked diligently to correct the errors that underlie them. Instead of following these erroneous paths, they gleaned another truth from the best of pagan culture about them, a fundamentally different approach that opened the mind to higher things. To this different cosmology known by reason I now turn.

Part II

THE VESTIGE OF EDEN

5 LIFE

Flat or Full?

Using commonsense knowledge of the world around us leads to two unexpected conclusions, at least from the point of view of modern materialism. One is that we can have practical certainty about many things apart from scientific research and opinion. The other is that the human intellect must be immaterial and capable of knowing immaterial things. Both these conclusions leave people steeped in modern materialism stupefied. How can any modern educated person not believe in the superiority of science? For a scientist not to believe this is tantamount to abandoning science. Not to believe that all reality is explainable in material terms is to retreat to the fanciful ideas of a prescientific world. Still, I maintain that not only are these two conclusions true, but also that the arguments for them are sound.

The arguments offered so far for the common experience of humanity and the immateriality of the intellect do not exhaust our armamentarium. Central to human inquiry, as well as to the biological sciences, is the question of life. Every biology textbook addresses the issue. For centuries, some of the most expansive thinkers in the Western world posed the following questions: How does one define life, and how can one know what is an adequate definition of life? Does a person need a textbook to learn what is life? Perhaps returning mentally to southern Indiana can help.

Seeing Life: Standing Still in the Snowy Woods

Heavy snows are somewhat uncommon in southern Indiana, but they do occur. They were always occasions of delight for me, as I would put on coat, hat, and boots and head into the woods. The woods during a heavy snow are largely an unseen world. The large flakes drift down through the trees while the branches and brush hang heavy with the snow, as if a large amount of whipped cream was just dabbled on them. The snow chokes everything. Here and there bits of brown twigs and brush poke through, and the green needles of the few pines provide one of the few contrasts with the dominant white blanket. Occasionally, among the flakes, larger aggregations of snow fall from the branches above. The cold bark of the trees lends its roughness to the cold of the air and the starkness of the landscape. The silver water of the creek cuts through the white and provides one of the few sounds one hears. If one moves away from the creek a bit, the snow hushes the sounds of movement.

Silence and stillness remain the unmistakable marks of the woods under snow; no sound or movement seems to penetrate. I experienced something similar in Mammoth Cave when the tour guide had everyone be quiet while he turned off the lights; the silence was broken only by someone unable to hold back his giggles. In the snowy woods, silence and stillness were dominant, or so it seemed. If I leaned against a tree and stood still for several minutes, small sounds, nearly inaudible at first, would punctuate the silence. Chickadees stir above in the branches or alight on the ground below. They would flit to and fro, scratching about the ground looking for some unseen morsel, interacting with other chickadees, or puffing out their feathers into an instant parka against the cold. Other songbirds would appear and do the same. Squirrels might jump through the branches or climb off a tree trunk and forage with their quick, jerky movements. They nervously pause and look about, tails twitching, then resume their business. If I was lucky and the sky overcast enough to make the light sufficiently dim in the trees, a great horned owl might float through the snow-covered branches, moving from one perch to another. After a time, the snowy woods would become quite alive. What caught my attention was movement. Chickadees and other birds, squirrels, and owls all move. Movement prompted discernment into the nature of the moving thing. What grabbed me most was that their movement was a directly intentional movement, discernibly different from the passive falling snow or the running water. The wind pushed the snow or the water ran down a slope, its course determined by rocks or fallen trees.

No one has captured the silence and sounds of a snowy scene in the woods better than Robert Frost describing his horse in "Stopping by Woods on a Snowy Evening." Here my own experience is echoed:

> He gives his harness bells a shake,
> to ask if there is some mistake.
> The only other sound's the sweep,
> of easy wind and downy flake.[1]

The horse is a cause of sound, while the snow is passively moved by the wind. Movements by animals are concentrated centers of self-effort. Life actively moves itself, as opposed to the passive movement of inanimate things.

No matter where one goes, the common experience of movement as a sign of life is the same. Living in Minnesota thirty-five years later, my children experience the same. So common in fact is the observation that life moves itself that our parks announce it; in a park within the city where I work hangs a sign by a pond that reads, *Look for any signs of movement in the water; can you see any types of life?* Most little children pick up immediately the truth that life moves itself. Like adults, they seem attuned to this occurrence. My own children on many occasions discover a worm or insect in the grass. "Poke it with a stick to see if it moves and or is dead," they say. Back in Indiana, wandering, I wondered about some object. Was it a dead branch or an animal lying there? I walked toward it. If it jumped up and ran away, it was alive.

Yet not all living things exhibit the same type of movement. Humans build many different things; they have language, discuss ideas; write philosophy, music, and plays; they play sports; and they believe in things higher, such as God, and have various religions. This is different from other species

1. Frost, "Stopping by Woods on a Snowy Evening."

in the world. There are similarities, but there are also profound differences. Animals may build things, but a given animal typically builds one thing one way. Robins build nests in only one way. On closer observation, they seem to build in a preprogrammed manner. No one has ever experienced an animal understanding the principles of structural engineering. Humans, by contrast, have large and diverse ways of communicating. Humans are generalists, animals are specialists. Human beings are rational and intelligent; they grasp the generic nature of things.

Still, the movement of animals is impressive compared to plants. Animals move about and are active, while plants seem to sit and grow. Humans occasionally "vegetate," that is, sit around eating all day like plants, but this behavior is likened to plants precisely because plants have a lower level of internally motivated movement. Movement is a basic characteristic of life. As such, ancient and medieval thinkers could not fail to notice its centrality to life itself, and they sought to construct a framework for understanding the universe.

What Is life? Life Moves (Completes) Itself

Modern biology texts define life with such phrases as "that which reproduces itself," "that which grows or eats and excretes waste," or "that which metabolizes."[2] All these are particular instances of change, or movement, in the broad sense of the term. They just never quite seem to get to the most generalizable observation of life as that which simply moves (changes) itself.

In the thirteenth century, Thomas Aquinas answered the question "What is life?" by taking a journey from nonliving things to the ultimate source of all reality, God. Thomas develops the basic observation made by human beings that life has a principle of self-movement – it moves itself.[3] Movement is the old term for change; in modern usage, it is the ability to change oneself. The term for this is immanence, taken from an immanent

2. See, e.g., Raven et al., *Biology*, 2–3.

3. *SCG* IV.11; *De Potentia*, q. X, 1c; *ST* I, q. 18, a. 1, c; I, q. 18, a. 2c. Specifically, a living thing is that which at its very core being, or substance, has the ability to move (or change in modern terminology) itself. The outward sensible manifestation of this substance is self-movement or self-change. For further discussion regarding levels of immanence in things, see also Toma, "Dionysian/Thomistic Framework," 87–113.

as opposed to a transitive verb.[4] A transitive verb needs another to complete it. An intransitive or immanent verb needs no other to complete it – it completes itself. St. Thomas noticed that the greater the immanence, the more interior it is to the organism, without reliance for the completion of its change on anything external to itself. He spoke of organisms as being more alive, the more internal the movement to the organism.[5] The ultimate self-moving act is intelligence, because in the highest of beings it does not need to rely on external things. In God, intelligence is the same as his existence and is who he is.[6]

The analysis of life based on movement naturally leads to the notion of the hierarchy of being.[7] The movement of nonliving things is a pure transfer of external motion to another. The most primitive living beings are plants,[8] where a transient interior action produces growth and reproduction. Next up the hierarchy are animals, defined by possession of the life of sense. In animals, sense experience terminates in the memory and not in an exterior thing like a new plant. The animals' experience of the world begins to resemble a type of union with what is known. Above animals, there are human beings with a rational intellect. While humans still depend on that which is outside of them to *begin* to think, the actual understanding is something interior. It is a purely interior act. Its product is the thing understood, and the image the knower has of himself. An intellect allows one to exist as a person, a being fundamentally ordered to another in relationships (e.g., friendship) and union. Later, I argue that the interior nature of human knowledge points to even higher beings who need nothing outside of themselves to know. Ultimately, the perfection of life is in God, who is his own cause and whose understanding is exactly the same as his infinite being.

It will probably surprise most modern readers that a medieval philosopher was able to gain profound insights into the nature of life without the experimental apparatus of modern science. A careful reading of Thomas

4. Sheen, *God and Intelligence*, 106–7.

5. *ST* I, q. 18, a. 3c.: "A thing is said to live in so far as it operates of itself and not as moved by another, the more perfectly this power is found in anything, the more perfect is the life of that thing."

6. *SCG* I.44–45.

7. *SCG* IV.11. 4.

8. Plants are simplest, according to St. Thomas. I ask the reader to wait until chapter 7 regarding such organisms as bacteria and protists, known as and called simpler by modern science.

Aquinas's *Summa contra Gentiles* shows that in Thomas's thought there is a synergy between implicit human understanding and analytical philosophy, which refines common experience into precise distinctions. Thomas uses this refined understanding to gain insight into the loftiest truth of Christianity, the life of the Trinity.

Thomas begins with the observation that we did, namely, that living things change and complete themselves. In other words, they are their own source of change. Just like children poking insects in the grass or investigating a novel object in the distance to see if it moves, the common criterion for life is self-movement. All people, both young and old, are fascinated by this observation: pulling the fish out of the water and watching it flop, watching horses run, or waiting for the snake to move in the cage at a zoo.

Another corollary of self-movement is self-maintenance.[9] Every day, you get up in the morning, eat breakfast, brush your teeth, go to school or work, learn and do things, eat two more times, play with your family, go to bed. You are working to maintain yourself. And *you* are initiating the change in yourself. Living things are their own source of change.

If the definition of life is that which moves itself, those things that change themselves in a deeper interior manner, particularly in completing themselves, are higher life forms.[10] In the modern conception of life, it does not make much sense to talk of higher or lower forms of life, except in terms of molecular or morphological complexity. Yet our common sense – or, better, common experience of life – indicates that higher forms of life are in some sense more perfect. The World Series, the Super Bowl, and the Olympics display this fact. Athletes of all types compete in the Olympics to see who performs best, and they rightly receive recognition because they show the perfection of their sport. The writer or the scientist who wins the Pulitzer or Nobel Prize does the same. They are recognized as the highest or greatest because they approximate perfection.

The same is true for natural life. To the degree a living thing can change and complete itself without another, it is more alive.[11] The more *independent*

9. Aquinas, *Commentary on Aristotle's De Anima* III.230–34.

10. *SCG* IV.11.1. "The higher a nature the more intimate [immanent, or interior] to the nature is that which flows from it."

11. *ST* I, q. 18, a. 3c.

or *internal* the organism is, the higher its form of life. So basic is this idea of self-movement to life that we do not even have in English a distinct word for those things that are nonliving. We understand living things and then define anything less as "*non*living" or inanimate. These observations, refined by empirical-philosophical analysis, led Thomas to distinguish three types of material life: plants, animals, and humans.[12] Nonliving things (subatomic particles, atoms, molecules, water, air, rocks, minerals, the sun, moon, and stars) are non-self-movers, collectively called "minerals" in the ancient and medieval world.[13]

Life from the Bottom Up: A Natural Hierarchy

The ancients called nonliving things minerals, but they were limited in their knowledge of nonliving things to earth, air, fire, water, rocks, minerals, and such. Today, many more nonliving things are known. A billiard ball hits another and transfers motion to it. The ball that will receive the motion is passive. It stays put until moved by another, which received its motion from another, and so forth. Where does the rock skipping across the water get its movement? From the thrower. The water hit by the rock gets its motion from the rock. Thomas uses the example of fire igniting wood.[14] It is transferred externally to the wood as the heat of one flame causes the wood to burn when it is near enough to it. St. Thomas notes two key points.[15] First, the fire gains nothing as it is completed in the wood, but the wood gains heat. Second, the wood does nothing actively to ignite itself but is ignited by the external action of the fire. The change of nonliving things arises from something external and is completed in something external.

Does modern science agree?[16] Take, for example, Isaac Newton (discussed in chap. 2), who is considered the father of classical mechanics. He

12. *SCG* IV.11.1.

13. The sun, moon, and stars were actually thought of as higher forms of material beings. I make my statement as if they had the understanding of these celestial objects as we have presently with our discoveries of modern science.

14. *SCG* IV.11.2; Toma, "Dionysian/Thomistic Framework," 87–113.

15. *SCG* IV.11.2.

16. Toma, "Dionysian/Thomistic Framework," 87–113.

formulated the famous three laws of motion that are taught in basic physics courses everywhere:[17]

1. Every body persists in its state of being at rest or of moving uniformly straight forward, except insofar as it is compelled to change its state by force impressed
2. The alteration of motion is ever proportional to the motive force impressed; and is made in the direction of the right line in which that force is impressed
3. To every action there is always an equal and opposite reaction: or the forces of two bodies on each other are always equal and are directed in opposite directions

Some distinctions are necessary to answer the question of agreement between Newton (science) and St. Thomas (philosophy). When it comes to nonliving matter and change of place (local motion), these laws are only somewhat consistent with the teaching of St. Thomas. When St. Thomas talks about change or motion, he is speaking about all forms of change, including local motion and change of quality or change in substance (coming to be and passing away).[18] Newton, however, restricts his analysis of motion to an idealized local motion, or change of place, and begins with the concept of inertial motion. With respect to local motion, Newton's concept of acceleration would approximate to Aquinas's understanding of the causes of local motion (it's not clear that Aquinas or Aristotle had a doctrine of acceleration).

St. Thomas held that for local motion to occur, a continuous force needs to be applied through the medium of motion.[19] This is a divergence from Newton's first law. If a shot arrow leaves the bow, the motive force is applied to the arrow through the medium (air). Newton, in contrast, held that the medium is a source of friction and does not transmit motive force. Thus, once an object is accelerated or set in motion, it will remain that way unless another force alters it. This represents a major difference between the two thinkers. But despite the differences of opinion on the simple motion of bodies,

17. Newton, *Mathematical Principles of Natural Philosophy*, 13–14.

18. Aquinas, *Commentary on Aristotle's Physics* III, lec. 1–5.

19. Aquinas, *Commentary on Aristotle's Physics* VII, lec. 3.

described by Newton's first law of motion, both Aquinas and Newton might agree on the cause of acceleration, as set down in Newton's second law.

Thus while there may be certain fundamental differences between these two thinkers, insofar as they do overlap, they could arguably agree on the general idea that nonliving things display for the most part an essential exteriority in their actions (the arrow's motion is imposed from without and terminates in the target, again exterior to it). In *this* sense, Newtonian ideas are simply more precise and mathematized descriptions of certain external actions, the motion per se of nonliving things. Similarly, modern science, having adopted the general view of forces from Newton, adopts this idea of external actions as well.

By the early 1900s, the Einsteinian theories of relativity and the theories of quantum mechanics began to supplant the Newtonian universe. Einstein posited space-time as the absolute reference for physical motion, not space or time by themselves, as did Newton.[20] Quantum mechanics is a body of information about the behavior of subatomic particles (and larger objects as well). I say more these more later, but the general observation that nonliving things interact by external influence is still valid in both fields. They are simply more sophisticated and precise understandings of our universe than Newton had. For instance, Einstein's work might ask, Which object is in motion and with respect to what frame of reference?[21] Quantum mechanics might show the probabilistic nature of our knowledge of the interactions of subatomic particles.[22] Chemistry is concerned with topics of atomic and molecular interactions, or precisely how a thing like fire transfers its heat to a piece of wood. It still deals with external actions but gives more precise descriptions of the mechanisms of the external change. In this respect, chemistry is the science of the mechanism of certain external actions.[23] None of this denies that inanimate things are not centers of self-change, however. Inanimate objects are not self-moving; that is, their actions end in another.

Modern physics and chemistry describe types of external actions. Objects are passive and only change if another changes them. Modern astro-

20. Greene, *Fabric of the Cosmos*, 68–75.

21. Greene, *Fabric of the Cosmos*, 51–80.

22. Heisenberg, *Physicist's Conception of Nature*, 34–42.

23. Toma, "Dionysian/Thomistic Framework," 87–113.

nomy tells us of incredible instances of these inanimate forces changing things: black holes destroying other stars, supernova explosions devastating regions of galaxies, high-intensity irradiation of planets, giant asteroids wiping out living beings such as the dinosaurs, our own moon with blisteringly hot areas in the sun and extremely cold regions in the shade of rocks, and the Big Bang itself, with the universe expanding faster and faster into a lonely void. Objects jostle and get farther and farther apart. Eventually, things will expand so far that few interactions will be possible.[24] The inanimate world of physics, chemistry, and astronomy reveals a universe expanding into a cold darkness driven by the mechanistic jostling of objects acting under external actions. Nonliving matter exists only for itself in a hostile expansion into a void.

Once living beings enter, the picture changes. Plants are the most basic level of life.[25] Why plant a garden? To wait for the plants to grow and produce seed and fruit, which in turn yields food. In large measure, nonliving things – CO_2, sunlight, inorganic nitrogen, phosphorus, and sulfur – cannot be turned into nutrients needed with a net gain in energy for the system. Plants can accomplish such a transformation. They draw in compounds from outside themselves, transform them inside, and cause themselves to grow and reproduce.[26] Inside, something radically different from the outside is made and organized into a plant tissue. There is a transient interiorization of action.[27] A plant enlarges or augments itself, and it produces another plant. A tree grows larger every year, and the end of this growth is simply to make itself more of a plant. As seeds are produced, the plant produces another plant, but this second plant is finally, totally separate from its parent; the action of a plant terminates in something exterior, the new plant. These ends – growth and reproduction – are determined by nature.[28] There is no freedom in what a plant does. Therefore, in plants, there is life at its most basic function of giving life to another of the same kind. Nevertheless, in plants, nonliving matter is fundamentally reorganized into something

24. Perlov and Vilenkin, *Cosmology for the Curious*, 125–41.

25. *SCG* IV.11.3. Again, I ask the reader to please wait until chapter 7 for a discussion regarding such things as bacteria and protists.

26. *SCG* IV.11.3.

27. *SCG* IV.11.3.

28. *ST* I, q. 18, a. 3c.

radically different: life. Matter is reoriented at its most basic level from a purely passive state existing only for itself and becomes, through the plants' offspring, that which is given (life from the parent) and that which is received (to the offspring). Life becomes a gift.

In this aspect of parents and offspring, we begin to see perhaps the deepest truth of things alluded to above. Union is productive of a third. It is not the fanatical absorption of two in each other that is the highest perfection of union, but rather their complete self-giving and union precisely in a third.[29] The perfection of life at the vegetative level – the production of offspring – gives us an insight into this. In material living things, physical union is for the sake of another.[30] How this plays out in intellectual union remains to be seen. Nevertheless, in a plant there are the beginnings of life, but not the perfection of life. Life can be much greater.

Animals are the next higher forms of life, both in modern science and in Thomas's system based on everyday human experience. Animals display something plants do not. They run, play, and traditionally performed much of our human labor. There is a kind of quickening in animals, and they approximate us humans to a much greater degree than plants do. This partly explains human affection for them, since people do not walk their plants or play fetch with them.

What makes animals different from a plant? In a word, they can sense: they see, smell, hear, taste, and touch.[31] Because they can sense things, they can perceive sensible objects: those objects having colors, odor, and so on. This power to know sensible objects allows them to fear or like certain things. If emotions are the aversion or attraction (affection) to things sensed, then animals have emotions.[32] They like people who feed them and care

29. Staniloae, *Holy Trinity*, 21–27. See also Damascene, *Christ the Eternal Tao*, 252–53.

30. This obvious truth needs restating in our pleasure-soaked society. Specifically, sexual reproduction is first and foremost for the sake of producing offspring. Aside from the self-evident nature of this fact, any review of biology texts will state the same; i.e., sexual reproduction is for the survival of the species, or the production of gametes (sex cells: sperm and eggs) is for the purpose of producing more offspring, or similar phrasing. The pleasure derived from it is secondary. While it may be pretty certain that higher animals other than humans derive pleasure from sexual reproduction, it is by no means certain with lower animals. But they do engage in this activity precisely to produce offspring.

31. *SCG* IV.11.4.

32. *ST* I-II, q. 22.

for them. They fear those who abuse them. The power of sensing and the desire (attraction or affection) or fear that comes from it are characteristic of animals. Animals also remember the things they like or fear; they have memory.[33]

Heliotropism may be cited as a counterexample to this generalization.[34] Doesn't the sunflower move with the sun? In fact, many plants do, and plants can "smell" and "hear" in a certain manner, too.[35] They also seem to remember these sensations. How, then, do we distinguish plants from animals?

We define a thing from what we know best.[36] Children learn what is gray based on black and white, not the other way around. Gray is a greater or lesser amount of black or white. Nectarines are a hybrid of peaches and plum. We define a nectarine from the two fruits from which it is derived, which we know better. Electricity in a wire is called a current, named after flowing water, which we know better. All knowledge proceeds by comparison with what we know better. We define sense based on what we, who are part animal, do. We sense. Sensing is the ability to know a sensible thing.[37] Once again, sensible things are made of matter; they have height, length, depth, and weight, and they exist in space and time. The general term for such a thing is an individual, as defined previously: that which is extended in space and time. Thus what an animal senses is *this* flower, *this* tree, *this* bowl of food, *this* dog, *this* human, or, going back to triangles, *this* particular triangle (not the idea). They know *this* individual sensible thing. The dog knows his master as *this* thing that cares for and feeds him. It has affection for a particular human being, but it does not know humanity or what it means to be a human. It doesn't know generalities or what a thing is, just *this* thing giving pleasure or pain. It is the lowest type of knowledge, knowledge of the

33. *SCG* IV.11.4.

34. The common observation that a plant turns toward the sun and tracks with it throughout the day.

35. Chamovitz, *What a Plant Knows*, 27–48, 71–89. This book is a fascinating account of the sensory capabilities of plants. Many aspects of their sensing capabilities appear to be similar to those of animals. But as the author admits up front, the term "sensing" is not exactly applicable in the same way in both plants and animals. As I will discuss, I think the key difference is that a plant does not *know* an individual.

36. Aristotle, *Physics* I, 315.

37. Aquinas, *Commentary on Aristotle's De Anima* II, lec. 5–12; III, lec. 2–3.

individual. This is what sensing is in its pure form, taken from our experience of the empirical world.

Plants "sense" in a much different manner.[38] They detect light, odors, and such for the purpose of their growth and reproduction. They detect the sensory stimulus itself and do not know per se the object that gives the sense. Their "memory" is similar. It moves toward the last place of the stimulus. They don't remember the individual thing. No one has ever seen a plant have joy or sorrow toward an individual.

But the dog has memory in a larger and more important way. It remembers the object of sense as a real individual that gives pleasure or pain, not as the plant that again has a memory of simply the "region" of "pleasure" or "pain." St. Thomas notes that in animals there is a deeper level of interiorization, or self-movement. Like plants, animals grow and reproduce; that is, they can vegetate. When animals sense, however, they begin using things external to them, the objects sensed, and the action of sensing ends in their memory. So in the case of animals, there is an action beginning on the outside – perceiving something sensible – that ends, is completed, on the inside, as a memory of the external thing.[39] A plant's action completes itself in something exterior, the new plant. With animals, there occurs a deeper action of self-movement, which is movement that does not depend totally on another. Sensing completes interiorly in the memory as a more intense type of self-movement; it is one step more independent of that which is outside itself, precisely because the animal stores the memory inside, remembering this or that *thing* as pleasurable or painful.[40]

The memory of an animal broadens the life of the animal to things outside of itself. This is another level of living beyond oneself, in contrast to mere reproduction in plants. In animals, there are the beginnings of true knowledge that we introduced in our discussion of the intellect. Knowledge

38. Chamovitz, *What a Plant Knows.*

39. *SCG* IV.11.4; *ST* I, q. 18, a. 3c.

40. This includes "lower" animals as well such as insects and fish. I use "lower" here in the common parlance; scientists would consider both of these as higher organisms. In scientifically lower organisms such as flatworms and rotifers, the answer to the question of whether they have memory is less clear. But as I argued above, one takes the standard from the obvious, not the gray borderlands. Insects and fish clearly do have memory. On a related point, insects also have brains (a question students occasionally ask). Indeed, they often have complex brains and nervous systems.

is something of the other possessed by the knower. Sense knowledge has sensible aspects of the other: the color of the other in the case of sight, or the sound of the other in the case of hearing. With sense knowledge, the animal contains aspects of the other and in an abstract sense is somehow more than just itself.[41] The experience of a rose with its deep red color and sweet scent leads to a fuller sense of the rose. Life is greater where there is greater knowledge, where the other abides in the knower. Such an experience leads to a type of reveling and resting in the known. And in animals there is a remote, albeit imperfect, reflection of communion or abiding in the other, a reflection of friendship that is the epitome of personal relations.

With human beings, life takes a gigantic leap. Sensation, memory, and intellect are now interrelated in a new way. Human beings share much with plants and animals. Centuries ago, Aquinas and others like him posited a substantial claim about the Hierarchy of Being: that which is above contains the powers of that which is below.[42] The Hierarchy of Being is not like stair steps that are all the same, each step simply above the next. The hierarchy means that most realities that are on the lower scale of the hierarchy are subsumed into those higher up. The sunflower tracking light is similar to sense experience in animals; it is approaching the power of that above it, the animal. Plants grow and reproduce; animals grow, reproduce, and sense; humans grow, reproduce, sense, and reason.

Reason is perhaps the most controversial difference between the Thomistic view of human beings and that of materialistic science. The intellect, and therefore humans, in modern science is seen as no different from animals.[43] From the Thomistic view, there is a fundamental difference. Scientism is highly reductionistic; it looks at life from the standpoint of its most primitive functions – growth and reproduction. Anything beyond that is extra stuff to aid survival. Thomistic thought views life from its most fundamental action (self-movement) and the deepening of this action as it moves

41. Aquinas, *Commentary on Aristotle's De Anima* II, lec. 5–12; III, lec. 2–3.

42. *ST* I, q. 57, a. 2c.

43. This is so widespread and accepted that it need not be supported by citation. Most standard texts in science make this claim. As discussed in chapter 3, the premise of modern scientistic thought, regarding the intellect, is that there is only material reality. The intellect of man is simply different in degree from that of animals.

toward perfection (completion).[44] So what type of self-movement is particular to humans?

We spoke of the intellect as immaterial. The natural objects of our thoughts are beings composed of matter. Because material things occupy space and time, they are external to us. Humans have a type of intelligence that needs external reality to gather information for the exercise of reason.[45] Once we have this knowledge, the act of thought itself is immaterial.[46] So like animals, humans depend on that which is outside them to know. Unlike them, they do not stop at individual knowledge but move on to the knowledge of the principles of material beings, especially the formal cause.[47] As the sensible aspect of things resides in the sense knower as memory, the intellectual knowledge of things resides in the intellect in its formal aspect, immaterially. This knowledge exists as immaterial in the intellect and not as material as it exists in external reality in the known thing.

Second, once an external object is known, humans further reflect on *themselves* by comparing themselves to what and how they know.[48] *They then know themselves precisely as knowing beings*. They are self-reflecting, able to muse upon and conclude new things from what they know. When humans think about things and their own action of thinking, they form an idea of self. We all have an idea of ourselves that is to a certain degree accurate, but not perfect or "complete," a kind of image of ourselves in our minds. Here we begin to see another type of reproduction. In addition to our biological children occurring from our vegetative powers, the life of the mind produces another self, our image of ourselves as knowers – the remote evidence of an internal intellectual fruition.[49] If, as we have claimed, the intellect becomes that which it knows, the higher the intelligent being, the more accurately that being knows itself. All things love themselves; they do things to augment their life and resist death. Therefore, once known, the more accurate the idea of self, the more it is loved. Thus in the intelligent act we begin

44. Aquinas, *De Potentia*, q. X, 1c.

45. *SCG* IV.11.5.

46. Aquinas, *Commentary on Aristotle's De Anima* III, lec. 4–8.

47. Once again, the formal cause is that which makes a thing to be what it is, as opposed to its material cause, which determines of what it is made.

48. *SCG* IV.11.5.

49. *SCG* IV.9–11.

to see three things reminiscent of a type of reproduction: the possessor of intelligence, the intellectual image of oneself, and the movement of the will (love) to that image.[50]

Perhaps the most important difference of all between the view proposed here and the materialist (reductionistic) view of human beings is that human beings are a bridge between material and intellectual reality, owing to their powers of sense and intelligence.[51] They possess the material powers of growth, reproduction, and sensing, and the nonmaterial or intellectual powers of knowing. They possess the powers of plants and animals in addition to their rational intellect. They are akin to beings lower through their material powers (or body in a generalizable sense) and akin to that which is higher through their intellects. In this sense, they are a microcosm of creation.[52] Our very constitution is the same as the universe around us. This similarity between us and the universe makes us able to know it. Our internal structure is a platform for knowing reality because it is like the rest of the cosmos. This is the real sense in which Christians and the Greeks before them thought of humans as the center of reality, not in the misguided popular sense as portrayed in misunderstandings of the Galileo controversy, of being the physical center of creation. In humans, we have a being able to know *ourselves* and enter into communities of knowledge and love.

Law of Assimilation

When we step back and view the actions of all four types of being in general—minerals, plants, animals, and man—the law of assimilation emerges.[53] This law helps us to understand the idea in chapter 3 that the intellect contains the other. Succinctly put, without the possession of the other in some

50. It is in this sense that certain Fathers of the Church, such as Augustine, used the internal operations of the human soul as a reflection of the Trinity (but not proving it by reason). See *ST* I, q. 32, a. 1, arg. 2 and ad. 2.

51. Scheeben, *Mysteries of Christianity*, 238–39, 357, 401, 401n54.

52. Golitzin, *Et Introibo*, 371–92. This idea of man as a platform of reality or, more specifically, a "little Church" Golitzin claims was prevalent in the Christian Syriac East and found its way into the Christian Greek East from there.

53. The term "law of assimilation" and its synthesis are taken from Sheen, *Philosophy of Science*, 108–11. Sheen in part bases this idea on *ST* I, q. 76, a. 2, ad. 4, and Aquinas, *Truth*, vol. I, q. 2, a. 1.

way, life in the universe as we know it would be impossible: vegetative life needs food, sensory life needs sensible things, and intellectual life needs intelligible being. But this ability to assimilate varies according to the nature of the assimilator. Each step up the hierarchy of being reveals a new and more perfect assimilation. Vegetative life draws in chemicals from outside and breaks them up for nutriment. In modern parlance, this is termed digestion, or catabolism, where a thing is broken down, and then anabolism, where new molecules are built up from these to unite to the organism assimilating. Vegetative life is so weak in its interiority that it must destroy what it assimilates before it unites.

Above vegetative life is animal life, the life of sense. Animals are not as destructive of their object of sense. They take in qualities (sensory aspects) of an object, such as color or sound. The animal then unites them for a composite sensory picture. In the end, its knowledge is only of juxtaposed parts (sensory qualities), just as that of vegetative life is parts of the chemical it has digested. At least in animal sensing, however, the quality as such is not destroyed, as is the chemical in vegetation.

In human intellection, we should expect to find a yet more perfect assimilation than in either plants or animals. And we do. The intellect of man still removes that which it needs for "nourishment," but in a much more perfect way. It unites with the formal principle, or cause, of the very nature of a thing. It does not take up qualities in parts as does the sense but becomes the other in a nonmaterial manner. In all three types of life, the end result is union, but only in the intellect is the cause of the thing assimilated preserved. And it is precisely because of its immateriality that it can do this.

Modern Science in a Medieval Framework?

Our tour of life is both refreshing and challenging. It shows us that philosophers who were keen observers of natural life were able to see many factual truths adumbrated in modern science. Those truths were based on common human experience, the same kind we all possess. Modern science gives us greater detail and precision but does not change the broad outlines of natural truth. Science itself is based on common experience. Common observations of nature cannot tell us about cellular structure or evolutionary linkages with the past history of the universe, but these details don't in any way lessen our certitude based on the things we know best: human experience of nature.

Yet modern scientism does stand in contrast to the notion of a hierarchy of being based on the greater internalization of self-movement. Modern biology resorts to a minimalistic understanding of life when it focuses on survival and reproduction. One might say that many modern thinkers have missed the obvious, namely, that there is a directionality to this natural hierarchy. It tends to move in a certain direction and not in another. The hierarchy of being points to the culmination of the material world in the immaterial intellect. The overarching, organizing principle of the cosmos is not survival but intelligence.

The neglect or denial of intelligence as an organizing principle or goal of the natural world may be rooted in a false understanding of how the material and immaterial relate to one another. The misconceptions about the body-soul relation, mentioned in chapter 3, are evidence of a mistaken understanding of material-immaterial relations. The Thomistic understanding of the hierarchy of nature shows that the material and immaterial are not opposites or irrelevant to each another. In that framework of thought, what is higher on the hierarchy contains or includes what is lower on the hierarchy. Thus animals with their memory in a small way approximate human beings, although they lack true intelligence. Humans are the material pinnacle of the hierarchy because they share in the material world with other organisms, while they are also able to transcend that world with their immaterial intellects. Life is more than survival or reproduction. Life tends toward intelligence. Still, are human beings the most perfect examples of intelligence and life?

6 THE PERFECTION OF THE COSMOS

Before addressing the question about more perfect forms of intelligence, the interrelationship of beings in the material cosmos needs to be addressed.[1] Do these beings exist in a static hierarchy? Do they relate to each other? Is there a dynamism, so evident in nature, to this hierarchy? And toward what does this dynamism tend? It has been argued that the key to ancient and medieval cosmology lies in the intellect. Not only does the distinction between exterior and interior change the frame for the hierarchy of being, but also this increasing tendency of life toward more interior actions is the driving force that relates material being and is the end toward which the whole material cosmos tends. At the same time, it is the thread that allows us to integrate modern science into the hierarchy of being and determine whether humans are indeed the most perfect forms of intelligence.

1. The discussion of the three perfections of nature and the perfect and imperfect ordering according to St. Thomas presented in this chapter follows in part the analysis of St. Thomas's thought on the universe given by Blanchette, *Perfection of the Universe*.

The Insects of Southern Indiana

The height of the summer heat in southern Indiana coupled with its abundant rain brings forth a profusion of grasses and flowers in an unmown field. When such a place butts up against the woodland, the best of both worlds is found. Insects are everywhere, in number and variety; grasshoppers and katydids proliferate. They fly into the air by the hundreds and land several yards away to continue their eating. Bees of all types—fuzzy honeybees, bumblebees, and colorful solitary bees—abound, marvelous creatures to watch. Painstakingly, they move toward and investigate each floweret of the flowers; in all this they display a single-mindedness of purpose. They are the envy of single-minded focus as they busily pick along a flower, dipping mouthparts for nectar or combing pollen into their pollen sacks on their back legs.

While bees are the denizens of the air, ants are their counterparts on the ground. Whole groups of ants move in large fans searching for food, following chemical scent trials. Especially striking are red ants that raid carpenter ant nests. At one moment, all is normal and peaceful in the carpenter ant nest; a few hours later, a large group of red ants attacks, killing and carrying off slaves; finally, silence and inactivity. They are the armies of the insect world. When I was still a young boy, I would kick a red ant mound and throw in a caterpillar. They would swarm over the poor creature and drag it away with ruthless efficiency. Similarly interesting creatures were the sleek wasps and hornets. They prowled about the flowers hunting for insect prey. Of the more fascinating types of such insects were the spider wasps and the large cicada killers. They would dig a hole by flicking the soil out of the way with their legs. After making the hole, they disappear and later come out front forward pushing more dirt. They nervously investigate their surroundings, fly about in a few circles, and go back to work. They might return with some hapless spider or cicada and drag it into their hole. I learned later they would lay an egg on it, seal the burrow, and the young would eat the victim alive, the prey having been paralyzed, not killed, by the sting of the mother, so it would serve as fresh meat for the larvae. Interestingly, they know exactly which part of the nerve along the bottom of their prey to sting to properly paralyze it.[2]

2. Grimaldi and Engel, *Evolution of the Insects*, 434.

Another menace is the European giant hornet, an inadvertent import to the United States. These are rather large insects that gathered on the roof of the house in the evenings where other insects would come because of the radiated heat from the shingles during the night. They would use this attractant to their advantage to hunt these insects. These giant hornets also had a fondness for the apples under our tree. It turns out that my dog Bliss liked the apples as well. These two facts were the basis for one of my favorite memories. Every fall, as the apples ripened and fell, a ritual repeatedly occurred. Bliss would extend her paw, flip the apple, and run back. She would wait a minute, and if no hornet came out, she would then consume it. I assume at some point she got stung in the mouth before learning to do this.

Perhaps my favorite was the robber fly, several species of which are found in southern Indiana. They seem to like the grass at the edge of the woods. They are a heavy-bodied, elongated fly, not totally unlike a giant heavy mosquito. Yet their aerodynamics and speed in flight are only equaled by their relatives, the hover fly. Robber flies would sit on grass, fly out at potential insect prey, deftly snatch them in midflight, and stab them with a wicked mouthpart. Then, settling down to consume the body juices of the prey, their eyes seemed to have an almost mechanical stare.

I miss the hot, humid evenings of southern Indiana, with the stretching rays of sun as the countryside hummed with the cicada song. This occurs in Minnesota but to a much more limited degree. A couple of times during my youth, I experienced the occurrence of the seventeen-year cicadas, a type that emerges from a larval stage in the ground, feeding on tree roots, every seventeen years as an adult in order to mate.[3] Their arrival would begin as a hum in the woods distinct from other cicadas and build like an advancing army. At full force, they were everywhere. Here again, an order similar to the seasons was evident; this was timed and occurred at a regular cycle.

While not an insect, another favorite of mine was the jumping spider. These delightful little creatures – many of whom had brilliant metallic colors – would sit on the propane tank under the walnut trees and hunt for insects. I would place my finger several inches away from them on the tank and move it slowly back and forth, which caught their attention. If I moved

3. Grimaldi and Engel, *Evolution of the Insects*, 308.

my finger slowly to my eye, they would fix on my eyes. If I looked at them and moved left, so would they; if to the right, they would move right.

The experience of these insects – bees, wasps, ants, grasshoppers, robber flies, giant hornets, cicadas, and jumping spiders – conveyed to me a definite sense of purpose and order in their behavior. Like my Airedale Bliss displaying purpose in turning over apples, I saw that the bees foraged, the other insects hunted, and the cicadas emerged with regular timing. All bespoke order and directed behavior. What is abundantly evident cannot be denied by rational beings open to evidence.

Final Causality: Affirmation and Denial

The directedness to an end and purposefulness in nature can be termed final causality. Probably no concept is more vigorously denied by the proponents of scientism, as they are committed to a materialistic philosophy. They know that final cause can only be justified in the end if there is a higher cause guiding things. Why? Insects, or events such as seasons, are ordered and work toward ends but are not intelligent. Yet our common experience tells us that intelligence is the cause of order and directedness. As an arrow reaches its target because of the mind and agency of the archer, so nonintelligent beings lower than humans work toward ends by some intellectual agent.[4] This is what materialism ultimately wants to deny.

While I was a PhD student, a prominent bee researcher visited our laboratory. At a potluck in his honor, as we sat around chatting, he stated that biologists must get rid of the terminology of final cause because it had no place in biology. Things do not work for an end, he insisted. He invoked the African tick bird to prove his point. This bird flies to a rhinoceros in order to pick off the ticks to eat. This behavior evolved in the ancestral tick bird happening to land on a rhinoceros and happening to eat the ticks. This food supply helped its young survive, and over generations of this repeated event, the bird gained this behavior. This biologist insisted that the tick bird's behavior should be described from this nonteleological historical standpoint: tick birds just happened to fly by and just happened to land on a rhinoceros.

4. *SCG* III.2.

The bird sees the ticks and just happens to eat them. Point proved? Quite the contrary! The very language of humans is laden with final causality precisely because it is so evident in nature. The physical universe, as we see it, is the proper object of our minds. That things work for an end is everywhere. Order and ends presuppose intelligence. My experience of nature in the southern Indiana of my youth did not permit me to accept these arguments against purposefulness in nature. Though they are common in scientific academia, they are as counterintuitive as anything I have ever encountered.

How could two scientists look at the same phenomenon and come to such opposite conclusions? Erazim Kohak offers an explanation.[5] He claims that scientific materialism has placed a construct, an obstacle if you will, between nature and the observer. The common experience of nature bespeaks purpose and ends. It is only by enculturation in a professional discipline or a vague academic culture that one is led to deny what is so evident to every observer. All living things in the material universe have in common birth (generation) and development to adulthood. Every spring in southern Indiana, new life appeared: flowering plants, budding trees, sprouting oaks, hickories, walnuts, fish and insects in the creek. The young of various animals, from deer to baby birds, were born or hatched. Generation and consequent maturation are about as evident and undeniable as anything in the spring and summer of the eastern woodlands. Purpose and ends in nature are everywhere, in the trees above us, on the earth around us, and in the water below us. The veritable explosion of life is an undeniable annual occurrence. Each of these beings develops in its own way and then comes to participate in a greater order about them. And all this is suffused with order, regularity, and purpose.

Part of the reason many modern people cannot see the validity and value of the cosmology I have been hinting at is that they have a wrong idea of what it consists in. They tend to think of a Hierarchy of Being as the idea of a stagnant ossified structure, which is at odds with the evident dynamism of nature. This is one of the most common critiques in both scientific and philosophical circles. Yet nothing could be further from the truth. This idea of hierarchy, coupled with order and final cause, contains an intrinsic dyna-

5. Kohak, *Embers and the Stars*, 11–12, 22–26.

mism and development that relate all creatures in a common, cooperative bond of mutual dependency and ascent to the highest of beings, God. But because many people living in urban areas have not had a detailed and regular experience of nature, let's turn to consider a creature known to everyone. Humans are undeniably as much a part of nature as any other animal. Nature needs us as much as we need it.

Human Development

Human individuals pass through several stages, beginning at birth and lasting until maturation. This can be called primary development.[6] In general, birth is the beginning, youth the intermediate, and adulthood the final stage. The stages of youth can be broken into baby, toddler, child, and teenager. Even in adulthood we recognize young, middle, and older adulthood. The end of one's youth is to become an adult. All young humans become a normal adult, barring some unforeseen accident such as premature death, disease, or some other type of incident. When these negative factors prevent the achievement of this end, we deem it tragic and contrary to natural maturation; this explains the large investment in medicine and psychology to overcome such difficulties. If we did not intuitively recognize the proper end of youth as adulthood, we would not try so hard to overcome impediments to this end. In nature, too, things achieve their end for the most part, barring some other thing inhibiting it. There is a true end to development, the adult. Becoming a normal adult is the natural end of youth. Nature works toward an end.

There is also a second type of development.[7] Once adulthood is achieved, and in part on the way to adulthood, we begin to complete ourselves in other ways beyond physical maturation. The natural desire of most humans is both to learn and to acquire skills. We go to school, read, write, earn a degree, or learn a trade. Being social animals, we interact with our parents first, then immediate relatives, friends, and society at large. The traditional term for these actions is the practice of the intellectual and moral virtues. These actions are distinct from those that simply grow us into an adult. Many of these are specific to humans, however; certain other animals can't learn as we do or are not

6. Blanchette, *Perfection of the Universe*, 55–57, 65–68, 70–73; *ST* I, q. 6, a. 3c.

7. Blanchette, *Perfection of the Universe*, 55–57, 65–68, 70–73; *ST* I, q. 6, a. 3c.

social. Few, if any, social skills are needed to be a clam. In the case of humans, this secondary development is viewed as necessary for being a person.

One might object that secondary development is the same as primary development. Becoming a normal adult requires education and social skills. While this is true, there is an important distinction to make. Primary development yields all the necessary structures and capacities to function normally. Natural programmed development occurs biologically and produces all proper functioning biological systems (e.g., circulative, digestive, muscular, neural) in order to acquire secondary development. Eyes are for seeing. The human eye is a detailed structure that allows one to perceive light and color with depth perception. Yet its function is seeing. There is a conceptual difference between its structure and its function. Primary development involves the structure, what a thing is. Secondary development involves the function in which that structure engages. We make a lawn mower to cut grass. Its structure is that of a lawn mower, but its function is to cut grass. So the structure of the eye is its primary development, while seeing is its secondary development.

Another example is learning to play a violin or any musical instrument. Many adults have the potential to play an instrument to some degree, and some of them actually do so. The potential is given by primary development, but the accomplishment of the task involves the secondary. One could be fully formed according to primary development and not ever achieve actual musical ability by secondary development. The same concerns sports. Most humans have the capacity to learn some type of sport, but some do not actually do so. Because some people are bigger, faster, more coordinated, have better mechanical abilities, or are smarter than others – they vary according to primary development – capacities according to secondary development vary as well. Of those who learn the violin, some play much better than others. This secondary development is the purpose of primary development and is as natural to us as the primary. Humans desire to engage in a variety of activities, such as learning, physical skills, and the arts. All normal people want to be successful in some regard and to have relationships with other people. A properly formed human being in the primary sense who only lounges and makes no effort to learn, socialize, or develop secondarily is rightly seen as having major problems. Primary development has its end or purpose in the secondary.[8]

8. Blanchette, *Perfection of the Universe*, 55–57, 65–68, 70–73; *ST* I, q. 6, a. 3c.

There is still another kind of development, the tertiary.[9] The tertiary is the use of secondary talents and abilities to actually participate in society, or a greater external good, whereas primary and secondary developments are proper to the individual. As proper primary development offers capacities for secondary development, which may or may not be actualized, so proper secondary development affords human beings the capacities to become contributing members of society at various levels. At the most basic level, individuals participate in the greater good of the family. The family as a whole completes us to a greater degree than is possible by ourselves. Another tertiary end is the community or state. Participation in the state completes us to a greater degree as well. This highest level is seen most clearly in an individual sacrificing himself for the greater whole, such as a father for the family or the soldier for the state. This sacrificial behavior evidences an intuitive recognition that the greater whole is something better than our own individual self and should be preserved more than us. It is therefore natural to learn for the purpose of engaging in larger groups than ourselves – an aversion to this would be seen as a social phobia. As primary development is for the secondary, so the secondary is for the tertiary.

Instead of primary, secondary, and tertiary development, ancient and medieval thinkers called these "perfections," but with a meaning different from the modern connotations of that word.[10] The modern sense of perfection is a loaded term, particularly in the sciences. Some additional rigor is needed to understand it as the premoderns used the term. The *American Heritage Dictionary* defines "perfect" in several ways, but as Blanchette argues,[11] the two primary meanings are:

1. Lacking nothing essential to the whole; complete of its nature or kind.
2. In a state of undiminished or highest excellence; without defect, flawless.[12]

9. Blanchette, *Perfection of the Universe*, 55–57, 65–68, 70–73; *ST* I, q. 6, a. 3c.
10. See Blanchette, *Perfection of the Universe*, 41–42, 75–76, for the following discussion of perfection.
11. Blanchette, *Perfection of the Universe*, 41.
12. *American Heritage Dictionary*, new college ed. (1980), s.v. "perfect."

While many people may think of perfection more in its secondary sense, it is the first definition that is closer to the original idea. The word "perfection" is taken from the Latin *perficere* (to complete), yielding the most basic meaning of completing a process. The original idea had more to do with completing something than with being without blemish or defect.[13] A human is perfect in the primary sense, according to the original definition of perfect, once it has achieved normal adulthood. The primary developmental process is completed. It is secondarily perfect upon having achieved certain intellectual and moral virtues, and tertiarily perfect when it has become a successful member of a family or society.

These three perfections, however, are not symmetrical or on a par. The first perfection is subordinate to the second, and the second to the third. There are within each of them intermediate perfections as well. Thus one can say there is a "perfect" baby because the baby lacks nothing for the proper functioning of a baby. One also hears the term "perfect" child, to define a child who lacks nothing for the proper functioning of a child. One must be a "perfect" baby in order properly to develop into a "perfect" child. The ideas of modern developmental biology fit this well, even though the word "perfect" is not used. There are discreet stages of development that one recognizes as successfully achieved and indicative of properly developing organisms in the fuller sense. The entire disciplines of prenatal and pediatric medicine assume as much. Why would one go for a physical exam if there were not recognized standards of development?

Each of these stages is subordinate to the one above, and the stages together result in an ordered whole. When we think of a whole system, such as an individual and his body, a family, or a society in this context, it is the integration of these various perfections — their order — that constitutes the whole.[14] A family has the parents as head, typically the father in most traditional societies. Individuals in the state are ordered to the whole: the city, then the state, then the nation. In the individual itself, we see cells ordered to tissues, tissues ordered to and constituting organs, organs ordered to the parts or systems, and these to the whole organism. Each level below is or-

13. Blanchette, *Perfection of the Universe*, 42.

14. Blanchette, *Perfection of the Universe*, 12–16; Aquinas, *Commentary on Aristotle's Metaphysics* XII, les. 12, no. 2627.

dered to the one above it. A cancer in an individual is precisely a group of cells growing out of control at the expense of the individual. The cells are out of order in subordination to the whole and literally consume the whole. Any such disorder in a system is therefore termed a "cancer," such as a "cancer in the body politic." Cancer cells are the "me generations" of the cellular world.

The subordinate parts are lesser in respect of the whole. Cells are lesser to tissues, tissue to organs, organs to parts or systems, and these to the whole. Various parts of any true whole are lesser to certain other parts.[15] A person intuitively recognizes this when nature reflexively raises the hand to protect the face.[16] Lessers and greaters are critical to the definition of order. Order is the harmonious integration of lesser parts to greater parts in a whole.[17] If a group of parts were truly equal in every way possible, there could be no order. While one might object that the president is really no better than any other person in a democracy, he is greater in a leadership role insofar as he is the head, regardless of his quality as a man. So in perfect equality, order is not possible. To be a properly functioning whole composed of parts, lessers, greaters, and subordination are necessary. A good analogy is an army, conceiving the whole army as an individual.[18] An army is composed of individual soldiers who interact to form the coordinated and ordered movements of an army, directed by the general. The trained soldier is the primary part of the army and is analogous to the primary perfection of an individual human. This primary perfection exists to act for the secondary level – the ordered harmonious interaction of the soldiers together to form a functional battle unit. This secondary perfection is ordered to its final end by the general (who serves in turn the state or king), the tertiary, or final, perfection. The secondary perfection of the army is for the end of the general or state. In a well-ordered and just society, the army is truly secondary to the state. The army will sacrifice itself for the good of the state or general, and in turn the individual soldier will sacrifice himself for the army, as the hand does for

15. *SCG* I.41; Blanchette, *Perfection of the Universe*, 124.

16. *ST* I, q. 60, a. 5c.

17. Blanchette, *Perfection of the Universe*, 118–27.

18. Blanchette, *Perfection of the Universe*, 12–19, 72–73; Aquinas, *Commentary on Aristotle's Metaphysics* XII, les. 12, no. 2629.

the face. So the primary perfection (the soldier) is subordinate to the secondary perfection (the army), which in turn is subordinate to the general or state. The army is thus an ordered whole, where the whole is greater than the sum of its parts. It is this very order that constitutes it an army. A disordered nonfunctional group of soldiers cannot properly be called an army. The essence of an army consists precisely in its well-ordered aim to its end. This order is the arrangement of lesser to great parts: the enlisted men to officers, the officers to the general, the general to the state.

Another example is an orchestra. The primary perfection is the trained musician. The secondary perfection is the integration of the various musicians to an ordered whole, and the third perfection is the conductor ordering the diverse parts to a harmonious piece of music. There are greater and lesser parts (e.g., a first and last violin), but together they produce an ordered piece of music. While one at times may want to hear a solo from the best musicians, it is typically the product of the whole that is most beautiful. And what is this product? It is the harmony of the order of the whole. The lesser parts in subordinating to the greater and they to the conductor produce an order, a harmony in this case. The essence of the whole is precisely this order.

In all these examples (the individual human, the army, the orchestra), the diversity of greaters and lessers is critical to the organization and beauty of the whole. In the individual human, if all parts were equal, each human would be a giant heart, or foot, or brain. None of these could exist by themselves; each needs the other. It is only because of the diversity of lessers and greaters that a true person, much greater than its parts, is possible. Everyone would willingly loose a foot over a brain, yet ultimately, without locomotion of any sort to procure food and other necessities, the brain could not survive. In an army, there are many soldiers having different specialties (armor, ordinance, reconnoiter, sniper, etc.), but each is more dispensable than the general. The same is true of the orchestra. A lesser violin is more dispensable than the first violin, but the coordinated playing of all these with the whole produces beautiful music. So while from the part's point of view it is better to be one of the greater parts, the greater good of the whole demands greater and lesser parts for it to exist. The same is true for human artifacts, be they cars or any mechanical thing. The car could lose windshield wipers with less consequence than losing a generator, but the necessity of lesser and greater parts is needed for the car to fully function. Nature displays the same reality. If all this were unique to humans or an imposition of their views on reality, as some think, humans would be an aberration. Yet humans are an integral and necessary part of nature and the universe. It is much simpler to admit we are natural, that we are based on and modeled after nature, and that the rest of nature is like us and is not an illusion.

Three Perfections in Nature

One might concede, perhaps reluctantly, that human life and social organization can be seen through the lens of these three perfections (primary, secondary, tertiary) but also insist that other parts of nature operate on a more basic level of survival and reproduction. But in our new cosmology, humans are an essential part of nature, an integral part of the universe. Edward O. Wilson, in his seminal work *Sociobiology*, points out that the evolution of organisms moves toward societies.[19] As he describes in his book *The Social Conquest of the Earth*, societies maximize organization, and so animal societies are the most successful organisms on earth.[20] Theirs has a division of labor like human societies, an organization allowing for a radical cooperation for the common good of the social group. The tertiary perfection of life is thus the general drive of organisms over the history of the earth. Why should we suppose them any different from humans and their organizations?

Our common experience of nature affirms Wilson's insight. Even in groups of organisms where tertiary perfection is not as obvious, it is still present. The creek community on my father's property is an integrated whole where all the parts have a role. Inorganic things such as water, rock, and air provide essentials for life. Plants produce bulk organic nutrients that animals need. Animals feed on plants or each other. Herbivorous animals keep the plants in check, and predatory behavior in animals keeps herbivores in check. A balanced, ordered whole is the product. Springtime in the creek ecosystem brings with it an array of flora (plums, ground flowers, cherries, honeysuckles, locusts) and fauna (insects, tadpoles, and minnows).

19. Wilson, *Sociobiology*.
20. Wilson, *Social Conquest*, 7–187.

Each of these has its primary and secondary perfections that allow them to emerge and develop in their internal nature, the final cause of which is the blooming and emerging that come with the lengthening of the day and the warming of temperatures. With respect to each other, their emergence is for the most part unrelated; it appears to occur by chance. Yet they are properly sequenced and timed because of the tertiary perfection of the system as a whole and its longer light and warmth.[21] Thus the beauty of a field of flowers is due to the tertiary perfection in much the same way that the beauty of the orchestra arises in the end from the coordination of the conductor. Seasons come and seasons go along the creek with an ordered sequence of processes and life. The system is hierarchically ordered. The lower serves the higher, but the higher needs the lower as well. In scientific jargon, this ordered system is called an ecosystem. Modern science has shown levels of order and integration in a detail previously unknown, only confirming the ancient and medieval idea of order and perfection.

A closer inspection of mammalian life unveils the same three perfections. The young of the raccoon undergo a certain amount of training and learning from parents and the environment in order to forage for food and thrive in their surroundings. Tertiary perfection for raccoons would be simply to fulfill their role in the ecosystem they are in, such as hunters or scavengers, and to maintain the species. Dogs provide a clearer example. Dogs are essentially domesticated wolves.[22] In the wild, the wolf displays a similar set of perfections. The primary perfection is the same, that is, pup to adulthood. They are taught to hunt and socialize in the pack by the other adult pack members (secondary perfection). Their tertiary perfection is in the service of the pack. Ultimately, the pack preserves the species. Individual wolves will die for the pack. An individual wolf attacking its own pack would not last long, as it would be disordered to the whole. In a domesticated context, the dog still shows the three perfections. We teach our dogs to socialize and live with us. We train them to defecate at certain times and places, we teach them basic obedience, tricks, to hunt, to guard us or our homes or livestock, to herd, or simply to be our companions and many other things as well. This is their secondary perfection. Because of these things, they live with us and

21. Aquinas, *Commentary on Aristotle's Metaphysics* VI, les. 3, no. 1205.

22. Nature, *Dogs That Changed the World*.

fulfill a role, thus fulfilling their tertiary perfection or final end. Tertiary perfection is implicit in any obedience training of a dog. Why would one train a dog for anything, if not to somehow integrate it into a family or a police force? A dog is out of place and disobedient in a family if it attacks its owner. Its final purpose is living with and serving us in some role.

Nonmammalian life shows social organization as well. Bees are a striking example. Individual bees mature in their cells and emerge as adults (primary perfection). They then perform various duties or jobs (secondary perfection) throughout their lives in the service of the colony, such as feeding the young, cleaning cells, foraging for nectar, and defending the colony.[23] The tertiary perfection of all their activity is the integrated service of the colony, their highest good. In fact, bees are a radical example of this because they are obligately social; tertiary perfection is an absolute necessity for life in that an individual bee separated from the colony will not live long.[24] When they get very old, they are simply stung to death and discarded from the colony. The diversity of greaters and lesser is also evident. Worker bees will die defending the colony, but the queen will never do so, as she is critically important for reproduction. The colony is so essential to bee life that scientists who study bees tend to think of the whole colony as an organism called the superorganism,[25] with the individual bees as cells.

Even inorganic entities such as rocks and minerals have these three levels, but they are not as obvious. Elements, minerals, and compounds were formed in the early stages of the universe, in stars, the interstellar medium, or on planets; these are the primary perfection of inorganic being.[26] Inorganic things are passive, but they have a capacity to be acted upon, the passive acceptance of external action from another, their secondary perfection. The service of inorganics in higher wholes (compounds, rocks, soils, planets, and living things) is their tertiary perfection.

23. Winston, *Biology of the Honey Bee*, 90–101.

24. Schulz et al., "Role for Octopamine," 350–59.

25. Wilson, *Sociobiology*, 383–86; idem, *Insect Societies*, 317–19.

26. For Big Bang nucleosynthesis (formation of elements in a prestellar universe), see Perlov and Vilenkin, *Cosmology for the Curious*, 189–92, and Shaw, *Astrochemistry*, 1–3; for stellar nucleosynthesis (element formation in stars), see Perlov and Vilenkin, *Cosmology for the Curious*, 193–94, and Shaw, *Astrochemistry*, 89–97; for the interstellar medium, see Shaw, *Astrochemistry*, 113–85; and for prebiotic chemistry of planets (and earth), see Shaw, *Astrochemistry*, 193–255.

The three perfections also apply to things below the threshold of everyday observation. The arrangement of cells, tissues, and organs in an individual reflects the same as an army, an orchestra, or all the natural examples cited above. We can extend all of this to everything in nature as a whole. Each of these integrated wholes has an intrinsic order, as described above. There is no reason to suppose that any of these are "out of place" in nature or an aberration. Quite the contrary, they are natural wholes or products of natural wholes. Organisms across nature are highly similar to each other in their organization, development, and behavioral maturation, from the genetic level to the mechanisms underlying such higher-order actions as memory, learning, and awareness.[27] Many animals have social organizations similar in structure, or at least with key common components to human families and societies.[28]

So there are three types of perfection in the material world: primary (basic development), secondary (actions arising from the capacities generated during primary development), and tertiary, the final perfection of a whole. Each lower perfection exists for and moves toward the higher perfection where it finds its end.[29] The final end of a being or system, the whole, in turn governs everything below it through the agency of the lesser perfections.[30] For instance, a general typically governs the soldiers not directly but through ordering the army division commander, who in turn orders the battalion commander, who in turn orders the soldier. The same is true of government. The president, senate, and congress govern individuals through lesser agencies, such as the state and cities. Likewise, in a natural whole such as our body, the whole immediately governs the various systems, such as the circulatory, nervous, or digestive, which in turn govern organs; these govern tissues, and tissues govern cells. Certainly, there are exceptions. As the general can at times directly command a soldier, so the whole body can directly influence cells. But these are more exceptions than the rule. At each of these levels, causality is evident.

All order in the material world presupposes a cause; in the three grades

27. Wilson, *Social Conquest of the Earth*, 10.

28. Wilson, *Social Conquest of the Earth*, 10, 133–90.

29. *ST* I, q. 47, a. 3c.; Aquinas, *De Potentia*, q. 5, a. 9c.

30. *SCG* I.83.

of perfection or development, the end of each perfection is its final cause, or its reason for being.[31] The higher perfection drives the lower, just as in human art. The artist is the final end that drives the whole process. It is through the desire for the shape of a glass triangle that the glass is molded to its full triangular form. The specific triangular shape (form) desired drives (is the end of) the particular use of glass (matter) and how it is worked. All capacities or "matter" (and lower levels of order) exist for the sake of the higher organizing principle, the form.[32]

Hierarchy: Top Down and Bottom Up

Thinking of the natural world as a hierarchy of increasing perfection—How else can it be viewed?—lends itself to the idea of completion. Now a hierarchy can be viewed from either the top down or the bottom up. These two vantage points can be called perfect (order of reason and intelligence) and imperfect (order of generation and time) ordering, respectively.[33] "Perfect" here implies that the entire hierarchy could be viewed as a whole (perfectly), and "imperfect" implies that it can be seen in its parts (imperfectly or incomplete). An analogy from human artistry illustrates this difference.

An artist causes the picture to appear both from the top down and the bottom up. From the perspective of the picture, the artist is the highest cause. In the mind of Leonardo da Vinci was the perfect idea of the Mona Lisa, the ultimate or final cause of the picture. He is the assembler, or the agent (the efficient cause), of the whole process of painting. He assembles the paints of various colors and the canvas (the material causes). He uses brushes of differing types and an easel, which are the unconscious agents (efficient causes) of a secondary nature. All these tools are guided by him, the highest and conscious agent. All the lesser causes are ordered to complete the ideal picture of the *Mona Lisa*. Because this ideal mental image guides the artist in everything he does, it is called the perfect ordering of the picture. The agent or efficient cause, the artist, is instantiating the idea into the material (paint, canvas). He orders everything so that it will all participate

31. Aquinas, *Commentary on Aristotle's Physics* II, lec. 5, no. 181; II, lec. 15, no. 272.

32. Aquinas, *Commentary on Aristotle's Metaphysics* XII, les. 2, no. 2438; *SCG* I.83.

33. Blanchette, *Perfection of the Universe*, 237–300; *ST* I, q. 85, a. 3, ad. 1.

in the perfect idea. Without this idea of the picture to guide him, nothing would be accomplished. There is, after all, an infinite number of pictures one could paint, but the single image in his mind guides the choice. A moment's reflection will reveal that this is the common experience of us all; without the initial idea and desire to do something, nothing would ever be finished. It is the idea in the mind that guides and specifies all other choices made by the agent. This mental image constitutes the perfection to which everything below it tends and in which the lesser things participate in the final version.

The process of Leonardo painting the *Mona Lisa* can also be viewed from the bottom up, or what the medievals would have called the imperfect order. Viewed from this perspective, each individual step in the course of painting approximates those above it and draws closer to the final form. Leonardo paints the generic human form, and then the human form of his model. This initial form – the general human form – determines the order and arrangement of the parts. For instance, the order of the application of the paint is specified by the choice of picture Leonardo wanted (the form). This general human form was done in view of a specific human, the form of Mona Lisa. The personal touches, expressions, and flairs reflect the style of the artist; it is *his* painting of Mona Lisa as opposed to another. Certain aspects about the primary perfection (e.g., female) would have been different if it were a picture of a man. The *Mona Lisa* is ordered to Leonardo's personal artistic expression and the image of her in his mind (the final cause). Viewed from below (or the imperfect order), each individual step is ordered to the particular step above it: it moves from the generic human form to the form of Mona Lisa that corresponds to the mental image in Leonardo's mind. Over time and with much effort, this painting develops, each step incomplete until the final end. Because of its incompleteness at various steps, the medievals called it an imperfect ordering in contrast to the perfect ordering, which contains the complete (perfect) idea.

This example of human genius is not an exception or aberration of nature because humans are a product of nature. The manner in which human beings accomplish tasks is indicative of their natural organization arising from nature outside of them. The development of organisms from intermediate states (e.g., toddler to child, child to adolescent, adolescent to adult) is the easiest example to observe. Each of these stages has the next stage as its goal. The end or perfection of each state and its consequent development is for the one above it. All things therefore change in order to find a state of completion, an end.[34] Any change (or movement, in philosophical terminology) is for an end. Any action is done for the sake of an end. Change, or movement, for itself is meaningless. Each stage of development occurs for the next. Each training or exercising of a capacity from primary development is to attain the habitual performance of the capacity. One develops the capacity to be musician not for the sake of practice but to perform the music. All things work for a stable end where the particular action has given way to "rest" (an abiding in) or a real performance of the behavior.

If all change is done for the sake of an end, what is the generic end to which all material nature tends? What is the stable state of all natural-material processes? More generally, what is the type of change characteristic of matter in general? And what does this type of change or development work toward, in what does it finds its completion? As walking finds its end in attaining a location, in what does the general movement of matter find its completion? Matter has the capacity to be changed or moved from the outside in contrast to internal or intellectual movement. Though all human knowledge is stimulated by observation of the material world, no intelligence, per se, is moved from without. For example, thought does not change place, nor does it increase or decrease in mass. From the point of view of matter, intelligence is the completion of all material actions, and therefore external change finds its completion in intelligence, true interior action.[35] The only being composed of both matter and intelligence is the human being. Therefore humans are the completion and end of all the natural processes in the material universe, both nonliving and living.[36]

It is this process of development over time – that is, imperfect ordering – that allows for a partial incorporation of natural evolutionary processes in this alternative worldview.[37] Because of the limited science of their

34. *SCG* III.2.

35. Aquinas, *Commentary on Aristotle's De Anima*, II, lec. 6.

36. Blanchette, *Perfection of the Universe*, 258–63; *SCG* IV.97; *ST* I, q. 85, a. 3, ad. 1.

37. Blanchette, *Perfection of the Universe*, 100n13, 148–54, 183–84, 230–32. Blanchette presents a compelling argument as to how thinkers like Aristotle and Aquinas, while following the science of the day, which suggested no new species, were nevertheless open to the possibility of new species in the

day, ancient and medieval thinkers did not know that new species actually occurred in cosmic history, but they were open to that possibility. The question they would have asked is why new species would emerge. In their frame of reference, they would have seen these natural novelties as steps in the preparation of matter for the occurrence of an intellectual soul in human beings. Intelligence makes up for the limitations in lower creatures, who in their individual natures are limited to certain times and places.[38] In a certain manner of speaking, intelligence allows human beings to be all things, and it elevates lower beings through humans to the life of the intellect and to union with the Final Cause of all things.[39] Only an intellect can truly know and will an end, and order other things to that end.[40] It is the nature of intelligence to order, and the existence of unconscious finality necessitates an Intelligence behind all things.[41]

In a worldview that contains the notions of hierarchy, multiple levels of causation, and ends, the human species appears as a natural and almost expected development. Human intelligence is the apex of material reality. The genius of a Leonardo or the creative brilliance of an Einstein is simply a heightened example of what every normal human being does – the exercise of an intelligence working toward ends. Why do human beings undeniably work toward ends and with final causes in their consciousness? Because the development of the universe, or what the medievals called imperfect ordering, had an end, too: the emergence of intelligence. In a worldview enriched by insights from the older sources, human life and intelligence do not appear as an aberration or surprising novelties.

---

context of their cosmology. Regarding a mechanism for evolution, see Aquinas, *Commentary on Aristotle's Physics* II, lec. 12, no. 253, where he proposes a mechanism of natural selection identical to the modern theory of microevolution. In the end, he rejects the mechanism. The broader point, however, is that thinkers in the medieval era were both open to the possibility of new species – rejected because of the science of the day – and had conceived of the idea of natural selection but rejected it as a purely accidental cause because of lack of final causality. In concluding, there is nothing per se contradictory in hierarchical cosmology that prohibits the idea of evolution.

38. Aquinas, *Commentary on Aristotle's De Anima* II, lec. 5, no. 283; Aquinas *Truth*, vol. I, q. 2, a. 2c.

39. Blanchette, *Perfection of the Universe*, 271–75; *SCG* I.44, II.46.

40. *SCG* II.24, III.2.

41. *ST* I, q. 2, a. 3c.

7 SCIENCE IN A NEW COSMOLOGY

Since the sixteenth and seventeenth centuries, there have been remarkable advances in the natural sciences. One of the hallmarks of modern science is the vastly greater amount of living and nonliving beings known in the universe. Compared to ancient and medieval thought, the variety of known elements, particles, stellar objects, and living things, along with the intricacies of their interactions, is unprecedented. The universe is about 13.7 billion years old, the laws of physics are valid, the fossil record shows a progression from simpler to more complex organisms, all living things are related to each other, complexity has increased. No one trained in the natural sciences has to doubt these things, although sadly there are many educated people in Western culture who only have a passing acquaintance with these natural truths.

Yet the facts and theories of science have often been presented in a philosophical framework that is deficient. Throughout this book, I have been explicating a seemingly new (and in fact very old) framework for interpreting the data of modern science that accords more with common human experience and the immaterial nature of human intelligence than other, newer frameworks. This framework acknowledges the grades of life in the material universe based on their immanence of interior actions, their relationships, and the orders of perfection. Although I have used numerous examples drawn from the history and practice of the sciences, it now remains to examine how the findings of modern science fit more tightly into this paradigm.[1] With pertinent examples, I illustrate that this framework, the Hierarchy of Being (hereafter abbreviated as HOB), can in fact accommodate the legitimate findings of the modern sciences. This claim contrasts with the philosophical framework of scientism, the interpretation of scientific data grounded in the philosophical tenets of materialism. I use key examples to show that the data of science need not be altered in the least to be accommodated into the HOB. It is only necessary to remove it from its current-day philosophical interpretation. *I do not alter any scientific data in the least.*

Many of my examples are biological in nature, for several reasons. At a practical level, I am a biologist specializing in genetics, my area of expertise. More importantly, the HOB affords us a view of material reality somewhat different from that predominant in modern science. In modern science, physics is assumed as the highest of the empirical sciences. This is because of the reductionistic assumptions of scientism claiming that elements both form and account for the properties of molecules, which in turn form and account for the properties of life; physics begets chemistry, which in turn begets life. There was even in classical thought a tendency to call philosophical physics a higher science, at least from the perspective of learning and thought, because it dealt with the causes of *all material being*, whereas philosophical psychology (the philosophy of life) dealt with only living material things.[2] Thus philosophical physics was higher in that it was more inclusive and the principles it found were common to both living and nonliving things.

In contrast, when dealing with the HOB, one looks at a rational ascent that begins with the lowest beings (nonliving) and ascends to higher beings, culminating in the human species. The more immanent the interior actions, the higher the being. In this framework, living things are higher than nonliving. Arranged thus, the more excellent object of science is life, specifically

1. Toma, "Dionysian/Thomistic Framework," 87–113. Chapter 7 in this volume constitutes an expanded version of the cited article, which covers the main points I discuss here.

2. Smith, *Philosophical Physics*, 3–25

human life. Biology, sociology, and psychology are the higher sciences from the perspective of the object studied, as they all deal with life.

Two Systems of Classification: Medieval and Modern

Thinkers throughout history have attempted to arrange beings according to common characteristics to see the order among them.[3] The system they used has changed over time, partly owing to the discovery of things that were previously unknown. I have referred on several occasions to nonliving things unknown to pre-Enlightenment thinkers, such as subatomic particles, atoms, the elements, galaxies, quasars, and theoretical objects such as black holes, among others. It may have occurred to the more biologically minded that I have ignored several types of organisms known to modern science, but not prior to it. Presently, there are many more living things known than before. Ancient and medieval thinkers classified material beings as humans, animals, plants, and minerals (nonliving beings). With the advent of modern science, a series of groupings of organisms had been settled upon based on broader to narrower relationships among sets of living things.[4] The broadest category was the kingdom. Recently, a yet broader grouping was added, called the domain. Modern classification therefore classifies living organisms by dividing them into three domains: Archaea, Eubacteria, and Eukarya.[5] Archaea and Eubacteria each have one kingdom under them: archaebacteria (primitive bacteria-like organisms) and eubacteria (true bacteria), respectively. Eukarya are divided into four kingdoms: protista (single-celled or simple multicellular organisms), fungi, plants, and animals. In all, there are six kingdoms of living things: archaebacteria, eubacteria, protista, fungi, plants, and animals.[6] Humans in modern science are generally not considered as essentially different from animals. So were ancient and medieval thinkers wrong in this regard?

We can cite two reasons why classification in modern science and the HOB differ. The first is historical. The ancients and medievals did not know

3. See Toma, "Dionysian/Thomistic Framework," 87–113, for further discussion of classification.

4. Raven et al., *Biology*, 13, 519–20.

5. Raven et al., *Biology*, 13.

6. Raven et al., *Biology*, 13.

of subatomic particles, molecules, galaxies, archaebacteria, bacteria, and protists. They did not have the technology to see these, as all have been discovered only in the past several centuries with such things as microscopes, telescopes, and various experiments to hypothesize or predict their existence. But that would not have changed their classification had they known of these, for a second and more important reason: because the HOB views things differently. It considers their most basic type of action: the type of motion either external or internal (self-movement) and the degree to which self-movement occurs. "What a thing is, is revealed by its action"[7] is a basic philosophical principle to which we all implicitly agree. One judges the next-door neighbor's dog as good or bad based on how it behaves toward you. If it approaches and wags its tail and licks you, it is good; if it snarls and aggressively lunges at you, it is bad. So the more basic the action, the more it reveals what a thing is at its core. In the HOB, material things are divided into those displaying external movement (nonliving) and three ways of internal or self-movement. These three are the growth and reproduction of plants, the sensory life of animals with their knowledge of the individual, and the rational intellect of man. According to this division, there are four material things: nonliving things, plants, animals, and human beings. This is a more basic aspect of things than that under which modern science views them, as the HOB is more general to things. That which includes more is more general or basic to it. That all people born in the United States are Americans is a more general and basic classification than to say they are from any one of the fifty states. But it is not wrong to say any person from these states is also an American.

Such is the case with these two frameworks for classification. Accordingly, modern classification arises not from this general approach of the HOB, but from things more specific: common ancestry based on their structure and certain specific functions. For instance, all bacteria (both archaebacteria and eubacteria) are distinguished from all other organisms (Eukaryotic) owing to their simpler cell type.[8] This is a structural difference. An example of differing function is that of the scientific definition of plants as those things that obtain food via photosynthesis (using light energy to fix carbon to pro-

7. *SCG* II.68

8. Raven et al., *Biology*, 541–42.

duce food), while fungi typically draw nutrients from dead organic matter.[9] The distinction of plants and fungi is an excellent example of the point at hand. Ancients and medievals did know of fungi but called them plants. In the HOB, plants are exactly what fungi are as they grow and reproduce – the definition of plants in the HOB. Only the means by which they procure food differs: plants by photosynthesis and fungi using dead or decaying matter. Neither is wrong, it is simply that the HOB sees a more general aspect of life. The two are perfectly complementary. The HOB correctly calls both plants (that which grows and reproduces), while modern science makes a distinction between how they procure food and bases its definition on that.

These two schemes of classification are not contradictory, but complementary: the modern can be easily absorbed into the HOB with all of its findings intact. Nonliving things (atoms, stellar objects) move exteriorly; they are minerals in the HOB. Archaebacteria, bacteria, and protists grow and reproduce; they are therefore plants in the HOB. Certain protists could possibly be considered animals, since they are highly mobile and can sense a variety of stimuli.[10] Fungi grow and reproduce – they are plants. Plants are plants, animals are animals. The only problematic beings are humans, since modern science in general denies the existence of a soul or immaterial principle. Therefore human beings represent the only and real philosophic problem between the two systems. It is the immaterial nature of the intellect, discussed in chapter 3, which sets man apart from the rest of animals.

Admittedly, there are also ambiguities in the HOB. There are some protists (discussed above) that seem to sense a variety of stimuli and are highly mobile. Are these plants, or could they be considered animals? Probably plants, but more study would be needed. Here modern science could help the HOB by setting up appropriate experiments, but modern science has its own ambiguities. What about viruses? Modern virologists are torn as to whether they are life or simply nonliving sophisticated toxins.[11] The HOB, which says that life moves itself, could help science at this point. Viruses do not replicate or do anything themselves.[12] Your own cells think viruses are

9. Raven et al., *Biology*, 147–49, 620–21.

10. Raven et al., *Biology*, 564–72.

11. Raven et al., *Biology*, 523.

12. Raven et al., *Biology*, 525.

part of themselves and replicate and build them.[13] Viruses will sit around forever without a host cell to do something for them.

In summary, there is a perfect consonance between scientific data and that of the HOB. No alteration or rejection of the data is required. It is simply a different frame of reference that can both subsume the science into it and give it a deeper meaning. This deeper meaning lies in understanding that the vast diversity of organisms discovered in modern science represents a general movement toward more immanent acts of life, specifically intelligence.

Physics and the Hierarchy of Being

In this system, nonliving things hold the lowest rank on the hierarchy. Nonliving things are passive in the classical distinction of internal versus external action. This includes such familiar things as rocks, minerals, iron bars, the sun, moon, and stars, and more unfamiliar things as well: atoms, subatomic particles, molecules, and galaxies. All of these react only when they come in contact with something else. They don't initiate their own actions. This even includes violent chemical reactions. Only when gasoline comes into contact with oxygen at the proper temperature will an explosion occur. Without the application of heat, the two will sit in each other's presence and do nothing. Consider also magnetism, where a field is generated that attracts another object. The magnetic field is simply a passive property of the magnet. The magnet will not seek out iron filings. The filings only move toward the magnet when the proper proximity is had. Perhaps the nearest physical example to living things is the growth of crystals.[14] Here again, crystalline growth is fundamentally different than life. Living things initiate their own change in many ways. Crystals will sit passively until placed in the proper environment with molecules or atoms of their own kind. These will then accrete together by locking in place, much as Lego blocks do in an ordered arrangement. The inherent dynamism of the self-motivating behavior of living things is absent.

It is sometimes said that the HOB of medieval thought contradicts the

13. Raven et al., *Biology*, 525.

14. Stein, *Finite and Eternal Being*, 237–39.

legitimate findings of modern physics. General and special relativity, quantum mechanics, Big Bang cosmology, and the old age of the universe have been seen as fundamentally surpassing classical thought.[15] But this is a false claim, and it arises from misunderstanding. The findings of quantum mechanics and particle physics do not contradict the HOB. These disciplines have shown us the much deeper particulate nature of reality and the specific behavior of the constituent particles in much greater detail. Yet for all that, at a foundational level, these fields have simply shown in more precise ways and in far more detail the general observation that nonliving things have external motion. Two of the more interesting results of quantum mechanics are the wave-particle duality of certain subatomic particles such as photons, and the discovery that one particle can influence another at a distance.

Subatomic particles such as photons and electrons have been found to behave in a manner similar to a wave at times and a particle at others.[16] When a water wave is passed through two spaced slits in a board placed in the water, it generates a series of bands on a target board. Light does the same. When electrons pass through in a similar setup, they are deposited on the target as individual dots (particles), but the combined effect of many such events produces the dots grouped together as wave bands on the target board. How can a thing be both particle and wave?[17] The wave is a potency field out of which particulate electrons emerge; the waves are the material cause that becomes informed by a formal cause producing individual electrons. The same goes for light or any other particle behaving similarly. Because these particles are so weak in their ability to exist independently from other particles or beings (electrons "want" to be in atoms), they are at the edge of reality, becoming actual things at times and at other times potential particles.[18] Such results led Werner Heisenberg to conclude that the evidence of physics suggests that matter at its most basic level is simply a potential to be, exactly what Aris-

15. Many books and papers of modern science at some point take a swipe at classical thought. Classical thought is often claimed to be at odds with modern science, or it is treated as a foil to show the superiority of modern science, or a recent finding of modern science is used to show classical thought in error. This is common across all disciplines of science: physics, chemistry, biology, psychology. A simple review of new releases in the science section of a major bookstore will show this.

16. Greene, *Fabric of the Cosmos*, 84–88.

17. Smith, *Philosophical Physics*, 190–96, 212–21.

18. Smith, *Philosophical Physics*, 190–96, 212–21.

totle termed the material cause. Heisenberg explains, "If we compare this situation with the Aristotelian concepts of matter and form, we can say that the matter of Aristotle, which is mere 'potentia,' should be compared to our concept of energy, which gets into 'actuality' by means of the form, when the elementary particle is created."[19] Heisenberg also thought that the statistical probability of the behavior of an atom, such as electron orbits, as elucidated by quantum mechanics, was a quantitative version of potencies for actual existence in the Aristotelian sense.[20]

Quantum mechanics also discovered that two particles separated at a distance can instantaneously influence each other's spin (all particles spin, or rotate).[21] If one passes an electron wave through a slit, causing it to split in two, each consequent wave can generate an electron. If the spin of these is measured by detectors widely spaced, one finds that each particle influences the spin of the other with no apparent connection between them. Such data have been claimed to invalidate causality, but this cannot be true because the experiment was set up, as described previously, under the agency of all four causes. Likewise, cause and effect in the splitting and the detection of the particles are assumed. Far from obviating causality, such data merely show that we must reconsider precisely the way causes can work in a physical system.

Even more "bizarre" predictions of modern physics, such as multiverses, do not absolutely pose a threat to the HOB. Multiverses are theoretical multiple universes (as yet with no data to support their existence) that bud off of the expanding space-time continuum, much as local mini-balloons could bud off a singular larger expanding balloon.[22] Such entities are predicted based on inflationary theory, which underlies our present cosmology of the expanding, or inflating, universe.[23] Inflationary theory itself is only possible and analyzable if one assumes cause and effect are operative as we know them. This includes both how the theory itself is known from causal laws of mathematics as well as experiments designed to test inflationary theory, which again depend on the self-evident principles discussed previously. Such

19. Edward Feser, "Heisenberg on Act and Potency," September 17, 2009, http://edwardfeser.blogspot.com/2009/09/heisenberg-on-act-and-potency.html.

20. Feser, "Heisenberg on Act and Potency."

21. Greene, *Fabric of the Cosmos*, 112–20.

22. Greene, *Fabric of the Cosmos*, 272–321.

23. Greene, *Fabric of the Cosmos*, 272–321.

multiple universes are hypothesized to have fundamentally different laws of physics and reality. But how truly different could they be if the supporting data of inflationary theory and their predicted existence upon such a theory are known through ideas assuming such self-evident knowledge for their very understanding? We can only know what reality gives us. While a multiverse, if it truly exists, may have bizarre entities in it, by any rational means to understand it, it would have the same self-evident principles undergirding it as ours.

Nothing in modern physics contradicts the outlines of the HOB, but certain interpretations of physical laws are contradictory to the view we propose. A good example is a recent book by Lawrence Krauss, A Universe from Nothing. Krauss maintains against classical thought that something, in this case a whole universe, can indeed come from nothing.[24] That nothing can come from nothing is a cornerstone of classical thought; it is the cornerstone of any rational thought. Being cannot arise from absolutely nothing. To obviate this problem, Krauss slyly redefines "nothing" throughout the book, completely missing both the philosophical and the theological definition. At his most extreme, Krauss defines "nothing" as empty space with a nonzero energy and the laws of physics, and claims that this empty space is the closest thing to "nothing" that ancient and medieval thinkers possessed.[25] This is simply a misunderstanding of Aristotle and Aquinas. Both had a clear idea of being versus nothing in the absolute sense. Aquinas clearly distinguished the idea of altering something preexistent – what he termed "making" – from creation, which is bringing something into existence from absolutely nothing. Krauss notes that modern physics has shown that this empty space is filled with energy and is rife with quantum fluctuations.[26] But energy and quantum fluctuations are something, maybe not in the exact same sense to which we are accustomed, but they are something and do exist. Of course, from this "nothing" arises subatomic particles and hence everything we see.[27] Thus, Krauss argues, something does come from "nothing." But his "nothing" of the space-time continuum is close to what Aristotle described

24. Krauss, *Universe from Nothing*.

25. Krauss, *Universe from Nothing*, 149–50.

26. Krauss, *Universe from Nothing*, 55–73, 91–104.

27. Krauss, *Universe from Nothing*, 150–59.

as potency, or material cause. Krauss sidesteps the question of whether any potency needs a higher causality to bring it into actual existence. Krauss later admits as much when he says that this idea of empty space (space-time) is not exactly nothing.[28] Then he proceeds to the idea that space-time itself comes from nothing through the laws of quantum gravity governing nothing.[29] But where do the laws of quantum gravity come from? In his putative answer, Krauss posits the notion of multiverses, that there are an infinite number of possible such ones with differing laws, and that our universe contains just one possible state of laws; with enough chances, anything is possible.[30] In this, Krauss fails to address two of the deepest questions: he assumes actual infinity in matter, and he fails to identify from where these laws come. Multiverses do not do away with the problem. In all of Krauss's semantic magicianship, he assumes that the only worthwhile knowledge is empirical verification (scientific knowledge) as the final arbiter of all knowledge. He has redefined the problem so that it falls within the sphere of his competence. The only problem is that he avoids the original (and true) question altogether.

The Age of the Universe

The evolution of the universe, according to the standard scenario, implies a cosmos of about 13.7 billion years.[31] The supporting data for this scenario include, among other things, the background radiation from the Big Bang, and its expansion rate.[32] Data show that at the origin of the universe, things were so hot that the parts of atoms could not come together.[33] As expansion continued, things cooled, allowing protons, electrons, and neutrons to form hydrogen, helium, and lithium, the three simplest elements in order.[34] Hydrogen and helium make up, respectively, 74 percent and 24 percent of

28. Krauss, *Universe from Nothing*, 58, 182–83.

29. Krauss, *Universe from Nothing*, 163–64.

30. Krauss, *Universe from Nothing*, 171–80.

31. Green, *Fabric of the Cosmos*, 226.

32. Green, *Fabric of the Cosmos*, 226–35.

33. Perlov and Vilenkin, *Cosmology for the Curious*, 155–62.

34. Perlov and Vilenkin, *Cosmology for the Curious*, 189–92; Shaw, *Astrochemistry*, 1–3.

baryonic ("normal") matter in the universe.[35] The remaining 2 percent comprises all the remainder of the elements in the periodic table.[36] The vast majority of these (including the elements that make us and most everything around us) were synthesized by the nuclear fusion of hydrogen to helium and helium to these heavier elements in the interior of giant stars that exploded in the earlier times of the universe (this still goes on today).[37] These elements formed into compounds in interstellar space, and clouds of these elements and compounds then coalesced into planets.[38] Appropriate conditions were had on these planets for far more complex compounds to form, which would be needed for life to arise.[39] Once planetary conditions were correct and sufficient complex molecules had formed, simple life such as bacteria or prokaryotes (plants in the HOB) appeared.[40] These simple life forms radically altered the conditions of the earth and paved the way for more complex cell types, called eukaryotes, to appear.[41] Eukaryotes are masters of living in community by forming multicellular life forms, such as higher plants, animals, and, finally, man.[42] Thus the fossil record shows simpler life forms first, followed by a sequential increase in the complexity of life forms, with humans as the most recent. This is a rough outline of the history of nonliving and living beings.[43] Upon this is based much of the superstructure of modern science and biology. Without altering the data in the least, let's see how this fits into the HOB.

An old universe is consistently used to bludgeon pre-Enlightenment thought, but many medieval thinkers (such as Aquinas) were less concerned about the age of the universe and more about its cause (e.g., that God produced it). They held to the truth of Scripture without necessarily adhering to a literalistic interpretation of it (in this case, six literal twenty-four-hour

35. Perlov and Vilenkin, *Cosmology for the Curious*, 187.

36. Perlov and Vilenkin, *Cosmology for the Curious*, 187.

37. Perlov and Vilenkin, *Cosmology for the Curious*, 193–94; Shaw, *Astrochemistry*, 89–97.

38. Shaw, *Astrochemistry*, 113–85; Perlov and Vilenkin, *Cosmology for the Curious*, 194–96.

39. Shaw, *Astrochemistry*, 225–55.

40. Shaw, *Astrochemistry*, 259–72; see also the entire work concerning a detailed discussion of how life might emerge from prebiotic conditions in Luigi, *Emergence of Life*.

41. Raven et al., *Biology*, 541.

42. Raven et al., *Biology*, 566.

43. Raven et al., *Biology*, 508.

periods for the creation of the world).[44] So, how do we reconcile a sequence in time according to science with a sequence according to being in the HOB? Does one intrinsically have to do with the other? The intrinsic link becomes evident through consideration of one of the principal strengths of ancient and medieval thought already discussed: causality. I maintain that an old universe is just what one might expect from a hierarchically arranged cosmos coming from the hand of a Creator.

Aquinas notes that things are caused slightly differently in immaterial things, in contrast to material things, which are things subject to time.[45] Recall the example of the artist in our discussion of perfection and ordering. Things in the mind are ordered according to what we termed perfect ordering. The artist first conceives in his mind the picture to paint. The final thing, the picture, comes first in his mind, as picture conceived, or the idea of it (hence the complete or perfect thing comes first – perfect ordering). Then he acquires the means to obtain it – his paints, easel, canvas, and brush. Finally, he paints it and produces the end, or the picture. But intellectually, it was first in his mind. So the final thing is both first and last in intellectual, or immaterial operations. This idea of the painting is most important; if the artist did not know of the thing to be painted, he would not paint it. In matter, however, things are somewhat different. In matter, the last thing obtained is the end, or the painting. From the perspective of matter, first the artist obtains the means (the paint, easel, canvas, and brush), next he assembles or paints it, and *finally* the picture is produced. So in matter, the order is means, assembly, and end. This was termed imperfect ordering, since the incomplete means are assembled first. This is everyone's experience of how things are done according to time; we never have the finished product first. We go from the basic things needed to make the finished product to the finished product.

Our intelligence is created by God, who modeled it after himself (Gn 1:26). When Intelligence (God) draws things to itself, it does this in matter by beginning with the least thing (the material building block) and

44. One should read the whole treatise on creation by St. Thomas Aquinas (*ST* I, qq. 66–74) to understand the medieval approach. Regarding the point of the truth of Scripture without the literal letter, see *ST* I, q. 67, a. 4c, and I, q. 68, a. 1c. In giving his own view, he cites and summarizes Church Fathers such as Augustine, Basil, John Chrysostom, and Dionysius. See also Aquinas, *De Potentia*, q. 4, a. 2c, for a similar explanation.

45. *SCG* III.18; *De Potentia*, q. 5, a. 1c; Aquinas, *Commentary on Aristotle's Physics*, lec. 5, lec. 15.

moving toward its end in matter. The least form of life, from which all life is "built" upon, is the lowest plant (a bacteria), which is the nascent beginning of matter preparing for the eventual reception of intelligence. The completion of this action toward intelligence in material reality is a human being, an intellectual creature with matter. In sum, the order of higher to lower according to being and intelligence in the hierarchy of being elicits the lower to higher in time and in matter.[46] While this does not prove that God created the universe in this manner, one should not at all be scandalized by an old universe, where beings are found in the fossil record from simpler to more complex. It is perfectly consonant with our experience of the manner in which an intellect (such as ours) works with matter. God himself is Intellect working in and with matter.

The History of Life: Simple to Complex

Both nonliving and living things become more complex over time. Scientism explains this evolutionary phenomenon as adaptations of increasingly complex attempts to survive.[47] Life started out simple and, through natural selection, added on structures and functions that enable its possessor to survive better in its environment.[48] These were passed on and altered through the ages as more and more sophisticated survival mechanisms appeared.[49]

46. Aquinas, *Truth*, vol. II, q. 14, a. 10c; *De Potentia*, q. 4, a. 2, ad. 33. Here, Aquinas states that the very order of nature is that things attain perfection through a succession of time. In *De Potentia*, q. 3, a. 6, ad. 16, he states that wisdom so orders things that they are brought from imperfection to perfection. Finally, I end with two quotes from *De Potentia*. The first is from q. 4, a. 2c.: "That the works of the six days according to the other saints were produced not simultaneously but by degrees, was not owing to lack of power in the Creator who could have produced all things at once, but was directed to the manifestation of God's wisdom in the production of things, in that when he made things out of nothing he did not at once bring them from nothingness to their ultimate natural perfection, but conferred on them at first an imperfect being, and afterwards perfected them, so that the world was brought gradually from nothingness to its ultimate perfection. Thus different days corresponded to the various degrees of perfection, and it was shown that things derived their being from God, against those who contended that matter was uncreated, and that moreover he is the author of their perfection, against those who ascribed, the formation of the lower world to other causes." The second, from q. 3, a. 10, states that in the beginning things were perfect, "as regards nature's causes from which afterwards other things could be propagated, but not as regards all their effects."

47. Raven et al., *Biology*, 403–10.

48. Raven et al., *Biology*, 417–52.

49. Raven et al., *Biology*, 417–52.

At its modern extreme, this evolutionary paradigm is taken as the fundamental idea of reality with which to be grappled.[50] The idea of survival as a possible mechanism need not be rejected, but the HOB also sees a higher purpose of finality.[51] This higher purpose is that material life is being moved toward intellectual powers, evidenced by increasing capacities of interiority and the ability to know.[52] The increasing ability of material structures to aid knowing is thus crucial. Let's examine some of the steps in the development of life.[53]

The first form of life was bacterial, featuring a primitive cellular structure called prokaryotic.[54] Prokaryotes arose around 3.5 billion years ago, according to the fossil record.[55] These cells have a phospholipid (fat- or oil- based) membrane acting as a wall, inside of which are the biomolecules necessary for life.[56] They are much like a balloon surrounded by a tough, rigid cloth filled with water and a dizzying array of biomolecules. Here is life in its most primitive state (plant life) performing the lowest of interior acts: transformation of external nutrients for growth and reproduction. Because these actions are partially interior (e.g., in a plant), at this most basic level, there must be a separation from what is outside. This separation is a barrier with the necessary material for life to function on the inside, thus producing an interiorizing subject. To produce an interior or self-moving action, there must be a separation from the outside. This is exactly what a bacteria cell is in its most basic form: a subject (cell) capable of a brief interior act, the most primitive life. Thus the very structure of life begins to represent this move toward interiorization.[57]

50. See in particular Dennett, *Darwin's Dangerous Idea*, as a case study in the nearly absolute universality of this idea.

51. See chapter 12 in this volume for a more complete discussion of survival as the condition of fallen human nature, acknowledged by the Church Fathers.

52. *SCG* IV.97, III.81; Aquinas, *Light of Faith*, chap. 171.

53. For further discussion of the history and development of life, see also Toma, "Dionysian/Thomistic Framework," 87–113.

54. Raven et al., *Biology*, 541.

55. Raven et al., *Biology*, 513–14.

56. Raven et al., *Biology*, 63–65, 89–93, 541–43.

57. A point of clarification may be needed here. All truly intellectual acts are interior (immanent), but not all interior acts are intellectual. That all living things have some type of immanence is the hallmark of life, however, and as I wrote in chapter 5, life consists of a greater or lesser degree of self-perfection, or completion. The interiority of lower nonintellectual beings, such as bacteria, is the first step in the progress of reality toward the most immanent form of life, intelligence.

The fossil record shows the next highest life form, the eukaryotes, as having appeared 2 to 1.5 billion years ago.[58] All cells in organisms higher than bacteria have eukaryotic cells, which have many internal compartments (organelles) where specific biomolecules (such as DNA in the nucleus) are housed and cellular functions are performed.[59] Prokaryotes are like a single-room house where all the normal functions (e.g., sleeping, cooking, eating, and entertainment) take place in one location. Eukaryotes, by contrast, are like a house with many rooms.

Compartmentalization in a house creates greater order and efficiency. Internal physical structures in eukaryotes produce a division of labor to enable organization for more complex structures and functions to come.[60] Just as a multiroom house easily surpasses the design and variety of a single-roomed house, eukaryotes easily surpass bacteria in the variety of forms. Why is this? It is not simply for survival, as modern theory suggests. Rather, life is acquiring a division of labor and greater variety of functions and structures in order eventually to support knowledge in its most basic form: the sensory capacity of animals, which consists in the knowledge of the individual. Life is moving toward intelligence.

One of the more interesting findings of molecular biology is that certain organelles in eukaryotic cells have structures and functions that are nearly identical to bacteria.[61] The energy-producing room (organelle) of eukaryotes (the mitochondria) looks like a bacteria, is structured like a bacteria, and has many bacterial biochemicals. Current theory holds that bacteria long ago invaded larger cells and took up residence in them, providing their host with energy and, in turn, gaining protection from enemies by being in the host.[62] Over time, these bacteria became totally integrated into the larger cell in a kind of hierarchical order. Thus in eukaryotic cells there is a highly ordered hierarchical arrangement where all the parts function for the whole. In higher eukaryotes, such as humans, this phenomenon increases many times in the hierarchical arrangement of these cells to tissues, tissues

58. Raven et al., *Biology*, 517–18.

59. Raven et al., *Biology*, 65–81.

60. Raven et al., *Biology*, 566.

61. Raven et al., *Biology*, 73–75.

62. Raven et al., *Biology*, 75, 562–64.

to organs, and finally organs to the whole individual.[63] It is this hierarchy that allows higher life and intelligence.

The original integration of the prokaryote into the larger cell was based on cooperation that resulted in a deeper capacity for interior functions. This cooperation becomes a basis for cooperative communities based on interior actions of knowledge and love, which are specifically human communities. The appearance of multicellular organisms between 2 and 1.5 billion years ago expanded this cooperation, leading to an integrated hierarchy for greater functions in eukaryotic cells.[64] Multicellularity contributed to a wide diversification of eukaryotes.[65] Such organisms deepen the increase in interiority seen in the transition from prokaryotes to eukaryotes. With their specialized cells, tissues, and organs, a greater interiorizing of actions and complexity of form becomes possible. This is evident in the progression of multicellular organisms from a single-cell stage to a complex adult organism. A major trend in development is an invagination of tissues to form tissues and organs that grow inwardly in a hierarchical arrangement for the deepening interiority of actions of life.[66]

The natural history of body plan development shows another striking pattern: over long stretches of time, life is organizing for sensory capabilities and for knowledge.[67] Evolution was preparing for the greater sensory knowledge capacity of the human brain, not simply for survival. Differing trajectories in development produce the various body shapes (annelids or worms, arthropods such as insects, fish, tetrapods such as reptiles and mammals, and others).[68] Primitive animals such as sponges have no symmetry in body plan: no right, left, top, or bottom. Just above sponges are creatures such as jellyfish that are radially symmetrical; they resemble a pie where several cuts can produce identical results. There is no right or left, only top and bottom. Most animals (such as humans) are bilaterally symmetrical. In bilateral symmetry, only one plane will divide an organism into roughly mirror image halves: such organisms have right, left, top, and bottom. In the

63. Raven et al., *Biology*, 2–4.

64. Raven et al., *Biology*, 518, 566.

65. Raven et al., *Biology*, 564, 592–93, 602, 607, 621–26, 646–47.

66. Raven et al., *Biology*, 518, 1110–29.

67. For further discussion of body plans, see Toma, "Dionysian/Thomistic Framework," 87–113.

68. Raven et al., *Biology*, 638–39.

progression from asymmetry to bilateral symmetry over deep time, there are changes allowing for the optimization of sensory organs.[69] Bilaterally symmetrical animals have a defined anterior and posterior, where most sensory organs are placed up front (a head) to immediately contact the environment. Asymmetrical and radially symmetrical organisms do not. A variety of forms and movements exists among animals to put these sensory structures in contact with sensible things. Why? Present biological theory claims that this better enables an organism to survive; that is, it can more rapidly and efficiently detect its food and avoid its enemies.[70] The HOB claims a different principal reason for this development: organisms are being organized to know optimally at the most basic level of knowledge, which is sensory life. Purely material life is preparing for an organism in which it can find its completion or rest, the human being who is intelligent. Intelligence, interior change, is the end of exterior change.

Once multicellularity arose, animal forms greatly diversified.[71] The most striking occurrence was the Cambrian explosion around 530 million years ago, in which animal body plans appeared in an "explosion" of variety and forms.[72] Within approximately 40 million years, all the animal body plans in the world today arose. Modern theories hold that they were exploiting many open niches in the environment with new means of adaptation and survival, or that new genetics evolved to provide a mechanism for diversification.[73] While these may be part of the explanation, one can also easily generalize and say that nature was experimenting with a variety of body plans with various sensory modalities in order to sense more efficiently. Life moves toward greater interior acts, culminating the ability to know.

Organ development and cellular specialization reached their apogee in the primate brain. As discussed in chapter 3, the human brain is among the most complex structures in the physical universe.[74] There are 200 billion nerve cells with 125 trillion connections. The number of possible connections is estimated at 101,000,000. By comparison, there are an estimated 10^{79}

69. Raven et al., *Biology*, 639.

70. Raven et al., *Biology*, 639.

71. See Toma, "Dionysian/Thomistic Framework," 87–113.

72. Raven et al., *Biology*, 509, 519.

73. Butterfield, "Macroevolution and Macroecology," 41–55.

74. Edelman and Tononi, *A Universe of Consciousness*, 37.

particles in the universe. What interpretation does the HOB offer for this incredible complexity? Humans are a type of primate, one informed by a rational soul that needs the objects of the material world to gain knowledge and understand itself. Consequently, such a primate needs a sophisticated "commonsense" organ, the brain.[75] The intellectual part of the soul or psyche (*anima*) thinks, not the brain. So what role does the brain play in the intellectual work of human subjects? Imagine two people on either side of a wall higher than each of them, so that they cannot see one another or communicate. Both see color differently. Far past the end of the wall is a dog that they both see. The only way for them to integrate their information for a proper understanding of the color of the dog is for a third party that can communicate with both – a common person. The brain is much like that third person. The brain is the organ that integrates or puts together all the sensory information. The eyes see, the ears hear, the nose smells, but it is the brain that integrates all these particular senses into a composite whole for the intellect of humans to use. Through the use of this image, the human intellect is aided in gaining a much deeper form of knowledge, that of the nature of the thing itself. The clearer and more accurate representation of the reality, the better the information the intellect can gain. So a common sensory organ is one that can integrate and assemble the sense input from all the senses to form a proper interior image of an external object.

The history of life and the contrast between two ways of viewing reality are seen as well at the molecular level of organisms. Consider genetics, the science of inheritance and variation. Some modern scientists attribute almost soul-like capacities to genes. In their narrative, not only do genes have information for biochemicals, but they also control development like a blueprint.[76] Sociobiology carries this thinking to an extreme by viewing genes as the driving mechanisms of life, almost as if they make an organism their house that will carry and propagate them.[77] Genes in this view do everything: they make the material that forms an organism, act as an assembler,

75. *SCG* IV.73.1: "Now the body is the instrument of the soul, and an instrument is for the use of the principal agent: therefore, the disposition of the instrument necessarily must be such as becomes the principal agent." See also *SCG* II.91.4. For the idea of a common sense, see Aquinas, *Commentary on Aristotle's De Anima* III, lec. 2–3.

76. Raven et al., *Biology*, 372–92.

77. Dawkins, *Selfish Gene*, v–vii, 2.

determine the structure to be made, and accomplish the goal of making the structure.

Not all scientists agree.[78] In a more moderate and, I would argue, more reasonable view, genes play a crucial but not omnipotent role. Genes are made of deoxyribonucleic acid, or DNA.[79] DNA by itself does nothing. It will sit inactive forever without a cell to read it. It is a molecule that contains biochemical information that the cell needs in order to make a given biochemical as needed. It is like a menu at a restaurant. The patron (organism) makes the order, not the menu (DNA). Furthermore, not all information is contained in the DNA. Some information passed on is contained in other molecular structures of the cell as well.[80] Second, DNA is passed on by the egg and sperm.[81] The sperm contributes only chromosomes, which carry the genes.[82] The egg, on the other hand, contains a set of chromosomes *and* the complete organization of the cell of the given type of organism. The egg is the first true unit of organization for the next generation and represents what it means to be the organism at its most basic level. It is the cell, as well as the whole organism in multicellular organisms, that decides when and which genetic information is needed. One can think of DNA functioning in the same manner as the heart. The heart beats according to the commands of the body. It is beyond anyone's personal control. Many systems in the body are such: liver, kidneys, digestion, and the like. In the same manner, genes are another system; they are used when needed in the manner dictated by the body or cell.

Modern genetics accords well with the HOB. Genetics, in its varying forms, studies aspects of the transmission of information for the growth, reproduction, complex structures, and behaviors of organisms. Although these are always explained in a purely materialistic manner in most of modern biology, the HOB views such material life as leading to an increase of the interiority of action. Growth and reproduction are simply the anabolic and catabolic capabilities of life. This information is stored and passed on by

78. Webster and Goodwin, *Form and Transformation*. See also Nijhout, *Metaphors*, 441–46.

79. Raven et al., *Biology*, 259.

80. Beisson, "Preformed Cell Structure," 1–8.

81. Raven et al., *Biology*, 208.

82. Raven et al., *Biology*, 1106–9.

DNA.[83] From DNA, a copy is made by the cell in the form of ribonucleic acid, or RNA.[84] The information in the RNA is read in another part of the cell by complex structures called ribosomes.[85] Ribosomes use this information to make basic protein structures.[86] Sometimes, however, genes just code for RNA without being read into protein.[87] Proteins and RNA are the tools of the cell to regulate other genes as well as to construct all the other molecular structures in the cells.[88] They are simply parts of the hierarchically arranged whole. The history of plants, particularly bacteria and the lower eukaryotes, shows that in them the basic biochemical pathways arose that all life employs. These were passed down through time to other life forms. Because lower eukaryotes were the first to have chromosomes, the eukaryotic mechanisms of inheritance were first established by them.

The inherent organization of an organism, with its various structures, is passed on by the female egg. DNA is needed in this process, of course, as it contains information for the tools (proteins, RNA) needed to carry out the work. The egg, typically not the DNA, contains the organization of a given organism at its most basic level, the first single cell that is fertilized to become the new organism. This organization governs the development of the whole, including its various complex structures.

At a yet higher level of organization and information transfer, beyond genetics[89] and the individual, strictly speaking, one finds cultural transmission. The passing on of culture, the product of the rational intellect, is seen in all human forms of knowledge and art: the sciences, philosophy, religious customs, language, writing, art, theater, music, and education. The basic structure of cultural transmission is the family with its members informed by a rational intellect.

Thus the information in the DNA provides the cell with the necessary

83. Raven et al., *Biology*, 280–81.

84. Raven et al., *Biology*, 280–81.

85. Raven et al., *Biology*, 280–81.

86. Raven et al., *Biology*, 280–81.

87. Raven et al., *Biology*, 317–22.

88. Raven et al., *Biology*, 37.

89. There is, however, a small nascent field of genetics concerned with cultural transmission. It is a subdiscipline of sociobiology. Instead of the gene, the unit of transfer is the meme, which is a short phrase or idea that conveys a powerful message and is considered by proponents to be selected upon, like a gene, and passed on to the next generation or group of people (Dawkins, *Selfish Gene*, 192).

biochemical information for growth and reproduction, which in turn provides nourishment for a given body plan (form), passed on by the egg. This all prepares life for the operation of intelligence, which manifests itself in human culture with material objects like tools and works of art, or with mental expressions in ideas like philosophy and literature. Hence the science of genetics fits the HOB well.

Among the vast amount of data in molecular biology, there emerges a general finding of great relevance: it shows that genes are hierarchically controlled.[90] Certain proteins, master switches called *transcription factors*, turn genes on and off in response to cellular needs.[91] Recent research, in fact, has shown mind-boggling levels of layer upon layer of complexity at the molecular level, where one level interacts with and controls another, which in turn controls another, and so on: the very definition of order and hierarchy.[92]

One of the distinctions I have made throughout this book is between scientific data and the conclusions drawn from them. The data from the fossil record show that organisms are arranged from simplest to more complex.[93] Within this record are many examples of certain organisms closely approximating those above them.[94] The accepted conclusion in most scientific circles about these data is that the lower organisms changed over time into the higher; they evolved, in the modern sense.[95] And yet the evidence of close approximations is exactly what is predicted as well from the HOB, where organisms are graded from lower to higher, and the immediately lower being finds an end in that which is higher. In his *Commentary on the Divine Names of Dionysius*, Thomas Aquinas states the principle of continuity of the HOB: "the superior nature in its lowest perfection touches an inferior nature in its highest perfection."[96] In other words, the lowest nature at its best approximates a higher nature at its lowest. Previously when discussing the HOB I

90. Raven et al., *Biology*, 14, 304–24.

91. Raven et al., *Biology*, 313–15.

92. Raven et al., *Biology*, 3–4. See also any number of books on the subject of complexity in various systems.

93. Raven et al., *Biology*, 508, 513–20.

94. Raven et al., *Biology*, 425–29.

95. Raven et al., *Biology*, 396.

96. Aquinas, *Commentary on the Divine Names of Blessed Dionysius* VII.4: "the lowest of the highest things, always conjoin to the principles of the secondary things, i.e., the highest of the lower things."

cited similar examples, such as the sunflower turning toward the sun as an approximation of animal sensing. Thus we have here two philosophical theories, modern evolution and the HOB, that both fit the fossil data.

But evolution from the view of scientism says that the lower actually becomes the higher. It must make a further inference that the data per se do not exactly show: that one organism changes into the other. Viewed in light of causal analysis, such an idea constitutes a real conceptual problem. Consider the following: When a glass triangle is melted, it is glass per se that is melted and not the shape. The craftsman does not literally change a triangular shape into a square. Triangles are not squares. Instead, he conditions the glass through the application of heat to be receptive of another shape. In this causal understanding of nature, it is the matter and not the form that changes. What it is, the form, comes to be or passes away. It is as impossible for the formal cause of something, such as an organism, to change into another as it would be to change the shape of a triangle into a square.

Now, the HOB can both accommodate evolution and overcome this problem, but it does so in a modified form. In addition to the craftsmen melting (conditioning) glass to change from a triangle to a square shape, two more examples may help. The first is a useful analogy found in the example of Damascus steel. Invented in the medieval Middle East, Damascus steel is a strong but plastic type of steel. In the mid-1700s, the original process for making it was lost to antiquity. Part of this process reportedly involved heating the steel to a high temperature, hammering it, and dousing it in water. Repetition of this process allowed for elaborate designs in the steel and some of its properties. At any point one could stop the process and finish it into a sword, but each hammering allowed for differing designs in the metal, and each prior hammering conditioned the metal for future designs. Clay apparently works the same way. Certain clay objects need varying levels of moisture to make them. Thus a lower amount of moisture might be needed to make a bowl, at which point the bowl could be beaten back down into a lump of clay, more moisture added, and a finer object such as a clay vase could be made. Yet the moisture for the bowl conditioned the clay somewhat for the vase.

Organisms in this understanding are similar. Evolution by natural selection can prepare matter for the reception of increasingly higher forms over time. Evolution is a mechanism that could condition matter for another type of organism, but it cannot literally change one type into another. Why? Once again, it is the formal cause that accounts for all the properties of a thing; the matter (i.e., material cause) simply provides it extension in space and time. Any anatomical or biochemical property of a thing is due to its formal cause. Things that are near each other hierarchically have similar forms and hence similar structure and properties. So any conditioning of matter due to evolutionary forces that allows a new closely related organism to arise would be expected through its similar form to have similar structures, just as it is found in both the fossil and DNA record. Quite the contrary to materialistic evolution, a hierarchically driven, causal evolution better fits human experience.

It is often claimed that a materialist view of evolution is supported by experiments in the laboratory involving the evolving of organisms or certain properties of them. Being familiar with such experiments, microevolutionary changes (changes within a species) are verifiable, but macroevolution (evolution resulting in speciation) is debatable. It partly depends on how a species is defined, which is a problem in biology. Further, all laboratory experiments are under the direction of a human agent and are performed according to the causal scheme outlined in chapter 2. By what intellectual right do those holding a strictly materialist view of evolution extrapolate to nature without claiming an intellectual agent or the four causes?

The existence of changes in organisms is consistent with the older traditions and the HOB as well. Several of the greatest Christian thinkers of the past have envisioned the possibility of new species arising. Nor was the possibility of (at least) microevolution and its mechanism of natural selection excluded. Two of the most influential thinkers in the West addressed the subject of speciation: Augustine in the fifth century and Aquinas in the thirteenth. In his longest commentary on the Genesis creation narrative, Augustine invoked the Stoic concept of *rationes seminales* (Greek = *logoi spermatikoi*) to explain how new forms could appear on earth even though Genesis 2:2 says that "God finished his work, which he had done and he rested on the seventh day." Augustine contended that God had put these "seedlike principles" in the original creation, which could in time yield new forms not previously observed.[97] While he probably had nothing like the modern notion of evolution per se in mind, he did not so narrowly believe that the only way God could work in creation was according to species.

Thomas Aquinas, too, perfectly describes microevolution by natural selection in the second book of his *Commentary on Aristotle's Physics*.[98] His account could be used in any modern textbook. Aquinas raised the question of whether the world was created instantly or in a succession of time.[99] He replied that temporal succession tended to bring out the order of divine wisdom better, in that bringing things from an imperfect state to a perfect one manifests order and wisdom better than simply appearing.[100] New species were possible, he thought, but they pertained to the "ornamentation" of the universe, not to its essential parts.[101] If they occurred, it would be somehow to aid the appearance of an intellectual being (humans), to which pertained the general purpose of matter as a whole.[102]

Human Evolution: Material and Beyond

The movement of life toward intelligence and immateriality is on grand display in human evolution as it moves from the purely material to immaterial intelligence, culminating in true culture and an awareness of transcendence and morality. Human history shows us that the genus *homo* (we are *Homo sapiens*) arose around 2 million years ago.[103] The first known member of the genus was *Homo habilis*. *Homo habilis* was around 4.5 feet tall, had a brain about half the size of ours (600–700 cc), possessed crude stone tools, and scavenged for much of his food.[104] Around 1.5 million years ago, there appeared *Homo erectus*, who was as tall, or taller, than modern man, had

97. St. Augustine, "St Augustine on Genesis," 145–88.

98. Aquinas, *Commentary on Aristotle's Physics* II, lec. 12.

99. See note 45 above.

100. See note 46 above.

101. *ST* I, q. 70, a. 1c.; Aquinas, *Light of Faith*, chap. 170; *Commentary on Aristotle's De Caelo et Mundo*, lec. 3, chap. 2, n. 21.

102. Aquinas, *De Potentia*, q. 5, a. 5, ad. 13. See the more complete discussion on this topic in chapter 8 in this volume.

103. Raven et al., *Biology*, 724.

104. Raven et al., *Biology*, 724; Tattersall, *Masters of the Planet*, 94–102.

a brain capacity of 900–1,000 cc, and possessed better tools and fire than *Homo habilis*.[105] Yet in neither *Homo habilis* or *homo erectus* do we find any definitive evidence of a rational intellect.[106] Neanderthals (*Homo neanderthalensis*), a more advanced type of human, lived from approximately 500,000 to 30,000 years ago.[107] Neanderthals were shorter but larger framed and much more muscled than modern humans, with a brain capacity larger than ours (1,400 cc).[108] While they buried their dead (with no ritual), there is nothing in this or other of their behaviors to strongly suggest some higher intuitions.[109] At roughly the same time as Neanderthals there lived a collection of humans called archaic *Homo sapiens* (*Homo heidelbergensis*).[110] They were taller than us, with a brain capacity roughly equivalent to our own (1,200 cc).[111] There is some evidence that they too buried their dead, but still no strong evidence of higher cognition.[112] Anatomically modern humans, *Homo sapiens*, appeared around 300,000 to 200,000 years ago, in northwest and eastern Africa.[113] By 20,000 years ago, *Homo sapiens* had spread across the Old World, and across the globe by 12,000 years ago, leaving behind their cave art and religious artifacts.[114] Here, evidence of true intelligence and culture becomes evident.[115]

Humans are divided into sexes, as are other higher forms of life. Certainly, a primary role of the sexes is for the propagation of the species. Another role might be posited, as well: the building up of society.[116] How so? A history of life and the development of sex roles points to a division of labor for

105. Raven et al., *Biology*, 724; Tattersall, *Masters of the Planet*, 96–116, 131–44.

106. Tattersall, *Masters of the Planet*, 94–144.

107. Tattersall, *Masters of the Planet*, 161–84.

108. Tattersall, *Masters of the Planet*, 161–84.

109. Tattersall, *Masters of the Planet*, 181, 183–84. The favored opinion is that Neanderthals had no symbolism and hence no higher thought. But recent evidence from Neanderthal cave "art" in France adds to the dispute (Jaubert et al., "Early Neanderthal Constructions," 111–14).

110. Raven et al., *Biology*, 725; Tattersall, *Masters of the Planet*, 145–52.

111. Tattersall, *Masters of the Planet*, 145–52.

112. Tattersall, *Masters of the Planet*, esp. 152.

113. Tattersall, *Masters of the Planet*, 184–202; Hublin et al., "New Fossils," 289–92; Richter et al., "The Age of the Hominin Fossils," 293–96.

114. Tattersall, *Masters of the Planet*, 184–202.

115. See "The Art in Caves and the Art of Intelligence" in chapter 3, in this volume; Raven et al., *Biology*, 203–28.

116. See Toma, "Dionysian/Thomistic Framework," 87–113, for further discussion of the sexes.

the life of the mind. Initially, life was propagated asexually by binary fission of simple cells: one cell splits into two.[117] All bacteria carry their genetic information in one large circular chromosome.[118] About the same time that eukaryotic cells appear, sexual reproduction arises in the protists.[119] These eukaryotes have, instead of one circular chromosome, pairs of chromosome for each type of chromosome they possess.[120]

With the appearance of multicellularity, among the earliest structures to appear are those producing or holding gametes (the sex cells).[121] Here, new life is being produced inside structures. As new plants appeared through time, true male and female parts developed.[122] In plants, these can be found on the same individual – many plants have male and female flowers – or separately.[123] Additionally, we find true young, or embryos, arising.[124] Initially, they were on their own for survival, but then provisioning with food in the seed occurred.[125] Life becomes interiorized and cared for by walling off the outside world. Organisms are producing life within, suggesting that the physical interiorization of life mimics its interior self-motion.

This becomes much more exaggerated, particularly in higher animals. The history of vertebrates (animals with backbones) is a revealing example. In many primitive vertebrates, such as most fish, the young develop outside the mother.[126] The male and the female release sperm and eggs, respectively, into the water where external fertilization occurs.[127] Amphibians, above fish, move about on land but return to the water for fertilization and development of young, as with fish.[128] Most reptiles and birds have internal fertilization, producing an external egg where the fertilized embryo is protected and

117. Raven et al., *Biology*, 187–88, 542, 565–66.
118. Raven et al., *Biology*, 542.
119. Raven et al., *Biology*, 565–66.
120. Raven et al., *Biology*, 189–91.
121. Raven et al., *Biology*, 587.
122. Raven et al., *Biology*, 603–11.
123. Raven et al., *Biology*, 844–45.
124. Raven et al., *Biology*, 586.
125. Raven et al., *Biology*, 600–601, 611–12.
126. Raven et al., *Biology*, 1087–88.
127. Raven et al., *Biology*, 1087–88.
128. Raven et al., *Biology*, 1088.

nourished.[129] Finally, in mammals, we find internal fertilization, followed by internal gestation.[130] Here, new life is completely interiorized, developed, nourished, and protected. The female mammal is particularly equipped for this with a womb for gestation and milk glands for feeding after birth.[131] Furthermore, long periods of rearing occur where the young stay with the mother, and sometimes the father, until early adulthood. In human females, the whole process becomes particularly interiorized, as even the ovulation signal is hidden.[132] In most other primates (and mammals), ovulation is only partly concealed or has evident external signs that it has occurred in order to facilitate mating.[133] Thus in mammals, the interiorization of life reaches its maximum. E. O. Wilson, the founder of sociobiology, argued that animal societies are the end toward which life is tending.[134] Societies are hierarchical organizations that promote efficient utilization of resources for the good of the individuals and species that possess them.[135] They are natural extensions of the hierarchical trend toward order and interiority that was seen in eukaryotic cells, with their increased compartmentalization.

It is in humans especially that the drive to intensify communal and relational living for the life of the intellect becomes unmistakable. The emergence of symbolic language, with its multifaceted components and rules, allows for a wide and diverse array of technologies and means of doing things.[136] The great cave painters of Europe certainly show rational thought and the ability to choose a variety of means to accomplish intended ends.[137] They know and understand the principles of things around them. Creating exquisite cave art and using religious artifacts show the cave dwellers to be self-reflecting and knowing beings.[138] In human beings, the definition of life as self-change shows itself in a truly novel manner for a material being.

129. Raven et al., *Biology*, 1088–89.

130. Raven et al., *Biology*, 1090.

131. Raven et al., *Biology*, 717.

132. Andelman, "Evolution of Concealed Ovulation," 785–99.

133. Andelman, "Evolution of Concealed Ovulation," 785–99.

134. Wilson, *Sociobiology*; *Social Conquest*, 7–187.

135. Wilson, *Social Conquest*, 7–187.

136. See "The Art in Caves and the Art of Intelligence" in chapter 3, this volume; Raven et al., *Biology*, 203–28.

137. See note 136 above.

138. See note 136 above.

Human intelligence yields true understanding of the world, self-knowledge, and awareness of higher realities. Far from intelligence being an add-on to life, the material universe finds its fulfillment and completion in the human intellect.[139]

The drive of life toward the intellect, knowledge, and love is supported from another perspective, the development of a nuclear family. In primate societies, there is a general tendency toward polygyny (the male having more than one female mate, with long-term rearing of offspring done by the females) and male dominance.[140] This is found in human hunter-gatherer societies as well, but there the family has become the nuclear unit, with long-term extended familial relationships.[141] Monogamy, where the male assumes a large role in child-rearing as well, is found in many humans, but in humans monogamy appears to arise partly from a strong cultural component rather than from biological origins.[142] Culture, as stated, is a product of the rational intellect. The father's role in this regard is particularly exaggerated toward his sons. Human males, as with most primate males and other mammalian males, have a drive to roam and be aggressive,[143] arising from their role as protectors of territories and resources.[144] The human father must channel (not remove) these drives toward higher things, such as tenderness to the family and an aggressive but controlled defense of families, homes, cites, states and nations, and of all that is good.[145] The ability to instill virtue and morality comes from the life of the mind, the human rational intellect, and its specific product, culture.

In sum, human culture can be defined as an animal society infused by the rational intellect with customs to understand and pass on truth to generations. The interior action of the rational mind thus tempers animal society into a hierarchical organization designed to nurture the life of the mind: education, rearing of children, and customs, or in other words the

139. See chapter 8 in this volume for a more complete discussion of this topic.

140. Wilson, *Sociobiology*, 515–46.

141. Wilson, *Sociobiology*, 547–75.

142. Low, "Ecological and Social Complexities," 161–76.

143. Wilson, *Sociobiology*, 515–46, 547–75.

144. Wilson, *Sociobiology*, 515–46, 547–75.

145. Special thanks to psychologist Richard Cross (Leominister, MA) for bringing up this idea, and for discussions on this topic. See also John Chrysostom, "Vainglory."

passing on of truth to the next generation. In humans, we see the apogee of the material universe in their biology, sexes, natural history, and customs, a fully integrated form of life reaching toward higher reality.[146] The human being is a social animal that forms structures and customs (true culture) to transmit truth and organize himself and his fellow man for the life of the mind and love. Given his rational intellect, which needs many examples to grasp reality, he forms philosophies, religious customs, art, literature, science, music, and all the forms and arrays of human knowledge enabling him and his descendants to rise to a higher reality and enter into communities of knowledge and love. The collection of these things is culture, or the transmission of knowledge and truth through particular things to the next generation.[147] Culture is a product of the rational intellect. So the rational intellect of humans provides a point of integration for these disciplines in the HOB. The mineral, plant, and animal life of the material universe is united in the intellectual life and soul of the human being, where the material universe finds its completion and unity in human nature and the intellect.

Jared Diamond's highly successful work *Guns, Germs, and Steel* synthesizes many types of data to show how human society arose.[148] Using a large collection of data from biological, anthropological, sociological, and geographic research, he explains how societies arose at different rates across Old World and New World arenas. Diamond asks why European civilizations came to dominate the world and why other civilizations, such as those of Papua New Guinea or of the New World, were technologically backward by comparison. His answer is that differing axes of trade routes across the Old World (east to west) versus those in the New World (north to south) made this possible, as well as greater availability of domesticable plants and animals in the Old World. He collates and explains an immense amount of data regarding basic materials needed to support human life and society (e.g., food, clothing, and shelter), the basic inventions and ideas to support them, and their ease of dissemination to other societies. If this development occurred at greater rates in some societies than others, it would give such societies that had these basic ideas and inventions the leisure time needed to

146. See also Toma, "Dionysian/Thomistic Framework," 87–113.

147. See Pieper, *Leisure*, for an excellent analysis of culture and its necessary basis.

148. Diamond, *Guns, Germs, and Steel*.

develop greater ideas, thought, and religion, because their basic needs were met. Yet, in a similar vein, Aquinas's explanation regarding material versus intellectual causation that was invoked to explain the simpler to more complex fossil record over time can also be applied here. An intellectual agent working with material reality begins with the parts and ends with the finished product. Human societal development would thus begin by procuring the basic needs of the body first, along with the skills necessary to maintain them. Then, later, humans begin to inquire into nature and reality, refine their experience of it, and develop sophisticated systems of thought and human organizations such as universities, states, and nations. Far from an argument that supports scientism, Diamond's work equally supports the HOB.

Here we can extend Aquinas's explanation to economics as well. Economics is the science of producing and using the basic needs of life. Some people argue that economics is the most important discipline for humans, as procuring these needs is done first in societies. Again, the simple and basic come first in an intellect working in matter, while it is the end that is most important. Once basic necessities are met, the life of the mind becomes practically possible.

The legitimate data of psychology can also be readily wrapped into the HOB.[149] Modern psychology deals with the life of the senses and is therefore common to animals and human beings, but it also deals with the intellect insofar as it quantifies the effects of an intellect on matter. I cite only three such sets of data. First, there is a growing consensus in clinical psychology that traditional ideas of the moral life and morality are important to the health and well-being of the individual.[150] Additionally, the regular practice of religion along with certitude of beliefs is a dominant factor in contributing positively to a person's well-being. The acceptance of relativistic beliefs (there is no truth) coupled with a lack of order in lifestyle adversely affects people. Second, psychological literature shows that children are "intuitive theists" by five years of age.[151] They have a natural idea that there is a higher

149. I would like in particular to express my thanks to Richard Cross, PhD (psychology), for bringing these examples to my attention and explaining them.

150. Snyder et al., "Hope Theory," 257–76; Seybold and Hill, "Role of Religion," 21–24; Sethi and Seligman, "Optimism and Fundamentalism," 256–59.

151. Rottman et al., "Cultural Influences," 17–26; Kelemen, "Are Children 'Intuitive Theists'?," 295–305.

being over all things, with an implicit understanding that reality is hierarchal as well. This has been shown *not* to be an idea imposed upon them by extrapolating from parents. While many of the specifics of their understanding of this being may be incorrect, they do understand that there is a Being who is provident (who looks after them), and who punishes wrong and rewards right. Human children are tuned to intuit hierarchy from an early age.

Confirmation of this notion of hierarchy comes from a surprising source. B. F. Skinner was one of the founders of behaviorism and a committed atheist.[152] His work has always been associated with materialistic thinking because he interpreted his data within a committed materialist philosophy. If one removes the data from its interpretation, however, the data can be seen in quite a different light. His research involved the motivating factors in animal behavior: rewards/punishment, the stimuli that elicit various behaviors in animals, and so on.[153] All of us know that we are attracted by various things and repulsed by others. Rewards and punishment are strong factors in rearing children and training pets. One particular aspect of Skinner's work involved the investigation into what motivates an animal to decline a present reward in the hopes of a future one.

Why would an animal turn down immediate gratification in the hopes of something better in the future? For instance, how much more food must a rat expect to get to induce him to turn down an immediate lesser amount? How much time delay is there in this perception? Will it wait hours or only minutes? One of Skinner's students, Richard J. Herrnstein, formulated these ideas into "the Matching Law," where choices were distributed according to rates of reinforcement for making those choices.[154] In his book *Crime and Human Punishment*, Herrnstein calls these rates "time horizons."[155] How much distance in time is one willing to endure for a future reward? This has immense practical applications to the moral life: Will one put off material rewards for future virtuous rewards? For how long and how much? Something similar appears in Thomas Aquinas's *Commentary on Aristotle's Sense*

152. PBS, "B. F. Skinner, 1904–1990."

153. PBS, "B. F. Skinner, 1904–1990."

154. "Richard J. Herrnstein (1930–1994)," website of the Department of Psychology, Harvard University, accessed December 7, 2018, http://psychology.fas.harvard.edu/people/richard-j-herrnstein.

155. Wilson and Hernstein, *Crime and Human Nature*, 41–66.

and Sensibles. Because Aquinas acknowledged that humans are part animal, he saw "anticipations" of this phenomenon of moral rewards in animals. He said that the longer an animal is willing to wait is an indication of how close it approaches to being intellectual.[156] Why? Only an intellect can truly understand something as future, as matter is locked into *this* time and place. The more an animal is willing to put off eating and mating to fight for territory in the hope of a future greater amount of food or mates, the more it indicates the animal's proximity to human intelligence. All these data are consistent with the drive of life toward intelligence, greater interiorization, and hierarchy.

Diversity, Complexity, and the Hierarchy of Being

The central concept illustrated in this chapter has been the Hierarchy of Being. It has been around for at least two thousand years, but I suggest that it may be the most powerful idea available for making sense of modern science in relation to our wider humanity. The data and to some extent the theories of modern science have greatly increased our understanding of the universe, but they have all too often been presented in a philosophical framework (worldview) that is not adequate to the task of worldview construction. Modern science has shown that nature is vastly more complex than previously thought, but there is something missing in truly intellectual discussions about science. The modern sciences are not only diverse and complex; they are also fragmented and isolated from one another and from the daily lives of ordinary people. Part of the reason, I believe, is scientistic materialism. It is simply barren of producing any sense of meaning of the universe that human beings can embrace. This is why so much of modern science, as presented by scientists and those who think of science in a material manner, is rejected in its larger meaning by the common man. It holds forth a world stripped of meaning, and our common experience tells us otherwise.

The way forward lies, I think, in returning to some ideas of our intellectual ancestors who lacked the specific details of modern science but were far better at capturing the whole in a coherent philosophy of knowledge and

156. Aquinas, *Commentary on Aristotle's "On Sense and What Is Sensed,"* 436a8.

life. One of the strengths of a framework for understanding reality is its inherent ability to integrate and unite various disciplines. The HOB can readily integrate, unite, and relate disparate fields of knowing, including the link between knowledge of material and immaterial reality. The basis for this integration is the observation of exterior versus interior change, and the consequent movement of and end of material change culminating in the human intellect. The HOB has the possibility to integrate and to unite a great array of human experience, precisely because it understands beings according to more general behavior than modern thought does and is *open* to immaterial reality. Based upon the knowledge of such beings exhibiting exterior or interior change, the various disciplines of knowledge of these beings in the hierarchy can be united into a coherent whole.

Any body of knowledge draws its character from the type of being it studies: geology is about rocks, minerals, and planetary structures, physics concerns nonliving forces, and biology is about living things. Molecular biology, physiology, and botany can be understood and united as facets of biology, the science of life. From unobservable subatomic particles to the most distant galaxies, the HOB can unite all types of knowledge into a coherent framework. Physics, geology, chemistry, quantum mechanics, and astronomy all have a common basis in the HOB in that their object is a type of being exhibiting exterior change. Some of these – such as physics, chemistry, and quantum mechanics – in part pertain to living things insofar as living things are composed of and subject to the laws governing nonliving things. Biology and all its subdisciplines (botany, zoology, physiology, genetics, evolution, et al.) have as their object living things, or aspects of living things. Living beings exhibit to a lesser or greater degree immanent (interior) actions, the unifying aspect of all these disciplines.

Psychology is the science of the emotions and the quantifiable effects of the intellect upon material things. So it is proper to both animals (which have emotions) and man, having both emotions and intellect. Sociology concerns societies of living things. So both psychology and sociology deal equally with higher-order aspects of animals and the juncture of animal/human life. At this juncture one also finds anthropology, the quantifiable study of human culture and the immediate ancestors of humans. Humans are persons, or material beings with a rational intellect and the power to love.

The bodies of knowledge resulting from the effort of the rational intellect to penetrate reality – the arts, sciences, philosophy, music, theater, history, literature, poetry, writing, politics, economics – all can be integrated into the HOB at the level of humans. Thus the deepest occurrence of true interior change in a material being – the rational intellect of humans – is the factor that unites all of these disciplines as the effort of the rational intellect to penetrate and grasp the object of study. When one steps back and looks at all of these disciplines and how they are ordered, the rational intellect of man is the skeleton that holds them into a unified whole and allows them to relate to one another.

Still, the HOB applied to the natural world leaves an important question unanswered. Are human beings with an immaterial intellect the only, or the most perfect, example of intelligence and life? The very existence of an immaterial knower and immaterial knowledge prompts a deeper search. The ascent of the mind, self-change (interior change), and humans as the pinnacle of the material cosmos lead one to ask this question. It is here that reductionistic materialism falls silent because it believes that nothing is bona fide knowledge that cannot be measured. The HOB with all its accompanying ideas of causation and diversity is more liberal minded. It is open to truth in immaterial things as well. Here it becomes possible to unite philosophy and theology with all the other disciplines so far mentioned. Philosophy, properly conceived, contains the highest form of knowledge based on our natural powers of knowing. It investigates all things, material and immaterial, under the aspect of being or existence in general and its causes, or Cause. Theology is the knowledge of that beyond our natural capacities and concepts, most specifically God.

8 THE TRUTH OF TWO TALES

It is time to step back and consider more explicitly what is at issue in the two worldviews we have been discussing. It is also crucial to realize that so far we have not made any substantive appeal to the Bible (or to sacred writings of other religions), to Judeo-Christian teachings, or to religious and Church authority. References to the Bible have been purely illustrative, with no real attempt to base anything on it. Appeals to Thomas Aquinas and other Church figures have been appeals to wise thinkers, not infallible authorities. This is necessary to emphasize, because modern people who are imbued with materialistic and secular modes of thought tend to identify any talk of such things as "religion," and thereby dismiss its relevance to science and cosmology. In fact, all that has been said is based on the experience of reality and rational inferences from these experiences.

Most of what has been discussed thus far can be known by reason, and much of it was formulated by Greek thinkers such as Plato and Aristotle before Christianity. Knowledge and understanding attainable by reason constitute our natural knowledge; we can reason to these conclusions because we have the natural ability to do so; one does not need revelation to reach the conclusions we have made. Yet the approach here seems foreign to modern people because it is so different from familiar ways of thinking. Most people, including Christians, have been taught to think about reality only in a strongly materialistic framework that assumes no other possible way of rationally approaching things. This exclusionary approach is a decisive factor leading to the bifurcation of reality into religious and nonreligious things; it contributes to the nearly complete breakdown of any intellectual approach to the former.

This book has been a study in contrasts between two worldviews. One is the reductionistic and materialistic scientism that reaches beyond the proper boundaries of science. The other is a worldview based on common human experience, into which science fits as one important part of the human quest for understanding and meaning. Throughout history, scientific theories often have been associated with worldviews that do not directly flow from science, but seem to fit it in many ways. In many sciences, it is h to distinguish different worldviews because the reasons for distinguishing between them are difficult to identify. Many of the reasons offered for a worldview may lie outside the strict competence of science. The ultimate question confronting us is not about science, but about how to discriminate between worldviews.

Two Conceptions of Knowledge and the Universe

A worldview that incorporates the Hierarchy of Being begins the inquiry process with the broadest question: What is life? This inquiry takes us on a journey from nonliving things to the ultimate source of all reality, God. Thomas Aquinas breaks down this question with the basic observation common to the human race that life is what moves itself. In his system, self-movement is seen as existing in a series of gradations from lower to higher. The more immanent the operation, the more interior it is (not relying on the external to complete itself), and the more it exhibits a higher or fuller sense of life. The ultimate self-moving act is intelligence, because its operation does not need to rely on external things. In God, intelligence is the same as his existence, and it is who he is.[1] Because human beings are ma-

1. *SCG* I. 44–45; *ST* I, q. 14, a. 4c. But it must be again emphasized that God is Intelligence *analogously*. He is infinitely above any created notion of intellect or intelligence. Because there is a *remote* similarity of ours to his, we call him Intellect or Intelligence. The same goes for any other attribute of his.

terial, they must depend on matter external to them to begin the intellectual act. The end product, self-knowledge, is not perfect either. But the act itself of knowing is immaterial.

This approach forms a rational basis of the traditional Christian view of reality and allows all types of modern knowledge, removed from their secular framework, to be easily grafted into Christian thought. Early Christian and medieval thinkers accomplished this by adopting the science of the ancient world and incorporating it into their worldview. They cast about and found in Greek thought data, theories, and conclusions compatible with their beliefs. Then they developed and perfected it with Christian revelation. In turn, they used these rational systems to probe more deeply into revelation in the discipline of theology. The cosmology presented here, the picture of the universe, is based on the common experience of the reality around all of us. It is the experience of people of various ages and cultures and is deepened with the self-evident principles that we gather from this contact with reality. That experience of reality around us is the common experience of both the medieval Christian thinker and the modern scientist: the universe is orderly, predictable, can be modeled with mathematics, and is undergirded by causal and other self-evident principles discussed in this book.

Scientism has a much more limited and restricted view of knowledge. Like the traditional inquiry sketched above, such thinkers begin with observations, but they limit bona fide knowledge to ideas that they claim are empirically verifiable (or falsifiable). They would reject many of the conclusions made in this book because they say that they are not testable.[2] They will reflexively critique the approach I am suggesting by arguing that we should defer to the findings of science, which in their minds requires the primacy of interpretation of scientific facts by the materialism of scientism. For instance, they might argue that science shows us that final causality does not exist. Such people tend to adopt a scientistic view of knowledge (i.e., worldview) in their graduate studies as they are preparing for professorships and

2. The scientific idea of testability flows from the nature of scientific data. Unlike valid philosophy, whose truths flow from the very nature of intuited first principles, scientific ideas do not. As discussed in chapter 2, scientific data arise from individual instances; there is no inherent reason a theory necessarily flows from them, as the theory must be tested against the data. It is precisely because of this that one must test a theory over and over. This is not a result of the strength of science, but rather its inherent weakness as a means of knowing truth.

professional research. This view is "in the air"; that is, it is part of the professional culture. Such a worldview is seen as the only way to avoid fanciful and superstitious thinking so characteristic of philosophy and especially religion.

Scientism is derived from materialism, the idea that only material things exist, and that anything worth knowing is made of matter. Particularly salient in materialistic accounts is the denial of purpose or an end (*telos*) in nature. The reason often offered for the denial of purpose is that it cannot be tested or measured. Still, there are multiple problems with scientism as a claim about what constitutes legitimate knowledge. First, how can science, which presupposes purpose in the very structure of its experiments, claim that purpose does not exist? Also, how can a discipline bound to individuality argue against principles that may be transcendent to material reality? Scientism consistently avoids the presuppositions under which it works.

Occasionally, one encounters a profound thinker who expresses scientism with unusual candor, one who admits that scientism is ultimately not about science. One such thinker is Richard Lewontin, the internationally famous Harvard biologist whose 1997 article in the *New York Times Review of Books* laid out the presuppositions of scientistic materialism with crystal clarity:

> Our willingness to accept scientific claims that are against common sense is the key to an understanding of the real struggle between science and the supernatural. We take the side of science *in spite* of the patent absurdity of some of its constructs, *in spite* of its failure to fulfill many of its extravagant promises of health and life, *in spite* of the tolerance of the scientific community for unsubstantiated just-so stories, because we have a prior commitment, a commitment to materialism. *It is not that the methods and institutions of science somehow compel us to accept a material explanation of the phenomenal world, but, on the contrary, that we are forced by our a priori adherence to material causes to create an apparatus of investigation and a set of concepts that produce material explanations, no matter how counter-intuitive, no matter how mystifying to the uninitiated. Moreover, that materialism is absolute, for we cannot allow a Divine Foot in the door.*[3]

Lewontin here in italics admits that science and its conclusions do not necessarily lead to a materialist view of the world. It is the prior commitment to materialism that leads to a materialistic interpretation of science:

3. Lewontin, "Billions and Billions of Demons." Emphasis added.

scientism. If not Lewontin's science, just where does this idea of materialism come from? What are his basic experiences of concrete reality that lead him to conclude to this? What is the rational basis – the evidence from this universe – that leads Lewontin to materialism? Lewontin's statement is not that of any cosmology based on rational inquiry. I have argued in this book that the true experience of reality leads to just the opposite conclusion, yielding insight into higher immaterial causality. And no science, just as Lewontin admits, can contradict this, including the ideas presented here of perfection, order, ends, and final causality. Quite the contrary, when viewed from the cosmology here presented, it agrees with and enriches it.

We must make a choice between a view of knowledge that is limited and restricted to matter and one that is liberal and open-minded, one that insists that matter is necessary as a substrate of knowledge in human beings but that also transcends the material world. In the end, intellectual honesty forces us to decide between a universe with no purpose or end, no *telos* to which it moves, or a universe in which things move toward some end, and from this end the universe derives its meaning and significance. A universe without direction and meaning simply exists in a mechanical state. It has no purpose from which the meaning of human life can be inferred. In this conception, the only meaning for humanity is what an individual or group baldly and boldly asserts, without any connection to the greater cosmos.

A Universe with Meaning

Lewontin's universe, the one espoused by scientistic materialists, reduces the complexities of nature to random and purposeless interactions. In such a view there is no meaning or purpose. In light of the natural human understanding of purpose, adopting the materialist view forces us to make a choice: either we deny a plethora of human experience – it must be a phantasm – or we seek to reduce all those complex human experiences to purely material causes – a vague hope for a distant future in the present state of our knowledge.

The worldview that I am advocating is replete with meaning and saturated with purpose. And that is precisely what bothers the reductionist, for he claims to be committed above all to Ockham's razor.[4]

4. Chervin and Kevane, *Love of Wisdom*, 206.

William of Ockham lived most of his life in the first half of the fourteenth century as a Franciscan friar who taught philosophy and theology. Ockham formulated the famous rule of parsimony that says, given data to be explained, the simpler explanation is to be preferred (Ockham's razor). This methodological principle has pervaded science ever since. One of the arguments traditionally given for accepting the Copernican (heliocentric) system over the Ptolemaic (geocentric) is that the former considerably simplifies the calculations and models of the planets. The reductionist takes such a case as symptomatic of all of science, and thus argues that a cosmology, such as I am advocating, violates Ockham's razor. But the rule of parsimony only applies when two explanations apply to a well-understood set of data, upon which all parties agree. The choice between a materialist or nonmaterialist worldview is far more complicated than a choice between two theories explaining an agreed-upon set of data. One who adopts the Hierarchy of Being acknowledges multiple causes and discerns *meaning* in both nonhuman nature and in human action. Such a thinker gleefully sees all these through the lens of realism, as realities to be explained, not explained away, not as human constructs dreamed up by fanciful desires for transcendence, but as real reflections of common human experience.

It is common human experience that has led us to define life as that which moves itself. The greater the form of life, the more interiorized it is. Though this simple fact is overlooked in a modern frame of reference, it is one of the most self-evident observations one could make. Purely interior actions are ultimately intelligence.

There are two types of intelligence. One is that of humans, whose thought is discursive and sequential. Humans reason from the particular to the general. But in a greater sense, one could ask whether intellects need to move at all from the particular to the general. Is it necessary to reason, in other words, or is it possible to simply know? This would constitute the second type of intelligence.

We have posed a related question several times already. Is it possible to go beyond human knowing? Even though human intelligence is per se immaterial and constitutes the end of movement in the material world, is it possible that there could be an intellect that simply knows? Could an immaterial being exist that knows things at once and without any discursive or sequential thought? Animals and plants possess purely material being but have no intellectual powers. Can there be beings with purely intellectual powers but no matter? There certainly is nothing irrational in this idea. It is the next logical step.

Up, Up, and Away

The existence of immaterial intellectual beings was not the invention of Christians. It was already articulated in ancient Greek thought. The Greeks were much attuned to the idea of an ordered universe, an idea that they gathered from their experience and observations of reality. If there were finite creatures (e.g., minerals, plants, and animals) whose existence was purely material, and humans who possessed both material and immaterial aspects, it made sense that there must be an infinite and purely immaterial Cause of Everything. Aristotle called this being an Unmoved Mover.[5] He reasoned that to complete the explanatory chain used in science, there needed to be a final explanation that was immaterial, because if it were material, it too would need to be explained.[6] And since such a being would be immaterial, it would not be bounded by space and time like other material creatures. Christians saw in Aristotle's Unmoved Mover a possible connection with the Infinite, Immaterial, and Uncreated Being that they called God.[7] In chapter 6, I pointed out that the existence of finality in nature in nonintelligent creatures such as insects necessitated an intelligent agent, because only an intellect knows an end and can direct something to it, just as an arrow is directed to its end by the archer. Greek thought, recognizing finality in nature, also noticed a certain gap in the Hierarchy of Being. Human beings were contingent material beings, finite in space and time yet possessing an intellect, knowing, immaterial reality. And the Unmoved Mover is a purely transcendent Immaterial Intellect. Could it be possible there also exist created immaterial beings who possessed purely intellectual powers?

5. Aquinas, *Commentary on Aristotle's Physics* VIII, lec. 7–13

6. Aquinas, *Commentary on Aristotle's Physics* VIII, lec. 7–13

7. *SCG* I.13, 15–28; *Catechism of the Catholic Church*, 31–32. This is by no means a necessary connection, as there are substantial differences between the two. The point is that human reason can attain to a demonstration of a type of Supreme Being, allowing us to understand that the God of revelation is not some arbitrary or irrational idea.

Aristotle called them Separated Substances (i.e., substances separated from matter), and Christians called them angels.[8] Here were finite immaterial beings without matter in between humans and the Unmoved Mover. When I first read the arguments for the possibility of such beings, I considered them weak arguments. Now, as a scientist studying nature and its order for thirty years, I think it one of the more airtight arguments if one holds that nature is *truly ordered*.

It is necessary to pause and understand two things before we can reason about the possibility of the existence of angels: the human quest for unified explanations and human reasoning about the existence and nature of God. The modern scientific enterprise is predicated on the search for unified explanations. Let's take Isaac Newton, sometimes called the final cause of the scientific revolution. Newton's mechanics was a startling achievement of unification. His law of universal gravitation applied to objects in free fall (e.g., apples), to trajectories (e.g., bullets), to planetary orbits, and to comets (e.g., Halley's). In the nineteenth century, Darwin's theory of evolution by natural selection was hailed because of its unifying power. In the twentieth century, the quest for unification took another step up, trying to unite all descriptions of the universe in one equation called the Grand Unified Theory. The goal was to formulate one mathematical equation that summed up the entire cosmos.

The search for unification is a remote reflection of our groping for God; as intellectual creatures, we look and long for this unity. We know that from one thing many things come; from the simple comes the complex. One and the simple is the source of multiplicity and complexity. Yet how can it be true that many things, many complex things, arise from one simple thing or idea? How do we understand the Many by the One? Thomas Aquinas addressed the same question in his *Summa contra Gentiles* in the thirteenth century, offering a beautiful example.[9] Aquinas, having shown that God knows only himself and everything else by knowing himself, then asks how God knows things outside himself if he only understands himself. Aquinas answers with the number 10, which can be thought of as ten units of one. In an analogous manner, say 10 is ultimate perfection, God. God would un-

8. *SCG* II.91.

9. *SCG* I.54.

derstand other things by approximations of perfections. Thus one creature might be thought of as 9, or 10 – 1 perfection of his nature. Another might be thought of as 4, or 10 – 6 perfections. Now, God is infinite, so even the greatest creature would be many subtractions below his nature. But this example shows that it is possible and plausible to believe that by understanding one thing (10), one can understand everything and multiplicity at the same time (all numbers less than 10). Even in the physical world we have analogous examples. For instance, sunlight produces multiple effects from the simple cause of light: heat, light, electrical flow, photosynthesis. But if even a finite knower such as a human being can grasp how multiplicity can arise out of unity, why would the Grand Knower not be able to do so?

To attempt to use reason about an Infinite, Immaterial, and Intellectual Being is to invite scorn from materialists. One of the most common questions they raise when any mention of God enters the picture has to do with the origin of God. If God created all these material things, so they say, who created God? This same objection lies behind a second insistence that a complex universe requires an even more complex God. Recently, one finds this argument in Lawrence Krauss's book *A Universe from Nothing.*[10] In one form or another, I have heard this objection repeatedly throughout the course of my life as a professional scientist. But the materialist question is based on a false understanding of what is being claimed about God. It is as if they imagine God to be just the next higher-up being in the universe but having many of the properties of matter. The ancient idea of God, especially the Christian idea, is completely different from what the materialists imagine. God is utterly Other than human beings can imagine him to be. Christianity has long affirmed the incomprehensibility of God by the human mind. Even though God can be known, he cannot be comprehended in rational categories alone. The problem for materialists lies in their inability or unwillingness to admit a Being whose *thatness* (existence) and whose *whatness* (essence) are the same.

Everything we know in the material world allows and requires a distinction between existence and essence. Let's take a simple example.[11] Imagine

10. Krauss, *Universe from Nothing*, xii, xv, 190.

11. The following example is not my own. I read it someplace at least twenty years ago, and despite my best efforts, I cannot find it again. I think it one of the more elegant explanations of the distinction between whatness and thatness (essence and existence). So I extend my thanks to whomever came up with it.

lying in your bed at night and hearing something rummaging around downstairs. What is it? It could be the dog, the cat, or a member of the family. All you know is that something exists, but you don't know *what* (essence) it is. Alternatively, imagine a friend who leaves a meeting by walking around the corner, and then you hear a gunshot. Is your friend alive? He may be. In this second case, you know what your friend is (a human), but not whether he *exists* now. You know his *whatness* (essence) but not his *thatness* (existence). All material creatures require a distinction between existence and essence. Scientists presume this distinction in the description of prehistoric animals; that is, they know *what* they are, and *that* they are not. Astronomers too might detect a wobble in the orbit of a planet or star and predict that some other object (another planet, planetoid, etc.) is causing it. They know *that* something is, but not *what* it is without further investigation. On a personal level, the *whatness* of my being human places a limit on the *thatness* of my existence; I am human and not a dog. Further, the existence of all material beings is contingent (not necessary).[12] They may exist, or they may not. So, all contingent beings need a cause to explain their existence, as it is not necessary that something (a what) exist (that it is); a cause is needed to bring essence and existence together.

With our rational faculties, it is possible to imagine a Being whose *whatness* (essence) is the same as its *thatness* (existence). This Being is its existence.[13] Its *whatness* is to be or exist. It cannot *not* exist. Its existence is not contingent but necessary. No cause is needed to bring essence and existence together; that is, they are the same in God. In contrast to all the examples of material life, this Being alone allows us to say that if you could know what it is, you would know that it is, and if you could know that it is, you would know what it is. Such a Being must exist even if we cannot name it or comprehend it with our rational minds. If such a Being did not exist, there would be no explanation for contingent beings like humans. We would have to relinquish the explanatory quest we call science and philosophy.

The ancient Hebrews seemed to grasp the same fact when an author recounted the story of Moses before the burning bush in third chapter of Exodus. Moses asks God what to tell the Israelites if they should ask, who

12. *SCG* II.15–16, 31; *ST* I, q. 44, a. 1c.

13. *SCG* I.22; *ST* I, q. 3, a. 4c.

it is that sent him (Moses) to them. The response from God is, "I AM has sent me to you." God calls himself, "I AM WHO I AM," or he who simply exists (Ex 3:14). God says "I AM" without a predicate. We all must say, I am a scientist, I am a man, I am an astronomer, or I am a being. His very Being is existence, and his properties (e.g., divinity, omnipresence, omniscience) are necessary and uncreated. It always was, is, and will be. God is an unlimited, perfectly simple Act of uncreated existence. Ours is a created and contingent existence. God needs no cause. It is nonsense to ask who caused him. He simply is; that is what he is. Having no parts and being pure existence, no cause is necessary. He is his own cause and the cause of everything else.[14]

Recall the definition of life as that which moves itself. This self-movement is ultimately an interior act called intellect or understanding from which the will and its act of love are part. To be *totally* self-moving, one would have to be pure infinite existence, in need of *no* cause. So in God, life, intelligence, will, love, existence, power, beauty, and truth are all perfectly one and the same thing: pure existence and therefore infinite.[15] God exists in a manner infinitely above and beyond creatures and as such is totally above, or transcendent, over creation. He is the completely *Other*.[16] Everything material in our world depends on something outside itself, but God has no need of anything outside of himself. He is totally happy in himself.[17] He knows all things outside of himself by knowing himself alone.[18] God knows and sees all things by understanding himself alone. He needs one idea: himself. His understanding is himself alone. His understanding or idea of himself is perfect, and is the exact same thing as himself. This is the ultimate act of intelligence, to understand all by one simple gaze. He is perfectly one with himself.

14. *SCG* II.16; *ST* I, q. 44; q. 47, a. 1c.

15. *SCG* I.22, 42, 43; *ST*, I, q. 3, 7, 11; q. 25, aa. 2–3.

16. Zizioulas, *Communion and Otherness*, 13–98.

17. *SCG* I.101; *ST* I, q. 26.

18. *SCG* I.45–59; *ST* I, q. 14; Aquinas, *Truth*, vol. I, q. II.

A New Angle on Angels

Yet in this cosmology, there is still a gap. Human beings are created material beings who have an immaterial intellect, and God is an Uncreated Immaterial Being who is Intellect Itself. The question naturally arises as to whether it is possible that there are created immaterial beings who know in a manner different from human beings but more closely to the manner in which God knows. Human knowledge moves from the particular to the general; it is discursive and sequential, properties that seem natural and even necessary for a material being. God's knowledge does not require time or sequence. God knows all things outside of himself by simply knowing himself. God's knowledge is the highest form of knowledge because it requires nothing outside itself. It is interiority writ large, depending only on itself for knowledge.

Can there be such beings? Consider that the actual act of *understanding itself* is independent of matter. In our deepest thoughts, we all know this is true. We can simply *understand* or *know*. So, above humans, it is possible to think of a pure act of understanding. This provides a rational base for what Christians call angels.[19] Angels are pure intellects, having no body (matter).[20] They do not depend on anything created outside of themselves for understanding. They know things by knowing themselves and the ideas put in them by God at their creation. So, their understanding of things is drawn purely from inside themselves. They have what is known as an intuitive (as opposed to a rational) intellect.

Angelic knowledge, or an intuitive intellect, is best understood by grasping a principle Thomas Aquinas stated in his reformulation of ancient philosophy, "the lowest of the highest things, always conjoin to the principles of secondary things."[21] In other words, the superior nature in its lowest perfection touches an inferior nature in its highest perfection. Or, conversely, that classes of entities lower on the hierarchy approximate the lower entities

19. Blanchette, *Perfection of the Universe*, 275–80. Blanchette maintains that St. Thomas holds to three ways of proving the possibility of the existence of angels by reason: substance as ontologically prior to corporeity, the order of the universe, and from the nature of intelligence.

20. For the entire following discussion of angels and their knowledge, see *SCG* II.49, 50, 96–101; *ST* I, q. 50, a. 1–2; I, q. 54–58; Aquinas, *Truth*, vol. I, q. 8.

21. Aquinas, *Commentary on the Divine Names of Blessed Dionysius* VII.4.

of a higher class. Recall heliotropism, the attraction of plants to light. It is similar to what we experience when we and animals sense something. Plants are lower than animals. But at their best, they approximate the behavior of animals. That which is lower will reach to that which is immediately above it. Sons do this in imitation of their fathers, daughters their mothers. Every amateur athlete wants to be like the professional. Since we are one step lower than angels, all of us likewise have a remote insight into how they know, but we don't realize it. We experience a faint reflection of intuitive angelic knowledge when we have an "Aha" experience. When you were in high school or college studying for a test, perhaps you spent hours or days trying to figure something out. After going over many examples in your mind, you suddenly had a flash of insight and understood the whole problem. This understanding clarifies all the examples you were going through and makes sense of them all together. You see them in light of the one big picture. Once the general idea of triangle is understood – a figure with three sides whose interior angles total two right angels – all types of triangles such as equilateral, isosceles, and scalene are implicitly understood.

This is a remote insight into angelic knowing. Angels know that big picture from the moment of their existence and understand everything in it. Upon hearing the word "mom," you will likely, as most people do, think of your particular mother. Experiencing your mother and other moms as you grow leads to a general idea of what a mother is when you are an adult. Your mother may be better than others in certain things, but others may be better than yours in other things. In experiencing many mothers, we gain an image of an ideal mother. Angelic knowledge is the reverse; it proceeds from the general to the specific. Suppose God wished an angel to know of mothers. At the moment of creation, God places the perfect idea of mother in the angelic mind. Instantly, without effort, the angel knows all possible instances of mother, and better than you know your own mother. Once the general idea is understood, all the examples are clarified and enlightened. This manner of going from the idea to the particular is the proper way an intellect should work.[22] Thomas Aquinas says that humans have a defective intellect when understood from the larger, more expansive idea of intelligence.[23] Yet it is the

22. *SCG* III.81; *ST* I, q. 89, a. 1c.

23. *SCG* I.57; *ST* I, q. 58, a. 3c; II, q. 49, a. 5, ad. 2.

type of intellect best for us as humans who exist in a world where we rely on material things to begin to know.[24] Our type of intellect learns from individual sensible objects (the particular thing) and concludes to the idea. The angel's is called an intuitive intellect, going from the idea to all the particulars.

The greater the ability of the angel to do this, the higher up and more powerful he is. To understand this last point, let's think of four types of mammals: dogs, cats, cows, and horses. Each of these can be divided into many breeds: dogs can be Airedale, Beagle, or Poodle; cats can be Siamese, Persian, or Calico; cattle can be Holstein, Angus, or Hereford); and horses can be Belgian, Thoroughbred, or Quarter Horse). Note also that cats and dogs are carnivores (eat meat), while cattle and horses are herbivores (eat plants). Let's think now of different possible angels knowing animals as an example. One angel would be given the idea of dog, cat, cattle, and horse and would know each type of the above breeds and all others in the respective category from the general idea of dog, cat, cattle, or horse. Another angel with a more powerful mind might know carnivore and herbivore and know all possibilities from these two ideas. By carnivore it would know dogs, cats, as well as bears, weasels, seals, and any other meat-eating mammals. By herbivore it would know cattle, horses, elephants, and all other plant-eating mammals. Another possible angel might know mammal. From this it would immediately know not only dogs, cats, cattle, and horses, but also bears, weasels, seals, horses, elephants, primates, rodents, and every other possible type of mammal. It would have to have the idea of reptile or fish (nonmammals) to know these, however. Yet another angel might know animal in general and know all possible types of mammals, reptiles, fish, insects, and the like from this one idea. So, the more powerful the intuitive mind, the fewer ideas it needs to understand all things. We find this reflected at a human level in that more intelligent people need fewer examples to learn, while the less intelligent need many.

The knowledge that angels have is similar to God's in that its intuitive nature is not discursive or sequential, but like humans' in that the ideas themselves did not originate in the angels themselves because the angels are created. In the Christian tradition, angelic intellects then stand as immateri-

24. *SCG* III.81; *ST* I, q. 89, a. 1c.

al created intellects between the Uncreated Intellect of God and the created material intellect of human beings.

An Upscale Universe

Prologue

Everything discussed so far has drawn on the resources of science and philosophy. Their methods of observation, reasonable inference, and experimental control have afforded a much richer storehouse of knowledge than many modern people realize. But we may have also reached a limit as to what human reason can tell us. The idea of limits to reason is essential to our hierarchical cosmology, but the problem today is not that people have too much confidence in reason, but that they have too little. Still, even with the expanded view of reason that I am advocating, there are limitations simply because our reasoning is so tied to the material realm.

In the following discussion, I must use a mixture of both knowledge accessible to the "unaided human intellect" and revealed (theological) knowledge. When distinguishing between what can and cannot be known by the human intellect, one must bear in mind that there is not and never has been such a thing as humans not aided by God's grace, to some degree.[25, 26] In the beginning, God created man with a supernatural vocation to be his children by union with his Son; that was always his intent.[27] So man has always had a supernatural end in God, and as such, his mind has been aided by grace. Even after the Fall of Adam, man has to an extent been aided by God's grace; this is particularly evident in the Old Testament history of the people of Israel.[28] So, in the higher musings of pre-Christian thinkers – even those not of Israel – God was most certainly still helping them by grace to some degree.

In addition, ancient philosophers made certain mistakes, especially as

25. De LuBac, *Mystery of the Supernatural*, is an excellent work regarding the idea that a "pure nature" never existed. Man's end was always in view of and in union with Christ. See also Popovich, *Man and the God-Man*.

26. I do not advocate here that it is not possible to know that certain things can and cannot be known by reason, but merely that, at the upper limits of reason, it is difficult at times to make such distinctions.

27. Regarding Adam, see the discussions in chapters 10 and 12 in this volume.

28. *Catechism of the Catholic Church*, 410.

they approached the limits of rational inquiry, as the subject matter became too difficult. And as discussed in chapter 4, there are certain revealed doctrines that can in principle be known by reason but are revealed to help our weak minds clarify them. I partly draw on medieval thinkers, who used this type of revealed knowledge to clean up the errors of the ancients.

The remainder of this chapter serves as a transition to Part III, which concerns knowledge by revelation. Therefore many things that follow are in theory possibly understood by reason, but owing to the condition of post-Fall man and his weakened intellect, these things need to be corrected and specified by Christian Revelation.

Discussion

All this talk of angels, intellects, and God comes from a cosmology based on a more liberal view of the human intellect, a view that sees a cosmos with meaning, purpose, ends, and ascending structure.[29] The limited, more restrictive, and conservative view of the intellect will have none of this. The putative reason is that knowledge must be based on empirical evidence. The dispute between these two worldviews, then, seems to rest on what counts as evidence. Scientistic materialists do not believe that nature has any end toward which it is tending. For them, to believe in purpose or ends is simply the fanciful attribution of human actions to nonhuman nature and is completely unjustified. It seems like a blatant anthropomorphism to attribute to (nonhuman) nature what transpires in human life. The fact that human beings make willful choices to do X rather than Y, to use intelligence to select for certain outcomes, to work toward ends with a sense of purpose—all that is perfectly normal in human life—does not justify the claim that nature works toward ends. But a moment's reflection shows that this is exactly what Darwin did in *Origin of the Species* in 1859. He observed pigeon breeders selecting for certain outcomes, and he then transferred the idea to nature. This is how he came up with natural selection. The question of whether his idea was justified in the final analysis is distinct from whether the transference from human selection to natural selection was reasonable in the first place.

29. The discussion in this chapter regarding the order and providence of creation derives in part from the analysis of St. Thomas's thought on these subjects given in Blanchette, *Perfection of the Universe*, 221–319.

The cosmos advocated here has three types of perfection (primary, secondary, and tertiary) and two orders of perfection (perfect and imperfect).[30] Can we apply this to the universe as a whole? Thomas Aquinas says that the primary perfection of the universe is the matter (taken in the classical sense of a pure potentiality to be material), and the basic elements that constitute the universe. In his day, the elements were earth, air, fire, and water; in ours, it would be the periodic table, the basic "stuff" of the cosmos. This is the ground or base "stuff" of material creation of which all else is made or needs. The secondary perfection of the universe is constituted by the nonliving things such as chemical compounds, planets, stars, and galaxies, but particularly plants and animals. Thus elemental inanimate being (primary perfection) is ordered to aggregate inanimate beings and nonintelligent living things (secondary perfection). The tertiary perfection is the intellectual substances, particularly humans as they are the end of material change, but also angels and then finally God.[31]

In a more restricted manner, we can apply these three perfections only to living things. Within the material cosmos, man again is the tertiary perfection (and beyond matter, angels and finally God).[32] Animals are the secondary perfection. Plants are the primary perfection since they are the base for the rest of material life. Either way, in the material cosmos, beings constituting the secondary perfection are ordered to the tertiary perfection of the human soul, as this is where matter finds its ultimate rest. It is therefore the drive toward intelligence that drives and guides the whole process of the material cosmos immediately and finally to God.

Such a universe would certainly make little sense unless it was a created

30. See Blanchette, *Perfection of the Universe*, 146–54, 228–63, for a synthesis of all the relevant citations from St. Thomas on this topic in this paragraph.

31. Regarding God as tertiary end, see *ST* I, q. 44, a. 4c. Regarding angels as a type of tertiary end, I would argue two points. First, insofar as they are the epitome of created intellectual life, they are a type of "cause" of lower intellects, by passing down their perfections of intellectual light to these lower intellects (man). Second, they order and govern all material creatures (*ST* I, q. 110, a. 1c). As St. Thomas argues, the perfection of the universe requires purely intellectual creatures (*ST* I, q. 50, a. 1c).

32. Within living things, this idea that plants, animals, and men represent the primary, secondary, and tertiary perfections of the material life is implicit in St. Thomas's discussion of hierarchy in *SCG* IV.11, discussed in chapter 5 of this book. Man unites all lower material creatures in himself (tertiary perfection), animals are the first level of knowing beings (of the particular), and plants order inorganic matter to something higher. See also Sheen, *God and Intelligence*, 122–24.

one. Creation is the doctrine, a core Christian one, that God created everything; specifically, that God alone brought things into existence from no previously existing substrate.[33] Bringing something about from a previous substrate, like a pot from clay, is termed *making*, as opposed to creating, a thing. Creatures can make things; only God can call something to be from *absolutely nothing*, or create things.[34] This does not mean the creature is fashioned out of nothing (as a substrate), but that God needs no substrate to bring something into existence. He who is "I AM" can say, "let it be," as he is of infinite power. Only he who is of infinite power can bridge the gap between nothingness (no being) and being. So God alone creates. And according to Christian tradition, creation from nothing is not ascertainable by reason per se because reason is ambiguous on this issue; it understands what creation is but cannot discern by its own power whether or not it occurred, the Big Bang notwithstanding.[35] Creation is literally from nothing, no matter, energy, particles, space-time continuum, *nothing*. The singularity before the Big Bang was a real thing, albeit much different than what we know at present.

The God who creates everything from nothing is intellectual and personal in his nature. Because he is infinite perfection and is in need of no creatures for his existence, he is absolutely free to create or not to create.[36] Given the fact that he has created, however, is it possible to ascertain his motive or plan of creation? The Christian tradition has given an unequivocal answer. God's motive for creating is simply his goodness and the communication of his goodness to creation that allows it to participate in his life and being.[37] Such participation is a kind of life and union with himself, who is the end of all things.[38] Now, as God is intellectual and personal, so the ultimate good of all things is somehow intellectual and personal.[39] God creates all things as a reflection of his own divine nature.[40] Each thing in its limited way reflects

33. *SCG* II.15–16; *ST* I, q. 44; I, q. 45, a. 1c, 2c, 5c.

34. *ST* I, q. 45, a. 5, c.

35. *SCG* II.31–38; *ST* I, q. 46, a. 1c, 2c.

36. *SCG* I.81; *ST* I, q. 19, a. 3c.

37. *Catechism of the Catholic Church*, 293–49; *SCG* I.81.

38. *SCG* III.16–21; *ST* I, q. 44, a. 1c, 4c.

39. *SCG* II.46, III.25; *ST*I, q. 65, a. 2c.

40. *ST* I, q. 44, a. 2c.

God's nature to a greater or lesser degree, but the greatest is the universe as a whole, the world of angels, humans, animals, plants, and nonliving things. God first desires the perfection (good) of the whole universe, the tertiary perfection of all things taken as an ordered whole.[41] The infinity of God is best reflected in a large diversity of finite lesser and greater creatures than in a large, undifferentiated homogeneity.[42] This universe may not be created as the best of all possible worlds in an absolute sense, but it is the best for the particular desire of his will.[43]

To speak of God's desires carries certain dangers if it is taken too literally, because it is easy to attribute to God human-like feelings. In speaking of God's desires, we are indicating the end or purpose of creation. God desires the good of the whole universe because the whole is greater than the sum of its parts.[44] This he loves above all created things. God loving the whole creation implies that he loves each part, even the nonintellectual creatures.[45] He wishes their good. This good finds its consummation in the Good of God himself. But God also desires the perfection and good of each of the parts of creation. The incredible diversity of the natural world is all good, but the parts exist in an ascending order of perfection, which climax in the intellectual order (humans and angels) since they are most like God.[46] Because angels and humans are ultimately of an intellectual substance, like God they can choose ends for themselves through free will. The choice of their good, their ultimate good, coincides in having the same end intended, God himself.[47] The intellectual parts of the cosmos, humans and angels, are directly

41. Blanchette, *Perfection of the Universe*, 97–98; *SCG* II.44; *ST* I, q. 49, a. 3c.

42. Blanchette, *Perfection of the Universe*, 139–40; *ST* I, q. 47, a. 1c.

43. Blanchette, *Perfection of the Universe*, 98–103; *ST* I, q. 25, a. 6, ad. 3; Aquinas, *De Potentia*, q. 5, a. 1, ad. 14.

44. Blanchette, *Perfection of the Universe*, 317–18; *SCG* III.64; *ST* I, q. 65, a. 2c; Aquinas, *De Caritatis*, a. 7, arg. 5, and ad. 5. Quoting arg. 5: "Moreover, God is loved out of charity. Therefore that ought to be more loved out of charity which is especially loved by Him. But among all created things, the good of the universe, in which all things are included, is especially loved by God. Therefore all things are to be loved in charity." Quoting ad. 5: "It must be said that there is contained, as a principle, in the good of the universe, rational nature which is capable of beatitude, and to which all other creatures are ordered. According to this, it is fitting both for God and for us to especially love the good of the universe out of charity."

45. *SCG* I.91, II. 45; *ST* I, q. 20, a. 2c; I, q. 44, a. 4c; I, q. 47, a. 2c; I, q. 65, a. 2c; I, q. 103, a. 1c.

46. *ST* I, q. 65, a. 2c.

47. *SCG* IV.55.

intended by God because they can directly desire him as their end, through their intellect and free will.[48] The individuals of a nonintellectual species, who cannot directly choose God, are intended by God only to support the species or to somehow serve humans.[49] Because they have in common with humans a material body, they find their end and completion in the human being who is intellectual as well.[50]

God is good not only in himself but also through his providence. He shows his goodness and love to creatures by providing for them.[51] He gives them both a being reflective of his own being, and he gives them a share in his providence toward other creatures.[52] His own goodness is manifested more in the being of creatures and the providential care they show others rather than simply in intimation of his being by itself. He allows creatures to participate in his providence by communicating his goodness to creatures through this hierarchy in a manner analogous to how Leonardo da Vinci communicated his good idea of the Mona Lisa to the canvas. It is providence through a governance of the higher to the lower.[53] A large family is an even better example. In families with many children, the parents might have the older children help in taking care of the younger. It is the parents who determine and ultimately provide for all the needs of the children, but their providence is acted out through the older children helping with the younger. The younger are no less cared for; it is simply the agency of caring that differs. That which is higher has a greater share in governance or providence.[54] The parents have the greatest share and give the oldest sibling more responsibility for the rest. The younger children have a lesser level of responsibility. As the parents can direct any of their children without intermediaries, so can God do so to his lesser creatures.

48. *SCG* III.112, 113; Aquinas, *Truth*, vol. I, q. 5, a. 3c.

49. Blanchette, *Perfection of the Universe*, 313; *SCG* III.112, 113; Aquinas, *Truth*, vol. I, q. 5, a. 3c.

50. Aquinas, *Truth*, vol. I, q. 2, a. 2c; *SCG* II.46.

51. *ST* I, q. 22, a. 3c; Aquinas, *Truth*, vol. I, q. 5, a. 8.

52. Aquinas, *Truth*, vol. I, q. 8, a. 8c; *SCG* III.77–79; *ST* I, q. 103, a. 6c. See also Dionysius the Areopagite, "Celestial Hierarchy." The entire work is in part an elegant argument for the idea of divine providence governing lower being through the agency of higher beings.

53. Aquinas, *Truth*, vol. I, q. 8, a. 8c; *SCG* III.77–79; *ST* I, q. 103, a. 6c; Dionysius the Areopagite, "Celestial Hierarchy."

54. Aquinas, *Truth*, vol. I, q. 8, a. 8c; *SCG* III.77–79; *ST* I, q. 103, a. 6c; Dionysius the Areopagite, "Celestial Hierarchy"; Aquinas, *De Potentia*, q. 3, art. 7c.

This is also a basis for miracles. Far from being irrational, miracles are simply the bypassing of the natural order by the very Maker of the order.[55] While impenetrable to our intellects, for God it is no more miraculous than a mother caring directly for the youngest child instead of relying on the older children. And in the context of understanding in the Hierarchy of Being, a miracle does not override the laws of nature; rather, it just inserts a little extra order into the universe.

God provides providentially for his creatures but carries out this providence – governance and the ordering of creation, gifts for his creatures – through the hierarchy in both its immaterial and material aspects. The Hierarchy of Being from highest to lowest (angels, men, animals, plants, and minerals) is internally arranged according to the three types of perfection, such that God provides for all things from the highest to the lowest.[56] Each creature communicates to that directly below it, as it is most proximate to it in likeness and most fittingly prepares the higher things for the creature immediately below.[57] To the highest angel, he gives most directly of himself, this creature communicates good things to that angel next lower than himself in the hierarchy, and so on down the hierarchy. The gifts of God come to lower creatures through the higher creatures – the perfect order. In reverse order, all things return to God through this hierarchy as well, not the least of which are the prayers of his intellectual creatures. Thus God is actively drawing all things to himself through this same hierarchy of being according to the imperfect order, where things find their completion in that above them.

Intellectual creatures have a special role in this because they, like God, can know ends. They have a special role in providence in that through their free wills they can order things in a superior manner and cooperate directly in divine providence. As the farmer plants a seed in the ground and waters it, he cooperates in divine providence. As God created the nature of the seed, the ground, and the water and ordered these for the human good of food production through the tending of the farmer, so does he use intellectual creatures to tend the cosmos as a whole.[58]

55. *SCG* II.98–101; *ST* I, q. 105, a. 6c, 7c.

56. Aquinas, *Commentary on the Divine Names of Blessed Dionysius* VII.4.

57. *SCG* III.79–81; *ST* I, q. 106, a. 3; I, q. 110, a. 1.

58. Blanchette, *Perfection of the Universe*, 315–16; Aquinas, *Truth*, vol. I, q. 5, a. 8, ad.4.

God providentially provides for all the needs of his greater and lesser creatures but executes this in a higher manner through intellectual creatures, both angels and humans. Angels are the conductors of creation as in an orchestra. They maintain order in the material universe and coordinate its laws. If humans with their limited understating can manipulate matter, so much more should the far greater angelic mind be able to manipulate the material universe.[59] And one should not think as a result there are no such things as "natural" laws because they are directed by something above matter. The carpenter, an intellectual agent, directs the hammer to its end in the building of the house. The carpenter is clearly a greater being than his tool, but both carpenter and hammer can truly be said to be a cause of the house. They are simply different levels of cause, the one intellectual, the other mechanical. Likewise, so is the angel to the laws of nature. Angels and the laws of matter are simply at a different levels of causality, the angel intellectual and the laws of nature mechanical.

Humans have a special role through law, which can be defined as the rational governance of humans and their societies.[60] Through law, human beings order the world around them in an efficient way to a greater end for society as a whole. This ordering of the nonintellectual world provides the basis for a balanced understanding of the stewardship of creation. The natural world, in and of itself, cannot possibly support the complexity and size of human activities and societies, but through the study of nature and technology, humans can put in place a more efficient system to aid nature in the service of humans.[61] The key to this is "to aid," not destroy, nature. Hence it is perfectly just to grow large amounts of food at the expense – to a degree – of other animals and plants. This reordering of nature must be done with prudence and a respect for the natural system and its natural laws of function, leaving a reasonable amount of wild areas to be preserved for the benefit of the greater whole of nature. This, in turn, allows humans to learn from and contemplate the natural world.

In this system, the human being occupies a special and central place.

59. Aquinas, *De Potentia*, q. 6, a. 3c.

60. *SCG* III.111–19; Blanchette, *Perfection of the Universe*, 282–85.

61. Blanchette, *Perfection of the Universe*, 283; Aquinas, *Commentary on Aristotle's Nicomachean Ethics*, lec. I.1.1.

Having a material nature like creatures below them and an intellectual nature like angels above, humans are a point of integration for the whole of creation.[62] While not the absolutely highest creature – angels occupy this place – humans have in a sense the greatest capacity for integration.[63] Material creation finds its rest and completion in an intellectual creature, the human being.[64] Human interaction with nature differs from that of any other material creature precisely because of man's intellectual and volitional powers. From the angelic standpoint, humans are a point of union because, like them, they have an intellect.[65] Further, angels direct the laws of the material universe, and the end of the material universe is in humans.[66] Reality lower than humans finds its end in humans, and the angelic world above men order the material universe toward this end in man. Therefore creation is ordered for the production of a certain amount of humans, because they are the locus of union for all of reality.[67]

The end of all of creation is the Creator.[68] Once again at the juncture of reason and revelation, we can make a few general summaries regarding the providence of God. Because God is providential, he has concern and care for his creation. Given he creates – and insofar as he creates, he is absolutely free to do so or not, as he has no necessity for anything created – he must supply for the needs of his creature.[69] For instance, because of his perfect justice, if he creates a certain organism having the need for food, he must give it the means to procure food. Thus God desires the good for his creatures – he loves them.[70] His desire is to enter into a type of providential care for them, constituting a type of community. Now, as stated previously, God is intellectual. Intellectual beings are personal.[71] By analogy, God is a personal being.[72]

62. Blanchette, *Perfection of the Universe*, 280–82; *SCG* IV.55, III.25.

63. Blanchette, *Perfection of the Universe*, 281; *SCG* IV.55, III.25.

64. *SCG* IV.97, III.81; Aquinas, *Light of Faith*, chap. 171.

65. *SCG* IV.55, III.25.

66. *ST* I, q. 110, a. 1c; Aquinas, *De Potentia,* q. 3, a. 10, ad. 4.

67. Blanchette, *Perfection of the Universe*, 260–62, 281–83; Aquinas, *De Potentia*, q. 3, a. 10, ad. 4; q. 5, a. 5c.

68. *ST* I, q. 44, a. 4; I, q. 103, a. 2.

69. *SCG* I.81–83; *ST* I, q. 21, a. 1c, ad. 3.

70. *SCG* I.91; *ST* I, q. 20, a. 3c.

71. *ST* I, q. 29, a. 1c.

72. *ST* I, q. 29, a. 3c. Here one is at the limits of reason. The Trinity of Three Persons in God is

Beings who are personal and of an intellectual nature desire to communicate and enter into communal relationships with other such beings. Extending this to God, we can loosely claim – by analogy again – that God desires a bond with his creatures, which is at the same time a type of community, or society, constituted by this.[73] This bond and community with creatures, glimpsed at by reason, are in no way similar to that known by revelation, to be discussed in Part III. Recall that God is infinitely above his creatures and creation. From a rational standpoint, this cannot be bridged. So the love and community between God and creatures constitute a just and caring stewardship over his estate (and personal from that standpoint), not the sharing by the creature in the very Personal Life of God in the most intimate depths of the divine nature, known by revelation.

This society is a perfect unified whole, the ultimate tertiary perfection. The universe – or the hierarchy as we presented it – is thus a dynamic structure precisely for the communication and personal friendship of intellectual beings to this end.[74] It is a rational structure where God communicates his

---

revealed knowledge, above reason. But because intellectual natures are personal, one may analogously apply this to God and conclude he has a personal aspect about him using reason. In this citation, St. Thomas answers using in part the revealed understating of the Trinity, and in part the rational idea of a "subsistent individual of a rational nature."

73. *ST* I, q. 22, a. 1–4; I, q. 103, a. 1–8; I, q. 104, a. 1–4. Question 22 regards providence, and questions 103–4, governance. The idea of an ordered universe (providence and governance) of creatures leads one to the idea of a society working together for a common end.

74. It may also be useful to quote in full Aquinas's summary of the providence and governance of things in *SCG* III.83:

> Now, from all the things that have been pointed out we may gather that, as far as the planning and order to be imposed on things is concerned, God disposes everything to Himself. And so, in his commentary on the text of Job 34:13 ("What other hath He appointed over the earth") Gregory says: "Indeed, He Who created the world by Himself rules it by Himself." And Boethius says, in *Consolation of Philosophy III*, "God disposes all things of Himself alone."
>
> But, in regard to the execution, He orders the lower things through the higher ones, and the bodily things through the spiritual ones. Hence, Gregory says, in his fourth Dialogue: "in this visible world nothing can be ordered except through an invisible creature." And the lower spirits are ordered through the higher ones. Hence, Dionysius says that "the heavenly intellectual essences first give divine illumination to themselves, and then bring us manifestations which are above us." Also, the lower bodies are ordered by the higher ones. Hence, Dionysius says that "the sun brings generation to visible bodies, and stimulates them to life itself, and nourishes, increases, and perfects, cleanses and renews."
>
> Moreover, Augustine speaks on all these points together, in book II of *The Trinity*: "As the grosser and lower bodies are ruled in a certain order by means of the subtler and more powerful

goodness to them, in order to draw them to himself. And it is precisely this hierarchical order of three types of perfection, garnered from our experience of the concrete world about us, that is the vehicle for this union.[75] As St. Thomas states, reality is ordered by God for the facilitation of a type of prayer that is the means of union with God: contemplation.[76] He notes that man is particularly suited to this type of action.[77] Once reality is properly ordered about man for contemplation, which as an intellectual action is purely interior, man needs nothing else to accomplish it.[78]

This Hierarchy of Being begins with nonliving things, whose movement is a transfer of external motion. The most primitive living beings are the plants, where a transient interior action produces growth and reproduction. Then animals are defined by the life of sense and knowledge of the individual. This action terminates interiorly and begins to resemble a type of union with what is known. Above animals there are humans with a rational intellect. While humans still depend on that which is outside of them to begin to think, the actual understanding is something interior. Understanding is a purely interior act, and its product, or completion, is the thing understood, the image of oneself. In this, we begin to see an intellectual production of another.

It is the intellect that allows one to exist as a person, a being fundamentally ordered to another in relationships, friendship, and union. This act is further intensified with the intuitive intellect of angels, who need nothing exterior in order to understand, but who do need a Creator to exist. The final perfection of life is in God, who is his own cause. In God, the thing understood is exactly the same as his infinite being: understanding and knowledge are the same as his Being.

The superiority of a worldview incorporating a Hierarchy of Being, over a reductionistic worldview, lies in its power to make common human experience and esoteric scientific knowledge more of a seamless garment. The

---

ones, so are all bodies by means of the rational spirit of life, and also the sinful rational spirit of the sinner by the righteous rational spirit."

75. Aquinas, *Commentary on the Divine Names of Blessed Dionysius* VII.4.

76. Aquinas, *Commentary on the Divine Names of Blessed Dionysius* VII.1–2.

77. *SCG* III.37.

78. That is, he needs nothing else in the material world to accomplish this. Contemplation, however, is impossible for man by himself—he needs God's grace to do it.

data of science in a materialist universe stand in tension with common experience, and to some degree militate against it. The scientific materialist inevitably ends up claiming that scientific knowledge trumps everyday human experience. The scientist must therefore be believed on faith, because the common human experience of all beings in reality contradicts what the scientist claims.

Conversely, a hierarchical and intelligence-centered worldview correlates with our common experience and thus makes science more intuitively plausible. If proponents of scientism relinquished a materialistic reductionism, one wonders whether they might find greater understanding and acceptance of science among the general public. In any case, I have argued that a rational analysis of scientific procedure shows that it is based on notions of common sense and common experience. If that is true, it places the scientist in an odd position at best. To claim that common experience is illegitimate and that only science is to be trusted is to kick the foundation out from under the science that claims to be the final authority. We must make a choice between a view of knowledge that is limited and restricted to matter and one that is liberal and open-minded, one that insists that matter is necessary as a substrate of knowledge in human beings but that also transcends the material world.

This choice is critically important for the discussion in Part III of the revealed nature of the universe. For it is in the created universe that God first speaks to man, laying the foundation for the rational acceptance of his revelation of his inner life and the order that proceeds from it. In the end, the universe accessible to our mind is the structure left from Eden, the vestige of what once was. It exists presently as an image (Part III) and in the end is to fully come. To understand this in its deepest sense, man needs to humbly submit himself to the God who reveals, found to be reasonable by observing the world about us. It is no small matter to choose between a universe closed to all but matter and a more liberal one open to higher things. We need a home field. As stated by St. Thomas in his *Summa contra Gentiles,*

> The consideration of creatures is also necessary to set aside errors, not only for the building up of truth, but also for the destruction of errors. For errors about creatures sometimes lead one astray from the truth of faith, so far as errors are inconsistent with true knowledge of God … Through ignorance of the na-

ture of things, and consequently, of his own place in the order of the universe, this rational creature, man, who by faith is led to God as his last end, believes that he is subject to other creatures to which he is in fact superior. Such is evidently the case with those who subject human wills to the stars [or I might add "genes" according to our modern lingo] . . . It is therefore evident that the opinion is false of those who asserted that it made no difference to the truth of faith what anyone holds about creatures, so long as we think rightly about God. For an error concerning creatures, by subjecting them to causes other than God, spills over into false opinion about God, and takes men's mind away from Him, to whom faith seeks to lead them.[79]

79. *SCG* II.3.1, 5, 6.

Part III

THE IMAGE OF ETERNITY

9 THE END OF HUMAN LIFE

The Holy Trinity

In a materialist worldview, it is impossible to say why human beings exist. It is impossible to say why there is a universe at all, or why there is something rather than nothing. Evolutionary developments might explain the appearance of the human race on earth, but such a historical retelling does not offer any end, any purpose, or any "higher" cause. In our new cosmology, the answer is not ambiguous at all, even if it is still hard to fathom. Just as we can know that a number called googol does exist, even though we cannot fathom its true size, so we can know our end as human beings, even if its total significance seems to be beyond our grasp. The end of our life is love, pure and simple.

The Human Family: The Training Ground for Love

When my parents bought our home in southern Indiana in my early teens, it was part of an old run-down farm. The house needed major remodeling, and there were many outbuildings and old fence rows overgrown with wild roses and young trees. Not too long after we moved in, my dad set me the task of tearing out these eyesores. I worked at it all day with tractor, axe, and chainsaw. When my dad arrived home from work, he was quite impressed, and commented on how much progress I had made. "Good job," he said. On one occasion, after I worked all day in the hot sun mowing the fields, I went outside after dinner to look at what I had accomplished. The rays of the sun were stretching out, and the day was cooling. My dad came by and said, "Good job."

Having responsibilities was nothing new for me at the time. From the time I could reasonably walk and move about the yard, I had jobs to do. My first was simply picking up sticks in a little wagon. These responsibilities progressed to taking care of chickens and my dog, mowing the yard and eventually the whole place, and cutting down trees and wood for the fireplace. During high school, I took care of most of the responsibilities outdoors on the thirty acres. Over time, I was given a progression of things that I was responsible for as well: I received my dog for my twelfth birthday, a shotgun for my thirteenth, a rifle for my fourteenth. During these years I asked, as any kid would do, why I had to do some of these things. The answer always given was that dad had to go to work to make money, and mom did as well (she started teaching high school when I was eleven), and mom had to keep the house, while dad also had to remodel the house; therefore I had to take care of the outside. Everyone in the family had some responsibility for the family. This developed in me a great feeling of responsibility to something greater. As a matter of fact, perhaps the greatest impediment to doing anything stupid in my teen years was worry of embarrassing the family. I think my experience was similar to other boys my age in that area as well. It may come as a surprise to people nowadays, but my high school had a gun club, where kids would shoot after school. Gun clubs were common in American high schools at the time. Students could leave guns in their cars or put them in the locker if they were kept in a case. Nothing bad ever happened. I think the reason was that most of the teenaged boys had similar levels of responsibility, came from intact families, and were aware that their actions reflected on their families. And their dads would not let them get away with anything foolish.

Thus from my earliest memories, dad gave me something that I consider the greatest value in my life, the reflexive desire to serve a greater whole. In this case, it was the family. My dad was the ultimate handyman. He could fix and do anything mechanical or skilled, and do it well. I grew up watching him do such things. Hearing him say "Good job" meant more than any amount of money I could have been paid. I had earned the respect of a master craftsman who also happened to be my dad. It was the affirmation by my own father that what I did was good. It was a job well done. Aristotle said that if you want to do something well, watch a person who is good at it. And in a small sense, I had served my family well.

Thomas Aquinas says that devotion to the family is the basis for devotion to God; it instills in one a natural reflex to be devoted to a higher thing.[1] These experiences I have just narrated paved the way for another great epiphany in an understanding of my Catholic faith, equal to that of reading Garrigou-Lagrange when I first entered college. At twenty-five, I read the complete works of the great Catholic saint and Doctor of the Church, St. John of the Cross, who is among the highest authorities in the Church regarding spiritual (mystical) theology. As one of the greatest poets of Spain, he composed *Romance 2: On the Communication among the Three Persons*. Alluding to the Baptism and Transfiguration of Christ, where the Father calls the Son his "beloved Son with whom I am well pleased" (Mt 3:17, 17:5; Mk 1:11, 9:7; Lk 3:22), John expands on the idea of love:

> In that immense love proceeding from the two, the Father spoke words of great affection to the Son, words of such profound delight, that no one understood them. They were meant for the Son and He alone rejoiced in them. What he heard was this: my Son only your company contents me. And when something pleases me, I love that thing in you. He who resembles you most satisfies me most and he who is like you in nothing will find nothing in Me. I am pleased with you alone, O life of my life! You are the light of my light, the image of my substance, in whom I am well pleased. My son, I will give myself to him who loves you, and I will love him with the same love I have for you because he has loved you, whom I love so.[2]

In these words, I intuitively found a completion to my experiences growing up in Indiana, a revealed analogue for the natural family. If Christ is he with whose company the Father is contented and who the Father is "pleased

1. *ST* II-II, q. 101.

2. John of the Cross, "Romances," 2.

with *alone*," yet we are told that he is our Father as well, then our end somehow must consist in becoming that which he loves (his Son) in some sense. We must be literally called to become Christ-like so that God can see only "his beloved Son, in whom he is well pleased," while at the same time we maintain our individuality. Catholic doctrine states that God is infinite, and hence happy in and by himself, [3] and yet condescends to his creatures. Human beings in turn are called to be God-like through Christ. This process of becoming God-like is a fundamental ancient Christian teaching that is termed deification, divinization, or, in the East, theosis.[4]

To the degree that the inner life (Father, Son, Holy Spirit) of God has been revealed to us, we can ascertain the highest purpose of creation. God's actions, those of a Being who is perfectly simple and one, are, with appropriate qualifications, the same toward his creatures as they are in the inner life of the Three Persons. God as the highest reality and the highest end of creatures sets the stage for the revealed structure of the universe, the role of which is to a greater or lesser degree to mediate this union of creatures with their Creator in Christ. Christ, true God and true man, conveys the inner life of the Trinity to creatures united to him in his mystical body, the Church. The Eucharist, his sacred body and blood, and therefore Christ himself, is the highest means of accomplishing that union. The Church is to bring forth the Eucharist in the liturgy (the Mass). This new society constituting the Church is organized for the liturgy and built around it to convey this Trinitarian life to creatures. As we will see later, the structure of the liturgy (or worship) is that toward which the Church is organized and, like the Church, reality as a whole is ultimately liturgical. All creation is called to mediate this union with God to the degree it can, and the liturgy is the archetype or model of this union of all things in Christ. The Church, the mystical body of Christ, thus becomes the revealed archetype, the ultimate or tertiary perfection of all things by assuming the created universe into it. Its earthly liturgy (the Mass) is the image of eternity because it is a participation in the fullness of the Heavenly Kingdom. From this more sublime vantage point, we can gaze down on the natural Hierarchy of Being, as the creation of God moving toward the Church. The Hierarchy of Being is the vestige of

3. *Catechism of the Catholic Church*, 213; *ST* I, q. 26, a. 1.

4. Arintero, *Mystical Evolution*, vol. 1, 16–41; Nellas, *Deification in Christ*, 15–42.

Eden modeled upon the revealed perfection of creation, the liturgy, which is the image of eternity. So we first discuss the revelation of the structure of the universe from its highest Cause, God the Trinity.

The Divine Family: The Trinitarian God

And thus the glory of the Son was the Father's glory, and the Father possessed all His glory in the Son. As the lover in the beloved, each lived in the other, and the Love that unites them is one with them. Their equal, excellent as the One and the Other; Three Persons, and one Beloved, among all three.

–St. John of the Cross, "Romances"

It [the Trinity] shows us that the very foundation of existence, the foundation of reality, the form of everything because it is its origin, is love, in the sense of interpersonal community. The foundation of being is a community of persons. Some say the foundation of being is matter, others, that it is a spirit, others that it is the one: they are all wrong. The foundation of being is communion.

–Jean Cardinal Daniélou, translated by Giulio Maspero in "Patristic Trinitarian Ontology"

Christian revelation vastly deepens the rational knowledge that God is his own existence as well as the perfection of life and intelligence discussed earlier. God's revelation of himself says that the essence of this Infinite Existence is love in a Trinity of Persons.[5] This is not three Gods but Three Persons in one God: Father, Son, and Holy Spirit, the perfect oneness of interpersonal communion.[6] Any valid approach to understanding the universe from a Catholic perspective must begin with the Trinity, God as Three Persons.[7] The very nature of this one God in Three Persons is love, as the Apostle John refers to God as love (1 Jn 4:8).[8] In this context, this is the same as saying God is the Trinity.[9] For us, then, the all-important first step is to deepen our understanding of love.

5. In addition to the following citations for this section on the Trinity, see Scheeben, *Mysteries of Christianity*, 25–197.

6. *Catechism of the Catholic Church*, 202; Scheeben, *Mysteries of Christianity*, 26.

7. *Catechism of the Catholic Church*, 234.

8. *Catechism of the Catholic Church*, 218–21.

9. Damascene, *Christ the Eternal Tao*, 251; Zizioulas, *Being as Communion*, 46.

A deep insight into God's love is described in the short treatise *On Purgatory* by St. Catherine of Genoa, among the most profound works in the history of the Church. As Catherine describes how the souls in purgatory are being prepared for union with God, she paints a beautiful description of God's love, portraying it as that to which these souls are being conformed:

> They are so contented with the divine dispositions in their regard and with doing all that is pleasing to God in that way which he chooses that they cannot think of themselves, though they may strive to do so. They see nothing but the operation of the divine goodness which is so manifestly bringing them to God that they can reflect neither on their own profit nor on their hurt. Could they do so they would not be in pure charity. They see not that they suffer their pains in consequence of their sins, nor can they for a moment entertain that thought, for should they do so it would be an active imperfection, and that cannot exist where there is no longer the possibility of sin. At that moment of leaving this life they see why they are sent to purgatory, but never again, otherwise they would still retain something private, which has no place there.[10]

This is love in its essence: total concern for the other with no regard for self to the point that even a thought of oneself is impossible ("an active imperfection" to think of oneself), and one cannot even "retain something private." One eminent Romanian Orthodox theologian has encapsulated this idea by stating that in the Trinity there is no "I," only "Thou."[11] Yet love by its very nature implies freedom.[12] Certainly, if we are forced to give ourselves, it is not love; no one wants to be forced into marriage. Ultimately, in its most pure form, love is a *completely free act* of self-gift to the other.[13] And because it is oriented to another, it presupposes persons or personal relationships. So God is a *completely free act of love existing as Three Persons: the Trinity.*[14] But in no way can God's Trinitarian life be known by reason.[15] It lies beyond human rationality. It is like the sun to the eyes, too powerful for

10. Catherine of Genoa, "Treatise on Purgatory," 300.
11. Staniloae, *Theology and the Church*, 88.
12. Scheeben, *Mysteries of Christianity*, 107.
13. Zizioulas, *Being as Communion*, 36–44; Aquinas, *SCG* I.91.
14. Zizioulas, *Being as Communion*, 36–44; *Catechism of the Catholic Church*, 221.
15. *Catechism of the Catholic Church*, 237.

our intellects or that of any creature, even for angels. But once God is known as love, both rational and revealed knowledge can complement and build on each other. How can we discuss this Infinite Being who exists as Three Persons? It will never be possible, even in eternity, to comprehend all that God is, because he is the deepest mystery, the ground and the end of all that exists.[16] Still, what can be known needs to inform and guide all else, since he is the ultimate reality.

St. Thomas says that even a small amount of knowledge of what is higher is more valuable than much knowledge of what is lower.[17] But the higher in reality that one ascends, the more difficult it is to describe; in the case of God, this becomes seemingly impossible, which is why the earliest theologians spoke of the *apophatic* knowledge of God.[18] Apophatic knowledge is the purifying of our understanding of something, by the sequential removal of what it is not.[19] It is knowledge through negation. We know what a living thing is, but since we do not know nonliving things to the same degree, we simply name them "non"-living or "in"-animate. We remove the living aspect of existence in our minds and apply them to nonliving things, such as a rock. We understand that it exists, but it is not alive. Now, the first objects of our minds are material creatures; all our terms in rational discourse are taken from them. By extension, we can apply this negation of knowledge to things above us, "im"-material or "in"-corporeal entities. We understand that they exist but are not bodily. Many of our terms – such as intellect, love, father, beauty – can be applied to God, but they are "contaminated" with the limitations of things as we experience them in their material condition. They are analogous, but not identical, when applied to God.

Applied to the Trinity, we can purify our understanding of Father and Son. What, then, do we ultimately mean when we call God "Father"? Our human reason by itself tells us that God is one simple act of existence. He has no parts.[20] Thinking of our earthly fathers, we know they all have bodies, interests (sports, gardening), habits good and bad, careers, and many other

16. *ST* I, q. 12, a. 7c.
17. *SCG* III.25.
18. *SCG* I.14.
19. *Catechism of the Catholic Church*, 42.
20. *SCG* I.18–27; *ST* I, q. 3.

aspects (or parts) about them. Are these things essential to "father"? Other things have bodies (such as mothers, or rocks, or horses). If a body were the essence of fatherhood, everything having a body would be a father. How about liking baseball or raising tomatoes? Certain people who aren't fathers like baseball and raise tomatoes as well. So if these were the essence of fatherhood, all who liked these things would be fathers. In fact, the only thing common about our human fathers is that they are males and have children. Humanly speaking, these are the two criteria for fatherhood. A human female who has a child is a mother. So is God a male, and does he have a child? Or can we purify this idea further?

Because God is nonphysical, we must remove the idea of sex, male or female.[21] In Genesis, we read that God created humans male and female (Gn 1:27). Both theologically and philosophically, sex is specific to material creatures, both male and female, and is for reproduction. Nonmaterial beings do not have sex, so we can remove that from God. So why not call God father and/or mother? Because we can go one step further. While God is not sexual, there is a specific aspect of being a parent that is embodied in maleness (minus sexuality) that we mean when we refer to parenthood in God as Father. Specifically, a father is he who gives life to and protects a child. Traditional human societies thought of the male parent as the highest provider for his children in the family. Ideally, he gave all good things to his family. Scripture in numerable instances describes God as the giver or provider. Of hundreds of examples, just think of the prayer "Our Father," when it starts, "Give us this day." The male is also the activator of life, a truth evident in modern science, as it is the sperm that actively seeks out the egg, from the female, in fertilization. The egg typically will remain passive until fertilized. So, ultimately, fatherhood refers to a specific type of parenting as that which activates, gives, and protects a child, summed up in a simple word writ large: "Paternity."[22]

"Paternity" totally defines the Father and nothing else,[23] save one thing,

21. *Catechism of the Catholic Church*, 239.

22. Mateo-Seco, "Paternity of the Father," 83. Mateo-Seco states that, according to St. Basil the Great, the name of Father is the first name of the First Person and is his most proper name, and that Paternity is the essential nucleus of the idea of Father.

23. *ST* I, q. 33, a. 2c; Scheeben, *Mysteries of Christianity*, 84.

his Son (and, as discussed, the Father is God but God as Father, i.e., God who has a Son).[24] To be paternal (a father) presupposes a child. Even to think of "father," we automatically have to refer to a child. As Father, God simply is he who gives to his child. All the Father's thoughts are found in his own Son. The Father is he who gives to his child (Son). The Father is the giver.[25]

Recall that I mentioned that God is completely free. The question arises as to whether God is free in his inner life to be Three Persons, or is he necessarily that way? The Cappadocian Fathers (Basil, Gregory Nazianzen, Gregory of Nyssa) and Maximos the Confessor expand on this idea to a much fuller degree to provide an answer: yes he is free to be Three Persons, but he also cannot be otherwise than Three Persons.[26] This idea comes from a completely different idea of freedom than the one to which we are accustomed. Humans exercise freedom of choice when they say "yes" or "no" to something.[27] But consider that this concept of freedom is rather limited. It follows from our weakness and limitedness. For instance, we should eat a good diet of a broad range of quality food. But we can choose not to do so, and thereby hurt ourselves. It would be best if we said "yes" to a good diet. That would help maximize our existence regarding physical health. Likewise, we can say "no" to an education. This would harm our mental health. The most extreme example of the effect of negative choices is suicide, where we say "no" to our own existence. The ability to say "no" to better things can actually seriously harm us. But shouldn't freedom of choice in the final analysis be that which always optimizes our life and our existence? We want to be free because we want to pick for ourselves what is best for us – health, careers, families, and the like – and not have someone else do it. But we fail at times in this endeavor by choosing to say "no" to what is best for us. The ability to say "no" to better things is actually a limitation of our freedom. It is a type of enslavement due to our limitation and weakness and is not the freedom possessed by God, for God has no limitations and weaknesses. God's

24. Gregory of Nyssa, *On the Holy Spirit*, 20. "We are not to think of the Father as ever parted from the Son . . . As it is impossible to mount to the Father, unless our thoughts are exalted there through the Son . . . The Father is always Father, and in Him the Son."

25. *ST* I, q. 42, a. 6, ad. 3; Perez, "Trinitarian Concept of Person," 139–45. Staniloae, *Theology and the Church*, 92–94.

26. Zizioulas, *Being as Communion*, 36–44; Zizioulas, "Trinitarian Freedom," 193–207.

27. Zizioulas, *Lectures in Christian Dogmatics*, 73–75.

freedom is not freedom of choice,[28] because freedom of choice is a limited freedom exercised by limited beings.

Freedom in its broadest sense is the ability to always do what is best for us. This is termed ontological freedom. Ontological freedom is the freedom to be oneself, uniquely particular, and not a moral freedom of choice.[29] This is the freedom of God – always freely to be his perfect, unlimited, infinite existence as the Trinity. But you may ask, How can something be free to exist? I exist, *then* I choose; this is so in us because our existence is given to us. In God nothing is given; he is before all else that is. He is eternal. God exists because he does so in perfect freedom. Being free and God's Trinitarian existence are simultaneous and the same thing; one was not *before* the other because God is one. At the same time, God could not "not" be in this way. All necessities or musts need to be removed from God. This is apophatic thinking in its extreme.[30] We have nothing in creation to compare to this. Quoting metropolitan John Zizioulas, "God is free if it is not nature that makes him exist, but he himself as a person. God is free if it is the person of the Father who makes God exist. If the Father wills to be, then God does not exist because he has to, but because he is willing to."[31] And in the case of the Person of God the Father, he is the Person who freely begets the Son, thus defining himself as *Father*.[32] The Father is the Father precisely because he freely exists as an infinite offering of himself in the Holy Spirit:[33] he freely exists not for himself, but for the Son. He cannot "not beget" the Son, but at the same time he begets in perfect freedom. This existing for another is precisely what love is; it is the way God is as a Trinity of Persons.[34]

What of the Son? Applying these same methods to the Son, we can ask

28. Zizioulas, *Communion and Otherness*, 121–22.

29. Zizioulas, *Communion and Otherness*, 121–22.

30. Maspero, "Patristic Trinitarian Ontology," 217–18.

31. Zizioulas, *Lectures in Christian Dogmatics*, 74–75. Again, "will" in this sense has nothing to do with the free will by which he creates. God is free to exist, but he never had a beginning, he was such from eternity.

32. Zizioulas, *Lectures in Christian Dogmatics*, 74–75; Maspero, "Patristic Trinitarian Ontology," 218–19, 224.

33. Maspero, "Patristic Trinitarian Ontology," 223.

34. Maspero, "Patristic Trinitarian Ontology," 224. See esp. Zizioulas, *Lectures in Christian Dogmatics*, 73–75, and *Communion and Otherness*, 121–22, for a detailed explanation from the Cappadocian Fathers.

what it means to be a child. A child is he or she who receives from his or her parent. To be a child, one must have a parent. The Son is he who receives (is begotten) from the Father.[35] Why a Son and not a daughter? Traditional human societies like those in the Bible see the Father-Son relationship as archetypal in the parent-child relationship. Because our concepts are based on our experience of creatures in the material world, the term "Son" is revealed to us in Scripture. Further, at a biological level, the male is larger and more muscular than the female because he guards territories and typically leads (especially in primates). Important as well, as discussed, he is typically the activator of life. And Christ, as the Son, is the Savior, Redeemer, and Head of the new creation (discussed in chaps. 11 and 12).

The knowledge of God revealed in Scripture yields the greatest penetration of the ideas of life and intellect previously discussed. If, according to the greatest reach of reason, life is ultimately an interior act of intelligence and the intellect is that which becomes another (or receives from another), then the language of Scripture becomes comprehensible and nonarbitrary. The Son is called the Wisdom and Word, or the Logos (rationality) of the Father.[36] The Son knows himself as "He who is from the Father" and is perfectly that which he knows (the Father).[37] As the Nicene Creed has it, the Son is "God from God, Light from Light, True God from True God, begotten, not made, consubstantial with the Father." The intellect is pure receptivity, or the ability to be relational, in the order of the spiritual, since the Son is the intellect (logos) of the Father. In the Trinity, the ability to be another (the image) is the height of the idea of a Person: to be so related as to be in perfect unity.[38] Both are equally God.

35. Carthusian Miscellany, *Wound of Love*, 175–76; Maspero, "Patristic Trinitarian Ontology," 223–24; *ST* I, q. 42, a. 6, ad. 3. "As the same essence is paternity in the Father, and filiation in the Son: so by the same power the Father begets, and the Son is begotten. Hence it is clear that the Son can do whatever the Father can do; yet it does not follow that the Son can beget; for to argue thus would imply transition from substance to relation, for generation signifies a divine relation. So the Son has the same omnipotence as the Father, but with another relation; the Father possessing power as giving signified when we say that He is able to beget; while the Son possess the power of receiving, signified by saying that He can be begotten."

36. *Catechism of the Catholic Church*, 241.

37. *Catechism of the Catholic Church*, 242

38. *Catechism of the Catholic Church*, 253; Zizioulas, *Communion and Otherness*, 113–54.

The Father, then, is pure giving.[39] He is the *arche* (αρχη) or origin of the Trinitarian life[40] and gives himself, completely, in the Holy Spirit to the Son.[41] He is the infinite poverty of giving as nothing is held back.[42] The only thing the Son is not that the Father is is paternity.[43] That defines the Person of the Father; he who gives completely, without being begotten himself, to generate a Son. "The Father loves the Son and has given all things into his hand" (Jn 3:35). He generates the Son in this manner from all eternity.[44] To be a Father, he must have a Son. There was never a time he was without one. The Son is freely pure receptivity from the Father. The person of the Son is "he who receives," the infinite poverty of receiving.[45] Being perfect receptivity, he "reflects the glory of God and bears the very stamp of his nature" (Heb 1:3). Being the perfect image of the Father, he who gives, the Son cannot keep anything for himself; he gives back anew everything to the Father.[46] Thus the Father loses nothing of who he is in his gift, as it is returned anew and he is confirmed in his Son, an eternal gift between the two results: "All mine are thine, and thine are mine" (Jn 17:10).[47] This gift exchanged is the Love of God or the Holy Spirit, the third person of the Trinity.[48] As that which is given, he is neither giver nor receiver but simply pure communication between the Father and Son.[49] He is the pure transparency of encounter or the bond and embrace of love between Father and Son.[50] This Holy Spirit is their glory, as St. Gregory of Nyssa states, based on the Gospel of John[51]: "The glory which thou hast given me I have given

39. Perez, "Trinitarian Concept of Person," 139–45.

40. *Catechism of the Catholic Church*, 245; Maspero, "Patristic Trinitarian Ontology," 218; *ST* I, q. 33, a. 1c; I, q. 33, a. 4, ad. 2.

41. *Catechism of the Catholic Church*, 246; Maspero, "Patristic Trinitarian Ontology," 223.

42. Carthusian Miscellany, *Wound of Love*, 175.

43. *ST* I, q. 32, a. 3c.

44. *Catechism of the Catholic Church*, 246.

45. Maspero, "Patristic Trinitarian Ontology," 223; Carthusian Miscellany, *Wound of Love*, 175.

46. Maspero, "Patristic Trinitarian Ontology," 223–24; Staniloae, *Theology and the Church*, 92–94.

47. Carthusian Miscellany, *Wound of Love*, 175–76; Maspero, "Patristic Trinitarian Ontology," 222–24.

48. Maspero, "Patristic Trinitarian Ontology," 222–24; Scheeben, *Mysteries of Christianity*, 64–65; *ST* I, q. 37, aa. 1–2.

49. Perez, "Trinitarian Concept of Person," 139–45; Carthusian Miscellany, *Wound of Love*, 176.

50. Carthusian Miscellany, *Wound of Love*, 176.

51. Maspero, "Patristic Trinitarian Ontology," 222–23.

to them" (Jn 17:22). And what does St. John say Christ gave? "Receive the Holy Spirit" (Jn 20:22). The complete self-giving and receiving of Father and Son is personified in the Holy Spirit, just as complete and perfect as them. The Holy Spirit is in a certain sense the culmination of the Trinity, the person of the love of God himself in the same way as the Father is the origin of the Trinity.[52]

Here the answer is found to the question about perfection posed in chapter 3: in order to be perfect, life, relations, and the intellect must ultimately be productive of another. Recall that the vegetative life in plants, animals, and humans results in another (offspring); St. Thomas states that to have offspring is the perfection of vegetative life.[53] The intellectual life found in humans gives us hints that another is produced in our idea of self. Vegetative life produces exterior offspring. Intelligence is an interior act, so ideally one should find an interior production of another. In the Trinity, we find the perfect free completion of this process. The bond between Father and Son occurs in a Third, the Holy Spirit, who is identical in nature with them.[54] Here again the Holy Spirit is the "culmination" of the Trinity, in that God's life of infinite Intellect is "productive" from eternity of a perfect inner Third Person. This idea prompted the Romanian Orthodox theologian Dimitru Staniloae to think of the Trinity from a psychological perspective.[55] Noting that one human person can become engrossed or obsessed with himself if alone, or two humans can become infatuated with each other in a relationship, he says a third is needed to "pull" humans out of themselves and radically orient them to another: psychologically, this third makes true love possible. In the Trinity, we therefore find three in this Perfect Union of Love.

Father, Son, and Holy Spirit are thus all equal and perfectly one.[56] All Three Persons are equally infinite love, understanding, beauty, wisdom, life, and existence, which in God are all the same thing. The only distinction is that of Paternity, Sonship, and Love. A father is a father because he has a

52. Maspero, "Patristic Trinitarian Ontology," 224n43; Scheeben, *Mysteries of Christianity*, 116; Staniloae, *Theology and the Church*, 66–67; Staniloae, *Holy Trinity*, 66–67; Durand, "Perichoresis," 187–88.

53. Aquinas, *Commentary on Aristotle's De Anima* II, lec. 7, 9.

54. *Catechism of the Catholic Church*, 245.

55. Staniloae, *Theology and the Church*, 92–94.

56. *Catechism of the Catholic Church*, 253; *ST* I, q. 42, a. 1c.

son, and for a son to be a son, he must have a father. Hence the Persons are called the Trinitarian relations.[57] This is our greatest mystery, how Three Persons can be one God. The infinite glory, beauty, and love of God are simply that of the Trinitarian relations. The essence of God is to be related as Persons, as a community or communion of Three Persons: Father, Son, and Holy Spirit in perfect freedom. Each is completely for the other; there is no "I," only "Thou" among them. No concern for I or me; each Person is distinct, but not an individual. Individual concerns and limitations are totally absent. All is given in love for the other; from the Father to the Son and from the Son back to the Father in the unity of the Holy Spirit. Infinite love, or freedom in relation. As Jean Cardinal Daniélou so poignantly put it, the foundation of being is a communion of three divine persons. In this eternal embrace, God is infinitely happy: "My Son, only Your company contents Me . . . I am pleased with You alone, O Life of my Life" (see also Mt 3:17; Mk 1:11; Lk 3:22), and the internal Trinitarian processions are the glory of God: "Father . . . glorify thy Son, that the Son may glorify Thee . . . Father, glorify thou me in thy own presence with the glory which I had with thee before the world was made" (Jn 17:1, 17:5).

And that brings us back to the mystery of creation. Why did God create? If God is infinite, it was not out of necessity, as he needs no creature to increase his happiness or glory. He has no reason to create or give things to his creatures except owing to pure liberality and love on his part, because nothing is needed in return. There is no possibility for selfishness, as there is in us. Yet by creating, God behaves toward creatures as he does in his inner life; he gives himself completely to us so that we can live his life.[58] This is our ultimate purpose, our deification. In his unique existence, God is able to enter into a personal union with us. This is our final (tertiary) perfection in a divine community of Persons. All reality is created by this God, and all things move toward a communion of persons in love. We were made out of love and for love.[59] This is our end.

57. *Catechism of the Catholic Church*, 255.

58. *Catechism of the Catholic Church*, 257.

59. John Paul II, *Familiaris Consortio*, no. 11.

Connecting Heaven and Earth: The Incarnation of Christ

God exists independently of us and does not need us.[60] If God wishes to enter into a relationship with us his creatures, how does he accomplish that union? In distinction from all other non-Christian religions, the Catholic faith believes in the Incarnation, God becoming man.[61] Heaven and earth are connected through the Incarnation of the Son of God.

The Incarnation can be a difficult concept for people to understand because it is absolutely unique. Almost all highly developed religions believe there is some commerce between God and the human race, so much so that one is tempted to think that it may be an inborn trait of the human makeup. The ancient Greeks, for example, thought of the gods coming down to earth, but this idea always involved either a lessening of divinity or a divinization of humanity. Yet the Incarnation differs significantly from this Greek idea in that it affirms that Jesus Christ was *fully* God and *fully* man.[62] Furthermore, many cultures think of religious belief and practice as the human ascent to the divine. Christianity reverses this idea by stressing the divine descent to the human race. The Incarnation was not a mingling of divinity and humanity but a union of divinity and humanity in *one man*, Jesus Christ, where both are kept distinct without alternation of the other.[63] Later I return to the Incarnation, but for now I want to ask about the motive for the Incarnation. Why would God become a man, or as the title of Anselm's famous work has it, *Cur Deus Homo*?

Almost all Christian theologies affirm the first three reasons summarized in the *Catechism of the Catholic Church*:[64] (1) to save us from our sins, (2) that we might know God's love, and (3) to become our model of holiness. While all Christian theologies stress that Christ came into the world to remove the stain on humanity due to the Fall of Adam and Eve and forgive the personal sins of each individual, Catholic theology, both in its Eastern and Western manifestations, also stresses a reunion with God, the fourth reason given in

60. The discussion in this section takes its material in large part from Scheeben, *Mysteries of Christianity*, 335–430.

61. *Catechism of the Catholic Church*, 461–63.

62. *Catechism of the Catholic Church*, 464–77.

63. *Catechism of the Catholic Church*, 464–69.

64. *Catechism of the Catholic Church*, 457–59.

the *Catechism* as to why God became man: "to make us partakers of the divine nature." This is implied also in the statement that we are to know God's love. What does it mean to know the love of God? To know God's love is to experience it, to be one with it. To say that the infinite God became man *only* to save us from our sins is to diminish the full meaning of the Incarnation.[65] The Fathers of the Church are unanimous in holding that God could simply have forgiven our sins as a judge absolves punishment for a crime.[66] The Fathers and saints typically start a discussion of the Incarnation with an emphasis on the redemption from sins, but the Incarnation was not absolutely necessary for this redemption.[67] God coming in human flesh took place in order to make sinners into God by participation, something that God alone can effect.[68] Athanasius of Alexandria famously stated this truth when he wrote, "The Son of God became the Son of man so that the sons of men may become the sons of God."[69]

Scripture certainly presents the Incarnation from the point of view of the Fall, and the Church Fathers developed this view as well.[70] Christ's person and work did remove original sin and our personal sins, but both Scripture and the Fathers indicate a greater purpose as well. The Gospel of John, chapter 17, is replete with statements that we may be one with the Son and the Father, that the love and glory that the Son has with the Father may be in us, and that all might be one to glorify the Son, who in turn will glorify the Father. While these lofty ideas reach their pinnacle in chapter 17, the remainder of Christ's farewell discourse in John, chapters 14–16, contains many of these ideas as well: that the Son and the Father may come to dwell in us, that we might be the branches of Christ the vine, that the Father might be glorified in the works of Christ, that the Son and Father may reveal themselves to us, that we might remain in Christ. Surely these ideas of the Indwelling, being one with the Father, and glorifying the Father, are higher ideas than simply the forgiveness of original and personal sins.[71] Following these scrip-

65. Scheeben, *Mysteries of Christianity*, 353–54.
66. Scheeben, *Mysteries of Christianity*, 344.
67. Scheeben, *Mysteries of Christianity*, 352–56, 418–22.
68. Scheeben, *Mysteries of Christianity*, 337–430.
69. *Catechism of the Catholic Church*, 460.
70. Scheeben, *Mysteries of Christianity*, 352–66, 418–22.
71. Scheeben, *Mysteries of Christianity*, 352–56; 418–22.

tural clues, the Church Fathers and Doctors, speaking of the Incarnation, affirm that while they may introduce it with original sin, they always conclude with something higher.[72]

So what is the loftiest motive of the Incarnation?[73] God is infinite; before all else existed, he *was*. He is the cause and end of all things. He is infinitely glorified and loved in himself by the procession of the Trinity, and he has no need to create. He created everything out of pure love and mercy, a completely gratuitous act. True love is to live for another, expecting nothing in return. Given that God does create, however, creatures on their part first owe him praise, glory, and love for what he did. All the works of God must love and glorify him because they are infinitely below and totally dependent on him, and "No one is good but God alone" (Lk 18:19). In glorifying or loving God, his creatures do not give him some new glory or love; if that were so, he could then be said to truly need us, and we could give him something he does not have.[74] When we say we "give glory to God," we manifest his glory in creatures or give a glory back to him that he gave us. This is similar to parents receiving great satisfaction in their toddlers giving back something that they (the parents) gave to them. But no creature is proportionate to God – all are infinitely below him. Again, when we say that God acts out of pure love for creatures, we mean there is no personal need on behalf of God. Nevertheless, God loves all things in himself, as stated insightfully by St. John of the Cross, "God loves nothing outside Himself, He bears no lower love for anything than the love He bears for Himself. He does not love things because of what they are in themselves, but because of what He is in Himself."[75] Or, as Scripture puts it, "In this is love: not that we have loved God, but that he loved us" (1 Jn 4:10).

The first reason for the Incarnation must be for God. *First*, God must love himself in the creature for *his* own sake. Christ could not be willed into existence purely for the creature, as he is God. The most exalted end of the Incarnation was that Christ became incarnate in order to extend the inner life of the Trinity to creatures with the result that creatures may glorify and

72. Scheeben, *Mysteries of Christianity*, 352–56; 418–22.

73. Scheeben, *Mysteries of Christianity*, 342, 357–64.

74. Scheeben, *Mysteries of Christianity*, 342, 357–64.

75. John of the Cross, "Spiritual Canticles," 32.6.

love God with the same glory and love that God possesses in his inner life.[76] Thus creation may partake of the inner life of God. Christ is the great medium or conduit on behalf of creation in that he conveys God's inner life, so that creation may participate in it and return it to him. The Incarnation is a real extension of the inner life of the Trinity to creatures.[77] Christ is the Son because he possesses the fullness of the Godhead in himself, and he is true man; Christ can give this inner life to men through his human body, the true body of the Son, "For as the Father has life in himself, so he has granted the Son also to have life in himself" (Jn 5:26).[78] The fullness of the Godhead is at our disposal, given completely to us as a gift. "The Son," who "can do nothing of his own accord" and does "only what he sees the Father doing" (Jn 5:19), sees the Father giving himself completely to him from eternity and in turn does the same for creatures. The Incarnation is nothing but an extension to the human race and to all of creation of the eternal generation of the Son.[79] Human beings are expected to completely give themselves, their life, back to Jesus, as Christ does to the Father ("All mine are thine, and thine are mine"). The Incarnation has its roots deep in the Trinity.[80] St. John of the Cross again summarizes this fact:

> It [the soul] is conscious there that God is indeed its own and that it possesses Him by inheritance, with the right of ownership, as His adopted son, through the grace of His gift of Himself. Having Him for its own, it can give Him and communicate Him to whomever it wishes. Thus it gives Him to its Beloved, who is the very God who gave Himself to it. By this donation it repays God for all it owes Him, since it willingly gives as much as it receives from Him.
>
> Because the soul in this gift to God offers Him the Holy Spirit, with voluntary surrender, as something of its own (so that God loves Himself in the Holy Spirit as he deserves), it enjoys inestimable delight and fruition, seeing that it gives God something of its own which is suited to Him according to His infinite being . . .
>
> A reciprocal love is thus actually formed between God and the soul, like the marriage union and surrender, in which the goods of both (the divine es-

76. Scheeben, *Mysteries of Christianity*, 391–92, 395–97, 406.

77. Scheeben, *Mysteries of Christianity*, 360–61, 379–80, 396–404.

78. Scheeben, *Mysteries of Christianity*, 368–71.

79. Scheeben, *Mysteries of Christianity*, 358–60, 396–404.

80. Scheeben, *Mysteries of Christianity*, 133, 359, 398, 446.

sence which each possesses freely by reason of the voluntary surrender between them) are possessed by both together. They say to each other what the Son of God spoke to the Father through St. John: All my goods are yours and yours are mine, and I am glorified in them [Jn 17:10]. In the next life this will continue uninterruptedly in perfect fruition.[81]

Here the inner Trinitarian life of God is beautifully expressed in creatures. As Father and Son are united in the Holy Spirit, so God gives the soul the same Holy Spirit (a third) as its "own" in which to establish a union with God as he possesses in himself. A later spiritual guide in the Church, equally as adept as John of the Cross, was Lawrence of Brindisi. He emphasized this truth of union through the Incarnation in direct terms: "Many learned theologians, therefore conclude that Christ would have become incarnate even if Adam had not sinned, for the mystery of the incarnation was revealed to Adam even before he sinned and he prophesied concerning it. St. Thomas teaches that Adam had explicit faith in the incarnation before the fall, because Adam prophesied concerning Christ insofar as his incarnation was ordained to the [completion of his deification in heavenly glory]."[82] Therefore the Incarnation could have taken place without the fall of Adam,[83] as its primary aim was the extension of the Trinitarian life to creation. It is from this viewpoint that Adam had the divine life of grace. As we will discuss, Adam had deification in a lesser form, a preparation for the greater deification to be found in Christ, which would have exceedingly elevated and perfected Adam's.

Two Roads Diverged

The worldview that emerges from divine revelation, or the disclosure of God's life to us, contains meaning and significance because it posits an end or purpose of human life. In a materialist worldview, it is difficult to find the end or purpose of life, except what we might make up out of thin air. According to this view, there is certainly no common end for all human life except to be absorbed into the dirt again. The traditional Christian language

81. John of the Cross, "Living Flame of Love," III.78–79.

82. See Tsakanikas, *Christocentrism of the Virtues*.

83. Scheeben, *Mysteries of Christianity*, 422–31.

of "Dust you are and to dust you shall return" takes on a whole new meaning in a materialist philosophy of life. For a transcendent worldview, however, the end of human life is to be ultimately in the heart of God, to live in the fullness of divine love, and to participate in that life and love with our full rational and faith powers. In this philosophy of life, God is the original and ultimate reality with which we must deal. The purpose of the entire cosmic order is to draw every human life up into something imaginably greater than any thought can comprehend. It is in that "something greater" that human happiness lies. Yet this divine life is so far above us that only God can bring it down to us. The Incarnation, the miracle of God becoming flesh, is the bridge between the material and the spiritual worlds. But the fact of the Incarnation in Jesus Christ is not an act to be admired and appreciated—it is a reality in which to participate. That participation is human deification or divinization.

10 ATTAINING OUR END THROUGH DEIFICATION

What is *our* purpose in relation to God? One answer, prominent among non-Catholic Christians in the United States, is that our purpose is to find salvation through the forgiveness of sins. For those who hold such a view, the biggest problem human beings face is the sin that keeps them from God. Catholics also believe that sins need to be forgiven, but their vision of salvation goes beyond forgiveness. For decades, children in Catholic schools memorized the *Baltimore Catechism*, which gave a simple and straightforward answer to this question about our purpose in relation to God: we are to know, love, and serve God.[1] Since children are likely to think in concrete terms, the question was sometimes phrased in localized language: What happens in heaven? The more or less standard answer was, "You will see God." Such an answer was based on Jesus's words, "Blessed are the pure in heart, for they shall see God" (Mt 5:8). The language of seeing God in the New Testament is based on the same idea among the Jews in the Hebrew Bible. But what could seeing God possibly mean? God is an immaterial, spiritual being. How is it possible to see him?

1. Kelley, *New St. Joseph Baltimore Catechism*, 9.

Deification Explained

As Catholic theologians pondered the meaning of "seeing God" through the centuries, they returned to some foundational biblical ideas of union, participation, and consummation. To "see God" was explained as meeting God, being united with God, and finding our fulfillment in God. Yet if the end or purpose of human life is union with God, the question naturally arises about how one gets to that final union. Deification is the process that begins in this life and is consummated in that complete union, a total participation in the divine life of God, living, as it were, in the love life of the Trinity.[2] Deification means growth in love, learning to love like God, but also loving with the same love that God has in himself.[3] Although the present *Catechism of the Catholic Church* is a hefty volume, it is designed as a summary statement of Catholic doctrine. In short form, the *Catechism* states, "The ultimate end of the whole divine economy is the entry of God's creatures into the perfect unity of the Blessed Trinity. But even now we are called to be a dwelling for the Most Holy Trinity: 'If a man loves me,' says the Lord, 'he will keep my word, and my Father will love him, and we will come to him, and make our home with him.'"[4]

The idea of entry into the unity of the Blessed Trinity far transcends the idea of going to heaven because one's sins are forgiven, or the slavish fear of a distant Master who will crush those who disobey. God the Trinity wants to enter into the same intimate union with us as he has in his Three-Personed self.[5] When understood properly, this concept of union with God is far different from a type of abstract relationship with him. Unfortunately, this latter idea is what even many Christians believe when they hear that we "were created to know, love, and serve God." This concept of an abstract and distant relationship, woefully incomplete as it is, still fuels the misconceptions of well-intentioned unbelievers who think of Christianity as a fear-mongering religion. But the true teaching of the Catholic faith is far different.

2. Arintero, *Mystical Evolution*, 1:58–60; Scheeben, *Mysteries of Christianity*, 316*ff*., 378*ff*., 654*ff*.; Staniloae, *Orthodox Spirituality*, 362–74.

3. John of the Cross, "Spiritual Canticles," 39.4.

4. *Catechism of the Catholic Church*, 260.

5. Scheeben, *Mysteries of Christianity*, 376–96.

God desires far more than to forgive our sins. He desires to give us his life, the only thing that is truly infinite and eternal. The Gospel of John is universally acknowledged as being the most theological of the four Gospels. It contains a depth of reflection and symbolism that resounds with the more profound meaning of salvation. When Jesus says, "I came that they may have life, and have it abundantly" (Jn 10:10), he is speaking of life in its fullest and most complete form. This life is more than simple forgiveness of sin and living with God; it involves living *in* God.[6] Catholic theology, picking up these scriptural cues, insists that God re-creates us such that his life is truly ours and is freely given, so that we share in his life.[7] One special passage in John's Gospel that emphasizes this life-giving love of God occurs in chapter 15:

> I am the true vine, and my Father is the vinedresser. Every branch of mine that bears no fruit, he takes away, and every branch that does bear fruit he prunes that it may bear more fruit. You are already made clean by the word which I have spoken to you. Abide in me, and I in you. As the branch cannot bear fruit by itself, unless it abides in the vine, neither can you unless you abide in me. I am the vine, you are the branches. He who abides in me and I in him, he it is that bears much fruit, for apart from me you can do nothing. If a man does not abide in me, he is cast forth as a branch and withers; and the branches are gathered together, thrown into the fire and burned. If you abide in me, and my words abide in you, ask whatever you will, and it shall be done for you. By this my Father is glorified, that you bear much fruit, and so prove to be my disciples. As the Father has loved me, so have I loved you; abide in my love. If

6. A significant development of this idea, which was brought to my attention after the writing of this book was nearly complete, is found in the writings of the Servant of God Luisa Picarretta. Fr. Tom Celso of Rochester, New York, generously gave me the most recent translation of private copies of her complete works (as yet not available to the general public), consisting of nine volumes containing all thirty-six volumes (plus letters), which were dictated to her by Christ while she was bedridden for sixty years. She speaks of living in the Divine Will (as opposed to doing the Divine Will). Living in the Divine Will is the completion of the clause from the "Our Father" – "Thy kingdom come, thy will be bone, *on Earth as it is in Heaven*" – and, according to her, it is the highest level of sanctity attainable. Her works seem to me a vast expansion of the *Spiritual Canticles* and particularly the *Living Flame of Love* of St. John of the Cross, with strong affinities with St. Thérèse of Lisieux, Blessed Elizabeth of the Trinity, and elements of Eastern Christian thought. It has been mentioned that she has written more about Adam's prelapsarian state than all the extant works of the Church on this subject combined. Having read at the point of writing this book the majority of her works, I would say it is certainly possible.

7. *Catechism of the Catholic Church*, 1213–15, 1265–66; Arintero, *Mystical Evolution*, 1:86–87.

> you keep my commandments, you will abide in my love, just as I have kept my Father's commandments and abide in his love. These things I have spoken to you, that my joy may be in you, and that your joy may be full. This is my commandment, that you love one another as I have loved you. Greater love has no one than this that a man lay down his life for his friends. You are my friends if you do what I command you. No longer do I call you servants, for the servant does not know what his master's is doing; but I have called you friends, for all that I have heard from my Father I have made known to you. You did not choose me, but I chose you and appointed you that you should go and bear fruit, and that your fruit should abide; so that whatever you ask the Father in my name, he may give it to you. (15:1–16)

Few passages in the Bible capture the essence of deification so well. The mutual indwelling spoken of means that Jesus's disciples (the branches) derive their life from the vine (Jesus). The key to this shared life is "abiding" or "remaining" in Christ, the very process of deification.[8] It is in this context that Jesus calls his disciples his friends, a designation used of Abraham as the father of Jews and Christians (Jas 2:23). This friendship with God is contrasted explicitly with a slave-master relationship. The underlying reason for such an intimate union with Christ lies in Jesus's words, "As the Father has loved me, so have I loved you; abide in my love. If you keep my commandments, you will abide in my love, just as I have kept my Father's commandments and abide in his love." The same love that the eternal Son of God experienced in the Trinitarian life before creation is now shared with humanity.[9] Not another love but the same love. It is participation in the self-giving life of God.

The same idea is found in the first letter of Peter, when he speaks of becoming "partakers of the divine nature":

> His divine power has granted to us all things that pertain to life and godliness, through the knowledge of him who called us to his own glory and excellence, by which he has granted to us his precious and very great promises,

8. John of the Cross, "Spiritual Canticles," 1.6–10. Also see Bacovcin, *Way of the Pilgrim,* and Lawrence of the Resurrection, *Practice of the Presence of God,* each of which gives an excellent introduction to the mystical tradition of both Eastern and Western Christianity and the need to "abide in" Christ and maintain constant prayer and recollection.

9. Jn 17:23–26.

> that through these you may escape from the corruption that is in the world because of passion, and become partakers of the divine nature. For this very reason make every effort to supplement your faith with virtue, and virtue with knowledge, and knowledge with self-control, and self-control with steadfastness, and steadfastness with godliness, godliness with brotherly affection; and brotherly affection with love. For if these are yours and abound, they keep from being ineffective or unfruitful in the knowledge of our Lord Jesus Christ. (2 Pt 1:3–8)

What John's Gospel portrayed in parabolic form, Peter's letter states explicitly: that those who know God become "partakers of the divine nature." Although Christian doctrine insists on the unbridgeable distance between the Creator and the creature, the essence of salvation is to participate in the divine life of God. We receive the very life and powers of God to live the life of God, to be "God" by participation. The *Catechism of the Catholic Church* picks up on this biblical theme: "The Word became flesh to make us '*partakers of the divine nature.*' For this is why the Word became man, and the Son of God became the Son of man: so that man, by entering into communion with the Word and thus receiving divine sonship, might become a son of God. For the Son of God became man so that we might become God. The only-begotten Son of God, wanting to make us sharers in his divinity, assumed our nature, so that he, made man, might make men gods."[10]

The reason that the Catholic Church insists on deification is that it is the universal teaching of the Fathers of the Church. In the distant past, the notion of deification was commonly known, but it has been largely forgotten among Christian faithful in the present age. In the twentieth century, Fr. John Arintero, OP, a great theologian of the spiritual life, emphasized the truth of deification. He wrote, "This deification, so well-known by the Fathers but unfortunately forgotten today, is the primary purpose of the Christian life. The entire Christian life demands a continual growth so prodigious that it has as its goal a perfection truly divine, for we must resemble God as a son does his father. 'Be you therefore perfect, as also your heavenly Father is perfect.'"[11] So, when Scripture refers to us becoming sons of

10. *Catechism of the Catholic Church*, 460. Emphasis added.

11. Arintero, *Mystical Evolution*, 1:23.

God by adoption, deification in its fullest sense is what is being referenced.[12] Yet it is impossible to explicate in minute detail what deification is exactly, because it is a profound mystery.[13] Recall that apophatic theology seeks to understand transcendent mysteries by way of analogy and negation. Direct descriptions are not possible. Nor is it possible by use of reason to discover the idea of deification any more than we could have guessed that God is a Trinitarian Being. Human reason is stymied in the face of such lofty realities. This is why the Bible often speaks in parables and figures of speech. Yet as theology attempts to explicate these high realities, we can say that God gives us the life of grace, or participation in a life that is vastly above our human nature.[14] This life, this love, is an absolutely unmerited privilege on our part.[15] Only God is God by nature, and we do not become God by nature; however, we do become like God by participation in the original divine life.[16] This means that deification is no mere moral alignment of our wills with God's will. The conformity of our will is essential, but we really participate in God's nature.[17] It is a mystery.

Mystery though it is, deification becomes somewhat clearer by a closer look through a different historical lens. Adam, the original father of the human race,[18] experienced a kind of deification as well, but to understand the first chapters of Genesis demands that we put aside our modern tendency to read literature as if it were a manual for car repairs, or a scientific or business textbook. The narration of Adam's creation and Fall into sin requires a mind-set more like the one Paul of Tarsus used. Paul calls Christ "the Last Adam" (1 Cor 15:45), suggesting that by understanding Adam's relationship with God, we clarify our own in Christ. Adam underwent a type of deification in the beginning, but one that differs from that of the Christian.[19]

12. Arintero, *Mystical Evolution*, 1:86–89, 1:144–48.

13. Scheeben, *Mysteries of Christianity*, 201–9.

14. Scheeben, *Mysteries of Christianity*, 201–9.

15. Scheeben, *Mysteries of Christianity*, 201–9.

16. Scheeben, *Mysteries of Christianity*, 201–9.

17. Scheeben, *Mysteries of Christianity*, 201–9. This is more of a Western Christian idea. Eastern Christianity would emphasize that we participle in the Person of Christ (Zizioulas, *Being as Communion*, 50).

18. I discuss Adam, Eve, Eden, the Fall, and Adam's relation to modern science and evolution more deeply in chapter 12.

19. *Catechism of the Catholic Church*, 374–75, 398; Scheeben, *Mysteries of Christianity*, 376–400.

Adam had his natural powers and received this life of deification as a seed to develop, which would come to fruition in the next life.[20] This gift to our original parent is termed Original Justice.[21] Original Justice was a gratuitous gift that Adam in no way deserved by his own merits.[22] What Adam possessed by nature consisted of two aspects: holiness and integrity.[23] Holiness is the life of grace we have been discussing, called deification. Integrity means he also found it easy not to sin, as he had total control over his body and its desires by his reason.[24] Integrity was another unmerited gift to support holiness. Because Adam was so exalted, it only followed that he should have mastery over that which was lower to support the ease of use of this gift of holiness. Thus his material life of sensation, growth, nutrition, and reproduction was totally regulated by reason, and no desire occurred until it was necessary.[25] For instance, he did not feel hunger until he deemed it the proper time and place to eat, nor did he have sexual desire until it was the proper time to reproduce. This was a gift of God by grace that enabled him to follow his reason, and hence God's will to a supreme degree, complementing his life of grace.[26] This control over nature was maximized exteriorly in that Adam did not have to worry about what to eat, as nature provided it for him, nor did he have anything to fear from beings lower than him, as he had mastery over the world about him.[27] One of the consequences of Original Justice was that Adam would not die, because his immortal soul, which we all have, had such power over his body through grace that it passed this immortality on to his body and kept it from decay and corruption.[28]

Original Justice would have been passed on to his descendants because they were Adam's children.[29] If he had had children with Eve before he sinned, he would have been their natural and supernatural father. This com-

20. *Catechism of the Catholic Church*, 375; *ST* I, q. 102, a. 4c.

21. *Catechism of the Catholic Church*, 376; Scheeben, *Mysteries of Christianity*, 221–28.

22. Scheeben, *Mysteries of Christianity*, 216–36.

23. Scheeben, *Mysteries of Christianity*, 216–21.

24. Scheeben, *Mysteries of Christianity*, 216–28; *ST* I, q. 94, a. 2c.

25. *ST* I, q. 94, a. 2c; *Catechism of the Catholic Church*, 377.

26. Scheeben, *Mysteries of Christianity*, 216–28.

27. Gn 2:9; *Catechism of the Catholic Church*, 376–77; *ST* I, q. 96, a. 1c; I, q. 96, a., 2c.

28. Scheeben, *Mysteries of Christianity*, 229–36; *Catechism of the Catholic Church*, 376; *ST* I, q. 97, a. 1c.

29. Scheeben, *Mysteries of Christianity*, 229–36; *ST* I, q. 100, aa. 1–2.

bination of nature and the state of Original Justice was the proper state, or nature, of the human race.[30] By "nature" in this respect we mean humans were created and intended to possess both their powers of nature (growth, reproduction, sensation, and rational intellect) and the state of Original Justice. Their duty in Eden was a type of contemplation of God, whereby they progressed in sanctity and ordered the rest of the world about them by uniting all things in them through their intellect; they were the prophets and priests of the material universe.[31] The full manifestation of deification and the life of God would occur in heaven.[32]

The Fall of Adam narrated in Genesis, chapter 3, speaks of Adams's eating of the fruit of the tree of the knowledge of good and evil. Why, in such an exalted state, would a creature refuse the gifts of the Creator? Adam nevertheless sinned and fell from his exalted state and brought down the whole of the human race to the condition we have today.[33] Original sin does not mean that we are responsible for Adam's sin, but it does mean that we live with the consequences of his disobedience.[34] To an individualistic mind-set, nothing could seem more unfair. Unfair, yes, in one sense, but not unreasonable. Consider two undeniable facts. Genetic dispositions (e.g., to cancer) are inherited; even behavioral patterns in families are passed down. Why, then, is the idea of inclination toward sin (concupiscence) so difficult to grasp? As head and father of the human race, when Adam sinned, he utterly spurned the gift of adoption as a son of God. He rejected God as his Father. That is why the Fall of Adam was so momentous: he rejected the source and meaning of life. He lost the state of Original Justice, both holiness (deification) and integrity.[35] But because he lost an unmerited gift far exceeding his nature, all humans lost theirs. In other words, he brought the state of humanity down to a level devoid of its supernatural qualities that should be

30. Scheeben, *Mysteries of Christianity*, 229–36.

31. *Catechism of the Catholic Church*, 378; Scheeben, *Mysteries of Christianity*, 237–39; *ST* I, q. 102, a. 4c; Larchet, *Therapy of Spiritual Illnesses*, 1:19–21.

32. Scheeben, *Mysteries of Christianity*, 679; *ST* I, q. 102, a. 4c.

33. *Catechism of the Catholic Church*, 397–403; see Scheeben, *Mysteries of Christianity*, 273–310, for an extended analysis of original sin and its effects, as well as Larchet, *Therapy of Spiritual Illnesses*, 1:37–46.

34. *Catechism of the Catholic Church*, 404–5; Scheeben, *Mysteries of Christianity*, 283–84.

35. *Catechism of the Catholic Church*, 400, 404; Scheeben, *Mysteries of Christianity*, 273–84.

present in human nature and, as a consequence, human nature became more akin to that of brute animals.[36] We lost the grace of divine sonship and deification and all it entailed, including mastery over ourselves and the world, as well as immortality. Through Adam, the whole material universe became warped and disfigured.[37] This is why "the last Adam," as Paul calls Christ, is the Redeemer of the cosmos, including the human race.[38]

Underlying the story of creation and the Fall is the notion of family and solidarity. We are all intimately tied to one another. Deification means that God wants a real familial life with us, to participate profoundly in the very interior and intimate life of the Trinity. We are called to enter into the familial life of God himself: children of the Father, brothers of the Son, and Spouses of the Holy Spirit.[39] God wants a relationship with us akin to that of a husband with his wife, by elevating us into his very life, so that we thus "become partakers in the divine nature" (2 Pt 1:4). It is as if an Infinite husband and wife brought you into, and made you part of, their own spousal intimacy and their relationship with their children. How can something infinitely above us have a familial relationship with something finite? To bridge this gap, God stoops down to make us, in a sense, his "equals."[40] He gives us everything he has. And God is perfectly simple, perfectly one. He loves us with the same love he has for himself: "All mine are thine, and thine are mine" (Jn 17:10). As John puts it in his first letter, "In this is love, not that we have loved God, but that he loved us" (1 Jn 4:10).

One of the greatest masters of the theology of love was, again, St. John of the Cross. John helps us to understand how deification grows out of and leads back to divine love:

36. *Catechism of the Catholic Church*, 400, 404–5, 407–8; Scheeben, *Mysteries of Christianity*, 301–2. See Nellas, *Deification in Christ*, 43–91, for an interesting discussion among the Church Fathers regarding the "garments of skin" in which Adam and Eve were clothed after the fall (Gn 3:21). These are interpreted as referring to the idea that in Adam's Fall, man fell nearly to the level of animal existence.

37. Rom 8:20–21. *Catechism of the Catholic Church*, 400, 407–8; Nellas, *Deification in Christ*, 48, 85–89.

38. *Catechism of the Catholic Church*, 410–11; Scheeben, *Mysteries of Christianity*, 323–30.

39. Arintero, *Mystical Evolution*, 1:140–94.

40. See notes 42 and 43 below.

> My son, I will give Myself to him who loves You, and I will love him with the same love I have for You, because he has loved You, whom I love so.[41]
>
> God makes use of nothing other than love ... The reason is that all our works and even our trials, even though they are the greatest possible, are nothing in the sight of God. For through them we cannot give him anything or fulfill His only desire, which is the exaltation of the soul. Of these other things He desires nothing for Himself, since He has no need of them. If anything pleases Him, it is the exultation of the soul. Since there is no way by which He can exult her more than by making her equal to Himself, He is pleased only with her love. For the property of love is to make the lover equal to the object loved.[42]
>
> Just as God loves nothing outside Himself, He bears no lower love for anything than the love He bears for Himself. He does not love things because of what they are in themselves, but because of what He is in Himself. Thus love is the purpose for which he loves. *With God, to love the soul is to put her somehow in Himself and make her his equal.* Thus he loves the soul within Himself, with Himself, that is, with the very love by which He loves Himself. This is why the soul merits the love of God in all her works, insofar as she does them in God. Placed in this grace, she merits God Himself in all her works.[43]

Thus God makes us his "equal" so that we can love him with his own love, know him with his own knowledge, beautify him with his own beauty, and glorify him with his own glory in the very freedom he enjoys: in a word, participate in the very inner life of the Trinity.[44] We can truly give him something he deserves (himself) and partake of his personal life.[45] And, in turn, God acts toward his creatures in the same way he acts toward himself in the Three Persons: he completely gives himself. Arintero states eloquently:

> God who desires to assimilate us to Himself as much as possible, communicates to us His inner life, His Spirit of love, so that we become participators in His divinity. He establishes with us a friendship as close and cordial as that of a father, spouse, and brother ... As true friendship tends to the presence of the beloved and the most intimate communication possible, so the friendship of

41. John of the Cross, "Romances," 2.7.
42. John of the Cross, "Spiritual Canticles," 28.1.
43. John of the Cross, "Spiritual Canticles," 32.6. Emphasis added.
44. John of the Cross, "Spiritual Canticles," 33.6, 39.3–4.
45. John of the Cross, "Living Flame of Love," 3.78–79.

> God, which incomparably exceeds human friendship, contracts that ineffable communication of the Spirit of love, who pours forth in our souls divine charity that we may be able to love God with the selfsame love with which He loves us and with which the three adorable Persons love one another.[46]

The notion of deification, however, faces a seemingly insurmountable problem from the ideas of God that are prevalent nowadays. Many people tend to think of God as simply one step above the human race, and of God as owing us something. The notion of deification may be initially attractive for these reasons. The problem is that God is infinitely above us. He is totally other than we are. God is happy in himself; he does not need us.[47] God's completeness or perfection is due to his being a Trinity of Persons, of possessing within himself relation.[48] Relation is at the heart of reality. If God is infinitely above us, if he is happy in and of himself, and if we are infinitely below God – for we are human and not divine, and even our human nature has been marred by sin – how can we be deified or divinized? How can the distance between God and us be bridged?

God's Answer in Christ: The Incarnation

God's answer to the insurmountable problem, the unbridgeable chasm, was to send his Son into the world to reconcile the world to himself. Divinity lowered himself to our humanity, uniting the human race to the divine life of the Trinity. What humanity could not achieve through all its religious yearnings, God did by lowering himself. This teaching, so pervasive in the New Testament, is beautifully summarized by Paul when he writes, "For our sake He [God] made him [Christ] to be sin who knew no sin, so that in him we might become the righteousness of God" (2 Cor 5:21). To become God's righteousness or justice is the heart of deification, and it is only achievable because Christ lowered himself to the state of our poverty: "For you know the grace of our Lord Jesus Christ, that though he was rich, yet for your sake he became poor so that by his poverty you might become rich" (2 Cor 8:9).

46. Arintero, *Mystical Evolution*, 1:133.
47. *Catechism of the Catholic Church*, 213, 295.
48. *Catechism of the Catholic Church*, 255.

John of the Cross, speaking in the voice of the heavenly Father, well captures this dynamic of love:

> Now you see, Son, that your bride was made in your image, and so far as she is like you, she will suit you well. Yet she is different, in her flesh, which your simple being does not have. In perfect love, this law holds: that the lover become like the one he loves. For the greater their likeness the greater their delight ... This is fitting Father, what you, the Most High, say; for in this way your goodness will be the more seen, your great power will be seen and your justice and wisdom.[49]

Because the Second Person of the Trinity assumed a human nature, deification becomes as much exalted above that of Adam's deification as Jesus Christ is above Adam, who for all his exaltedness was still a finite being.[50] In order truly to understand man's purpose in deification, we must investigate the God-Man himself, Jesus Christ. Who, then, is Jesus Christ? This question may not be as easily answered as most people think, so we must turn to the collective wisdom of two thousand years of Christianity.

The classic definition of Jesus Christ comes to us from the Council of Chalcedon, which took place in 451 AD.[51] The most formidable problem facing the council was how Jesus Christ could be said to be both God and man. How could there truly be two natures, one of God (truly God) and one of man (truly human), and yet one Person in Christ? The Gospel of John issued the answer from the earliest days of the Christian Gospel, stating that "the Word became flesh and dwelt among us" (Jn 1:14). The council was anxious to balance both the divinity and the humanity of Jesus Christ because it rightly perceived that a diminution of either would undermine the entire Christian proclamation.

Thus the council insisted upon the full divinity of Jesus Christ that had been determined at the Council of Nicaea in 325.[52] In the face of the Arian heresy, Nicaea said that Jesus Christ was "true God from true God, consub-

49. John of the Cross, "Romances," 7.3–5, 7.8.

50. Scheeben, *Mysteries of Christianity*, 354–55.

51. See Carroll, *Building of Christendom*, 9–262, for a thorough discussion of the Councils of Nicaea I, Ephesus, and Chalcedon and the events surrounding them.

52. *Catechism of the Catholic Church*, 465.

stantial with the Father." Now the task for the Council at Chalcedon was to precisely define the proper relationship between the divine and human natures of Jesus Christ. It said that in Jesus Christ there was one person, the person of the divine Son of God, the Logos spoken of in John 1:14: "For in him the whole fullness of deity dwells bodily" (Col 2:9).[53] But Jesus Christ was also truly and completely man, with one exception: he did not have sin.[54] In the first century, the author of the Letter to the Hebrews stressed that Jesus was like his brothers in every way but sin (Heb 2:17, 4:15). As a man, Jesus had a human soul with its intellect and will, and a human body with all its consequent powers, which was taken from a real person of the human race, Mary, his mother.[55] He also had perfect integrity far above that of Adam; there was no inclination to evil desires as well. He was perfectly ordered.[56]

In theological terms, the union of the divine and the human in Jesus is called the hypostatic union.[57] The word *hypostasis* has a range of meanings in ancient Greek, but in this context it is the word the Fathers of the Church chose to designate "person" (the Latins used *persona*). Chalcedon said Jesus had only one person, the Second Person of the Trinity, the Son. He had no human person.[58] Human nature was so taken up into the Son that the Person of the Son is the Person of that humanity.[59] God did not displace a human person with the Divine Person, but so assumed humanity into the Person of the Son that that Person is the true Person of that human nature.[60] So when Jesus the man spoke to his Apostles, it was truly the Son of God that was speaking to them. When he acted, it was truly the Son of God acting.[61]

Probably one of the best scriptural quotations attesting to this occurs in the Gospel of John: "Truly, truly, I say to you, the Son can do nothing on his own accord, but only what he sees the Father doing; for whatever he does, that the Son does likewise. For the Father loves the Son and shows him all

53. *Catechism of the Catholic Church*, 467.
54. *Catechism of the Catholic Church*, 467.
55. *Catechism of the Catholic Church*, 466, 471–77.
56. Scheeben, *Mysteries of Christianity*, 327–30.
57. Scheeben, *Mysteries of Christianity*, 316–22.
58. *Catechism of the Catholic Church*, 467–68; *ST* III, q. 4, aa. 2–3.
59. *ST* III, q. 4, aa. 2–3.
60. *ST* III, q. 4, aa. 2–3; Scheeben, *Mysteries of Christianity*, 316–22.
61. *Catechism of the Catholic Church*, 468.

that he himself is doing" (Jn 5:19–20). Thus Jesus's actions on earth were those of the Second Person of the Trinity. Later, theologians developed these ideas by saying that Jesus also had the Beatific Vision, which is his union with God the Father in eternity.[62] He constantly beheld the glory of God in his mind on earth. This meant that Jesus willed to do good for all humanity in his every action on earth, be it healing, teaching, listening, suffering, dying on the Cross, or rising from the dead. His entire life and ministry on earth were dedicated to uniting humanity with the Father. He gave of himself completely in the same manner that the Father gives himself completely to him. And Jesus's devotion to the Father, total acceptance of everything from his Father's hand, is the model for our behavior. His life can be summed up in the words in the garden of Gethsemane: "not my will, but thine, be done" (Lk 22:42), a perfect reflection of the idea that there is no "I," only "Thou," in the Trinity. On earth, Jesus simply continued the perfect act of receiving and self-giving, or self-oblation, that occurs in God's inner life.[63]

This is how our deification is possible. Jesus's humanity was united to his divinity, and a similar union with God – certainly not the hypostatic union of Christ – takes place in us.[64] His union with the Father was natural, but ours is only by God's grace and gift. Jesus's human nature, since it was united, but not confused, with the eternal Son, was truly the human nature and human flesh of the Son of God, and thus it is "absolutely and *per se* the flesh and body of God's Son."[65] Therefore the human nature of Christ could truly call God his Father in the same way that the natural Son of God could in the Trinity, because the Person involved was the Son of God, and it enjoyed all the same rights and privileges as the natural Son.[66] In other words, the human nature of Christ could literally stand before the Father and "demand" everything the Second Person had by being the natural Son of God.[67] This is a pure mystery of the faith, because no creature could ever expect such a degree of union with God; indeed, no greater union is possible. As a result,

62. Scheeben, *Mysteries of Christianity*, 325–26, 448.

63. *Catechism of the Catholic Church*, 470, 473; Scheeben, *Mysteries of Christianity*, 359–60, 391–92, 445.

64. Scheeben, *Mysteries of Christianity*, 383–85.

65. *Catechism of the Catholic Church*, 467; Scheeben, *Mysteries of Christianity*, 368.

66. Scheeben, *Mysteries of Christianity*, 377.

67. Scheeben, *Mysteries of Christianity*, 377.

while Adam could and did lose all his privileges of grace, including deification, it is impossible for the human nature of Christ to do so.[68]

Christ's Work of Sacrifice

When Paul used the phrase "the last Adam," he was teaching that Christ was the only Savior of the human race. The whole human race is held together by him and summed up in him.[69] Christ's personality was the unlimited infinite Person of the Son, and he is therefore the Creator, Principle, Soul, Crown, and End of all humanity.[70] Christ is the bearer of the human family down to each and every individual, precisely as it is contained in each individual.[71] This is the basis for the Church's teaching that we are the mystical body of Christ.[72] The whole race belongs to the person of Christ as his body is assimilated to him, becoming in a sense a great extension of his body in space and time. As Christ is united to the Father by the divine nature in common with him, so he is united to us by having a common flesh. And as the Son receives from the Father and gives everything back to him here on earth as in eternity, so his mystical body does the same. The whole of creation united to Christ, his mystical body, the Church, is called to the same relationship with the Father as Christ has by nature.[73] By extension, therefore, in the same manner that the human nature of Christ has the same rights before the Father as the Son does by nature because his human flesh is the true flesh of the Son, so any human united to the body of Christ has, in Christ, the same rights before the Father as the Son does by nature.[74] What this means is that while deification was purely gratuitous for Adam, in Christ, it is ours by the rights and merits of Christ.[75]

Christ's union with humanity is what makes it possible for him to offer his life as a sacrifice for the sins of the whole world, for all humanity, even

68. Scheeben, *Mysteries of Christianity*, 322–30.
69. Scheeben, *Mysteries of Christianity*, 368–69.
70. Scheeben, *Mysteries of Christianity*, 365–69.
71. Scheeben, *Mysteries of Christianity*, 365–69.
72. Scheeben, *Mysteries of Christianity*, 369.
73. Scheeben, *Mysteries of Christianity*, 376–84.
74. Scheeben, *Mysteries of Christianity*, 376–84.
75. Scheeben, *Mysteries of Christianity*, 376–84.

those who reject him.[76] The crucifixion of Christ is the greatest manifestation of the Trinitarian life we have.[77] He loved both us and the Father without reserve. In a condition of sin and fall, where the world is fundamentally disordered, the world cannot have the love required for final perfection. It is no longer fit to contain its Creator. But Christ's death was a complete act of self-giving, to the point of even feeling forsaken by the Father in his human nature: "My God, My God, why hast thou forsaken Me" (Mk 15:34). He experienced the pain of body and soul on behalf of the human race that was joined to him in the mystery of the Incarnation. Yet, in the end, Jesus's death on the Cross expressed a complete trust in the Father: "Father, into Thy hands I commit my Spirit" (Lk 23:46). Christ truly immolated his body on behalf of us for the love and glory of the Father. But in death's very victory, by the power of the Holy Spirit, Christ overcame death and used it to redeem and sanctify mankind, not just restoring it to its Adamic state, but to an infinitely greater level of life.[78]

Christ's suffering and death open the path to our deification in the next life. Baptism is the normal means by which we begin this process of becoming holy.[79] Our primary Christian duty is to mature our deified state (holiness) by working to gain integrity back through reception of the sacraments, prayer, mortification, almsgiving, and penance.[80] How does this work? Holiness is first and foremost a condition of our soul. Our bodily holiness will be completed after the resurrection of our bodies and will be obtained through our soul.[81] Remember that the soul is spiritual, and the powers of the spirit are interior – intellect and love. By working to order ourselves, or gain integrity, we teach our senses to focus on the interior.[82] This disposes our nature for grace from God, to increase our holiness.

76. Scheeben, *Mysteries of Christianity* , 432–45.

77. Scheeben, *Mysteries of Christianity*, 431–47. See page 445: "Christ's sacrifice, in the very form in which it was actually offered, namely, in the shedding of His blood to the last drop, [is] the highest expression of the Trinitarian relations and the most perfect vehicle of their extension to outer world."

78. Scheeben, *Mysteries of Christianity*, 419, 455.

79. Scheeben, *Mysteries of Christianity*, 374–75, 572; *Catechism of the Catholic Church*, 628, 1214–16, 165, 1266.

80. *Catechism of the Catholic Church*, 2015; Scheeben, *Mysteries of Christianity*, 631–35.

81. Scheeben, *Mysteries of Christianity*, 666–84.

82. The Eastern Christian ascetical work the *Philokalia* (see chap. 3 in this volume) is a particularly excellent and classical Christian compendium of this idea.

The key component in deification is our human will, the ability to choose good or evil. We have a free will because we are rational creatures; we can freely choose different ends. Deification grows by the increasing choice to turn our wills toward God. But because of the Fall of Adam, our will is injured and failing. We need help to strengthen our will to choose what is right. One the most wonderful truths of the Christian faith is that God not only commands what to do, but also provides us the resources to be able to do it. That is one reason why the institutional Church exists on earth.

Earlier, I mentioned that in the Incarnation, Christ united all humanity with himself. In a sense, all humanity is in Christ, but only some people know this; they belong to the Church, the mystical body of Christ.[83] The institutional Church is an outward, visible expression of that mystical body.[84] The grace of Christ that is invisible and intangible becomes visible and tangible through the ministry of the Church.[85] As the Father chose to send his Son into the world to redeem it, so the Son of God on earth chose to send his Church – his body – into the world to communicate his life and love to the world through the liturgy and sacraments.

83. *Catechism of the Catholic Church*, 775–76; Scheeben, *Mysteries of Christianity*, 438–39.

84. *Catechism of the Catholic Church*, 771, 954.

85. *Catechism of the Catholic Church*, 774, 1116, 2014.

11 THE CHURCH AND HER LITURGY

Already present in figure at the beginning of the world, this Church was prepared in marvelous fashion in the history of the people of Israel and in the old Alliance.
–*Lumen Gentium* I.2

The liturgy is the summit towards which the activity of the Church is directed, it is the font from which all her power flows.
–*Sacrosanctum Concilium* 1.10

The Church exists to get people to heaven, to bring every human being back to his final end, which is union with the Triune God.[1] Every human activity, whether it be scientific research, artistic creation, or contemplative prayer, has the same final purpose of glorifying God through the offering of one's labors back to the Creator.[2] The Church functions to help people in their tasks of offering their lives and labors back to God. Many people think of the Church in one of two faulty ways. One involves seeing the Church as an institution that is bent on self-propagation, self-protection, and control of people's lives. In this view, the Church is much like a secular organization,

1. See Flannery, "*Lumen Gentium*," I.1–8; *Catechism of the Catholic Church*, 850.
2. *Catechism of the Catholic Church*, 299, 358, 901.

such as a corporation, a government, or a university. People who hold this view of the Church tend to distinguish between spirituality and formal religion; they typically say "Yes" to spirituality and "No" to formal religion. Oddly enough, the other deficient view sees the institutional Church in roughly the same light as the first but distinguishes between the institutional Church and the real mystical Church. This view sees the essence of the true Church as purely spiritual. The institutional structures of the Church are unnecessary add-ons. Offices, honors, and rituals are all man-made creations, not divine authorizations.

Even those who love the institutional Church, can be frustrated and stymied at times. They believe that the Church is the Bride of Christ, his body on earth, and that her ministries are ordained by God, but they too can find themselves disillusioned with particular ministers and misguided policies that are not at the core of the Good News of Jesus Christ. For them, the antidote to cynicism is twofold: metaphysics and hope. Unlike the two views mentioned above, they hold a sacramental view of reality. Just as nature embodies higher realities in physical matter – the soul is always expressed through the body – so the Church has within her bosom the mystical realities of Christ and his love. For them, spirituality is not in spite of the Church but through the Church. And no matter how decimated the Church may look at any given time, they always hold out the hope of reform, of change for the better. This hope is not a vague wish for a better day; rather, it is a supernatural power (virtue) they hold within themselves.

A Sacramental Worldview

A sacramental view of reality is startling and little understood. Earlier, I claimed that readers have probably not heard the Catholic story of the universe before. In many years of discussion with people of widely different beliefs, I have only rarely encountered those who understand this cosmology in its sacramental starkness. For a person who views reality through the lens of sacrament, everything speaks of God and higher realities; everything contains a higher dimension and a deeper meaning. The cosmos and the Church are two sides of the same coin; they are complementary realities, one in the order of nature, and the other in the order of grace. Both are ultimately designed to bring humanity and all of creation back to the Creator and Redeemer. This is why the Church has sacraments. The Church holds within its grasp the mystical realities of heaven, the very things needed for deification. It is not accidental that the *Catechism of the Catholic Church* likens each sacrament to an aspect of bodily growth and societal life.[3]

1. Baptism: the re-creation of the person and analogous to conception or birth.
2. Confirmation: analogous to maturing or growth, and which completes baptism.
3. Eucharist: divine food to nourish the soul, analogous to natural food.
4. Reconciliation (also called Confession or Penance): the forgiveness of sins when one falls from God, analogous to natural forgiveness.
5. Marriage: natural marriage raised to the order of grace.
6. Holy Orders: bishops, priests, and deacons who effect the sacraments and govern the Church, analogous to civic leaders.
7. Anointing of the sick for health of soul and body and forgiveness of sins for the chronically ill and dying: analogous to natural medicine (physical healing).

Sacraments cover every stage of life and every walk of life. The minister of every sacrament is ultimately Christ, through the Holy Spirit, who acts through human ministers.[4] In the Eucharist, the priest stands in the place of Christ as his agent in transforming the bread and wine into the body and blood of Christ. All this is accomplished by Christ as the head of the Church, the mystical body.[5] Because Christ is human as well as divine, his redemptive and sanctifying actions extend to the heart of matter itself.[6] Animals, plants, and nonliving things find their union in Christ, but they do so through human life in union with Christ; all things find their completion in Christ.[7] Christ is the "firstborn of all creatures" (Col 1:15) and through

3. *Catechism of the Catholic Church*, 1210–12, 1420–21, 1533–35, 1537, 1601.
4. *Catechism of the Catholic Church*, 1120.
5. *Catechism of the Catholic Church*, 787–96.
6. *Catechism of the Catholic Church*, 1142, 1359; Scheeben, *Mysteries of Christianity*, 401–2.
7. *Catechism of the Catholic Church*, 668, 792; Scheeben, *Mysteries of Christianity*, 401–2.

his body the Church, all things — angels, humans, and other material creatures — have their purpose and end.[8]

All creatures united to Christ constitute a great supernatural organism, the Church, the body of Christ, the new kingdom of God.[9] As Christ is the head of the Church and the Spirit of Christ is the Holy Spirit, the Holy Spirit is the soul of the Church, the active agent who brings about Christ's saving actions through the sacraments.[10] All creation united to Christ becomes a liturgical act in Christ and offers all reality back to his heavenly Father, as an act of praise under the form of the Eucharist.[11] Thus the Church primarily exists for this liturgical act of the Eucharist, which is simply the extension of Christ's eternal offering to the Father in the Holy Spirit; in this way, all reality returns to the inner life of God and becomes "the new creation" willed by the Father, such that he may see all things in his Son, "with whom he is well pleased" (Mt 3:17).[12]

The Liturgy: The Heart of the Church

"Liturgy" derives from the Greek *leitourgia*, which originally meant "public service."[13] It became the word that Greek-speaking Christians adopted to designate their public worship and that was taken over into Latin and the West. The liturgy is the primary work of the Church because the goal of life is worship of the Triune God.[14] The sacraments, the liturgy surrounding them, and the whole structure of the Church are directed toward the worship and service of God.[15] The study of liturgy, its history, and theology is a lifelong task, but the foundational meaning of such study is all rooted in the liturgy of heaven. The Church in heaven is one continuous liturgy of worship and functions as the archetype for the Church on earth and for

8. Scheeben, *Mysteries of Christianity*, 401–4.

9. *Catechism of the Catholic Church*, 792–96, 1474.

10. *Catechism of the Catholic Church*, 774–76, 792, 797–98.

11. Scheeben, *Mysteries of Christianity*, 398–404, 438–40.

12. *Catechism of the Catholic Church*, 1074, 1138, 1324–27; Scheeben, *Mysteries of Christianity*, 396–404.

13. In addition to the following references in this section on the liturgy, see Flannery, "*Sacrosanctum Concilium*," 1.1–13.

14. *Catechism of the Catholic Church*, 1074, 2084–85.

15. *Catechism of the Catholic Church*, 2096, 2114.

all creation.[16] The liturgy of the earthly Church is a real embodiment and participation in the heavenly liturgy, the act of eternal offering and praise to the Father done here on earth.[17] The earthly liturgy constitutes a present realization of the future and eternal liturgy.[18]

The liturgy is the best means of looking into heaven. Its arrangement and ordering of things are the best insight into heaven we have. It is the Image of Eternity. In the Eucharist, the glorified body and blood of Christ as it is in heaven, is also present on earth.[19] The highest act of this oblation (offering) is the sacrifice of Christ present in the Eucharist.[20] The earthly liturgy contains the essence of heaven itself, Jesus Christ, the God-Man. The Church is never more the Church than when it is at worship, because it is then that the Church is most an image, an embodiment, and a microcosm of heaven.

Contrary to the secularist separation of everyday life and religion, the Christian who truly understands the Church and her liturgy knows that all creation is at heart liturgical.[21] All of creation as it unfolded was a sequential instantiation of the Church into creation:[22] the creation of the angels was the

16. *Catechism of the Catholic Church*, 1090, 1136–39, 1326.

17. *Catechism of the Catholic Church*, 1089; Flannery, "*Sacrosanctum Concilium*," 1.8; Hahn, *The Lamb's Last Supper*. The whole thesis of Hahn's book is that the earthly liturgy is a participation in the heavenly and the principal aim of the Book of Revelation is the description of the heavenly liturgy.

18. Hahn, *Lamb's Last Supper*, 116–18.

19. Scheeben, *Mysteries of Christianity*, 514–22.

20. See the beautiful and profound treatise on the Eucharist in Scheeben, *Mysteries of Christianity*, 469–535; also 542–45.

21. *Catechism of the Catholic Church*, 347: "Creation was fashioned with a view to the Sabbath and therefore for the worship and adoration of God. Worship is inscribed in the order of creation." See also Benedict XVI (Joseph Ratzinger), *In the Beginning*, 31–32. Note especially: "Creation is designed in such a way that it is oriented to worship. It fulfills its purpose and assumes its significance when it is lived, ever new, with a view to worship. Creation exists for the sake of worship" and "The creation accounts of civilizations point to the fact that the universe exists for worship and for the glorification of God."

22. In addition to the references in note 21, see also *Catechism of the Catholic Church*, 759–62, and references therein regarding the centrality of the Church in God's plan. In particular, see 760: "The world was created for the sake of the Church" and The Church is the goal of all things." See also Puhalo, *Creation and Fall*, 1–14, and references therein. There are several things in Puhalo's book with which I disagree and that may be at odds with Catholic teaching. But this part about the Church is a good, succinct summary of the Eastern Fathers on the preexistence of the Church and its form in creation. Several citations overlap with the *Catechism of the Catholic Church*. In *ST* Suppl., q. 34, a. 1c, St. Thomas states that all things are arranged by God according to the hierarchical order described

placement of the Church in heaven,[23] and that of Adam, Eve, and Eden the placement in the material universe.[24] The liturgy is the heart and core of the Church, since it is the precise structure that brings God in the Eucharist to creation.[25] It thus constitutes the pattern, or blueprint, for the Church and all of creation.[26] The original state of creation was a preparation for the new, just as the Old Testament was preparation for the New Testament.[27] In this perspective, the natural world and knowledge prepare the way for revealed reality and knowledge. So God's original creation was modeled on and designed on the liturgy in a direct manner. This is the structure on which a Christian view of reality should be ordered; it includes science and every other form of knowledge of the world. It is the core framework that God had in mind when

by Dionysius the Areopagite, "Ecclesiastical Hierarchy," V. Finally, see Maximos the Confessor, *The Church*, 68–71, and Hahn, *Father Who Keeps His Promises*, 51–53.

23. See notes 21–22 above and Dionysius the Areopagite, "Celestial Hierarchy." The whole work explains this idea, but see especially chap. III, on the definition of hierarchy; chaps. VII–X, on the types of angels and their order; chap. VIII.3, on the three hierarchies of angels; and chap. XII, on human hierarchs (bishops) and their relation with angels. Compare to Dionysius the Areopagite, "Ecclesiastical Hierarchy," especially chap. I, on the purpose of the ecclesial hierarchy; chaps. II–IV, on the three rites in the liturgy; and chaps. V–VI, on the active and passive hierarchies. It is obvious that the angelic orders and the Church are structured the same. *ST* I, q. 108, a. 1c; I, q. 108, a. 6c. In the last *ST* citation, St. Thomas describes the three hierarchies of angels and the role of the first, second, and third as union, illumination, and purgation, respectively. Also see *SCG* II.80, where St. Thomas specifically states that the angelic hierarchy is patterned according to end, form, and order. From the citation in note 32 below, this is understood to be union, illumination, and purgation, respectively.

24. See notes 21–22 above; John of Damascene, "Orthodox Faith," 230–38, and the commentary by Puhalo, *Creation and the Fall*, 21–25. Here, St. John of Damascene, following Scripture, describes Eden, where man walks with God, and the material conditions, which are beautiful, as serving the purpose of lifting man to God. The architecture, ornamentation, and sights and sounds of the liturgy in a church building do the same. See also Ephraim the Syrian, *Hymns on Paradise*, II, III (88–96); Hahn, *Father Who Keeps His Promises*, 55.

25. Flannery, "*Sacrosanctum Concilium*," 1.7, 9.6.

26. See notes 20–24 above. Note the Dionysian definition of hierarchy ("a sacred order, a state of understanding and an activity approximating as closely as possible to the divine. And it is uplifted in imitation of God in proportion to the enlightenments divinely given to it") and consequent explanation of hierarchy's purpose as that of purifying, illumination, and perfecting ("Celestial Hierarchy" III.164D). This is precisely the explanation given of the liturgy by Maximus the Confessor, *The Church*, 90–117; *Catechism of the Catholic Church*, 760.

27. See notes 20–24 and 26 above; Flannery, "*Lumen Gentium*," I.2. St. John of Chrysostom: "And he himself made the temple [Jewish Temple, i.e., a type of the Church] in the image of the whole kosmos, both visible and invisible" (*Homily on the Birth of Christ*, trans. Dr. Kenneth Howell, personal communication, 2016).

he created everything, and it constitutes the most powerful organizing principle for all our thought and labors. As Leonardo had the complete *Mona Lisa* in mind when he painted her, so God had the liturgical act of the Church in mind as he created. It is the ultimate and perfect order of all things.

Creation is therefore the unfolding plan of the Church. The original natural world is being transformed into the newer one called the body of Christ, the Church. This original natural world is modeled after the final idea of the Church.[28] Therefore the Church is reflective of what we see in nature. The mystical body of Christ is the supernatural whole that God loves the most, as the universe is in the natural order.[29] Instead of an intellectual end of all things with some remote notion of a personal relationship ascertained by reason reflecting on the natural universe, we see a personal union developed to the highest degree in our supernatural end. The whole is the body of Christ, the second Person of the Trinity. The end of each intellectual creature coincides with a personal union with this Person of Christ. Here is found the perfect completion of the intellect and the drive of love in creatures, culminating in personal union with the Persons of the Trinity.

But as there are greater and lesser parts in the natural order, so there is in the body of Christ. These parts are constituted by a threefold development, or perfection, analogous to that of the natural order. But each is elevated far above what they are in the natural order. These are the three general parts of the liturgy upon which all of creation is based: union (end or remotion), illumination (type or disposition), and purgation (conversion or ordering to God), corresponding to tertiary, secondary, and primary perfections in nature, respectively.[30] These three parts are the principal steps in the Christian theology of the spiritual life (deification).[31] Thus the Church was founded as a means of union with God organized upon the parts of the liturgy, which itself (via the Eucharist) is the greatest means of union with God. This structure reflects down on the rest of creation as well, informing us that all things are built with the Church in view (perfect order).[32]

28. *Catechism of the Catholic Church*, 760.

29. See Eph 22–23, where husband and wife are compared to Christ and the Church, respectively. Obviously, a husband loves his wife more than a part of her.

30. On the three parts of the liturgy, see note 35 below.

31. Arintero, *Mystical Evolution*, 2:50–251.

32. Aquinas, *Commentary on the Divine Names of Blessed Dionysius* VII.4: "The entirety of the

All things in some way must mediate this union with God. What else could creation ultimately be in view of the infinite love of God for us? The liturgy of the Church, the body of Christ, is the archetype and model toward which all things tend, as it is *the* means of union with God. As stated by St. Paul (Col 1:15–18), "*He is the image of the invisible God, the firstborn of all creation; for in Him all things were created, in the heavens and on the earth, visible and invisible, whether thrones, or dominions, or principalities, or powers, or authorities – all things were created through him and for Him. He is before all things, and in Him all things hold together. He is the head of His body, the Church; he is the beginning, the firstborn from the dead, that in everything he might be pre-eminent.*"

Many of the Church Fathers refer to union, illumination, and purgation as parts of the liturgy. Among the most notable is Maximos the Confessor, one of the greatest Greek theological thinkers, whose work *Mystagogy* addresses this subject.[33] *Mystagogy* is a concise explanation of how the liturgy is composed of these three parts. Another great thinker in the same tradition, from whom St. Maximos drew significant inspiration, is Dionysius the Areopagite. Dionysius's entire corpus revolves around this idea of the liturgy.[34] St. Maximus says that the progression of the liturgy is built on union,

---

creatures is set by God for us that we would know God through it, insofar as the entire order possesses certain images and imperfect assimilations (or likenesses) of divine things that are compared to themselves as principal exemplars to images. Thus, therefore, out of the order of the universe, just as by a certain way or order, we ascend through the intellect, according to our power to God, who is over all, and this in three ways: first and principally in the removal of everything insofar as we think of God or as fitting for God nothing of those things which we observe in the order of creatures [*union*]. A second way is through excess: [i.e.] for not such creaturely perfections such as life, wisdom, and things of this type do we remove from God because God had a defect; but rather because he exceeds every perfection of the creature [*illumination*]. Further, we remove from him wisdom because he exceeds all wisdom; third, by the causality of everything as long as we consider that whatever is in creatures proceeds from God as from a cause [*purgation*]" (emphasis mine). Once again, from the other works of Dionysius (see note 23 above for relevant citations from his "Celestial Hierarchy" and "Ecclesial Hierarchy"), it is understood that St. Thomas's terms removal (remotion), excess, and cause correspond to union, illumination, and purgation, respectively.

33. See Von Balthasar, *Cosmic Liturgy*, for an analysis of the general liturgical view of creation held by Maximos the Confessor.

34. See Golitzin, *Et Introibo ad Altare Dei* and *Mystagogy*. Both works are beautiful and profound analyses of the Dionysian corpus and were an inspiration for me to study and learn this tradition and write this book. In addition, Golitzin's works taught me that the key to the entire corpus of Dionysius's works is "Ecclesiastical Hierarchy," not "Mystical Theology," as many Western thinkers claim

illumination, and purgation.[35] One begins with Scripture readings to purge people of worldly concerns (purgation) and focus their attention on God. The Nicene Creed transitions from purgation to illumination by educating about the higher doctrines of the faith. Then occurs the consecration, where Christ comes in the Eucharist to enlighten or illumine the faithful, as he did to the disciples on the road to Emmaus (Lk 24:30–31). The "Our Father" is the transition from illumination to union as one begins to call God, "Father." Finally, one receives the Eucharist, attaining union with God.[36]

The Old and New Testaments are replete with this liturgical structure. A well-known commentary regarding this idea is Gregory of Nyssa's *Life of Moses*, in which Gregory explains Moses's ascent of Sinai as a type of the liturgy.[37] Purgation is represented by Moses's abandonment of the life of the senses and the cares of the world, exemplified when he leaves behind the people of Israel and their purification. Exodus 19:17 states that Moses told the people to station themselves at the foot of the mountain after sanctifying and washing themselves (Ex 17:10). They were not to break through to see the Lord (Ex 19:21). Next, Moses hears trumpets and sounds (Ex 19:16, 19:19). These represent all of creation proclaiming God (illumination). Finally, he encounters the unseeable God in a cloud (union) (Ex 19: 9, 19:18), where he sees God's dwelling and uses it as the model according to which he builds the Jewish tabernacle and temple (Ex 25:9). The Jewish temple is

(Golitzin, *Et Introibo ad Altare Dei*, 42). In addition to the citation in note 22 above, see Dionysius the Areopagite, "Celestial Hierarchy," especially chaps. III, VII–X, VIII.3, and XII; Dionysius the Areopagite, "Ecclesiastical Hierarchy," chaps. I–VI; and *ST* I, q. 108, a. 1c; I, q. 108. A. 6c.

35. See Maximos the Confessor, *The Church*, 90–117, for the remainder of the paragraph. This theme of purgation, illumination, and union is repeated over and over in these pages.

36. There is a distinction between Dionysius and Maximos the Confessor in the emphasis placed on the parts of the liturgy for purgation, illumination, and union. Dionysius and Maximos seem to be in agreement that the liturgy of the Word is the purgative part of the liturgy. The difference comes in illumination and union. Dionysius sees the Eucharist as the illuminative part, and the sacred Myron (oils) of the bishop that remain reserved behind the veil for the use of the clergy as union. Maximos, by contrast, sees the creed and institution as illumination, and the reception of and transformation by the Eucharist as union. It is important to notice, however, that the threefold structure of the liturgy is held by both. I tend to follow Maximos the Confessor's approach, as it is more presentable to modern Catholics, but in so doing, I am not at all denying the validity of the Dionysian approach.

37. Gregory of Nyssa, *Life of Moses*, 152–88. See Dionysius the Areopagite, "Mystical Theology," 134–41, for among the most famous of all commentaries on St. Gregory of Nyssa's work.

but a figure of the liturgy as well.[38] It consisted of three general parts. The inner sanctuary consisting of the Holy of Holies where God dwells (union), the veil covering the Holy of Holies represents illumination, and the outer court where the priests purify themselves figures purgation. Exodus 26:31–34 states:

> You shall make a veil of blue and purple and scarlet material and fine twisted linen; it shall be made with cherubim, the work of a skillful workman. You shall hang it on four pillars of acacia overlaid with gold, their hooks also being of gold, on four sockets of silver. You shall hang up the veil under the clasps, and shall bring in the ark of the testimony there within the veil; and the veil shall serve for you as a partition between the holy place and the holy of holies. You shall put the mercy seat on the ark of the testimony in the holy of holies.

Church Fathers such as St. Augustine, St. Bede, and Origen summarize this passage as follows.[39] The veil was hung across the wall that divided the inner temple—the Holy of Holies, where the Ark of the Covenant was placed—from the outer section of the temple called the sanctuary. The inner temple, which was invisible to all but the High Priest, represents heaven, and the ark represents the Lord. The outer section was visible and served as the place where the sacrifices were offered. This was accessible to all the priests and represents the Church in the world. The outer courtyard was where the priests sanctified themselves. If the priest was not sanctified (purged), he could not enter into the Holy of Holies where God dwelt (union).

Chapter 12 of the Letter to the Hebrews directly refers to the Church as the heavenly Jerusalem (the structure of heaven – the temple or liturgy).[40] The entire Book of Revelation refers to this idea and is therefore simply describing heaven as a perpetual liturgy, or Mass, the eternal offering of Christ and his body, the Church, to the Father.[41]

Scripture as a whole is arranged to figure the liturgy. For example, the liturgical structure of Noah's Ark consisted of animals on the lower deck (purgation), birds in the middle (illumination represented by their ability to fly

38. Ephraim the Syrian, *Hymns on Paradise*, III.

39. Lienhard, "Exodus, Leviticus, Numbers, Deuteronomy," 127–28, 134–36.

40. Heb 12:22. Note also in Heb 18–22 the description of the Sinai event and Moses, again a type of the liturgy.

41. Hahn, *Lamb's Last Supper*.

upward), and Noah, like a deity, on top (union).[42] The whole journey of Israel from Egypt to the promise land shows a liturgical structure. The Israelites leave Egypt and start to be purged of slavery (sin); the wanderings in the Sinai Desert are a continuation of this purge. Illumination occurs on Sinai with the Law. Finally, union is the entering of the promise land. Yet another example is the Transfiguration of Christ: Elijah represents purgation as he preached repentance to Israel, Moses is illuminator as he gave the Law to Israel, and Christ is union, as he is God and Elijah and Moses adore him.[43] Everything in Scripture is a development of this liturgical structure (the Church) from Adam to Christ, what we in general call salvation history: after the Fall of Adam until Abraham is purgation, from Abraham to John the Baptist is illumination, and with the coming of Christ, union is possible.[44]

And so we return full circle to the Church, the supernatural organism willed for eternity by God to draw all of creation into personal communion with himself, raising us up in Christ into the very inner life of the Trinity.[45] Here we are at the heart of the Hierarchy of Being, the ultimate core of which is the liturgy. On the altars of churches around the world, during the liturgy, the infinite natural Son offers himself perfectly to the Father in sacrifice. The whole of reality is presented perfectly in Christ to the Father. Perfect praise, adoration, and love are offered to God the Father, and hence the Holy Trinity in the liturgy, because God is offered to God, the only being capable of truly pleasing and loving him. Everything comes down from God here as well, since we receive the Eucharist, which is Christ, the God-Man. This is the ultimate perfect order of things.

42. Ephraim the Syrian, *Hymns on Paradise*, II.

43. Toal, *Sunday Sermons*, 37–73.

44. Thus purgation, illumination, and union, the three stages of the spiritual life, and the three parts of the Liturgy can be reduced as follows, according to Arintero: "In purgation a man understands himself, in illumination, he understands God, in union he works to be united and transformed into God. Purgation is attributed to the Father, illumination the Son, and union, the Holy Spirit. Quoting Bonaventure the three stages are reduced to Who am I, Who Is God? How can I become united to Him through love?" (*Mystical Evolution*, 1:49). Is this not simply salvation history? While no Divine Person is limited in what he does in creation, we can attribute the roles of the Three Persons in creation: God the Father creates and Israel is chosen (typically attributed to the Father revealing himself), Christ redeems (the Son's revelation), and the Holy Spirit forms the Church (revelation of the Holy Spirit).

45. Eph 1:3–5; Scheeben, *Mysteries of Christianity*, 539–42.

The Structure of the Church as Hierarchy

If the structure of the liturgy and deification are patterned upon purgation, illumination, and union, the structure of the Church reflects this reality as well. Now we can also view the structure of the liturgy from the standpoint of the two visible hierarchies of the Church. The first is the ecclesial, or active hierarchy, consisting of bishops, priests, and deacons,[46] those who are the active source of grace by dispensing the sacraments. The second is the passive hierarchy of monks, baptized laity, and catechumens, those who receive the sacraments.[47] Here, one can see that the idea of union, illumination, and purgation is exactly reflected. This is particularly evident in more ancient versions of the liturgy, where the positioning of the clergy reenacted deification.[48] Bishops would stand immediately in the central place at the altar, the throne of God, in imitation of union with God in the spiritual life. Priests would receive the Holy Mysteries from the bishops, representing the middle stage, illumination. They stood at the altar, flanking the bishop, representing their lower position. Finally, deacons would stand between the priests and the laity, where, by proclaiming the Gospel, they would draw the laity (through purgation) to the priest for illumination. The monks, those coming out of the lay ranks for special consecration to God (union), would be seated between the deacons and the rest of the baptized faithful, who are those illumined by the light of Christ. Finally, the catechumens would stand toward the back of the Church and remain present only through the reading of the Gospel and homily, thus being purged by listening to the Word of God.

As I discuss in chapter 12, the angelic hierarchies in heaven are also arranged in this manner. We see this in the liturgical structure of the Church's rituals. At the Great Entrance of eastern liturgies, such as that of the liturgy of John Chrysostom, one hears the acclamation "Let us who mystically represent the Cherubim, and sing the thrice-holy hymn to the life creating Trinity, now set aside all earthly cares that we may receive the King of all." There are reflections of this in the Roman rite: during the first eucharis-

46. Dionysius the Areopagite, "Ecclesiastical Hierarchy," V; Golitzin, *Mystagogy*, 210–17.

47. Dionysius the Areopagite, "Ecclesiastical Hierarchy," VI; Golitzin, *Mystagogy*, 212–13.

48. Dionysius the Areopagite, "Letter Eight," 1089A; Golitzin, *Mystagogy*, 211–12, 213–17.

tic prayer, one hears, "we humbly beseech you, almighty God, to command that these offerings be carried by your angel to your altar in heaven." All liturgies sing the *Holy, Holy, Holy* of the Seraphim and Cherubim from Isaiah (6:1–4) and Revelation (4:8) before the consecration. The progression of the liturgy reflects this as well.

In addition to their positioning in the liturgy, the holy orders (bishops, priests, and deacons) and the passive hierarchy (monks, baptized, and catechumens) that constitute the hierarchical structure of the Church themselves represent these three parts of the liturgy. Bishops represent union, priests illumination, and deacons purgation in the active hierarchy,[49] while the monks represent union, the baptized laity illumination, and the catechumens purgation in the passive hierarchy.[50] All of reality centers on Christ, his incarnation, the liturgy, and union with him in the spiritual life.

The bishop is the successor to the Apostles.[51] He has the fullness of ecclesial powers and can effect all seven sacraments, which are the primary sources of grace in the New Covenant of Christ. He is the head and governor of a territory in the Church, the diocese or eparchy. As an individual, his office represents unity in the spiritual life.[52] Priests are the dispenser of the seven sacraments and can affect all but holy orders.[53] Because the sacraments are the primary sources of grace instituted by Christ for the New Covenant, priests are the dispensers of divine providence and through the sacraments illumine the faithful. Thus their role is analogous to illumination in the spiritual life.[54] Deacons are the lowest level of holy orders, and their role is the preaching of the Gospel and the temporal affairs of the Church.[55] Through preaching, they are to draw the faithful toward higher things and away from excessive attachment and absorption in worldly affairs. They

49. Dionysius the Areopagite, "Ecclesiastical Hierarchy," V, 504C–508B; Golitzin, *Mystagogy*, 210–12. See also *ST* Suppl., q. 34, a. 1c; Suppl, q. 37, a. 2c, and ad. 1.

50. Dionysius the Areopagite, "Ecclesiastical Hierarchy," VI, 529D–533A; Golitzin, *Mystagogy*, 212–13.

51. *Catechism of the Catholic Church*, 86–862, 1555–61.

52. Dionysius the Areopagite, "Ecclesiastical Hierarchy," VI, 529D–533A; Golitzin, *Mystagogy*, 212–13.

53. *Catechism of the Catholic Church*, 1562–68.

54. Dionysius the Areopagite, "Ecclesiastical Hierarchy," VI, 529D–533A; Golitzin, *Mystagogy*, 212–13.

55. *Catechism of the Catholic Church*, 1569–71.

purge the faithful from things leading them away from God. They represent purgation in the spiritual life.[56]

Regarding the passive hierarchy, the monk is the archetype of the Christian life.[57] In the most extreme form of monastic life, the eremitical, his life is a consecration to God to do all things for God alone. All activities and desires give way to doing things purely for the love of God in himself. This is the highest of all creaturely activities, constituting love in its most pure form, and is the essence of union with God. The life of all in heaven will consist in this. The baptized laity represent illumination, because by baptism they have been enlightened and brought into the life of Christ.[58] They strain toward the ideal of the monk to the degree that their situation in life allows them. The catechumens represent purgation, as they are purging themselves of their desire for the world and of their former evil ways as they progress toward baptism.[59]

Bishops and monks represent the higher levels of the Church hierarchies (union), but this does not mean that they are the only ones called to union with God. All people are called to union with God.[60] By definition, anyone in *heaven* is in union with God.[61] In the earthly Church, the ministers of the Church represent these realities because *ecclesial* positions *represent and/or mediate* union, or illumination, or purgation. But in the heavenly Church, placement in the *heavenly* hierarchy of union, illumination, and purgation is based on the level of charity, or love, one attains here on earth, not whether one is a bishop, a priest, a deacon, monk, or a layman.[62] All angels or men in all three parts of the Hierarchy of Being in heaven have attained union with God. Nevertheless, their position or placement in the heavenly hierarchy is based on the intensity of this union. Neither all human beings nor all angels are equal in heaven.[63] The deciding factor is love.

56. Dionysius the Areopagite, "Ecclesiastical Hierarchy," VI, 529D–533A; Golitzin, *Mystagogy*, 212–13.

57. Dionysius the Areopagite, "Ecclesiastical Hierarchy," VI, 532D–537C; Golitzin, *Mystagogy*, 212.

58. Dionysius the Areopagite, "Ecclesiastical Hierarchy," VI, 532A–532B; Golitzin, *Mystagogy*, 212–13.

59. Dionysius the Areopagite, "Ecclesiastical Hierarchy," VI, 532B–532C; Golitzin, *Mystagogy*, 213.

60. *Catechism of the Catholic Church*, 2013–14, 2028, 2045.

61. *Catechism of the Catholic Church*, 1045.

62. *Catechism of the Catholic Church*, 772–73. *ST* Suppl., q. 94.

63. *Catechism of the Catholic Church*, 1021; *ST* Suppl., qq. 93–94; Suppl., q. 96. See also I, q. 26,

The liturgy and the structure of the earthly Church are so important because God desires to deify us, and the Eucharist is the core means of contact with the whole scheme because it brings us Christ in the liturgy. The pattern of the liturgy is the structure of the mystical body of Christ. Christ as the God-Man acts as he has done eternally by offering himself completely to the Father. In this way, Christ extends the inner life of God to all things. The liturgy captures the meaning of the words "All mine are thine, and thine are mine."

The Eucharist: The Sacrament of Sacraments

If the Church exists to get people to heaven, as it surely does, then its most important gift to the human race is the Eucharist.[64] As the Incarnation was God's answer to unite himself with humanity through the person of Jesus Christ, so the Eucharist is God's answer to bring people to Jesus Christ. As the Incarnation is the extension of the Trinitarian life to creation, the Eucharist is the extension of the Incarnation.[65] This is why the Eucharist is the source and summit of Christian life.[66] Without the Eucharist, the Church is nothing, but with the Eucharist, it is everything; it makes the Church.[67] All the sacraments are contained in and oriented to the Eucharist and in it is "contained the whole spiritual good of the Church."[68] It therefore completes the offering of the life of the Trinity and completes the idea of deification.[69]

The synoptic Gospels record for us the institution of the Eucharist.[70] On the last night of his life before his crucifixion, Jesus took his twelve disciples into an upper room where he said, "'Take, eat; this is my body.' And he took a cup, and when he had given thanks, he gave it to them, saying, 'Drink of it,

a. 3c, explaining that the object of beatitude, God, is the same for all, but as regards the act of beatitude (understanding or union with God), this differs for each creature. *SCG* III.58.

64. Scheeben, *Mysteries of Christianity*, 469–535, 542–45.

65. *Catechism of the Catholic Church*, 790, 1003, 1391, 2845; Scheeben, *Mysteries of Christianity*, 477–79, 481, 485–86, 496–97, 522.

66. *Catechism of the Catholic Church*, 1211, 1324.

67. *Catechism of the Catholic Church*, 1396.

68. *Catechism of the Catholic Church*, 1324.

69. *Catechism of the Catholic Church*, 950, 1074, 1212, 2845; Scheeben, *Mysteries of Christianity*, 479–97, 512–33.

70. *Catechism of the Catholic Church*, 1337–44.

all of you; for this is my blood of the covenant, which is poured out for many for the forgiveness of sins'" (Mt 26:26–28). In these few words the entire meaning of salvation and eternal life is contained. The Church professes that the Eucharist is the same substance as Jesus Christ himself and that through communing with him, human beings are able to be deified, made more and more into the image of Christ.[71] Yet because this sacrament entails so much that is foreign to the modern secularized mind, it is necessary to comprehend more exactly what the Eucharist is and why it transforms everything.

The Eucharist is the sacrament whereby the priest, during the liturgy (the Mass), acts in the person of Jesus Christ and changes the bread and wine into the body and blood of Christ.[72] The appearance (technically called accidents) is still that of bread and wine, but the substance of the bread and wine has become the body and blood of Christ.[73] The Church makes no apology for the miraculous character of this event; there is simply nothing like it in the natural realm, but natural analogies can help us understand the event. Every living thing changes appearance as it grows. A puppy has many features it loses or acquires as it matures, as does a young corn plant as it becomes a mature plant. The changes in a natural organism are changes in the accidents (appearance) of the organism, not in its substance.[74] The substance of each naturally occurring thing is what gives it identity over time. The puppy is the same animal as the grown dog. Now, in the course of nature, the appearance of a thing does not change its underlying substance. The appearance of a thing, or what is referred to in Aristotelian philosophy as its accidents, is supported by what the thing is (its substance).[75] By its nature or substance, a dog never looks like a corn plant or vice versa. Something abides (its nature) and something changes (its appearance or accidents).[76] In the changing of the bread and wine into the body and blood of Christ, it is the substance that is miraculously changed; the appearances

71. *Catechism of the Catholic Church*, 950, 1074, 1212, 1374, 2845; Scheeben, *Mysteries of Christianity*, 479–97, 512–33.

72. *Catechism of the Catholic Church*, 1376. Scheeben, *Mysteries of Christianity*, 497–511; *ST* III, qq. 75–77.

73. *ST* III, qq. 75–77.

74. Aquinas, *Commentary on Aristotle's Physics* I.11–13.

75. Aquinas, *Commentary on Aristotle's Physics* I.11–13.

76. Aquinas, *Commentary on Aristotle's Physics* I.11–13.

are miraculously held in place by the nature of Christ.[77] He who created all can alter the way things work; the externals are held constant while the substance changes. So in the Eucharist, the nature or substance of bread and wine is changed into the body and blood of Christ. Nature is not replaced, but changed.[78]

It is through Holy Communion that our human natures are restored to their divine origin and brought more closely to the divine end.[79] As the bread and wine are changed into something infinitely greater, so are we changed in an analogous manner toward greater deification.[80] Recall that in the Incarnation there is a union of the divine and human natures in *one* person, the Second Person of the Trinity. When people receive the Eucharist, they are receiving the Person of Jesus Christ, not simply his body and blood in a limited sense.[81] The expression "body and blood" is often expanded into the fuller form of "body and blood, soul and divinity."[82] Jesus's divine nature and person are communicated through his human nature to the one who receives him in the sacrament of the Eucharist.[83] The Eucharist is God among us.[84]

It is beyond belief that God would humble himself and become so vulnerable to human beings. He uses a human sinner like all of us (the priest) to pronounce the words of Christ – words from the mouth of God himself – that effect this change.[85] Now, the priest has no power in and of himself to effect this change, this transubstantiation, but the priest puts his mouth at the disposal of Christ, who through the Holy Spirit transforms the bread and wine into Christ's body and blood.[86] This complete transformation by Christ and into Christ with the words "Take . . ., this is my body" is reminiscent of the perfect giving of the Father and Son in the Trinity in the

77. Scheeben, *Mysteries of Christianity*, 497–511; *ST* III, qq. 75–77.

78. Scheeben, *Mysteries of Christianity*, 497–501.

79. Scheeben, *Mysteries of Christianity*, 479–97, 512–33.

80. Scheeben, *Mysteries of Christianity*, 479–97, 512–33.

81. *Catechism of the Catholic Church*, 1374, 1377.

82. *Catechism of the Catholic Church*, 1374.

83. *Catechism of the Catholic Church*, 1212, 1391–92; Scheeben, *Mysteries of Christianity*, 479–97, 512–33 (esp. 526).

84. *Catechism of the Catholic Church*, 1404.

85. *Catechism of the Catholic Church*, 1367, 1411.

86. *Catechism of the Catholic Church*, 1333, 1348, 1353, 1357, 1410, 1545, 1548. See also Scheeben, *Mysteries of Christianity*, 509–10, on the Holy Spirt effecting the Eucharist.

words, "All mine are thine, and thine are mine." These words, *Take this*, in their stark meaning enacted by Christ, can be argued to be the same action by Christ on earth as those that he does eternally in the Trinity, when he says, "All mine are thine." As the infinitely perfect act of complete giving of himself in the Holy Spirit by the Father generates Christ, who is begotten, from eternity, so analogously the perfect self-giving of Christ in the Liturgy transforms the bread and wine into Christ by the infinite power of the Holy Spirit. Thus it is Christ as God that is totally given to us. He is absolutely at our disposal ("For to us a child is born, to us a son is given," Is 9:6) in the pure silence and plainness of the appearance of bread and wine. As the Persons of the Trinity give themselves absolutely to each other, so is Christ given to us. The Eucharist is therefore the greatest sign and symbol of the Most Holy Trinity and constitutes the best view into the fires of the divinity.[87]

The same Jesus Christ who once lived on earth and had every appearance of being a true man is the same one who is received in the Eucharist, the difference being that in the Eucharist the glorified body and blood of Christ in heaven are received.[88] While Jesus's death on the Cross was the sacrifice of his own life in a bloody fashion in his earthly flesh, the Eucharist is the same sacrifice of Christ (not a new one) but in an unbloody fashion.[89] As Christ was sacrificed once and for all on Calvary, the sacred liturgy (the Mass) is the application of this sacrifice through time and space to all individuals.[90] The Eucharist, then, is the primary agent of deification.[91] It is food for the soul.[92] We eat natural food for nourishment and for enjoyment, and we only possess and enjoy it transiently as it is changed into us through our metabolism. In the Eucharist, however, Christ absorbs us and changes us into himself.[93] The primary purpose of this "marvelous exchange," as it is called in the liturgical prayers, is the mutual possession and enjoyment of two lovers: Christ and the human soul.[94] Here the law of assimilation,

87. Van Breman, *God Who Won't Let Go,* 85.

88. Scheeben, *Mysteries of Christianity*, 509–22.

89. *Catechism of the Catholic Church*, 1362, 1367.

90. *Catechism of the Catholic Church*, 1369.

91. Scheeben, *Mysteries of Christianity*, 480–81, 512.

92. *Catechism of the Catholic Church*, 1212, 1275, 1436, 2837; Scheeben, *Mysteries of Christianity*, 504–30.

93. Scheeben, *Mysteries of Christianity*, 500, 513–14, 523–25.

94. Scheeben, *Mysteries of Christianity*, 527–30.

discussed in chapter 5, is found exercised in a perfect manner. Whereas the life of nutriment in plants and other material organisms broke up that which they assimilated as food, the individual is perfectly assimilated into unity in Christ but keeps his distinction as a human person.

The Eucharist is first and foremost food for the soul, since the soul is the highest part of us. Throughout this book, I have stressed that the concept of the soul has been misunderstood. In traditional philosophy and Christian thought, the psyche or *anima* (soul) has everything to do with the intellect and love. The Eucharist brings about a progressive union of God with our intellect or soul by infusing divine love into it.[95] And rightly so, because the intellect is the faculty of union with spiritual things: love ends in union. So as God unites himself with our intellects (personal union), we are slowly changed into him. As John of the Cross wrote so incisively, "with love the soul pays to God what she owes Him; with the intellect, on the contrary, she receives from Him."[96] This is analogous to the natural Son of God being the Intellect or Word of the Father, and he who both receives and is what he receives.

Deification Refocused

We now have an answer to our question about the means for deification. The liturgy of the Church, and especially the Eucharist, is the divinely given primary means to attain deification and final union with God. The great spiritual theologian John Arintero has beautifully summed up this truth:

> He infuses us with a participation in His own being and He transfigures us into the image of His only-begotten Son, so that we might be a living splendor of the divine Word just as the Word is "the brightness of His glory and the figure of his substance" (Heb 1:3). Then seeing His own Son resplendent in us, He sees Himself in us and can look upon us with that infinite complacency which He enjoys in His adorable and absolute perfections.... The true supernatural order consists, then, in God's humbling Himself to the level of His creature and the creature's being elevated, so far as possible, to the level of the Creator. It consists, in short, in the incarnation and humanization of God and the deification of man. Such is the sublime order to which we have been raised by the divine liberality.[97]

95. *Catechism of the Catholic Church*, 1392; Scheeben, *Mysteries of Christianity*, 523–30.
96. John of the Cross, "Spiritual Canticles," 38.5.
97. Arintero, *Mystical Evolution*, 1:43–44.

Arintero has drawn on a long history of spiritual wisdom that goes to the heart of our theme. Love has its origin in God and leads back to God. In fact, the only love that can be worthy of God is what he himself gives in Christ, as John of the Cross stated long ago. Recasting the love of the Father for the Son, John of the Cross speaks of the Church as the bride of Christ, writing: "My Son, I wish to give You a bride who will love You. Because of You she will deserve to share our company, and eat bread at Our table, the same bread I eat, that she may know the good I have in such a Son; and rejoice with Me in Your grace and fullness."[98]

Deification will reach its completion only in heaven.[99] The body of Christ in the Eucharist will have prepared the soul for the full reception of God as its nourishment and end.[100] The soul will be expanded and given the capacity of direct union with God and full participation in the divine life, where it will possess the unmediated and intuitive intellectual vision (the Beatific Vision) of the divine essence.[101] "We shall be like Him, for will shall see him as he is" (1 Jn 3:2), and "this is eternal life, that they know Thee [Beatific Vision] the only true God, and Jesus Christ, whom Thou hast sent" (Jn 17:3). This vision is proper by nature only to the Persons of the Trinity itself, but creatures share in the vision by grace.[102] Here, the entire Church, the body of Christ with Christ as its head, embracing all creation, will present of itself an eternal oblation and offering of praise before the Father.[103] This will simply be the final extension of the Trinitarian life to creatures offered back to the Father. The Church will be a great supernatural organism in which it will act as both offerer and offered to the Glory of God the Father.[104] Because the Holy Spirit vivifies this body as its soul, he will permeate the entire edifice as one great Temple of God.[105] Here the end of human life and of the entire created order is finally realized in all its fullness.

98. John of the Cross, "Romances," 3.1–2.
99. Scheeben, *Mysteries of Christianity*, 523–27.
100. Scheeben, *Mysteries of Christianity*, 523–27.
101. Scheeben, *Mysteries of Christianity*, 651–65; *SCG* III.58–63.
102. Scheeben, *Mysteries of Christianity*, 659.
103. Scheeben, *Mysteries of Christianity*, 397, 402, 438–39, 443.
104. *Catechism of the Catholic Church*, 1356–72.
105. *Catechism of the Catholic Church*, 797–98; Scheeben, *Mysteries of Christianity*, 394, 544–45.

12 THE COSMOS AS A LADDER OF LITURGICAL PERFECTION

The liturgy of the Church is built around the progression from purgation to illumination and from illumination to final union with God. The unique claim made in this book—unique at least to modern ears—is that the whole universe is similarly structured.[1,2] As union is the end of the Church's litur-

1. As cited in chapter 11, note 26, see Dionysius the Areopagite, "Celestial Hierarchy," III.164D, on the definition of hierarchy and his explanation of it in terms of purification, illumination, and perfection. The specific role of hierarchy is to perform these operations in order to draw as close to God as possible, which is precisely the point of the liturgy and the hierarchy of creation. The *Catechism of the Catholic Church*, 299 and 342, states that creation is ordered and a hierarchy. See *ST* Suppl., q. 34, a. 1c, where St. Thomas states that all things are arranged by God according to the hierarchical order described by Dionysius the Areopagite, "Ecclesiastical Hierarchy," V (purgation, illumination, union).

2. A point should be noted here regarding purgation. In this chapter, I cite several instances where both the immaterial (angelic) and material universe reflect purgation, illumination, and union. To most people, the reflexive idea is that purgation has to do with a moving away from sin. Purgation *in the context of sin* means a turning away from sin toward God, but purgation is not necessarily tied to sin. As Arintero states, "In purgation, man understands himself"; therefore anything that allows one to know his relation to God is purgation (*Mystical Evolution*, 1:49). Similarly, Nichols notes that the Church Father Irenaeus of Lyons wrote that the world is a "divinely appointed milieu" for "soul-making" and "producing mature persons to reflect the life of God" (*Shape of Catholic Theology*, 69–70, 200). The world was thus created as a place of trial (purgation) to join men to God. Purgation

gy, so the Hierarchy of Being has as its goal the union of all creation with the Creator in reflection of and assimilation into the liturgy, its model. Because human beings are the pinnacle of the material created order, they serve as the integration point for the whole universe; in human life and labor, the universe can be offered back to its Origin as an act of worship. It is in this new worldview that science takes on a wider and more meaningful sense, a sense in which all human labor, including science, finds its purpose beyond the material world in the End of all things.

I wrote earlier of the imperfect and perfect orders as a way of scoping out the whole of the cosmos. The imperfect was a perspective from the bottom up that viewed the material world from the standpoint of individual facts and patterns. This imperfect order parallels the progression from purgation through illumination to union. The imperfect order is like standing on the bottom rung of a ladder and ascending step by step to a higher level. The perfect order is the perspective from the top down that views the cosmos from the standpoint of the whole. Once we have a greater knowledge of the universe through the revealed plan of God, we can view the entire cosmos from above. God's revelation aids us in recasting all our scientific knowledge in the light of its ultimate purpose. This perfect order is like standing on the top rung of a ladder and looking down on each step in relation to the vantage point of the top. The whole of creation is illuminated as a reflection of the Creator's goodness and love. The perfect or complete order parallels the top-down view from union to illumination to purgation.[3] The imperfect order is how limited human beings approach the world; the perfect order is

is a trial in which man progresses to greater dependence upon God, whether in sin or not. Jesus himself could undergo purgation. In the temptation in the desert, the first temptation was to turn stone into bread. The reply of Christ was, "Not on bread alone shall man live." Here is a turning away from a material good by ordering to that which is higher. Jesus *as man* could be perfected (he "increased in wisdom and in stature, and in favor with God and man," Lk 2:52). As I discuss below, Adam before the Fall was to undergo a trial (purgation) that would eventually lead to entry into heaven. In its broadest sense, then, as defined by Thomas Aquinas (*Commentary on the Divine Names of Blessed Dionysius* VII.4), purgation is "whatever in creatures proceeds from God as a cause." Therefore the universe can be created "very good" and yet still be brought to a higher level of perfection. And the first step in this process is a trial or a reorientation to that which is higher (purgation). These steps – purgation, illumination, and union – are the very nature of reality and being.

3. See also Toma, "Dionysian/Thomistic Framework," 87–113, for further discussion of this tripartite order in creation.

how God sees the cosmos. How, then, does the universe look from the perspective of perfect ordering?

The Immaterial Universe

The highest of creatures (God is not a creature) in the immaterial universe are angels.[4] The English word "angel" derives from the Greek *aggelos*, which originally meant a "messenger," whether human or superhuman. As such, it was an appropriate translation of the Hebrew *malak*, which had the same systematic ambiguity. In time, the Christian usage of *aggelos* (Latin *angelus*) came to designate a generic preternatural being that communicated God's messages to human beings, as well as a specific type of angel that was the lowest in the angelic hierarchy, the one closest to the created material order.[5]

As I argued in Part II, human reason can infer the possibility of the existence of angels as pure thought. As spiritual substances, they possess intellect and will, or thought and love, such that they exist as persons that can enter into communion with other such beings: they are personal. To the degree something is spiritual, its nature consists to a greater degree of intellect and will and is more personal. Contrary to a materialist worldview, spiritual realities are hardly irrational; a spiritual substance is the very definition of intellectuality, love, and communion, just as the human intellect is capable of love and communion precisely because of its immaterial (spiritual) nature. God's revelation in Scripture and throughout the history of the Church deepens these conclusions and informs us of the precise kinds of angels, their orders, and their duties. This tradition assigns them a place in God's plan for union with him. The hierarchy of angels is therefore made by God to represent and mediate union (the end), illumination (type or disposition), and purgation (means), constituting the liturgical structure in heaven.[6] Drawing on numerous references in the Old and New Testaments, there are three general classes or hierarchies.[7]

4. *Catechism of the Catholic Church*, 330.

5. *Catechism of the Catholic Church*, 331 (messengers), 336 (aids to men). Regarding lower angels more specifically as aids to men, see notes 10 and 11 below.

6. Dionysius the Areopagite, "Celestial Hierarchy," III; *ST* I, q. 108, a. 1.

7. *ST* I. q. 108, aa. 5–6. There are several different names for the ranks of angels throughout Catholic thought. I follow St. Thomas, who reviews these differences and comes up with a resolution and orders the ranks as I have written.

1. The highest hierarchy has three types (choirs, or orders):
   - Seraphim (Is 6:1–7)
   - Cherubim (Ex 26:1; Ez 10:15, 10:20)
   - Thrones (Col 1:16; Rv 20:4)
2. The second hierarchy has three choirs:
   - Dominions (Eph 1:21)
   - Virtues (Eph 1:21)
   - Powers (Rm 8:38; Eph 1:21)
3. The lowest hierarchy has three choirs:
   - Principalities (Rm 8:38; Eph 1:21)
   - Archangels (Tb 12:6, 12:15; Dn 9:21–27; Lk 1:28; Jn 5:4; Rv 1:7–9)
   - Angels (multiple references)

The first hierarchy is highest because the choirs gaze upon the End of all creatures, God himself.[8] So, in general, this hierarchy represents union with God. They all have a purpose with only God purely as an end: they exist purely for God and his praise, the highest role of creatures. The seraphim praise him for his love and goodness. God's absolute goodness (love) is the highest revelation of himself, most perfectly expressed in the revelation of Jesus Christ through his passion, death, and resurrection for sinful men. They burn with the ardor of pure love for God and exist solely as a representation of union with the pure love of God for his own sake, the ultimate End of all creatures. Within this highest hierarchy, the seraphim therefore represent union. The cherubim praise God for the knowledge of all creatures in him, or how God is the archetype of all things; thus within this highest hierarchy they represent illumination. They see the types or disposition of all things in God. The thrones praise him for the order with which all things are arranged. The thrones represent purgation.

The second hierarchy in general represents illumination.[9] Its choirs govern all of God's creation because that governing disposes all things toward an end. Within this hierarchy the first order of angels are the dominions. God uses them to appoint those things that are to be done (the end) in creation. Because they oversee final purpose in this hierarchy, they represent

8. Dionysius the Areopagite, "Celestial Hierarchy," VII; *ST* I. q. 108, aa. 5–6; *SCG* III.80.

9. Dionysius the Areopagite, "Celestial Hierarchy," VIII; *ST* I. q. 108, aa. 5–6; *SCG* III.80.

union within this hierarchy. The next order is the virtues, whom God uses to carry out what is to be done. The virtues are those beings that regulate the natural laws of the universe, governing all things falling under these laws, such as our galaxies, stars, physical laws, and material life in general. They dispose things to the end (type). Thus they represent illumination in this second hierarchy. The third order are the powers, which order how the things to be done are carried out, as well as protecting creation against disorder from the demons (angels who have sinned). They deal with the means and so represent purgation in this hierarchy.

The lowest hierarchy in some manner deals with the affairs of men.[10] They represent purgation by ordering men to receive God's grace, and purge them from things that do not bring them to God. The highest natural end of man is the good of a nation or state. So the principalities are the guardian angels of cities, states, and nations, representing the end or union in their hierarchy. The next order in this hierarchy constitutes the archangels, who announce the great things of men, thus illuminating them. For instance, we see the Archangel Gabriel announcing the conception of John the Baptist to Zacharias and the conception of Jesus Christ to Mary. Finally, the lowest are the angels, who are the guardian angels of individual men. They order individuals to God, and by these actions represent purgation in the lowest hierarchy. All of us receive a guardian angel at birth, whose sole job is to watch over us and adapt God's gifts to us and bring our prayers to him.[11]

There are parallels between the angelic (celestial hierarchies) and the ecclesial hierarchy of bishops, priests, and deacons, as discussed in chapter 11.[12] The angelic is the instantiation of the church in heaven, so one would expect that the ecclesial church and that of heaven to be part and parcel in structure. Dionysius the Areopagite, other Church Fathers, and Thomas Aquinas noted that the bishops and first hierarchy of seraphim, cherubim, and thrones are analogous. This is followed by the analogy of priests and the middle angelic hierarchy of dominations, virtues, and powers. At the lowest level, the deacons are analogous to the lower hierarchy of principalities, archangels, and angels. The first angelic hierarchy and bishops both repre-

10. Dionysius the Areopagite, "Celestial Hierarchy," IX; *ST* I. q. 108, aa. 5–6; *SCG* III.80.

11. *ST* I. q. 113, aa. 1–5.

12. See "The Structure of the Church as Hierarchy" in chapter 11.

sent unity with God in their respective manner. The second hierarchy and priests represent illumination, as both are directly involved in disposing for union. Finally, the lower hierarchy and deacons represent purgation, as both in some manner order their subjects to illumination by detaching them of their inordinate attachments to this world. This angelic sense is also intended to be conveyed in the order (position) of the clerical ranks in the liturgy, as discussed in chapter 11.

We can find this same parallel in the passive hierarchy as well.[13] As the first hierarchy of seraphim, cherubim, and thrones exists solely for the praise and love of God, for who he is in himself, so is the life of the monk intended to reflect this. The middle angelic hierarchy of dominations, virtues, and powers illumines all of creation by ordering it and distributing the gifts of God, so the baptized layman is one who is illumined through the life of Christ conveyed in the sacraments. Again, as the lower angelic hierarchy represents purgation, so does the catechumen. He is being purged in order to be brought to the sacrament of baptism for illumination.

God reflects himself in his creatures both by creatures being a reflection of who he is and by having them pass on to others what he gives them in imitation of how he himself gives all things to his creatures. Therefore all the orders listed above pass on what they know from God to those below. In fact, all the graces and gifts of creatures are received from those above. The very definition of hierarchy – both celestial and ecclesial – according to Dionysius the Areopagite and Thomas Aquinas, is "a sacred order which cleanses, enlightens, and perfects, and is cleansed, enlightened, and perfected."[14] Gifts and graces from God come down to us from our guardian angels, who received them from archangels, who in turn received them from principalities, who received them from powers, and on up the hierarchy. Things come to creatures from God through hierarchy, and the creature returns things to him through it.[15]

13. See "The Structure of the Church as Hierarchy" in chapter 11.

14. Dionysius the Areopagite, "Celestial Hierarchy," III.164D; *ST* I. q. 108, a. 4, obj. 1; Suppl, q. 34, a. 1c.

15. See chapter 8, note 74, with the beautiful quote from *SCG* III.83, summarizing God's order and disposition of things. As St. Thomas states and quotes from Dionysius, it is precisely the role of each rank in a hierarchy to pass on what they receive from above to those lower. Creation, as I have argued, is an ordered hierarchy. Because it is created by God, it is the normal means by which he governs

The Material Universe

In comparison to the immaterial universe, the material universe is a more remote reflection of the liturgical pattern of union (end), illumination (type or disposition), and purgation (means). Still, in a broad way the material universe reflects these realities:

> union represented by human beings,
> illumination represented by animals,
> and purgation represented by plants.

Revelation from God tells us what we also discovered by the use of natural reason, namely, that humans are the pinnacle of material creation, bringing all things together.[16] Through our being and through our intellect, we are able to be the integration point for all the material world.[17] We have the powers of all material being in us and represent unity in the material universe. But it is also true that our intellectual knowing powers allow us to become one with the thing known, living its life in a sense, and uniting all things immaterially in our intellect.[18] As such, humans are a remote reflection of the unity of all things in God and the unitive way of the spiritual life. We unite the spiritual and material worlds in us.[19] It was fitting, then, that the Incarnation of Christ occurred with humans instead of angels.[20] Because God is the creator and sustainer of all things who contains all things

---

and cares for his creatures. It is the typical order he desires. Certainly, being God, he can circumvent this order, as discussed in chapter 8, but that is not the norm. As the *Catechism of the Catholic Church* states, there is a hierarchy of creatures (342), God wills the interdependence of creatures to complete and serve each other (340), and there is solidarity among all creatures as they all have the same Creator and are all ordered to his glory (344). Again from *SCG* III.83, God disposes (wills) all things by himself alone but distributes these things from higher to lower by the agency of creatures. In this visible world, nothing can be ordered except through invisible creatures. Finally, in *SCG* IV.1, St. Thomas then states that as things descend from the highest summit of things, man rises to God by beginning with lower things and gradually ascending.

16. *Catechism of the Catholic Church*, 343, 355–61, 364.

17. Second Vatican Council, *Gaudium et Spes*, I.14.

18. See chapters 3, 5, and 8, on the nature of the intellect and its purpose in man.

19. See chapter 5, notes 51–52.

20. *ST* III, q. 4, a. 1; *SCG* IV.42; Scheeben, *Mysteries of Christianity*, 357–404; Nellas, *Deification in Christ*, 35–36.

in himself, it was fitting that he should become one with the very creature who has the potential to bridge both material and spiritual worlds to unite them.

The unitive function of human beings led early Christian thinkers to speak of the human being as a microcosm of reality and the Church, the heart of which is the liturgical structure of union, illumination, and purgation.[21] The human being sees in the universe his own very structure.[22] Ultimately, every human person is like a little liturgy, a being whose nature is built as a platform of praise and adoration of God. He belongs in a liturgical setting and society, in union with a community of persons. His home is ultimately in the Church, united to the Persons of the Trinity. His very structure allows him to know and understand the universe, which itself participates in the liturgical structure of the Church and is a means of ascent to God.[23]

Although human life in one manner is like that of lower creatures – ordered to growth, reproduction, and the senses – human life is ultimately regulated by and ordered to the life of reason, the life of the mind. It is their own ordered structure that allows humans to perceive the same order in nature; the meaning in nature is a part of common human experience. And this perception of meaning in reality forces a choice between right and wrong, that is, the moral life.[24] This was one of the greatest insights discovered by the ancients, both Christian and pagan, that has been lost in significant parts of modern thought and education regarding nature and reality. Much modern thought has disconnected morality from nature, and human moral decisions from reality. There has been a loss of the critical interplay between the life of the mind and that of morality. But the choice of the good life leads through creatures to the threshold of faith, which allows him to perceive again in the supernatural society of the Church a likeness to himself.

The practical choice to embrace divine revelation given in the society of the Church finds its ultimate and highest purpose in union with the Persons of the Trinity. As the life of reason shows that our end is a type of intellectual contemplation of God, so the life of faith perfects this and shows a personal

21. See chapter 5, and notes 51–52; Nellas, *Deification in Christ*, 29–30.

22. Smith, *Wisdom of Ancient Cosmology*, 12–13.

23. Smith, *Wisdom of Ancient Cosmology*, 13.

24. See chapter 1.

union with the Persons of the Trinity, ordered to their praise and adoration in the society of the Church. Human nature itself draws everyone to investigate the universe – Aristotle said all human beings desire to know[25] – and at each step, from the natural universe to the revealed society of the Church, the human mind perceives an order and perfection like its own: union, illumination, purgation. If a human being allows the lower powers of sense, growth, and reproduction to hold sway over reason, he will have trouble perceiving the very order of things about him. At every encounter with reality, this tripartite structure forces us to make a choice, to reject or accept it. What we do and how we think are inseparable. As St. Augustine states famously in the first book of his *Confessions*, "Our hearts are restless until they rest in you, O Lord."

In this multilayered cosmology, the remainder of the material universe below human life – animals, plants, and minerals – leads back to human life and intelligence.[26] These lower forms of life are essential to the human growth of knowledge, because animals can be thought of as illumination (the life of the sense), and plants can be thought of as purgation (the life of growth and reproduction). The hallmark of animal life is sensing. And sensing is a type of knowledge, knowledge of the particular or individual. Sensory knowledge is thus the lowest of all possible knowledge, but it is knowledge nonetheless. Animal knowledge, as with all knowing, is a type of illumination.[27]

Plants are composed of matter and a noneternal (nonintellectual) soul

25. Aristotle, *Metaphysics*, 1552.

26. In chapter 8, I noted that there are two possible means of viewing the primary (purgation) and secondary (illumination) perfections of the material universe. With humans as the tertiary perfection (union) of material creation, the first possible ordering would be animals and plants as illumination, then inorganic matter as purgation. The next would be to order strictly from the viewpoint of living things: humans as union, animals as illumination, and plants as purgation. As a biologist, I have chosen to emphasize the latter.

27. *Catechism of the Catholic Church*, 2415–18. I argued in chapter 5 and chapter 8 that from reason one can know animals as a secondary perfection of the universe (a secondary perfection is illumination in revealed knowledge). St. Thomas describes animals as a type of ornamentation of the material universe, and the material universe serves for the production of humans, the end and purpose of material creation. An aspect of this service is the use of animals for human needs. This is explicitly stated in the context of proper human stewardship of creation by the paragraphs cited from the *Catholic Catechism*. Thus there is an implicit connection on this point between reason and revelation; i.e., animals are a secondary perfection (illumination of material creation). Beyond this point once again,

capable of growth and reproduction. They have the function common to all other types of material life: they grow and reproduce. They produce a "gift" at the most basic level: plants take impersonal matter and transform it into something higher, "life," and give this life to another, its offspring. Thus plants purge matter of its total orientation and closedness to itself. They are a remote reflection of purgation in the spiritual life.[28]

Adam, Eve, and Eden

Our goal here is to describe a cosmology according to the sources of divine revelation, and therefore it is crucial to address the question of the original human pair.[29] In the history of Western science, especially since the birth of the historical sciences (biology, anthropology, linguistics, etc.) in the nineteenth century, perhaps no aspect of biblical thought has suffered so much from the hands of scientism. There has been in every generation since about 1800 those who attempt to use science to prove the falsity of the biblical story of Adam and Eve. There have equally been those in every generation who have given credible answers to these attempts, but one rarely hears about such responses. The result is that the chimera of the conflict of science and religion is promoted and sustained despite its implausibility on historical and conceptual grounds.

---

the hallmark of animality is sensory knowledge and memory. Any knowledge, no matter how slight, is a type of illumination.

Using the alternative order (see note 26 above) — humans, animals/plants, nonliving matter — poses no problem. Plants, as with animals, would be ornamentation because they too serve for the production of humans both immediately for food and clothing and remotely as the first step or basic "stuff" of organized life.

28. See chapter 5 and chapter 8. Purgation in the spiritual life is to purge that which is lower, to order or orient to that which is higher. It is the ground or base state. In material life, plants are the ground or base state, and, as argued, they uptake and fundamentally orient nonliving matter to something higher (life).

Alternatively, nonliving matter could fill the purgative role (see notes 26 and 27 above) as the basic "stuff" of material existence (material cause) that must be ordered to that which is higher. See note 2 above (Aquinas, *Commentary on the Divine Names of Blessed Dionysius* VII.4) and chap. 11, note 32, for cause as a type of purgation.

29. The literature regarding Adam and Eve, both for and against their existence, is vast and beyond the scope of this book to completely review. I therefore confine myself to a few relevant points and citations.

Revelation asserts that there were in fact two progenitors of the human race.[30] Adam and Eve existed as those progenitors, and the entire human race originated from them.[31] This is true for several reasons, but one of the

30. Gn 2–3; *Catechism of the Catholic Church*, 359–60; Pius XII, *Humani Generis*.

31. Despite all the arguments for and against the literal interpretation of the Adam and Eve story in Genesis, from both ecclesial and secular sources, I take the position that Adam and Eve truly existed. I do so for three primary reasons: first, the tradition of the Church is seemingly in favor of humanity's being descended from two parents; second, the state of science regarding the human fossil record (dynamically changing) and genetic record (variable) do not contradict this position; and third, the valid ways of reconciling the science with the tradition of the Church support the position.

As to the tradition's affirmation of the existence of Adam and Eve, see Pius XII, *Humani Generis*, 37: "When, however, there is question of another conjectural opinion, namely polygenism, the children of the Church by no means enjoy such liberty. For the faithful cannot embrace that opinion which maintains that either after Adam there existed on this earth true men who did not take their origin through natural generation from him as from the first parent of all, or that Adam represents a certain number of first parents. Now it is in no way apparent how such an opinion can be reconciled with that which the sources of revealed truth and the documents of the Teaching Authority of the Church propose with regard to original sin, which proceeds from a sin actually committed by an individual Adam and which, through generation, is passed on to all and is in everyone as his own."

The key is the statement of Pius XII that the belief in Adam follows from original sin. The *Catechism of the Catholic Church*, 404, states, "The whole human race is in Adam as one body of one man. By this the unity of the human race all men are implicated in Adam's sin, as all are implicated in Christ's justice." Paragraph 403 also notes St. Paul's argument that human misery "cannot be understood apart from Adam's sin and the fact that he transmitted to us a sin." This is in part a reference to St. Paul in Rm 5:12–18, where he states that as sin came into the world through one man, so through one man – Jesus Christ – was man redeemed. St. Paul builds upon this in 1 Cor 15:42–50 by making a comparison in multiple areas between Adam and Christ. Catholic Tradition likewise follows St. Paul by calling Christ the new Adam (discussed in chap. 10), using a close parallel between the idea that as all men were contained in Adam and fell with him, so all were contained in Christ and are a new creation in him. See *Catechism of the Catholic Church*, 355–421, 1736, on the creation of man, first parents, Adam and Eve, and the Fall. See also *Catechism of the Catholic Church*, 359, 388, 402, 404, 504–5, 518, 532, 538–39, 635, regarding Jesus Christ and Adam. Scheeben, *Mysteries of Christianity*, 201–310, offers an excellent summary of the mystery of our first parents, Adam and Eve, their original condition, and the Fall. See Benedict XVI (Joseph Ratzinger), *In the Beginning*, especially for the dangers of doing away with the creation accounts.

See Tattersall, *Masters of the Planet*, for the conditions of the fossil record of ancient hominids. Many of these are compiled from a "type" specimen (which might consist of a small piece of the skeleton, such as a jaw bone and part of the cranium) and other assorted fragments. Ewen Calloway, "Genetic Adam and Eve," reviews the genetic "mitochondrial Eve" and "Y-chromosome" Adam, which generated so much news. This is from a secular standpoint, which one would expect from *Nature*. But from this article, written by a scientist and published in one of the most prestigious of scientific journals, one can clearly see the variability of scientific data (i.e., the molecular clock). While I think such studies are fascinating (as I am a geneticist), present scientific findings do not compel a change to or call into question the idea of an original first two parents.

most important is that this historical fact is implicated in a higher doctrine. It provides the historical foundations of Adam and Eve. This higher doctrine is original sin.[32] The doctrine of original sin, recounted in the third chapter of Genesis, is that our first parents sinned grievously and transmitted the *effects* of this sin (not their personal sin itself) to all their human descendants.[33] This is an object of our faith. This idea logically necessitates that two original parents must have existed: Adam and Eve. Thus their existence follows from the theology of original sin.[34] Now, this is one area where the proponents of scientism see an "obvious" falsehood in the Bible, but it is worth considering that the question of one or multiple origins of the human race is still unsettled from the evidence of numerous sciences.[35]

Perhaps even more importantly, Adam was the head of the human race.[36] The Bible would call him the covenant head.[37] The human race was concentrated in one man, who represented and acted for all that would follow. Recall that Adam was created in original justice, meaning he had the life of grace (holiness) and integrity.[38] With the life of grace, he possessed the divine life of God to a supremely exalted degree.[39] He also found it easy not to sin owing to his "integrity."[40] His material life of sensation, growth, nutrition, and reproduction was totally regulated by reason, and no desire

---

Regarding science in general, see Horn and Wiedenholer, *Creation and Evolution*, 12–13: "The clay became man at that moment in which a being for the first time was capable of forming, however dimly, the thought 'God.' The first Thou that – however stammeringly – was said by human lips to God marks the moment in which the spirit arose in the world. Here the Rubicon of anthropogenesis was crossed. For it is not the use of weapons or fire, not new methods of cruelty or of useful activity, that constitute man, but rather his ability to be immediately in relation to God. This holds fast to the doctrine of the special creation of man; herein also lies the reason why the anthropogenesis cannot be possibly determined by paleontology: anthropogenesis is the rise of the spirit, which cannot be excavated with a shovel. The theory of evolution does not invalidate the faith, nor does it corroborate it."

Finally, see Austriaco et al., *Thomistic Evolution*, 203–38, for an interesting speculation on a possible reconciliation between modern science and the testimony of Scripture.

32. *Catechism of the Catholic Church*, 396–409; Scheeben, *Mysteries of Christianity*, 273–310.

33. *Catechism of the Catholic Church*, 404–5.

34. See note 31 above regarding the quote from *Humani Generis* of Pope Pius XII.

35. See note 31 above.

36. *Catechism of the Catholic Church*, 404; Scheeben, *Mysteries of Christianity*, 233–35, 365, 386.

37. Hahn, *Father Who Keeps His Promises*, 49, 54–55.

38. See chapter 10, notes 18–32.

39. See chapter 10, notes 18–32.

40. See chapter 10, notes 18–32.

occurred until necessary.[41] Because of this integrity, his body in this state would have appeared different than at present. It may have radiated the excellence of his soul in a manner analogous to how a light bulb radiates the filament inside.[42] Interestingly, St. Thomas Aquinas states that Adam would have known about Christ, since he (Adam) was married.[43] Marriage is a sacrament and takes its grace from Christ, whether before or after Christ in time. Adam's marriage was therefore the primary channel of graces for him, and as head of the race, he would have known from whence the fruitfulness of his marriage came. Because he knew of Christ, he would have known the Trinity as well.[44] What he didn't know was why the second Person of the Trinity became man, since he did not know in advance that he (Adam) would sin.

Adam and Eve's abode was Eden, a particular place created for men in the state of Original Justice, and not the general state of creation before Adam's Fall.[45] A lesser tradition in the Church, held by several saints, including St. Thomas, is that both Elijah the prophet and Enoch ("Enoch walked with God; and he was not, for God took him," Gn 5:24) are presently in Eden until the second coming of Christ, when they will have a special duty to undertake.[46] If Eden still exists, why don't we see it? Probably because its properties are somewhere between our physical state and that of a spiritual state. As the proper place of men in the state of Original Justice, it would exist in a much more spiritualized state than our present fallen condition.[47]

41. See chapter 10, notes 18–32.

42. Nellas, *Deification in Christ*, 52.

43. *ST* II-II, q. 2, a. 7c.

44. *ST* II-II, q. 2. a. 8c.

45. *Catechism of the Catholic Church*, 378; *ST* I, q. 102, aa. 1–2, 4c.

46. *ST* I, q. 102, a. 2, ad. 3; III, q. 49, a. 5. See also Montgomery, "Two Witnesses," for an interesting summary of this tradition. The author mentions in addition to St. Thomas the following Fathers, saints, and thinkers as contributing to the Enoch/Elijah tradition: St. Irenaeus, Tertullian, Pope St. Gregory the Great, St. Ephraim the Syrian, St. Augustine, St. John Damascene, Francisco Suárez, and St. Robert Bellarmine.

47. *ST* II-II, q. 2, a. 7c. As summarized by Larchet, *Therapy of Spiritual Illnesses*, 1:15–36, a sizable body of literature exists from the Church Fathers, particularly the Eastern Fathers, holding that the physical state and conditions of Adam and Eve were not like our present one in the physical universe. Eden, being a place for men in the state of Original Justice – whose spiritual and physical state was greatly exalted above ours – existed to accommodate this state of humanity, as stated by St. Thomas. It was the place proper to these conditions. Perhaps in our modern parlance we might state it occupies

It would be somewhat subject to the laws of physical matter, but not to the degree we are.

Ephraim the Syrian, a great Doctor (teacher) of the Church, says that Eden was structured upon a three-tiered model of union, illumination, and purgation.[48] This was the instantiation, or beginnings, of the Church in the material universe. The Tree of Life was analogous to the Eucharist and represented union with God ("To him who conquers, I will grant to eat of the tree of life, which is in the paradise of God," Rv 2:7, and "To him who conquers, I will give some of the hidden manna," Rv 2:17). Equating the two statements "To him who conquers, I will grant to eat of the tree of life" and "to him who conquers, I will give the hidden manna," it follows that the manna is a type of the Eucharist (Jn 6:31–34), as is the Tree of Life. It occupied the highest reaches of Eden. The Tree of the Knowledge of Good and Evil represented illumination ("the tree was good . . . and that the tree was to be desired to make one wise," Gn 3:6). The lower reaches of Eden, with the trees permissible from which to eat, represented purgation, as here the bodily needs were taken care of so that Adam and Eve could be oriented to God ("the Lord God made to grow every tree that is pleasant to the sight and good for food," Gn 2.9). Ephraim also compares this structure to the Jewish temple.[49] The Tree of Life is analogous to the Holy of Holies, the Tree of the Knowledge of Good and Evil is analogous to the veil over the Holy of Holies, and the lower reaches of Eden that represent purgation are analogous to the courtyard area of the temple where the Jewish priests purified themselves. This clearly illustrates the emergent idea of organizing all reality around the Church: first in Eden and then in the Jewish temple and rites. Summarizing, Eden was the form around which the remainder of the material universe was to be organized. The threefold structure of the liturgy and the Church – union, illumination, and purgation – was the organizing principle for the rest of the material universe and reality as a whole.

Genesis states that Adam was placed in Eden to care for and cultivate

---

another "dimension," somewhat outside of time and space, above the conditions of purely material limitations.

48. Ephraim the Syrian, *Hymns on Paradise*, II–III.

49. Ephraim the Syrian, *Hymns on Paradise*, III, XV; See also Hahn, *Father Who Keeps His Promises*, 55, for a similar comparison.

it (Gn 2:15). What does "cultivate" mean in this context? Simply tilling the ground? If, as is related in Genesis, he had the fruit of the plants that grew there to eat, he did not really need to cultivate soil and grow things. Remember that in the state of Original Justice, humans and creation were different from the present, so much so that a comparison is sketchy and oblique at best. Adam's sin was an event of unmitigated catastrophe on an unimaginable scale for humans and the material universe as a whole. But the Fathers, saints, and Doctors of the Church have provided insights about and fleshed out the idea of the cultivation of Eden.[50] According to many of them, Adam was placed in Eden to worship God, to perfect himself, and to grow in deification toward final union with God. He was there to help his children in Eden and to order the rest of creation outside of Eden. He also would have governed Eden as a benevolent, all-wise father and head of his family.[51]

Adam would have engaged in the begetting and rearing of children and their similar perfection.[52] Being the master of material reality, he would have ordered the rest of creation upon the liturgical structure of Eden. How precisely the ordering of creation would have been done by Adam is one of the areas where the greatest difference with post-Fall man occurs. He would have accomplished them primarily through a type of contemplation of God.[53] In Eden, Adam's life consisted in a type of habitual prayer, but he would still have acted in a sense similar to us, governing Eden and raising a family in an analogous manner, for example.

Adam's ultimate goal, however, was contemplation leading to cultivation of union with God.[54] By continual union through prayer and worship, the graces obtained by Adam, as the father of the human race and master of material reality would have spilled over into these three other areas that were his duty: personal perfection, familial perfection, and the perfection of the world about him.[55] It was in Adam that Jesus's later words would have been most

50. *Catechism of the Catholic Church*, 378; Scheeben, *Mysteries of Christianity*, 237–39; *ST* I, q. 102, a. 4c; Larchet, *Therapy of Spiritual Illnesses*, 1:19–21.

51. *Catechism of the Catholic Church*, 374–79.

52. *Catechism of the Catholic Church*, 374–75; *ST* I, q. 98, qq. 100–101.

53. See chapter 10, note 31.

54. See chapter 10, note 31.

55. An interesting development of the idea of Adam's purpose appears in the writings of the Servant of God, Luisa Picarretta (see chapter 10, note 6). Luisa says that Adam's role was to bring all of

perfectly enacted: "But seek first his kingdom and his righteousness [kingdom and righteousness = deification], and all these things shall be yours as well" (Mt 6:33). Eden is the archetype and prototype of seeking first the kingdom of God.[56] What Adam was in Eden we must all become. We too need to

---

creation back to God as a great offering. God is one and creates a multitude of creatures to reflect his divine nature. In these creatures he sees his attributes. Adam is described as "doing the rounds" of creation and uniting the multitude of creatures and all of creation in himself – including the image of God's attributes contained therein. He gives these back to God as one great offering. Hence Adam is the priest of the universe and makes a great unified offering of it to God (an offering that is therefore liturgical).

How does he do this? Precisely as described regarding the intellect in chapter 3 of this work. His intellect knows creatures and creation, and they take on an immateriality in his intellect and become one in him. This is offered back to God.

Unfortunately, I cannot do this justice here. Luisa Picarretta's description is quite beautiful and among the loftiest literature I have ever read.

56. I will take the liberty of a small divergence here. As a scientist, I have had several occasions to hear the argument that beliefs in Adam, Eve, Eden, and even angels (particularly the belief that they watch over us and order the material universe) are leftover "children's stories" from a bygone era when people were more ignorant. While I traditionally have not professionally associated with Catholic thinkers as much as with scientists, I have done so on occasion and am doing so more recently. Sadly, I have heard these same ideas from certain professional Catholic thinkers as well. But I have argued for the existence of angels and their mission from both reason and revelation. I think the tradition of the Church supports the existence of Adam, Eve, and Eden. Therefore I ask, Why are they so unpopular?

First, I think their unpopularity springs from our times. We are materialists and scientific rationalists. We try to explain away the mysteries of the faith using natural phenomena. The dialogue of reason and revelation is a strong tradition of the Church, and I am not trying to minimize it, as readers of this book know. But there are things above our natural powers of thought that will always remain a mystery. Such are some of the doctrines regarding Adam, Eve, Eden, and angels. No amount of rationalization can explain away the mystery. There are some things that cannot be fully penetrated by reason.

Second, as a pointed response to the dismissal of these doctrines as "children's stories," I wish to ask, Has anyone considered that reality may ultimately be structured in part like that for which a child wishes? And that this is a reasonable stance based on the history of human experience?

A basic truth of the Faith is that God is a "Family" of Persons. This Family wants us to be a part of its most intimate family life: to have a share in its life and to call the first Person of this Family "Father." Further, this Father creates earthly fathers as a reflection of who he is. All that is most dear and wonderful to us about our fathers and mothers, which mankind has expressed in literature, poetry, and children's stories (and dreams), is magnified infinity in our heavenly Father, with whom we will one day be united. The eastern icon called *Mother of the Divine Kiss* shows an intimate mother-child relationship. It depicts the Christ child close to Mary's face, staring in her eyes and giving her a kiss. If one meditates on this poignant depiction, one comes to understand that Christ became part of the most intimate aspects of human family life, placing himself in the most personal exchanges of a human family. It only stands to reason that this is an image of the relationship he wants to have with us, placing us in the most intimate exchanges between the Three Persons of the Trinity, the heavenly

throw ourselves fully into reliance on God as our Father and not worry about our needs. The God and Father who provided integrity and Eden to Adam to maximize his prayer life is the same God who aids us in the absence of Eden and our integrity. This enables us, like Adam, to focus fully on God.

Paradise Lost: A Singular Fall

Scripture and the Tradition of the Church relate two falls, that of Lucifer (the devil) and that of Adam.[57] Lucifer was the highest of all angels and hence the greatest of God's creation.[58] Tradition has it that he looked upon his exalted beauty and greatly admired it.[59] When God offered him deification, the divine life that is infinitely above creatures, he saw how infinitesimal he was compared to God.[60] Proud as he was of his own beauty, he hated God for his beauty and rejected God. Scripture says he took one-third of the angels with him by inducing them to reject God as well.[61] This test occurred immediately after the first moment of their creation.[62] For the fallen angels (demons), no possibility of redemption can occur because of the intuitive intellect.[63] Through this they know everything they need at the moment of their creation. As such, they have full knowledge and cannot learn anything new by their natural powers. In turn, they fully know their decision to do right or wrong. If they commit evil, they cannot therefore learn anything new to see more deeply into what they did. With humans and their rational intellects, they can learn from new experiences.[64] We have the possibility of understanding more deeply what we did wrong and can "try again."

---

family. As he came down to us, so he wants to bring us up to him. Heaven is a child's dream, that is, to be cared for in the most personal way by infinitely perfect parents who will never disappoint and will satisfy every need beyond one's wildest dreams.

Why not, then, have doctrines that seem on the surface somewhat child-like? "Unless you turn and become like little children, you will never enter the kingdom of heaven" (Mt 18:3).

57. *Catechism of the Catholic Church*, 391–93, 396–400.

58. *ST* I, q. 63, a. 7.

59. *ST* I, q. 63, a. 3; Scheeben, *Mysteries of Christianity*, 259–64.

60. Scheeben, *Mysteries of Christianity*, 259–64.

61. Rv 12:4.

62. *ST* I, q. 63, a. 6.

63. *Catechism of the Catholic Church*, 393; *ST* I, q. 64, a. 2.

64. *ST* I, q. 64, a. 2.

We have already addressed to some degree the original sin of Adam as a loss of Original Justice (both holiness and integrity) and the consequent loss of Original Justice by the rest of the race as well.[65] Again, we are not guilty of *Adam's personal sin*. The actual nature of this sin remains somewhat a mystery; it is figured in Scripture by the eating of the apple from the Tree of the Knowledge of Good and Evil. Scott Hahn has analyzed this idea and thinks it is more detailed.[66] Specifically, while Adam was free from harm by those things lower than him – plants, animals, physical forces – he was not free from harm by higher things (demons or the fallen angels). Hahn notes that when Eve was tempted, Adam was silent. Because Adam was master of Eden and protector of all in it, what was he doing? Was the perfect master of the house absent when his family was attacked? Hahn thinks that Adam was afraid of Satan. He knew that it was possible to be harmed by him. Thus Adam's test was to stand between his wife and evil and protect her (and possibly get harmed or killed). He should have trusted in God, but instead he trusted himself, failed, fled, and left his family vulnerable. The fall then (according to Hahn) actually occurred before the temptation of Adam by Eve. St. Ephraim the Syrian relates it more mystically.[67] He says that Adam was the great high priest of Eden and reached to touch the Eucharist (Christ) before his time. He pushed through the veil (the Tree of Knowledge of Good and Evil) into the Holy of Holies and committed sacrilege. Just as touching the Ark of the Covenant meant death in the Old Testament, because one was not properly consecrated for temple service, so similarly did Adam incur guilt. Had he been patient, he would have been allowed to do this in the fullness of time and his development. Whatever the particular nature of Adam's fall, it held catastrophic consequences for men and the universe.

This fall was a disaster of epic proportions, unlike anything else that had happened.[68] Adam and all humans fell out of their intimacy with God and the freedom they enjoyed in him in all aspects of life: toward the Persons of God, in their integrity, toward nature, physical laws, and bodily needs.

65. Scheeben, *Mysteries of Christianity*, 303–6.

66. Hahn, *Father Who Keeps His Promises*, 58–59, 63–72.

67. Ephraim the Syrian, *Hymns on Paradise*, III–IV.

68. On both sin and original sin and their effects, see Scheeben, *Mysteries of Christianity*, 243–310. On original sin and the general pathologies arising in man as a consequence, see Larchet, *Therapy of Spiritual Illnesses*, 1:37–123.

In other words, we became for the most part subject to our biological and physical limitations. We began to live as individuals enclosed in our self, our "I," instead of beings focused on the other, "Thou." The individual and his problems became paramount. Our thoughts were fettered by our bodily needs – it was (is) hard to focus. Our emotions, aches, pains, and disordered desires distracted us. They took over as our leader. Worries and concerns consume us. Nature was no longer subject to us since it and the whole universe became disordered when its head, Adam, to whom it was subject, became disordered. Physical calamities, disease, animals, fleas, flies, poison ivy, and the like began to bother us. Heat and cold afflicted us. We needed food, as nature in Eden would no longer feed us. Worst of all, our union with God and the ease of contemplating him ceased. Life became a fight for survival.[69] Survival, instead of interpersonal communion and intimacy with God, men, and angels, became the preeminent concern. *Our* needs, as *individuals*, our psychoses, neuroses, and concerns became first instead of love of the other. Put simply, we fell from the life of the intellect to that of the animal.[70]

Further, because Adam was master of material creation, his sin also caused an alteration of the material universe as a whole.[71] A disorder crept in. As St. Paul says, "For creation waits with eager expectation the revelation of the sons of God; for the creation was subjected to futility, not of its own will but by the will of him who subjected it in hope; because the creation itself will be set free from its bondage to decay and obtain the glorious liberty of the children of God. We know that the whole creation has been groaning in travail together until now" (Rm 8:19–22). So not only Adam but also animals, plants, galaxies, stars, planets, atoms, and molecules were affected in some way.

Despite the fall, however, not everything was ruined.[72] While the fall of Adam was a truly catastrophic event, it did not destroy everything. First, man can neither create nor uncreate; only God can do these things. Therefore, despite the radical alteration of humans, they remained fundamentally good as God created them.[73] Just as the fall of the angels didn't destroy their

69. Nellas, *Deification in Christ*, 47.

70. See "The Way Back Home" below.

71. *Catechism of the Catholic Church*, 400, 408.

72. *SCG* III.12; *ST* I, q. 48, a. 4.

73. *Catechism of the Catholic Church*, 374, 405, 1701–7.

nature, so man didn't destroy his nature but, like the demons, radically inclined himself toward evil.[74] Likewise, the universe and all in it remained fundamentally good but altered.[75] And as the fall of the angels did not destroy the angelic hierarchy, so one of the things remaining in the material universe was the rooted order seen among living things: plants, animals, and humans, or purgation, illumination, and union. The vestige of what once was remained: the Vestige of Eden, the Hierarchy of Being. And this was but a lesser participation in the liturgy of the Church, the Image of Eternity.

A Disordered and Dangerous World?

Discussion of the Fall inevitably raises the question of evil, especially in the minds of those who see little or nothing beyond the physical.[76] I do not intend to engage the question in any depth here, as it is beyond the scope of this book, but a few words about the chaotic violence and destruction found in the universe as a whole seem appropriate. I have seemingly painted creation as a place of beauty, order, and goodness while ignoring evil and its consequences. Has not modern science shown the universe to be "red in tooth and claw"?

Recall once again that while God providentially determines the being and goodness of each thing, providing all that they need, he principally carries out the distribution of his goods through the higher creatures to the lower ones.[77] Only God is perfect, as even the highest seraphim have limitations because they are finite. Thus the possibility exists for any creature with a free will to fall.[78] This free will is given to intellectual creatures because God wants to be in union with them for eternity, and love demands freedom or it is not love. God can never do any true evil, but he does permit evils

74. *Catechism of the Catholic Church*, 391, 404–5, 407, 978, 1707, 1714, 1849; *ST* I, q. 63, a. 4; I-II, q. 85, a. 2.

75. *Catechism of the Catholic Church*, 400.

76. Among the best short treatises I have read on evil, particularly as it is present in material creation, is David Bentley Hart's *The Doors of the Sea*, an excellent account of this subject written largely from within Eastern Orthodox tradition. I have outlined a slightly more Thomistic approach than I think Hart favors, keeping in line with what I have written previously in this book.

77. See chapter 8; *Catechism of the Catholic Church*, 306–8.

78. *Catechism of the Catholic Church*, 368, 392, 1854.

insofar as he creates creatures with free will.[79] Thus the source of evil in creation is the evil or disorder committed by intellectual creatures.[80]

The consequences of these actions do not affect only the guilty agent. They affect all other creatures as well, both higher and particularly those lower, since the higher governs the lower in creation.[81] The acts of a ruler influence all his subjects, just as a musician in an orchestra who plays off-key not only errs himself but also distorts the whole piece. An evil committed by an angel has broad ramifications because of the angel's high place in the hierarchy. This includes distorting the physical universe, since certain choirs of angels have as their duty the governing of physical laws.[82] Because man was created as the governor and head of the material universe, and in man the material universe is to be united to its Creator, any evil committed by man turns the material universe against him.[83] Peace is the tranquility of order, and it was this order of which the peace of Eden primarily consisted, namely, that all things lower than man were turned toward God as a means of helping man attain union with God and with man in turn uniting these lower beings in himself to God.[84] So to a large degree, the orientation of so many things against us is our own fault and continues to be magnified any time we do evil, however minor.

The lower a thing is and the further from the source of all good (God), the more frequently it can do wrong, while the higher a thing and the closer to God, the less it may do wrong, although (as I have noted) any given wrong it does has graver consequences.[85] Thus physical disasters of exceeding magnitude with large numbers of people dead in part may result from higher creaturely causes, such as demonic forces.[86] At the physical level, however, things can easily become disordered themselves, apart from any higher influence, low as they are in being and goodness themselves.

In addition to objective evils, there are purely physical deficiencies,

79. *Catechism of the Catholic Church*, 309–14.

80. *Catechism of the Catholic Church*, 309–14, 400.

81. See chapter 8.

82. *ST* I, q. 63, a. 7c.

83. *Catechism of the Catholic Church*, 400.

84. *Catechism of the Catholic Church*, 353; *ST* II-II, q. 29, a. 1, ad. 1.

85. *ST* I, q. 63, a. 7.

86. Hart, *Doors of the Sea*, 59–60, 88–90.

which strictly speaking are not evils in the same sense as moral evils. God not only permits them, but he can also directly cause certain of them (but not necessarily).[87] Illnesses, loss of employment, or certain accidents (among other things) can be caused by God in order to correct his creatures, in a manner analogous to the way that parents punish children for the child's own good. Yet some of these things are caused by the limitations of our natures and again by other higher agents.

Lower on the hierarchy are the deaths, travails, and pains of nonintellectual creatures, such as animals and plants. St. Thomas writes that God created creatures that according to their very nature were not subject to death and decay, such as the angels, and others that were partly subject to death (the body) and partly not subject to death (the soul), such as men, and God also created beings that according to nature were totally subject to decay and death (animal, plants, inanimate things).[88] This was part of the hierarchy of being and the ordering of higher and lower beings in it. Thus the teeth and claws of carnivores, as well as fossils found of animals that died in combat or perished in tar pits, are not inconsistent with this doctrine. Their problems are innate to their nature but can also be magnified partly through the disordered actions of higher creatures (both angels and men).

This brings us to the incredible powers of disorder and violence found particularly in the universe beyond earth (but on earth as well). Modern science has shown us disorder and chaos in the universe at levels unimagined in the ancient and medieval world: exploding stars, black holes with titanic gravitational force destroying everything around them, extreme radiation cooking hundreds of worlds at once, colliding planets, and unimaginable heat and cold, just to name a few. Only a few miles above or below us, the physical environment is completely inhospitable to life. We live on a thin, highly selective ribbon of life surrounding the planet. The universe is not very friendly to life. Anyone with the least bit of familiarity with modern science has to acknowledge this fact. Ignorant of these phenomena, ancient and medieval thinkers looked up at the heavens and saw the regularity of the cycles of the sun, moon, and stars and inferred perfection in extraterrestrial matter. They certainly experienced the violence on earth as we do, physically

87. *ST* I, q. 22, a. 2, ad. 2; I, q. 48, a. 2.

88. *ST* I, q. 22, a. 2, ad. 2; I, q. 48, a. 2.

probably to a greater degree owing to the absence of the benefits of modern medicine, agriculture, and other applied sciences. But the point is that they saw primarily order and beauty in the *physical* cosmos as it supposedly approached "nearer" to God. Thus, understandably, they emphasized the order and goodness of things while possibly at times ignoring the disorder in nature at their feet. But they did acknowledge the still greater disorder at the moral and spiritual level as they held to the existence of beings (angels and demons) far greater in power than the physical cosmos as whole.

Materialistic minds do the opposite. Learning of the disorder found by science, many people today tend to overemphasize it and ignore the question of where order and beauty come from. It is legitimate to ask why there are such titanic forces opposed to us. But the presence of such forces cannot dispense of the equally (if not more) important question, From what does this order and cause derive? While teaching us of things about the physical universe that would wither the soul, science also teaches that even the most spectacular instances of such apparent disorder follow strict physical laws of order and cause and effect in their operations.[89] Underlying the disorder is order. While premodern people were largely ignorant of such destructive forces in the universe and might be excused for failing to take them into account, materialists know of both the destructive forces and the order underlying them and are therefore less excused because they do know both. No amount of chaos and disorder in the cosmos dispenses with the central questions of whence everything came and what causes of order, beauty, and goodness are to be found. These are the perennial human questions, and no new finding, however daunting, can ignore them. The very nature of science involves investigating the order of things.

As the Psalmist states, "Thou prepared a table before me, *in the presence of my enemies*" (Ps 23:5). Christian cosmology does not naively dismiss evil or goodness in the manner scientism does. It understands evil as a present part of reality and expects God to care for us in its midst (as well as eventually defeat it).

89. Gleick, *Chaos*.

The Way Back Home

God in his mercy did not abandon man. He promised him a redeemer and adapted man to the conditions of the fallen universe: those of survival.[90] Genesis states that after the fall, "the Lord God made for Adam and for his wife garments of skin, and clothed them" (3:21). By "leather garments," or "garments of skin," more than just clothes are meant. Several Church Fathers, most prolifically St. John Chrysostom, take this to mean that God thus gave man the capacity for all sorts of skills: initially hunting and the making of tools, weapons, and cloth, and eventually agriculture, crafts, and the organization of societies higher than families, such as cities and nations.[91] All these things were needed to get along in a fallen world where man must procure food, clothing, and shelter, and manage affairs with others who are absorbed in themselves. These "garments of skin" might possibly refer to our very physical condition as well. According to this interpretation, Adam was reduced physically and mentally to a more primitive state in order to survive among wild beasts.[92] It was Adam's free choice to reject the pre-Fall conditions. God's "respect" for Adam's freely chosen decision "cooperated" with Adam and mercifully placed him in the conditions he needed for survival, including the altered physical and mental conditions necessary to compete with animals. It was as if God said, "If you insist on being like an animal, I'll give you what you need." While Adam did not "devolve" into another species, he was radically altered from the exalted physical and men-

90. Nellas, *Deification in Christ*, 47.

91. See Nellas, *Deification in Christ*, 43–102, for an excellent summary of interpretations of the "garments of skin" and their meaning for the condition of Adam after the Fall according to various Eastern Church Fathers. There is one exception in this Eastern interpretation to a Catholic understanding, however. Nellas argues, along with certain Church Fathers, such as Gregory of Nyssa and John Chrysostom, that reproduction in the biological sense of sexual union is an effect of the Fall. Nellas also cites St. John Damascene as arguing that God created human beings male and female in anticipation of sin. St. Thomas disagrees with this and expresses the opinion that sexual reproduction was present in Eden before the Fall and was created by God as good. According to Thomas, sexual reproduction in Eden would have been conducted completely under the influence of reason with no lust involved and would have been more pleasurable (*ST* I, q. 98, a. 2). Thus it is not a consequence of the Fall. Finally, it is a teaching of the Church that both sexual individuation and sexual reproduction are a great good from the origins of human creation (*Catechism of the Catholic Church*, 355, 369–70, 371–72, 383, 1603–15).

92. Nellas, *Deification in Christ*, 48–51.

tal state he enjoyed in Eden. It is also at this juncture, where the idea that Adam fell into a greater concern for survival—one of the sources of animal motivation—that evolutionary theory's emphasis on survival as the motivating force of nature can be partially reconciled with the Church Fathers' interpretation of Adam's fall.[93]

Scripture relates that one-third of the angels fell from the angelic hierarchy.[94] Humans in one respect were created by God to restore the hierarchy of being.[95] What does this mean? Because of the intuitive intellect, the grace received from God by an angel is in proportion to his nature.[96] For instance, a throne will always be below the cherubim, but higher than dominions. If God gives grace to a throne, it will always be more grace than that he gives to a dominion, but less than what he gives to a cherubim. Each angel is fixed in his place with regard to other angels. But for men, because of the human rational intellect, which learns from new things presented to it, a certain fluidity is possible.[97] Not only can we learn a new reason why we did something wrong and be forgiven, but God can endow us with his life, the life of grace, which is far above who we are by nature. We are more plastic than an angel.

And because God's life is infinitely above the life of any creature, a man infused with such life can move up the hierarchy in heaven beyond his nature, or natural place.[98] With the Incarnation and redemption bringing baptism and the life of grace, men are called to places above their natural abilities; again, the very order of grace assumes a life far above the natural capacity of any creature. Thus men will take the place of the fallen angels, restoring the old angelic hierarchy by grace.[99] God uses men to restore the

93. As discussed in chapter 7, the purpose of evolutionary changes according to modern biology is to enhance the ability of the organism and species to survive. Adam fell from a greatly exalted state of friendship with God, where the needs of the body were not a concern, to the ordinary day-to-day life of animals (i.e., survival). Thus he (and man in general) became preoccupied with those things needed for survival – food, clothing, shelter – and the excessive acquisition of these as well, owing to concupiscence. To survive, or to succeed in life according to modern human standards, became the driving force of his existence.

94. Rv 12:4.

95. Lk 20:16; *ST* I, q. 62. a. 9; I, q. 108, a. 8; Scheeben, *Mysteries of Christianity*, 403.

96. *ST* I, q. 62, a. 6; I, q. 108, a. 4; I, q. 108, a. 8.

97. *ST* I, q. 62, a. 6; I, q. 108, a. 4; I, q. 108, a. 8.

98. *ST* I, q. 62, a. 6; I, q. 108, a. 4; I, q. 108, a. 8.

99. The Gospels speak of men "like the angels in heaven" (Mt 22:30) who have become "equal to

original structure of heaven. The final glory of all angels and men in heaven with God is structured upon this threefold division of union, illumination, and purgation for all eternity – the Church in heaven.

Mary: Icon of Divinity

In a world under the curse due to original sin, is there any human creature who can reflect and display our true human end? One might say that Jesus Christ can reflect such an end because he is truly human; but of course Christ is also truly God. But there is another who perfectly reflects all that it means to be human: Mary, the Mother of God.[100] She is the highest creature, far above the highest seraphim.[101] In her human nature, Mary is lower than the lowest angel, but in the order of grace, she is the God-bearer (*Deipara*, or *Theotokos*).[102] Speaking of the Mother of God, the liturgy of St. John Chrysostom states, "More honorable than the Cherubim and beyond compare more glorious than the Seraphim, You a virgin gave birth to God the Word, You the Mother of God we magnify." Of this relation of low nature and high grace in Mary, St. Bernard of Clairvaux writes, "Thus it is right that Mary who was made the last of all when she was the first, was lifted from the lowest to the highest rank; it is right that she became the mistress of all, it is fitting that she was elevated above the angels themselves."[103] In Mary we find a concentrated image of the Catholic universe: in the icon of Our Lady of the Signs, a Russian icon dating from the 1100s, Mary is depicted with Christ in a medallion at her center, with his arms outstretched and uplifted, giving all of his gifts to her. In turn, she holds her arms up, giving

the angels . . ., sons of God, being sons of the resurrection" (Lk 20:36); St. Thomas develops this point further. See *ST* I, q. 108, a. 8.

100. *Catechism of the Catholic Church*, 466, 495, 509, 2677.

101. *Catechism of the Catholic Church*, 492–93, 508, 2030, and the remainder of the paragraph, with accompanying notes. See also Albert the Great, "We grant that her Son surpasses her in all privileges: but this, far from diminishing the praise of the mother, exalts it in that she has not only engendered a Son equal to her, but a Son infinitely better than herself. Under this aspect the goodness of the mother is rendered, in a sense, infinite. Each tree is known by its fruit: hence if the goodness of the fruit makes the tree good, the infinite goodness of the fruit manifests an infinite goodness of the tree," quoted in De Koninck, "Ego Sapientia," 18.

102. *Catechism of the Catholic Church*, 495.

103. De Koninck, "Ego Sapientia," 44.

all the gifts she receives from her son to two seraphim, the highest angels, one at each hand. These in turn will pass the gifts down to the rest of creation. All things come from God and return to Him through Mary, his most exalted creature.[104]

In Mary, the Mother of Signs, the Christian worldview perfected by revelation sees Jesus Christ and the Most Holy Trinity at the center of Mary, the highest creature by grace. Christ creates out of the pure goodness of who he is, Goodness and Love Itself, by no necessity on his part. By pure liberality, God desires to draw all angels and men into union with himself and participation in the personal life of the Trinity. He is the Source of all, of both creatures themselves and their actions, and head of his mystical body, the Church. Mary is the God-bearer, so all things come from God through her. She is the "neck" of the body of Christ. She distributes all the gifts and graces of God to the highest angels, the seraphim, depicted at her fingertips. They in turn pass these down to the order of angels below them and on to humanity, constituting the body of Christ.

Mary also serves as a transitioning focal point that brings this discussion back to science and modern knowledge, and toward a conclusion. Mary is the mother of Christ, hence the Mother of God. She is the burning bush from which God spoke to Moses, the Ark of the Covenant, the Temple in Jerusalem, the Temple of God, the God-bearer.[105] She is the perfect dwelling of God. And she is a human and therefore material: she is made of matter. Earlier we said that the whole history of the material universe is developing toward the human race. In its deepest meaning, the whole story of the 13.7 billion years of the material universe, with all its laws of matter and the development of galaxies, stars, planets, and the entire history of life from bacteria to humanity, is one large effort by matter to provide a temple for its Creator. The fruit of this entire history is therefore Mary.[106] She is the flower and fruit of matter offering itself to its Creator as a worthy temple. Conceived without original sin,[107] she was ordered (purged) to God in the

104. *Catechism of the Catholic Church*, 968–70.

105. These are but a few of the myriad titles of Mary from Church tradition. A reading of the litanies and akathists to Mary from the Latin and Eastern traditions will state these and many more.

106. De Koninck, "Ego Sapientia," 19. De Koninck's work cited here and previously is a short but profound treatise on Mary. See also Toma, "Dionysian/Thomistic Framework," 87–113.

107. *Catechism of the Catholic Church*, 411, 491.

greatest manner. Her words "Let it be to me according to your word" (Lk 1:38) are the greatest wisdom creation can speak to its Creator. Here, illumination reaches it apogee, and final union occurs through the Incarnation of the Son of God. In this sense, Mary is herself *the* icon of the Church, the liturgy, and all of reality.[108]

Thus creation in its fullest extent is a giant liturgical structure of purgation, illumination, and union analogous to the primary, secondary, and tertiary perfection in the natural world. All is received from and given to Christ through this hierarchy. This is the view God had from all eternity, that of the liturgy of Christ to be consummated in heaven. This allows us to make much more sense of the Incarnation of Christ. Far from being dropped into a sterile, purposeless universe of interacting atoms, molecules, and stars, he came as a champion[109] to restore the very order of creation, broken by the fallen angels and man, and to redeem and reorder us to our higher purpose of personal intimacy in the life of the Trinity.

108. *Catechism of the Catholic Church*, 967, 972; De Koninck, "Ego Sapientia," 19.
109. Ps 78:65–66; *Catechism of the Catholic Church*, 385.

Part IV

CONCLUSION

13 ANAPHYSICS

Understanding from the Height of Reality

Now that we have sketched a cosmology based on what God has revealed through Scripture and its official interpretation in the history of the Church, it is possible to return briefly to science itself and reconsider it in the light of that revelation. To the modern secular mind, to examine scientific data or theory in the light of revelation is to return to a supposedly prescientific—and to that frame of mind, "medieval"—mind-set. But we have contended that not only can scientific data and Christian faith be reconciled, but also a cosmology with a Hierarchy of Being is the only kind that can account for the immateriality of the intellect and the immateriality of Ultimate Being. It is the only kind that can offer any sense or meaning for the universe.

The philosophical approach in Part II invoked a rational ascent to God, an approach that makes faith reasonable. It led to reason's highest realization: that God is Being and Intellect. Accordingly, life is ultimately an intellect. Life and intellect in God are the same. And at the far reaches of reason, one might glimpse hazily that God is personal, but personal insofar as to be intellectual means that one can be related radically to another. The Chinese philosopher Lao Tsu in his *Tao Te Ching* seems to have had a sense of God (the Way) as personal; his work could be interpreted as the zenith of rational ascent.[1] But to know that this Personal Being is a Trinity of Persons requires a revelation from God; it is beyond our rational capabilities. The Christian revelation of the Trinity as Three Persons in one nature provides the final ground for understanding reality and the universe, both spiritual and material. All beings participate to a greater or lesser degree in the Personal Life of God, life that is both Intellect and Will. Once human beings receive that revelation, they can view and understand everything from this vantage point. Our most proximate contact with this reality is the God-Man, Jesus Christ. As the Three Persons are united in a bond of Love, so all things are united in the body of Christ, by the Holy Spirit. Personal union means a free gift of self-love resulting in its most perfect union, through a third.

Taking our stance on this high summit, we can speak of an *anaphysical* understanding of reality, from the Greek *ana*, meaning "above." It differs slightly from the more common "metaphysical," which means the search for knowledge of things beyond (*meta*) the physical. Introduced by the Italian physicist and theologian Giulio Maspero, "anaphysical" denotes understanding all reality, not only those truths above the material universe, from up above, or top down.[2] If the highest truth is that of the Trinity, insights into the Personal Relations of the Trinity ought to provide the groundwork for the deepest understanding of all other persons, human and angelic, as well as all other, lower creatures. Thus the primary way of understanding things from an anaphysical standpoint is similar to the process described in chapter 7, with the intellect as the driving force: one lifts the facts of science from a material framework and places them in a more rational one. But instead of the intellect, it is the person as the center of the relational being of intellect and will that is the end toward which all things tend. One simply employs the same argument of chapter 7 but substitutes personal being for the intellect, keeping in mind the backdrop of revelation.

1. Damascene, *Christ the Eternal Tao*, 77–78, 242–71. This is an excellent book of Eastern Orthodox theology that attempts to outline a theology of Christian revelation in the light of the best of ancient Chinese philosophy.

2. Maspero, "Life as Relation," 31–52.

A Brief Review of the Cosmos

I previously argued that material change has its end or *telos* in interior or intellectual change. I showed that the highest understanding of the data of science, according to reason, shows that the material universe is moving toward intellectual (human) being, as all things are being drawn by God into unity with himself. Thus the dominant trend in the material universe, according to our rational insight, is the general development of all things toward the capacity to support intellectual life in the human species. All other facts in the material universe are in some way subordinate to this end, and at the same time undergird it.

This development was based on a distinction known to pre-Enlightenment thinkers between living and nonliving things, according to exterior versus interior actions. The hallmark actions of nonliving beings occur through the transfer of change from one thing to the next, exemplified by the collision of billiard balls. By contrast, living things initiate and complete change themselves; they are their own source of change. The highest exemplary form of interior change is that of intelligence or understanding. It is toward intelligence that exterior change tends, and where it finds its completion. When the history and dynamics of the material universe are examined, the overarching tendency of things to facilitate intellectual operations becomes clear. This viewpoint supersedes the primacy of survival, the dominant scientistic and materialistic paradigm for understanding the universe.

To show this, I examined several areas of discovery and research in modern science: the classification of beings, modern physics, the fossil record, the developmental history of organisms, the evolution of the sexes, societal evolution, and psychology. All of these can be viewed according to the framework of the Hierarchy of Being and understood as leading toward intelligence.

All the new discoveries of modern science (subatomic particles, various molecules, galaxies, bacteria, protists, etc.) are easily reconciled by the fourfold division of beings in the material universe of the Hierarchy of Being according to minerals, plants, animals, and humans. Modern science classifies natural beings based on structure and function, while the Hierarchy of Being uses the essential operations of exterior versus interior change. There is no conflict between these two, as the latter is broader and can encompass the divisions of the former. All creatures known by modern inquiry can fit into the organization of the Hierarchy of Being, whose very structure is based on exterior and interior change leading to intelligence.

The discoveries of physics (including quantum mechanics), of astronomy, and of chemistry are simply sophisticated and precise understandings of exterior change and its mechanisms. One of the key means of incorporating such findings into the Hierarchy of Being is the causal system of Aristotle. Many of the findings of quantum mechanics, field theory, and cosmology can be understood within his potency-act philosophy. The ability of the Hierarchy of Being to incorporate such findings shows its explanatory power and fecundity. The age of the universe, for example, not only is not contradictory to the Hierarchy of Being, but also actually makes sense as a product of the manner by which an intellect (specifically God's) works in matter by assembling the simpler things first with an eye to building the desired end product. That end is an intellectual creature.

Natural history accords with the Hierarchy of Being as simpler life forms arise first, followed by lower multicellular organisms, and ending with higher complex life forms, such as mammals and the human race. In evolutionary history, matter was being organized to support complex structures for knowing material reality in a sophisticated manner.

The trend to interiorization is seen in the increasing complexity of cells, from non-compartmentalized prokaryotic to highly compartmentalized eukaryotic cells. In prokaryotes, cells reproduce by simple fission. In eukaryotes, fission occurs as well, but sexual reproduction also makes its first appearance. The advent of multicellularity found organisms initially asymmetrical in body plan, but with cellular specialization increasing. Some of the first specialized structures were those supporting reproduction. Initially, these were simply cells that budded off the whole, but special structures occurred later to support the proto-offspring.

As multicellular organisms became more sophisticated, complexity, body plans, and the sexes changed to support greater abilities to know and to cultivate knowing. The physical increase in complexity and interiorization allowed for greater division of labor within the body, to support the intensified interior actions of organisms. The body plan became radial (able to be cut like a pie) and supported basic neural networks and sensory abilities. The sexes slowly developed toward distinctly male and female.

With the advent of truly higher multicellular organisms, there arose highly complex organs, division of labor, bilateral symmetry, true sexuality, and communities. The most complex organ and sophisticated system in higher organisms is the primate/human brain, as a commonsense organ that efficiently integrates the sensory input from all the senses so that an intellectual soul (*anima*) may properly perceive its world for understanding. The complete evolution of body plans from asymmetric and radial to bilateral finds the senses more or less concentrated in the anterior of the organism and the visceral functions in the posterior. With the senses concentrated in the front to efficiently sense their surroundings, organisms could more efficiently coordinate all the senses for a composite picture of reality.

A hallmark of animal behavior is emotionality. The sophisticated emotional ability of higher organisms is yet another example of life preparing for the intellect. Why? Because the intellect makes one a person, a being who is both material and intellectual, and the intellectual faculty needs fine-tuned abilities to interpret and read another person, allowing the individual to function in families and societies.

True sexes appeared. They become the basis for the family and societies, and ultimately for culture. They support, cultivate, and extend the life of the mind. In all of these instances, the process of evolution consequently becomes not the principal driving force of living beings, but a means to tweak living systems to fine tune their ability to know.

The Hierarchy of Being provides a powerful rational framework to integrate the findings of modern scholarship into a system able to accommodate material and immaterial reality, and to provide a rapprochement between the best of modern and premodern thought. In this frame of reference, the intelligence is seen as the driving force and end of all things. But in the light of our discussion of revealed knowledge, is it possible to go beyond the pure notion of intelligence as the unifying factor for science and modern scholarship? Let us briefly revise the above approach to reason and the intellect in the light of Anaphysics.

A Brief Sketch of Anaphysics

Anaphysics makes the substantive claim that all life is relational and it offers the Divine Trinity as the ultimate ground or final explanatory structure for this fact.[3] What light does this shed on the material universe? Nonliving things exhibit only external change in their interactions with another. There is no interiorization of actions. If we closely examine these interactions, however, we begin to hints of a progress toward relational being.

The general tendency of inanimate being over the development of the universe through deep time is to become more and more complex. Subatomic particles interact to form atoms, atoms interact to form molecules, and molecules interact to form stars, planets, and galaxies. In the interactions of parts, one finds a rudimentary type of relational existence. These things come together under the laws of physical and chemical interactions to form loose aggregates. Then, physical and chemical bonds form yet stronger unions, giving rise to more complex structures. As a bridge can in part be accounted for by the relational positioning of the various stones, so the interaction of parts acts to form greater wholes.

The science of quantum mechanics also reveals a deeper insight into this phenomenon.[4] Quantum mechanics states that the very observation of a system can alter the system; the very act of measuring an object alters the known object. And one particle can influence another at great distances, so that there is a fundamental relational aspect to the interactions of things. At the subatomic level, particles cannot simply be defined by what they are, their essence, but in part must be defined by relations.

Life is arranged historically from the simplest to more complex organisms. The sequence of life in the fossil record is bacteria, protists, plants, animals, and humans or, from the standpoint of the Hierarchy of Being, plants, animals, and humans. How does anaphysics illumine the Hierarchy of Being?[5]

Plants, as defined by the hierarchy of being (bacteria, protists, and plants, according to modern science), are the lowest level of life. Plants take

3. This entire section on anaphysics takes its inspiration and some of its examples from Maspero, "Life as Relation," 31–52.

4. Maspero, "Life as Relation," 31–52.

5. Maspero, "Life as Relation," 31–52.

inorganic material and transform it into living matter. They exist to grow and reproduce, and the outcome of this process is another plant. Plants take matter, oriented purely toward itself and capable of only exterior actions, and reorient it through their offspring to something greater, such as another plant. As a consequence, matter, existing for itself at its most base level, is purged of total absorption in self to begin to exist for and be productive of another. By analogy with higher forms, one can use the terms "parent" and "offspring" to characterize this relation. While not a relation of love, it certainly is radically different from relations found among inanimate objects.

Such simple life began with bacterial fission involving no sexual reproduction or sexual individuation to produce two new individuals. With the advent of the eukaryotic cell, possessed by all higher types of life, life came into existence owing to the union of two sets of genetic information (chromosomes), or sexual reproduction. One chromosome of each pair is inherited from one of the parents. From this point on, all life begins as a communion of two that leads to unity in a new individual. This is because two chromosomes, one from each parent, are needed for conception of the new organism. From the outset, all eukaryotic life, even at a biochemical level, is relational.

Modern biological theory holds that early eukaryotes arose through a symbiotic relation between bacteria and larger cells, where bacteria invaded and resided in a larger cell to provide it with energy, and in turn to receive protection. An initial symbiotic relation is subsumed into a hierarchical relationship where the bacteria are the organelles at the service of the greater whole, the eukaryotic cell. This cooperation (relation) between cells is ultimately laying the groundwork for life to have a greater ability to give of itself and receive from another. Life is a unitive relation that lays the material groundwork for love.

Animals take the next step with true sensory capacities and knowledge of the individual. Their body plan develops over deep time from an asymmetric through a radial to a bilateral plan, with the senses slowly becoming generally concentrated in the anterior and the visceral functions in the posterior region. This concentration allows for more efficient knowing. Knowledge of any other, no matter what it is, is a type of relatedness and is essential for a personal being to exist. In the sensory act itself, animals become one with the sensory aspects of reality, another foreshadowing of the oneness with another through intellection, which characterizes persons.

Emotions arise from the sensory life. They are an expression of attraction or aversion to sensory stimuli. The complex emotional interactions of animals and humans uncovered by psychology can be thought of as necessary to produce relatedness and communities. The extreme intricacy of these emotions in higher animals, particularly higher mammals and humans, is yet another body of evidence consistent with the idea that life is moving toward personal being at the material level.

Broadly speaking, higher animal life exists as separate sexes, a male and female that can enter into a relation with one another. In mammals, maleness and femaleness represent true parenthood in the fullest sense, where the young are nourished, protected, educated, and cared for during long periods, a further intensification of relational existence. Animal societies and communities are in part the product of the separation of the sexes and the need to come together to produce another, that is, to find completion in a third and to rear and educate offspring.

All of these are a foreshadowing of and preparation for human life. The general trend toward the development of complex systems, atomic, molecular, and vital is a necessary prerequisite for the capacity to support personal beings (human) that have both intellect and free will. One needs extremely sophisticated molecular and genetic systems, complex organs such as the brain, and highly efficient systems such as sensory and memory capacities to integrate all the subtle inputs (physiological, emotional, and sociological) required to enter into friendships, families, societies, and culture with other personal beings. These, science has discovered, are unimaginably complex. The increase in complex systems over the eons of the universe can simply be interpreted as laying the necessary groundwork for a truly personal being. Likewise, the evolutionary mechanisms found in nature that lead to more complex living systems (with the caveats I posited in chapter 7) can be thought of in the same manner as contributing to personal being.

What in the end is the reason for knowledge and intellectual abilities in the human person, a true intellectual creature? True knowing allows one to enter into in union with another at the intellectual (nonmaterial) level. It allows one to be truly personal toward another. Also, it gives one knowledge of the end of one's action and hence the good or bad. Because of the intellect and will, the element of freedom appears truly for the first time in evolutionary history. One is able to freely choose the good. In Genesis, one hears the words "So God created man in his own image, in the image of God he created him, male and female he created them" (1:27). From the outset, man and woman were created as personal beings, beings created for love. The basic human unit of life is the family, where all higher-order human interactions are initially formed: with other men as well as angels and God, and higher units of human society, such as universities, cities, states, and religions, and the Church. What relationships are more intimate than that of the husband-wife, father-child, mother-child, and siblings? Each of these is the model for our relations with the Persons of the Trinity, or rather the relationships within the Persons of the Trinity are the archetype of these human interactions. Knowledge of the end or purpose allows one freely to be a gift of self to another, to love in such a way that it ultimately terminates in personal union via the intellect. Love makes the two equal. This is the final purpose of the material universe: to produce an intelligent creature who can be one with its Creator. In the greatest manner, it is to produce a temple like Mary, in which God becomes incarnate in the ultimate Gift, the Son. The creature can enter into eternal union with the Creator in the highest manner possible, deification in the Person of the Son.

All biological life is an integrated form of relatedness that achieves its highest state and terminates in the free relatedness or personal being of humans.[6] As material change finds its completion in the intellect – the intellect is an interior action not undergoing true exterior change – so relational being, under the *necessary* laws of the universe, finds its completion in the *free* relational being (person) of the human. Necessity terminates in freedom. Material development throughout the history of the universe ultimately terminates in the free personal existence of human beings, where the rest of the material universe can unite with its Creator through the free gift of the human. The general movement of life in matter is therefore preparing to free itself from its individuality in order to exist in the true freedom of persons in union with God. The archetype for this unity is the Personal

6. Maspero, "Life as Relation," 31–52.

Relations of the Trinity. Here is the ultimate insight of anaphysics, which explains the inherent relationality of the material universe.

The Hierarchy of Being clearly places the human race at the apex of the material world, the only species that possesses true intelligence. If all cosmic history has been moving toward the emergence of such a species, then the appearance of humanity on earth is not an accident of biology or a meaningless brute fact. Such a conclusion accords well with the nearly universal perception that there is something unique about humanity. The purpose of humanity is not bare survival akin to that of other species; it is the operation of the intellect with its accompanying volitional powers that opens the human person up to something more than the material, to transcendence itself. Such a conception contrasts sharply with a view that sees the human race as *primus inter pares*, the first among equals. Survival, of course, is an essential prerequisite to the appearance of intelligence, but it is not the end of existence. If mere survival as a species were all that mattered, there are many other means to survive without the necessity of intelligence. The unique and singular fact of human intelligence in the classic sense cries out for explanation.

There is nothing in the revealed aspects of the Christian and Catholic worldview that contradicts the global natural history of the fossil record of man. All the discoveries of physical anthropology do not in any way set aside or make superfluous its claims about the uniqueness of humanity. There is, however, irreconcilable conflict between a materialistic view of the human race as a cosmic accident without end, purpose, or meaning. And I consider one conglomerate fact of human life to be irrefutable evidence for the anaphysical view, namely, that human beings have always perceived themselves more in accord with the anaphysical view than with the reductionistic materialism advocated today. But such universal consensus is not evidence for a materialist philosophy because it rejects the common experience of humanity as so many self-constructed myths. It seems that the most important question still facing us today is one of Immanuel Kant's famous four: *Was ist der Mensch*?

Reality: Scientistic, Rational, or Anaphysical?

In each of these perspectives—the scientistic, the rational (Hierarchy of Being), and the anaphysical—the data of our universe would appear such as is recorded in standard scientific presentations. Facts are facts. Yet something is different with human beings. A chimpanzee walking through a laboratory with test tubes, or observing measurements of speed or mass, or playing in a fossil quarry, sees the same facts as a human scientist, and yet no chimpanzee has ever discerned a scientific law. It simply lacks the ability to synthesize, correlate, and raise facts to higher knowledge. It lacks intelligence in the true sense of the term. Only humans can discern and understand meaning. Scientism seems utterly incapable of explaining this difference. Perhaps it is only by stepping out of the ballpark of scientism into another worldview, one with reason derived from common human experience, that the meaning of our lives can be ascertained. An understanding of the nature of things, or *natura rerum*, as the ancients called it, can only be carried out by an intellect. Intuiting the meaning of things, not from the raw facts of science or the senses—after all, a chimpanzee has those, too—but from the common human experience of nature, is uniquely and gloriously human. This anaphysical view, I argue, is much more satisfying than the scientistic view, as it explains the full spectrum of human experience at a much deeper and more complete level. All human disciplines—art, history, music, poetry, literature, theater, philosophy, science, and the like—can be seen as shadows of the attempts of a rational being freely to grasp and express his experience, as a person desiring communion and union with the God-Man within a liturgical framework. Intelligence, will, love, and personhood in matter—*what it truly means to be human*—are understood in a much deeper manner when understood anaphysically, because they become open to explanation beyond matter. In contrast to materialist explanations that ignore meaning in material reality, the anaphysical worldview gives the final purpose to existence. It is true humanism.

14 BACK TO THE WOODS AND BEYOND

Walking the fields and forests of southern Indiana taught me that there is more to nature than the materialist story tells us. The lichens and leaves, the dragonflies and denizens of the forest all bespeak purpose and meaning. My persistent reflection on human experience showed me the poverty of scientism, the reductionistic construct that holds that the only legitimate knowledge is what comes from a laboratory. The human spirit perceives meaning immediately in nature, and philosophical reflection only clarifies and articulates that meaning already given. In contrast to the flat and monochrome reserve of certain modern constructs, the *plus quam* (more than) of the ancient and medieval thinkers answers to the plenitude of human experience. There *is* more to reality than the exponents of scientism pretend.

Nor am I alone in my belief in the primacy of nature and human experience. Erazim Kohak, the philosopher of nature whose time in the virgin woods of New Hampshire spoke the same truths, has identified the source of the problem and the solution awaiting those bold enough to seek it:

> The miracle of nature is the power and grace of God which confront the dweller therein. That is the most basic given ... The recognition of that given is at the same time our most basic conceptual task. Both in principle and as a

> matter of historic fact, alienation sets in when humans lose their awareness of the presence of God and persuade themselves to view the cosmos no longer as a creation, endowed with value in the order of being, a purpose in the order of time and a moral sense in the order of eternity, but as a cosmic accident, meaningless, and mechanical. Then nature comes to appear as absurd and we ourselves as futile within it . . . If we are to escape [this absurdity and futility], no conceptual task is more urgent then that of recovering our awareness of the presence of God and of nature as His creation. A book concerned with the conceptualization of nature ought surely to speak prominently of the presence of God, whether or not such is the current philosophic fashion.[1]

Arguably the most prominent intellectual trend of the last few centuries has been the slow, steady erosion of God from nature, ourselves, and human culture. The famous biologist Theodosius Dobzhansky coined the phrase "nothing in biology make sense except in the light of evolution." I say that nothing makes sense anywhere except in the light of God. Nor have the immaterial realities of angels, souls, and the transcendentals escaped the corrosive influence of materialism. This has had devastating consequences for humans trying to understand themselves and the world about them. One of my central contentions is that this erosion has been neither necessary nor consistent with human experience, reason, and revelation. Rather, one of the principal causes of this erosion has been the misuse of the findings of science. But this is a result of the misuse of science through the interpretation of data in a materialistic framework, which itself is not derivable from the data of science. Quite the contrary—not only is science not in contradiction with immaterial reality, but also, within the proper framework, such as a rational Hierarchy of Being, it can be subsumed into and reconciled with immaterial reality. Such a framework both places science into its proper context within the scope of human experience and knowledge and opens the human mind to transcendent being in all its aspects. This reinterpretation allows humans access to the highest knowledge of reality by making the ascent of faith in revelation a reasonable action. From these heights, humans can look back on reality and understand all things, including themselves, in the highest light of God.

1. Kohak, *Ember and the Stars*, 183.

The error in the modern materialist approach to nature and reality lies at the very beginning of human thought regarding how we know; a small error in the beginning has major consequences in the end. This error constitutes perhaps the major difference between the modern materialist and ancient/ medieval approaches to reality. Materialist thought claims that empirical research done by the scientist in the laboratory or field is the foundation for knowledge of reality. The scientific method and its findings are sacrosanct. The common experience of mankind is fundamentally in error and must be corrected. Daniel Dennett claims in *Darwin's Dangerous Idea* that evolution is a "universal acid," against which every other idea must be tested.[2] I would add that this is the view of scientism regarding science in general. But long reflection on the process of science and my own scientific labors has shown me that science assumes this human common experience, which we know from our first contact with reality, prior to any experiment or finding of science.

Twenty-three hundred years ago, Aristotle's *Physics* set out the true basis for this contact with reality and any subsequent system of thought: "The natural way of doing this, is to proceed from that which is best known to us."[3] All knowledge known by proofs or inference is derived from some preexistent knowledge. This cannot go on forever; an infinite regress would never deliver any certitude because nothing certain would ever be attained. So there must be something we simply know, that is, the self-evident truths derived from human experience. These self-evident truths are not simply truths of logic that we artificially impose on nature, but rather are truths of logic *because* they are basic truths of all reality, material and immaterial. We are knowing beings, and so there is a direct consonance between reality and our minds. Contrary to skepticism, we truly *know* things and their principles. Foundational truths are simply known from our initial contact with reality.

A critical mistake in materialist thought is to confuse self-evident principles with "urban legends" or common misunderstandings, like the world being flat. Because good science traffics in knocking down these misunderstandings, many thinkers assume that all ideas based on common experience

2. Dennett, *Darwin's Dangerous Idea*, 61–84, 521–22. The idea of the whole book is that Darwin's theory of natural selection is the universal standard for all ideas and theories.

3. Aristotle, *Physics*, 315.

are open to rebuttal. Nothing could be further from the truth. What are some of these self-evident principles? There is order in the universe, reality is hierarchical (since order is the subsuming of lesser to greater parts), a whole is greater than the sum of its parts, or the principles of identity, of noncontradiction, and of causality, and the notion of a Presence of something higher behind nature. These are not subject to critique, because all human rational discourse first depends on them. No scientific experiment ever discovered these principles; they have always been presupposed by all science. These are the "universal acids," to invoke Dennett's language, against which every idea must be tested. Everything in science is subject to them, including evolution.

What is imposed on nature is the mechanistic assumptions of modern thought through scientism. The idea that nature is simply the sum of the material forces of its parts and their interactions in a cold Newtonian universe is not human experience. Contrary to Aristotle's wisdom, scientism holds that our true test of theories is based on entities extremely distant from our contact with reality – things least known by us (atoms, quarks, quantum reality, electrons, genes) rather than what is most known. So it comes as no surprise that a graduate level biochemistry text opines, "Despite the advances in knowledge in recent years, for many people the notion of a vital force of some sort still survives. The view taken here is that such a notion is not needed for an understanding of living systems – that all actions and reactions that occur in living systems can be explained in terms of their chemistry."[4]

Against such scientism and in support of Aristotle, our natural reflex for knowing shows us the opposite. We know things less accessible to our knowledge by those things more accessible. This is why we call electricity a "current" (after water), or why we teach our children that the color gray is a shade of black and white. Deeper still, modern physics supports this insight of Aristotle. Werner Heisenberg perceptively asked what exactly electrons and other quantum objects are upon which scientism bases its worldview.[5] Our observations of such small entities fundamentally alter them, as the very means of studying them requires interactions with objects of similar size and energy. For instance, the photons that bounce off a large object such

4. Zubay, *Introduction to Biochemistry*, 1.

5. Heisenberg, *A Physicist's Conception of Nature*, 32–46.

as a dog, allowing us to see it, have little effect on the dog. But to another subatomic particle, such photons could be highly destructive. Heisenberg recognized that the product of these interactions, these "realties" studied by science, are just as much artificial as they are natural. Upon these somewhat subjective/objective objects, scientism bases its knowledge of reality.

Therefore, quite the contrary to scientistic claims that those who derive meaning from nature are projecting subjective human meaning onto it, it is in fact scientism that is projecting onto nature an artificial, machine-like quality devoid of intrinsic meaning. Humans are taught this in educational programs from an early age and begin to think of themselves as alien to nature, as they have a natural insight that they themselves have meaning. Eventually, humans themselves are thought to be pure mechanisms, the "atoms" of which are the genes and neurons that reduce our intellects and wills to pure subjective projections of mechanical meaning onto our nature. In the end, the very immateriality of our intellects is denied. We are no more than machines.

Once our immaterial nature is denied, we are cut off from higher things. As Thomas Aquinas realized, it is by the immaterial nature of the intellect that we principally come to know immaterial things. The denial of the highest part of ourselves drives the stake into the core of our being. We become like the perception of the natural world about us, a mechanical cog in a meaningless universe. The action of this "mechanical" mind – "reason" – becomes itself mechanical, like the rest of reality. Rationality becomes equated with matter and empiricism. The stage is set for the denial of immaterial reality, and thus faith in a supreme being, as something inherently irrational.

On the contrary, the rational framework of the universe understood by ancient and medieval thinkers is the Hierarchy of Being. At a perceptual level, the Hierarchy of Being in the material world – minerals, plants, animals, and humans – is obvious, as any human immediately understands when he considers that he is different from and superior to other living beings in the world. One does not need to teach a child this fact; they grasp it early on. They have to be taught to deny it later. A key insight of this structure is that nonliving things change by external actions, whereas living things change by deepening acts of interiority. These interior actions lead the way toward and are ultimately manifested as intelligence. From reason's standpoint, life is ultimately intelligence. Intelligence becomes not the calculating machine of modernity, but a faculty of the soul capable of union with another reality. Indeed, to truly know is to become one with or live the life of another. This power gives us the capacity to be persons, or beings made for communion and union with other persons, including God.

In the final analysis by our rational understanding, God is Intellect itself. Because we are intellects as well, this gives us the rational insight that the universe is created with purpose. We have the potential for friendship with God, but this insight lies at the far end of reason and needs the help of revelation to grasp, clarify, and elevate it. The greatest gift of the rational approach to reality, afforded by the Hierarchy of Being, is that the mind enjoys the freedom to expand and accept a higher truth revealed by God, a gift materialism excludes from the outset, a priori. The gift of reason and creation is perhaps best summarized by St. John of the Cross: "[The soul] begins to walk along the way of the knowledge and consideration of creatures, which leads to the knowledge of her Beloved, the Creator."[6]

The Travesty Called Modernity

If the greatest gift of nature is to prepare us to accept revelation, then the greatest travesty of modern thought is the misuse of nature to sunder us from assenting to the revelation of our Creator. More specifically, one might say that the greatest intellectual hoax of the modern age is the use of the tremendous insights into the beauty and order of the universe that science has provided to teach us that the world we call home is a meaningless mechanism with no Person behind it. It is absolutely false and unnecessary to use knowledge in this manner. As I have shown, it is perfectly possible to incorporate legitimate scientific data into a framework open to higher things. Scientific facts per se have no meaning, but they only receive meaning from the philosophical framework in which they are discussed and debated.

In the end, we are faced with a crisis of meaning based on a battle not over science but over competing philosophies. Our natural frames of ref-

6. John of the Cross, "Spiritual Canticles," 4.1.

erence that teach us are under assault. Nature in all its forms is disfigured: the world about us is thought of as a machine of pure atomic and genetic physicality. Arguably, much of modern ugliness and banality is a result of this philosophy. Faced with this meaninglessness, the human heart loses itself because it is only in its very relationship with God that it finds its highest meaning. As stated by the Second Vatican Council, "The dignity of man rests above all on the fact that he is called to communion with God. The invitation to converse with God is addressed to man as soon as he comes into being. For if man exists, it is because God has created him through love, and through love God continues to hold him in existence. Man cannot live fully according to truth unless he freely acknowledges that love and entrusts himself to his Creator."[7] We are not bipolar creatures, intellectual schizophrenics, if you will; the man of nature is not separate from the man of grace. We are unitary beings, and what happens with one aspect of our lives affects the whole of our life. It is impossible for minds bent low in mechanism to expect to grasp transcendence, whether they are inclined to religion or not. Our grasp of nature is critical for our proper appreciation and understanding of God, who reveals himself as the highest good. Mechanism and pure physicality drag down to the level of banality the mind that was created to be united with its infinite Creator.

From Reason to the Revealer

In the early twentieth century, a young Jewish woman sought out the founder of phenomenology, Edmund Husserl. Becoming the first female student of philosophy under Husserl's tutelage, she went on to become a philosophical luminary in her own right. As she reveals in her autobiography, the driving force of her life was the search for truth. Through all her meanderings and musings, Edith Stein would go on to be known as St. Therese Benedicta of the Cross. Both in her rational investigations and in her spiritual yearnings, she cast a unique light on the relationship between reason and revelation:

7. Second Vatican Council, *Gaudium et Spes*, I.19.

> The will naturally occupies itself with what is provided through the senses, finds in this its joy, seeks to take possession of it, feels pain over its loss, hopes for possession, and fears loss. *But it is not the spirit's calling to recognize created things and to enjoy them.* To be thus involved is a perversion of the spirit's original and actual purpose for existence. It must be liberated from this captivity [purgation] and elevated to the true being for which it was created. Its gaze must be directed to its Creator [illumination]. It must surrender itself to him with all its faculties [union]. This will be achieved progressively, step by step, through a work of education and detachment.[8]

Edith Stein came to see the synergy between what we believe about nature and how we respond to God. We simply cannot forget nature. It is the prerequisite to revelation. Why? Among the principal reasons for the order in creation as constituted by God the Father is specifically this purpose: to educate or, as the etymology of the Latin root *educare* suggests, "to draw out." The intellectual life draws us out of ourselves to participate in the great whole of nature and gives us the highest knowledge of the Creator apart from what he himself reveals. Its greatest wisdom is to teach us to humble ourselves and turn toward God and say with Mary, "be it done to me according to your word." In the words of the Camaldolese reformer Paul Giustiniani, one must "Live alone with God, and live for God alone,"[9] or detach oneself from all things in complete dependence on God. The work of detachment, as Therese Benedicta later says, is the work of God himself.[10]

This is why creation is structured upon the pattern of the liturgy, which in the Church, the mystical body of Christ, brings us Christ in the Eucharist, God himself. This liturgical structure is a threefold ladder that is the archetype of all things: it detaches us from inordinate attraction to material things, educates us to the greatest degree from creatures possible about God, and finally opens the door through a radical detachment from all things and dependence completely upon God, in order to unite us with himself by a participation in his Trinitarian life, which is called deification. The very purpose of the liturgy is to extend the life of the Trinity to all creatures so that in Christ all may form one great supernatural organism to participate in the

8. Stein, *Science of the Cross*, 114, brackets and italics added.

9. Leclercq, "Alone with God," 563.

10. Stein, *Science of the Cross*, 114–31.

eternal act of perfect self-oblation to the Father that gives infinite glory to God: the perfect liturgical act of the Persons of the Trinity. It was this pattern that God had in mind from eternity and upon which all is patterned—angels, Eden, ourselves, and the material universe. The point of creation is to aid in the consummation of this act to the greatest degree possible according to the capacity of each entity. In the end, "when all things are subjected to him, then the Son himself will also be subjected to him who put all things under him, that God may be everything to everyone" (1 Cor 15:28).

This end in God is yet another infinite magnification of what our natural world gives us, such as our family relationships, as described in the Book of Revelation:

> "Behold, the dwelling of God is with men. He will dwell with them and they shall be his people, and God himself will be with them; he will wipe away every tear from their eyes, and death shall be no more, neither shall there be mourning, nor crying, nor pain any more, for the former things have passed away." And he who sat upon the throne said, "Behold, I make all things new." Also he said, "Write this, for these words are trustworthy and true." And he said to me, "It is done! I am the Alpha and the Omega, the beginning and the end. To the thirsty I will give water without price from the fountain of the water of life. He who conquers shall have this heritage, and I will be his God and he shall be my son."[11]

The greatest loss for the intellectual life resulting from scientism and materialism is that the understanding of the transcendence of this God, existing as Three Persons whose essence is perfect love, is lost to the human mind and heart. This God is utterly transcendent and infinitely above his creation, but he is also a loving Being in Three Persons, three infinite Persons who know no limits of love and grace. So the highest human act is simply to adore and love God for who he is in himself. As so many saints remind us, God is to be adored simply because he is God. The adoration of God lies in simply being he who deserves perfect praise precisely because he is the infinite Father. The highest human vocation is summed up in Scripture: "You shall love the Lord your God with your whole heart, with your whole soul, and with your whole mind. This is the first and greatest commandment" (Mt. 22:37–38).

11. Rv 21:3–7.

"And a second is like it: You shall love your neighbor as yourself" (Mt 22:39). Or, as stated by the Carthusian monk Augustin Guillerand,

> A want of reverence is by no means rare. It paralyses the majority of souls. It is what wounds God's relations with His children; the idea of a Father is spoiled. He is a companion, a friend, a confidant whom we treat as equal. A father is altogether different. He is someone from whom we receive everything; to whom we give only what he gives to us. In his presence a child remains, and must remain, one who comes from him, and can act only by his power. The father is the source, the author without whom the child is nothing and can do nothing. The child depends on him for everything and in everything, and lives in a state of complete and constant submission to him. Love changes nothing of this; it tempers the submission with a confiding love, but it does not do away with it or diminish it in any way.[12]

The seventh-century monk of Constantinople Maximos the Confessor beautifully expresses our human end in terms reminiscent of Dionysius the Areopagite. Yet these terms strike at the heart of all reality in its splendor:

> Being the bread of life, or wisdom, spiritual knowledge and righteousness, He arouses in us an insatiable desire for Himself. If we fulfill His Father's will He makes us co-worshippers with the angels, when in our conduct we imitate them as we should and so conform to the heavenly state. Then he leads us up still further on the supreme ascent of divine truth to the Father of lights, and makes us share in the divine nature (2 Pt 1:4) through participation by grace in the Holy Spirit. By virtue of this participation we are called children of God and cleansed from all stain, in a manner beyond circumscription, we all encircle Him who is the author of grace and by nature the Son of the Father. From Him, through Him, and in Him we always will have our being, our movement and our life (Acts 17:28).[13]

Here St. Maximos the Confessor captures the Hierarchy of Being from an anaphysical standpoint. This standpoint is of the Father of all lights and goodness, who, from above, draws his lowest of intellectual and personal creatures, man, through the ranks of his highest creatures, the angels, to

12. Guillerand, *Prayer of the Presence of God*, 94.

13. Maximos the Confessor, *The Lord's Prayer*, Al Moutran, October 7, 2011, http://almoutran.com/2011/10/4309.

participation in his very nature. Here, united with the Trinity in a perfect singular Vision, the Beatific Vision, we see that all there is, all we are, all our desires, all our actions, and the ability to carry these out are caused by God. Karol Wojtyla (St. John Paul II) in *Rays of Fatherhood* succinctly states the same as follows: "And everything else will then turn out to be unimportant and inessential except this: father, child, and love. And then, looking at the simplest things, we will all say: 'Could we not have learned this long ago? Has this not always been embedded in everything that is?'"[14]

There is an essential reason why unmediated contact with nature is so important. Knowledge begins with wonder and consummates in praise of the divine, as Plato so perceptively captured it. And well into the modern era we still find voices echoing this profound human longing. A voice not easily heard in Victorian England, Mary Anne Evans (George Eliot),[15] veiled her own femininity but unveiled her human heart in her famous work *Daniel Deronda*:

> A human life, I think, should be well rooted in some spot of a native land, where it may get the love of tender kinship for the face of earth, for the labors men go forth to, for the sounds and accents that haunt it, for whatever will give that early home a familiar unmistakable difference amid the future widening of knowledge: a spot where the definiteness of early memories may be inwrought with affection, and kindly acquaintance with all neighbors, even to the dogs and donkeys, may spread not by sentimental effort and reflection, but as a sweet habit of the blood. At five years old, mortals are not prepared to be citizens of the world, to be stimulated by abstract nouns, to soar above preference into impartiality; and that prejudice in favor of milk with which we blindly begin, is a type of the way body and soul must get nourished at least for a time. The best introduction to astronomy is to think of the nightly heavens as a little lot of stars belonging to one's own homestead.[16]

14. John Paul II, *Radiation of Fatherhood*, Part III, 2.

15. While I use this quote from *Daniel Deronda* in support of the idea of the transcendent (see next paragraph), it should be pointed out that Evans was not at all religious. She lost her faith around age twenty and was agnostic at best. See Gordon S. Haight, "George Eliot," *Encyclopaedia Britannica*, last updated December 18, 2018, www.britannica.com/biography/George-Eliot. Nevertheless, I think this passage expresses great insight into the proper order in which we learn and is very much in line with a transcendent understanding of reality.

16. Eliot, *Daniel Deronda*, chap. 3.

The experience of the natural world as it is, with no artificial veil to conceal it, conveys the sense of the transcendent. The deepness of the woods, the countryside, the order in the seasons, the relationships of all the things contained therein, indicate that there is something greater than itself. Behind the artificial veil cast by materialism, there still lies a world of beauty, order, and goodness, understood by the intellect and loved by the will. Legitimate science deepens that appreciation by adding particulars, but does not in any way add to its fundamental reality, much less detract from its depth and wonder, wonders perceived not by the senses, but by the intellect. In this world, human beings and nature are not at odds but rather co-dependent. Nature lifts the human mind to its Creator. In turn, humans lift the totality of nature below them to its Creator above them. "*There are more things in heaven and earth,* Horatio, than are dreamt of in your philosophy."[17]

I found this goodness, order, and beauty on my thirty acres in the hills of southern Indiana. Here were my beloved hills and valleys, woods, meadows, and streams, where the autumns are walls of russets and golds, the winters quiet with covert life, the springs vibrant with the scents of flowers, the heat shimmering in the summer against the backdrop of locust and mockingbird song, and where materially my dog Bliss rests peacefully under the spreading branches of a chestnut tree but immaterially in my mind for eternity. These were my teachers at a key moment in my life of a reality beyond that of merely what presented itself before my eyes. I am so grateful.

17. Shakespeare, *Hamlet*, Act I, Scene 5.

BIBLIOGRAPHY

Adler, Mortimer J. *Intellect: Mind over Matter.* New York: Collier, 1990.

Andelman, Sandy J. "Evolution of Concealed Ovulation in Vervet Monkeys (*Cercopithecus aethiops*)." *American Naturalist* 129, no. 6 (1987): 785–99.

Aquinas, Thomas. *Commentary on Aristotle's De Anima.* Translated by Kenelm Foster, OP, and Silvester Humphries, OP. London: Routledge and Kegan Paul, 1951.

———. *Commentary on Aristotle's De Caelo et Mundo.* Translated by Fabian R. Larcher and Pierre H. Conway. Priory of the Immaculate Conception at the Dominican House of Studies, accessed December 27, 2018. http://dhspriory.org/thomas/DeCoelo.htm#1-3.

———. *Commentary on Aristotle's Metaphysics.* Translated by John P. Rowan. Notre Dame, IN: Dumb Ox Books, 1995.

———. *Commentary on Aristotle's Nicomachean Ethics.* Translated by C. J. Lutzinger, OP. Notre Dame, IN: Dumb Ox Books, 1993.

———. *Commentaries on Aristotle's "On Sense and What Is Sensed" and "On Memory and Recollection."* Translated by Kevin White and Edward M. Macierowski. Washington, DC: Catholic University of America Press, 2005.

———. *Commentary on Aristotle's Physics.* Translated by Richard J. Blackwell, Richard J. Spath, and W. Edmund Thirkel. London: Routledge and Kegan Paul, 1963.

———. *Commentary on the Divine Names of Blessed Dionysius.* Translated by Harry C. Marsh, Jr. PhD diss., Vanderbilt University, 1994.

———. *De Caritatis.* Translated by Lottie H. Kendzierski. Milwaukee: Marquette University Press, 1960.

———. *Light of Faith, Compendium of Theology.* New York: Book of the Month Club, 1993.

———. *The Literal Exposition on Job, a Scripture Commentary Concerning Divine Providence.* Translated by Anthony Damico. Interpretive Essay and Notes by Martin D. Yaffe. American Academy of Religion Classics in Religious Studies 7. Edited by Carl A. Raschke. Atlanta, GA: Scholars Press, 1989.

———. *On the Power of God (De Potentia).* Translated by Laurence Shapcote. Westminster, MD: Newman Press, 1952.

———. *On the Truth of the Catholic Faith* (*Summa contra Gentiles*), 5 vols. Translated by Anton C. Pegis. Garden City, New York: Doubleday, 1955.

———. *Summa Theologica*, 5 vols. Translated by the Fathers of the English Dominican Province. Westminster, MD: Christian Classics, 1981.

———. *The Trinity and the Unicity of the Intellect.* Translated by Sister Rose Emmanuella Brennan, SHN. London: Herder, 1946.

———. *Truth*, 3 vols. Translated by Robert W. Mulligan, SJ. Cambridge: Hackett, 1994.

Arintero, John G., OP. *The Mystical Evolution in the Development and Vitality of the Church*, 2 vols. Translated by Jordan Aumann, OP. Rockford, IL: Tan Books, 1978.

Aristotle. *Metaphysics*. Vol. 2 of *The Collected Works of Aristotle*, edited by Jonathan Barnes, 1552–1728. Princeton, NJ: Princeton University Press, 1984.

———. *Physics*. Vol. 1 of *The Collected Works of Aristotle*, edited by Jonathan Barnes, 351–446. Princeton, NJ: Princeton University Press, 1984.

Augustine. *On Christian Doctrine* (*De Doctrina Christiana*). Translated by D. W. Robertson Jr. Upper Saddle River, NJ: Prentice Hall, 1958.

———. "St Augustine on Genesis. Two Books on Genesis against the Manichees and On the Literal Interpretation of Genesis: An Unfinished Book." In *The Fathers of the Church*, vol. 84, translated by Roland J. Teske, SJ. Washington, DC: Catholic University of America Press, 1991.

Aurelius, Marcus. *Meditations of the Emperor Marcus Aurelius Antoninus.* Translated by George Long. Boston: Estes and Lauriat, n.d.

Austriaco, Nicanor Pier Giorgio, OP, James Brent, OP, Thomas Davenport, OP, and John Baptist Ku, OP. *Thomistic Evolution: A Catholic Approach to Understanding Evolution in the Light of Faith*. Dominican Friars of the Providence of St. Joseph: Cluney Media, 2016.

Bacon, Francis. "The Great Instauration (Part 1 of the Novum Organum)." In *The English Philosophers from Bacon to Mill*, edited by Edwin A. Burtt, 5–23. New York: Modern Library, 1939.

Bacovcin, Helen, trans. *The Way of the Pilgrim and the Pilgrim Continues His Way*. New York: Image Books, 1978.

Beisson, Janine. "Preformed Cell Structure and Cell Heredity." *Prion* 2, no. 1. (2008): 1–8.

Benedict XVI (Joseph Ratzinger). *In the Beginning . . . A Catholic Understanding of Creation and the Fall.* Translated by Boniface Ramsey, OP. Grand Rapids, MI: Eerdmans, 1990.

———. *The Spirit of the Liturgy*. Translated by John Saward. San Francisco: Ignatius, 2000.

Blackwell, Richard J. *Galileo, Bellarmine and the Bible.* South Bend, IN: University of Notre Dame Press, 1991.

Blanchette, Oliva. *The Perfection of the Universe According to St. Thomas: A Teleological Cosmology.* University Park: Pennsylvania State University Press, 1992.

Bohr, Niels. "Quantum Physics and Biology." *Models and Analogues in Biology: Symposia of the Society for Experimental Biology* 14 (1959): 1–5.

Butterfield, N. J. "Macroevolution and Macroecology through Deep Time." *Palaeontology* 50, no. 1 (2007): 41–55.

Calle, Carlos. *Superstrings and Other Things: A Guide to Physics*. 2nd ed. Boca Raton, FL: CRC Press, 2010.

Calloway, Ewen. "Genetic Adam and Eve Did Not Live Too Far Apart in Time." *Nature*. August 6, 2013. doi:10.1038/nature.2013.13478.

Carroll, Warren. *The Building of Christendom*. Front Royal, VA: Christendom College Press, 1987.

Carthusian Miscellany, A. *The Wound of Love*. Herefordshire: Gracewing, 2006.

Catherine of Genoa. "Treatise on Purgatory." In *The Spiritual Doctrine of St. Catherine of Genoa*, complied by Don Cattaneo Marabotto, 299–334. Rockford, IL: Tan Books, 1989.

Catholic Church. *Catechism of the Catholic Church*. 2nd ed. Vatican: Libreria Editrice Vaticana, 2012.

Chamovitz, Daniel. *What a Plant Knows: A Field Guide to the Senses*. New York: Scientific American/Farrar, Straus and Giroux, 2012.

Chervin, Rhonda, and Eugene Kevane. *Love of Wisdom: An Introduction to Christian Philosophy*. San Francisco: Ignatius, 1988.

Chesterton, G. K. *Orthodoxy*. Mineola, NY: Dover, 2004.

Damascene, Hieromonk. *Christ the Eternal Tao*. Platina, CA: Valaam, 2004.

Darwin, Charles. *The Origin of Species*. New York: Penguin, 1958.

Dawkins, Richard. *The Selfish Gene*. 2nd ed. New York: Oxford University Press, 1989.

De Koninck, Charles. "Ego Sapientia: The Wisdom That Is Mary." In *The Writings of Charles De Koninck*, 2 vols., edited and translated by Ralph McInerny, 1–62. Notre Dame, IN: University of Notre Dame Press, 2009.

De Lubac, Henri. *The Mystery of the Supernatural*. New York: Crossroad, 2016.

Dennett, Daniel C. *Darwin's Dangerous Idea: Evolution and the Meanings of Life*. New York: Simon and Schuster, 1995.

De Sales, Francis. *Treatise on the Love of God*. Translated by Dom Henry Benedict Mackey, OSB. Rockford, IL: Tan Books, 1997.

Diamond, Jared M. *Guns, Germs, and Steel: The Fates of Human Societies*. New York: W. W. Norton, 1999.

Dionysius the Areopagite. "The Celestial Hierarchy." In *Pseudo-Dionysius: The Complete Works*, translated by Colm Luibheid, 143–91. Mahwah, NJ: Paulist Press, 1987.

———. "The Ecclesiastical Hierarchy." In *Pseudo-Dionysius: The Complete Works*, translated by Colm Luibheid, 193–259. Mahwah, NJ: Paulist Press, 1987.

———. "Letter Eight." In *Pseudo-Dionysius: The Complete Works*, translated by Colm Luibheid, 269–80. Mahwah, NJ: Paulist Press, 1987.

———. "The Mystical Theology." In *Pseudo-Dionysius: The Complete Works*, translated by Colm Luibheid, 133–41. Mahwah, NJ: Paulist Press, 1987.

Draper, John Henry. *A History of the Conflict between Religion and Science*. New York: Appleton, 1874.

Durand, Emmanual, OP. "Perichoresis: A Key Concept for Balancing Trinitarian Theology." In *Rethinking Trinitarian Theology: Disputed Questions and Contemporary Issues in Trinitarian Theology*, edited by Giulio Maspero and Robert J. Wozniak, 177–92. London: T & T Clark, 2012.

Easterbrook, Greg. "Forgotten Benefactor of Humanity." *The Atlantic*. January 1997. https://www.theatlantic.com/magazine/archive/1997/01/forgotten-benefactor-of-humanity/306101/.

Edelman, Gerald M., and Giulio Tononi. *A Universe of Consciousness: How Matter Becomes Imagination*. New York: Basic Books, 2000.

Eliot, George. Chapter III. In *Daniel Deronda*. Dictionary of Victorian London. Accessed March 2, 2019. http://www.victorianlondon.org/etexts/eliot/deronda-0003.shtml.

Ephraim the Syrian. *Hymns on Paradise*. Translated by Sebastian Bock. Crestwood, NY: St. Vladimir's Seminary Press, 1990.

Euclid. *The First Three Books of Euclid's Elements of Geometry*. Translated by Thomas Tate. London: Longmans, Green, 1966.

Faculty of Arts and Sciences. *Report of the Task Force on General Education*. Cambridge, MA: Harvard University, 2007.

Finocchiaro, Maurice A. *The Galileo Affair: Documentary History*. Berkeley: University of California Press, 1989.

———. *Galileo on the World Systems: A New Abridged Translation and Guide*. Berkeley: University of California Press, 1997.

Frost, Robert. "Stopping by Woods on a Snowy Evening." In *The Poetry of Robert Frost*, edited by Edward Connery Lathem. New York: Henry Holt, 1969.

Gleick, James. *Chaos: Making a New Science*. New York: Penguin, 2008.

Golitzin, Alexander. *Et Introibo ad Altare Dei: On the Mystagogy of Dionysius the Areopagite and His Predecessors in the Eastern Christian Tradition*. Thessalonika: Patriarchikon Idryma Paterikon Meleton, 1994.

———. *Mystagogy: A Monastic Reading of Dionysius Areopagita*. Edited by Bogda G. Bucar. Collegeville, MN: Liturgical Press, 2013.

Greene, Brian. *The Fabric of the Cosmos*. New York: Vintage Books, 2005.

Gregory, Brad S. *The Unintended Reformation: How a Religious Revolution Secularized Society*. Cambridge, MA: Belknap Press of Harvard University Press, 2012.

Gregory of Nyssa. *On the Holy Spirit: Against the Macedonians*. Pickerington, OH: Beloved Publishing, 2014.

———. *The Life of Moses*. Translated by Abraham J. Malherbe and Everett Ferguson. New York: Paulist Press, 1978.

Grimaldi, David, and Michael S. Engel. *Evolution of the Insects*. New York: Cambridge University Press, 2005.

Guillerand, Dom Augustin. *The Prayer of the Presence of God*. Manchester, NH: Sophia Institute Press, 2005.

Hahn, Scott. *A Father Who Keeps His Promises*. Cincinnati: Servant Books, 1998.

———. *The Lamb's Last Supper: The Mass as Heaven on Earth*. New York: Doubleday, 1999.

Harre, Rom. *Great Scientific Experiments*. Oxford: Phaidon Press, 2011.

Harre, Rom, and E. H. Madden. *Causal Powers: A Theory of Natural Necessity*. Totowa, NJ: Rowman and Littlefield, 1975.

Harrison, Peter. *The Bible, Protestantism, and the Rise of Natural Science*. Cambridge: Cambridge University Press, 1998.

Hart, David Bentley. *The Doors of the Sea: Where Was God in the Tsunami?* Grand Rapids, MI: Eerdmans, 2005.

Heisenberg, Werner. *The Physicist's Conception of Nature*. Translated by Arnold J. Pomerans. New York: Harcourt, Brace, 1958.

Herbert, Nick. *Quantum Reality: Beyond the New Physics*. New York: Anchor Books, 1985.

Horn, Stephan Otto, and Sirgfried Wiedenholer, comp. *Creation and Evolution: A Conference with Pope Benedict XVI in Castel Gandolfo*. San Francisco: Ignatius Press, 2006.

Howell, Kenneth J. "Copernicanism and the Bible in Early Modern Science." In *Facets of Faith and Science*, edited by Jitse van der Meer, 4:261–84. Lanham, MD: University Press of America, 1995.

———. "Galileo and the History of Hermeneutics." In *Facets of Faith and Science*, edited by Jitse van der Meer, 4:245–60. Lanham, MD: University Press of America, 1995.

———. *God's Two Books: Copernican Cosmology and Biblical Interpretation in Early Modern Science*. Notre Dame, IN: University of Notre Dame Press, 2002.

———. "Natural Knowledge and Textual Meaning in Augustine's Interpretation of Genesis: The Three Functions of Natural Philosophy." In *Interpreting Nature and Scripture: History of a Dialogue in the Abrahamic Religions*, edited by Jitse M. van der Meer and Scott M. Mandelbrote, 117–45. Leiden: Brill, 2008.

Hublin, J. J., A. Ben-Ncer, S. E. Bailey, S. E. Freidline, S. Neubauer, M. M. Skinner, I. Bergmann, A. Le Cabec, S. Benazzi, K. Harvati, and P. Gunz. "New Fossils from Jebel Irhoud, Morocco and the Pan-African Origin of Homo Sapiens." *Nature* 546 (2017): 289–92.

Jaubert, Jacques, Sophie Verheyden, Dominique Genty, Michel Soulier, Hai Cheng, Dominique Blamart, Christian Burlet, Hubert Camus, Serge Delaby, Damien Deldicque, R. Lawrence Edwards, Catherine Ferrier, François Lacrampe-Cuyaubère, François Lévêque, Frédéric Maksud, Pascal Mora, Xavier Muth, Édouard Régnier, Jean-Noël Rouzaud, and Frédéric Santos. "Early Neanderthal Constructions Deep in Bruniquel Cave in Southwestern France." *Nature* 534 (2016): 111–14.

John of Chrysostom. "Vainglory and the Right Way for Parents to Bring Up Their Children." In *Christianity and Pagan Culture in the Later Roman Empire*, translated by Max L. W. Laistner, 85–122. Ithaca, NY: Cornell University Press, 1951.

John of the Cross. "Living Flame of Love." In *The Collected Works of St. John of the Cross*, translated by Kieran Kavanaugh, OCD, and Otilio Rodriguez, OCD, 577–649. Washington, DC: Institute of Carmelite Studies, 1979.

———. "Romances." In *The Collected Works of St. John of the Cross*, translated by Kieran Kavanaugh, OCD, and Otilio Rodriguez, OCD, 724–37. Washington, DC: Institute of Carmelite Studies, 1979.

———. "Spiritual Canticles." In *The Collected Works of St. John of the Cross*, translated by Kieran Kavanaugh, OCD, and Otilio Rodriguez, OCD, 408–565. Washington, DC: Institute of Carmelite Studies, 1979.

John of Damascene. "The Orthodox Faith." *In The Fathers of the Church St. John of Damascus Writings*, vol. 37, translated by Frederic H. Chase Jr., 165–406. Washington, DC: Catholic University of America Press, 1981.

John Paul II. *Familiaris Consortio*. Vatican Translation. Boston: Daughters of St. Paul, 1981.

———. *Fides et Ratio*. Vatican Translation. Boston: Pauline Books and Media, 1998.

———. *Radiation of Fatherhood*. 1964. Don Bosco Salesian Portal. Accessed February 24, 2019. https://donboscosalesianportal.org/wp-content/uploads/Radiation_of_Fatherhood.pdf.

Joyce, G. F. "Toward an Alternative Biology." *Science* 336 (2012): 307–8.

Kelemen, D. "Are Children 'Intuitive Theists'? Reasoning about Purpose and Design in Nature." *Psychological Science* 15, no. 5 (2004): 295–305.

Kelley, Bennet, CP. *The New St. Joseph Baltimore Catechism*. 2nd ed. New York: Catholic Book Publishing, 1969.

Kepler, Johannes. *The Harmonies of the World*. Translated by Charles Glenn Wallis. Annapolis: St. John's Bookstore, 1939.

Klug, William S., Michael R. Cummings, Charlotte A. Spencer, Michael A. Palladino, and Darrell Killian. *Concepts of Genetics*. 11th ed. Hoboken, NJ: Pearson Education, 2015.

Koch, Christof. *Consciousness: Confessions of a Romantic Reductionist*. Cambridge: Massachusetts Institute of Technology Press, 2012.

Kohak, Erazim. *The Ember and the Stars: A Philosophical Inquiry into the Moral Sense of Nature*. Chicago: University of Chicago Press, 1984.

Koyré, Alexandre. *Newtonian Studies*. Chicago: University of Chicago Press, 1965.

Krauss, Lawrence M. *A Universe from Nothing*. New York: Free Press, 2012.

Larchet, Jean-Claude. *Therapy of Spiritual Illnesses: An Introduction to the Ascetic Tradition of the Orthodox Church*, 4 vols. Translated by Fr. Kilian Sprecher. Montreal: Alexander Press, 2012.

Lawrence of the Resurrection. *Practice of the Presence of God*. Translated by Salvatore Sciurba, OCD. Washington, DC: ICS Publications, 1994.

Leclercq, Dom Jean. "Alone with God." Translated by Elizabeth McCabe. In Dom Jean Leclercq and Paul Giustiniani, *Camaldolese Extraordinary: The Life, Doctrine, and Rule of Blessed Paul Giustiniani*, edited by Camaldolese Hermits of Montecorona, 526–940. Bloomingdale, OH: Holy Family Hermitage, 2003.

Levering, Matthew. *Engaging the Doctrine of Creation Cosmos, Creatures, and the Wise and Good Creator*. Grand Rapids, MI: Baker Academic, 2017.

Lewontin, Richard. "Billions and Billions of Demons." *New York Review of Books*. January 9, 1997. http://www.nybooks.com/articles/archives/1997/jan/09/billions-and-billions-of-demons/.

Lienhard, Joseph, T., SJ, ed., "Exodus, Leviticus, Numbers, Deuteronomy." In *Ancient Christian Commentary on Scripture*, vol. 3. Downers Grove, IL: InterVarsity Press, 2001.

Lorkowski, C. M. "David Hume: Causation." *Internet Encyclopedia of Philosophy*, accessed December 28, 2018. http://www.iep.utm.edu/hume-c.

Low, B. S. "Ecological and Social Complexities in Human Monogamy." In *Monogamy: Mating Strategies and Partnerships in Birds, Humans and Other Mammals*, 161–76. Cambridge: Cambridge University Press, 2003.

Luigi, Pier Luigi. *The Emergence of Life: From Chemical Origins to Synthetic Biology*. Cambridge: Cambridge University Press, 2006.

Masci, David. "Scientists and Belief." Pew Research Center, Religion and Public Life Project, November 5, 2009. http://www.pewforum.org/2009/11/05/scientists-and-belief/#1.

Maspero, Giulio. "Life as Relation: Classical Metaphysics and Trinitarian Ontology." *Theological Research* 2, no. 1 (2014): 31–52.

———. "Patristic Trinitarian Ontology." In *Rethinking Trinitarian Theology: Disputed Questions and Contemporary Issues in Trinitarian Theology*, edited by Giulio Maspero and Robert J. Wozniak, 211–29. London: T & T Clark, 2012.

Mateo-Seco, Lucas Francisco. "The Paternity of the Father and Procession of the Holy Spirit: Some Remarks on the Ecumenical Problem." In *Rethinking Trinitarian Theology: Disputed Questions and Contemporary Issues in Trinitarian Theology*, edited by Giulio Maspero and Robert J. Wozniak, 69–102. London: T & T Clark, 2012.

Maximos the Confessor. *The Church, the Liturgy, and the Soul of Man: The Mystagogia of St. Maximos the Confessor*. Translated by Dom Julian Stead, OSB. Still River, MA: St. Bede's, 1982.

Montgomery, Scott. "The Two Witnesses." *Daily Catholic: Diadems of the Decade* 18, no. 63 (2007): http://www.dailycatholic.org/issue/10Mar/030407sm.htm.

Morris, William, ed. *The American Heritage Dictionary of the English Language*. New College ed. Boston, MA: Houghton Mifflin, 1980.

Nature. *Dogs That Changed the World*. Narrated by F. Murray Abraham. Chicago: Questar, 2011.

Nellas, Panayiotis. *Deification in Christ: Orthodox Perspectives on the Nature of the Human Person*. Translated by Norman Russell. Crestwood NY: St. Vladimir's Seminary Press, 1987.

Newton, Isaac, *Mathematical Principles of Natural Philosophy*. Translated by Andre Motte. Berkeley: University of California Press, 1934.

Nichols, Aidan, OP. *The Shape of Catholic Theology*, Collegeville, MN: Liturgical Press, 1991.

Nijhout, H. F. *Metaphors and the Role of Genes in Development. Bioessays* 12, no. 9 (1990): 441–46.

Nikodimos of the Holy Mountain and Makarios of Corinth, comp. *The Philokalia: The Complete Text,* vols. 1–4. Translated by G. E. H. Palmer, Philip Sherrard, and Kallistos Ware. London: Faber and Faber, 1979–1995.

Origen. "Letter to Gregory Thaumaturgus." Translated by Frederick Crombie. In *Ante-Nicene Fathers*, vol. 4, edited by Alexander Roberts, James Donaldson, and A. Cleveland Coxe. Buffalo, NY: Christian Literature, 1885. Revised and edited for New Advent by Kevin Knight in 2017, http://www.newadvent.org/fathers/0415.htm.

PBS. "B. F. Skinner, 1904–1990." A Science Odyssey: People and Discoveries, accessed December 28, 2018. http://www.pbs.org/wgbh/aso/databank/entries/bhskin.html.

Perez, Angel Cordovilla. "The Trinitarian Concept of Person." In *Rethinking Trinitarian Theology: Disputed Questions and Contemporary Issues in Trinitarian Theology*, edited by Giulio Maspero and Robert J. Wozniak, 105–45. London: T & T Clark, 2012.

Perlov, Delia, and Alex Vilenkin. *Cosmology for the Curious*. Cham, Switzerland: Springer, 2017.

Petrides, George A., and Janet Wehr. *Peterson Field Guide to Eastern Trees.* Boston: Houghton, Mifflin, 1998.

Picarretta, Luisa. *Complete Unpublished Works*. Provided by Fr. Tom Celso, Rochester, NY.

Pieper, Joseph. *Leisure the Basis of Culture.* San Francisco: Ignatius Press, 2009.

Pinheiro, V. B., A. I. Taylor, C. Cozens, M. Abramov, M. Renders, S. Zhang, J. C. Chaput, J. Wengel, S. Y. Peak-Chew, S. H. McLaughlin, P. Herdewijn, and P. Holliger. "Synthetic Genetic Polymers Capable of Heredity and Evolution." *Science* 336 (2012): 341–44.

Pius XII. *Humani Generis*. Vatican City: Libreria Editrice Vaticana, 1950. http://w2.vatican.va/content/pius-xii/en/encyclicals/documents/hf_p-xii_enc_12081950_humani-generis.html.

Popovich, Archimandrite Justin. *Man and the God-Man*. Alhambra, CA: Sebastian Press, 2008.

Puhalo, Archbishop Lazar. *The Creation and the Fall: A Lecture Series on Genesis*. Dewdney, BC: Canadian Orthodox, 2006.

Raven, Peter H., George B. Johnson, Kenneth A. Mason, Jonathan B. Losos, and Susan R. Singer. *Biology*. 10th ed. New York: McGraw-Hill, 2011.

Rice, George. "Are Viruses Alive?" Microbial Life Educational Resources, accessed December 28, 2018. http://serc.carleton.edu/microbelife/yellowstone/viruslive.html.

Richter, D., R. Grün, R. Joannes-Boyau, T. E. Steele, F. Amani, M. Rué, P. Fernandes, J. P. Raynal, D. Geraads, A. Ben-Ncer, J. J. Hublin, and S. P. McPherron. "The Age of the Hominin Fossils from Jebel Irhoud, Morocco, and the Origins of the Middle Stone Age." *Nature* 546 (2017): 293–96.

Rottman, J., L. Zhu, W. Wang, R. Seston Schillaci, K. J. Clark, and D. Kelemen. "Cultural Influences on the Teleological Stance: Evidence from China." *Religion, Brain & Behavior 7, no. 1* (2017): 17–26.

Russell, Bertrand. *Religion and Science*. Oxford: Oxford University Press, 1961.

Scheeben, Matthias Joseph. *The Mysteries of Christianity*. Translated by Cyril Vollert, SJ. New York: Crossroad, 2006.

Schulz, David J., Andrew B. Barron, and Gene E. Robinson. "A Role for Octopamine in Honey Bee Division of Labor." *Brain, Behavior, and Evolution* 60, no. 6 (2002): 350–59.

Scott, Alwyn, ed. *Encyclopedia of Non-Linear Science*. New York: Taylor, Francis, 2005.

Sears, Francis W., Mark W. Zemansky, and Hugh D. Young. *College Physics*. 5th ed. Reading, MA: Addison-Westley, 1982.

Second Vatican Council. *Gaudium et Spes: Pastoral Constitution on the Church in the Modern World*. In *Vatican Council II: The Conciliar and Post Conciliar Documents*, edited by Austin Flannery, OP, 903–1014. Northport, NY: Costello, 1975.

———. *Lumen Gentium: Dogmatic Constitution on the Church*. In *Vatican Council II: The Conciliar and Post Conciliar Documents*, edited by Austin Flannery, OP, 350–432. Northport, NY: Costello, 1975.

———. *Sacrosanctum Concilium: The Constitution on the Sacred Liturgy*. In *Vatican Council II: The Conciliar and Post Conciliar Documents*, edited by Austin Flannery, OP, 1–282. Northport, NY: Costello, 1975.

Seeley, Thomas D. *Honeybee Democracy*. Princeton, NJ: Princeton University Press, 2010.

———. *Wisdom of the Hive: The Social Physiology of Honey Bee Colonies*. Boston, MA: Harvard University Press, 1996.

Sethi, S., and M. E. P. Seligman. "Optimism and Fundamentalism." *Psychological Science* 4 (1993): 256–59.

Seybold, K. S., and P. C. Hill. "The Role of Religion and Spirituality in Spiritual and Mental Health." *Current Directions in Psychological Science* 10, no. 1. (2001): 21–24.

Shakespeare, William. *The Complete Works of William Shakespeare*. Vol. 2, edited by W. G. Clark and W. Aldis Wright. New York: Nelson Doubleday, n.d.

Shaw, Andrew M. *Astrochemistry: From Astronomy to Astrobiology*. West Sussex: John Wiley and Sons, 2007.

Sheen, Fulton J. *God and Intelligence*. New York: IVE Press, 2009.

———. *Philosophy of Science*. Milwaukee: Bruce Publishing, 1934.

Smith, Vincent Edward. *Philosophical Physics*. New York: Harper and Brothers, 1950.

Smith, Wolfgang. *The Wisdom of Ancient Cosmology*. Oakton, VA: Foundation for Traditional Studies, 2004.

Snyder, C. R., K. L. Rand, and D. R. Sigmon. "Hope Theory." In *Handbook of Positive Psychology*, edited by C. R. Snyder and S. J. Lopez, 257–76. New York: Oxford Press, 2002.

Staniloae, Dumitru. *The Holy Trinity: In the Beginning There Was Love*. Translated by Roland Clark. Brookline, MA: Holy Cross Orthodox Press, 2012.

———. *Orthodox Spirituality*. Translated by Archimandrite Jerome Newville and Otilia Kloos. South Canaan, PA: St. Tikon's Seminary Press, 2003.

———. *Theology and the Church*. New York: St. Vladimir's Seminary Press, 1980.

Stein, Edith (Therese Benedicta of the Cross). *Finite and Eternal Being*. Washington, DC: ICS Publications, 2002.

———. *The Science of the Cross*. Washington, DC: Institute of Carmelite Studies, 2002.

Tattersall, Ian. *Masters of the Planet: The Search for Our Human Origins*. New York: Palgrave MacMillan, 2012.

Toal, M. F., ed. and trans. *The Sunday Sermons of the Great Fathers*, 4 vols. San Francisco: Ignatius Press, 1996.

Toma, Daniel P. "A Dionysian/Thomistic Framework for the Integration of Science into Catholic Tradition." *Logos* 16, no. 3 (2013): 87–113.

Toma, Daniel P., Kevin P. White, Jerry Hirsch, and Ralph J. Greenspan. "Identification of Genes Involved in *Drosophila melanogaster* Geotaxis, a Complex Behavioral Trait." *Nature Genetics* 31, no. 4 (2002): 349–53.

Tsakanikas, Matthew. "The Christocentrism of the Virtues According to Santa Caterina da Siena." Doctoral thesis. Pontificium Institutum Ioannes Paulus II Studiorum Matrimonii ac Familiae apud Pontificium Universitatem Lateranensem, 2013.

Van Breman, Peter, SJ. *The God Who Won't Let Go*. Notre Dame, IN: Ave Maria Press, 2009.

Villareal, Luis. "Are Viruses Alive?" *Scientific American* 291, no. 6 (2004): 100–105.

Von Balthasar. *Cosmic Liturgy: The Universe According to Maximus the Confessor*. Translated by Brian E. Daley, SJ. San Francisco: Ignatius Press, 2003.

Von Frisch, Karl. *The Dance Language and Orientation of the Bees*. Translated by Leigh E. Chadwick. Cambridge, MA: Belknap Press of Harvard University Press, 1967.

Ward, Peter, and Donald Brownlee. *Rare Earth, Why Complex Life Is Uncommon in the Universe*. New York: Copernicus Books, 2004.

Webster, Gerry, and Brian Goodwin. *Form and Transformation: Generative and Relational Principles in Biology*. Cambridge: Cambridge University Press, 1996.

Westfall, Richard S. *Never at Rest: A Biography of Isaac Newton*. Cambridge: Cambridge University Press, 1980.

White, Andrew D. *The History of the Warfare of Science with Theology in Christendom*, 2 vols. New York: Appleton, 1896.

Wilson, Edward O. *The Insect Societies.* Cambridge, MA: Belknap Press of Harvard University Press, 1971.
———. *The Social Conquest of the Earth.* New York: W. W. Norton, 2012.
———. *Sociobiology: The New Synthesis.* Cambridge, MA: Belknap Press of Harvard University Press, 1975.
Wilson, James Q., and Richard J. Herrnstein. *Crime and Human Nature.* New York: Simon and Schuster, 1985.
Winston, Mark L. *The Biology of the Honey Bee*. Cambridge, MA: Harvard University Press, 1987.
Zizioulas, John D. *Being as Communion: Studies in Personhood and the Church*. Crestwood, NY: St. Vladimir's Seminary Press, 1985.
———. *Communion and Otherness.* New York: T & T Clark, 2006.
———. *Lectures in Christian Dogmatics*. London: T & T Clark, 2008.
———. "Trinitarian Freedom: Is God Free in Trinitarian Life?" In *Rethinking Trinitarian Theology: Disputed Questions and Contemporary Issues in Trinitarian Theology*, edited by Giulio Maspero and Robert J. Wozniak, 193–207. London: T & T Clark, 2012.
Zubay, Geoffrey. *Introduction to Biochemistry*. 2nd ed. New York: Macmillan, 1988.

INDEX

abstraction, 30, 70, 72
act, highest human, 312
action, revelatory, 145
Adam and Eve, 271–78; existence of, 277n56
Adler, Mortimer, 64n19
agent, principal, 79, 159n75; as efficient cause, 138
Albert the Great, ix, 287n101
anaphysics, 293–303, 313; origins of, 294
ancient thinkers, 12n20, 30, 32–39; acceptance of natural causality, 35; definition of intelligence, 61; dismissal by modern thinkers, 14, 28; open to evolution, 141, 164–65; relationship to modern science, 55–56; relevance of, 14; understanding of matter, 71; understanding of perfection, 130–31; understanding of reality as a hierarchy, 14; understood philosophy to draw on reality, 28
angels, 98, 182–83, 187–90; fall of, 278–281, 286; guardian, 267; hierarchy of, 264–71; tertiary end of, 192n31
animals, 33–34, 111; ability to sense, 115–118; different from persons, 59; in the hierarchy of being, 111–120, 268–271, 299; and the law of assimilation, 121; memory of, 117–118; movement of, 109; organization of societies, 134–136; secondary perfection, 270n27
anointing of the sick, 244
Anselm, 84; *Cur Deus Homo*, 219
anthropology, 174, 302
Arintero, John, OP, 229, 234, 260–61, 262n2
Aristotle, x, 8n8, 12n20, 22, 34–35, 55, 72, 73, 74, 85, 89, 112, 149–50 , 176, 207, 270, 307; analogy of sight to explain intellect, 61–62; *De Anima*, 8n8; and *episteme*, 40; and the four causes, 35–36, 47, 54, 75, 296; moderate realism, 79; *Physics*, 8n8, 306; and *theoria*, 35; Unmoved Mover, 182
art, 70, 71, 168; cave art, 66–68
asceticism, 21, 23
assimilation, law of, 120–21, 259
astronomy, 48–51, 114, 314
Athanasius of Alexandria, 220
atheism, 1, 84, 172
atoms, 51–53, 64–65, 148–51
attributes of God. *See* divine attributes

Augustine, 12n20, 84, 86–88, 93, 95, 96, 101, 251; *Confessions*, 86, 270; *De Doctrina Christiana*, 87–88; *De Genesi ad Litteram*, 93; *rationes seminales*: 164–65

Bacon, Francis, *Great Instauration*, 91
Baptism, 244
beatific vision, 238, 261, 314
Beaumont, William, 45–49, 51, 52, 53
beauty: delight of the good, 23, 30–31; diversity critical to, 133; of natural reality, 32, 58; as a transcendental, 32
Bede, 251
belief in God, reasonable, 4, 182n7
Bellarmine, Robert, 93, 95; *Letter to Fr. Paolo Foscarini*, 95
Benedict XVI, Pope, 14n22
Bernard of Clairvaux, 287
Bible. *See* Scripture
Big Bang, 114, 136n26, 151, 193
biology: definition of life, 108; definition of species, 164; and evolution, 305, focus on survival and reproduction, 122; and human development, 131; molecular, 54, 156, 162; nonlinear, 54; sociobiology, 159–160, 168; study of living things, 174
bishop, role of, 254
Blanchette, Oliva, 130, 140n37
body: human, does not preexist the soul, 76, 81; instrument of the soul, 79, 159n75; of Christ, 222, 237; requires a formal cause, 76; resurrection of, 240
Boethius, 13n21, 88–89, 101; *Consolation of Philosophy*, 89
Bohr, Niels, 41, 52–53
Borlaug, Norman, 4n5
brain, 6; complexity of, 80, 158–159; organ of "common sense," 79; processes sensory information, 62, 79–81; role in activity of intellect, 79–81; versus the soul, 159

capitalism, 27
Catechism of the Catholic Church, x, 77n40, 219–20, 226, 244
Catherine of Genoa, *On Purgatory*, 210
cause and effect, 33–35, 82, 99, 307; in Darwin's observations of species, 53–55; derived from common human experience, 36n29, 37, 49; and Isaac Newton, 49–51; in nature, 33–34; presupposed in empirical research, 47, 54; universality of, 50
causes, Aristotle's four, 35–36, 52, 53, 75
certainty: degrees of, 41–43; practical, 105
Chalcedon, Council of, 236–37
change, 110, 140; exterior and interior, 295–96, 308; moves toward intelligence, 295. *See also* movement
chemistry, 40, 113, 307; basis in the hierarchy of being, 174; changes in, 55; relationships to physics, 113, 143
Church: archetype of creation, 208, 248, 275; exists for the Eucharist, 245; and the Galileo Affair, 92–96; hierarchy of, 253–56; and Eden; liturgical structure of, 15, 208; liturgy of, 242–61; microcosm of heaven, 246; misconceptions about, 242–43, 275; and moderate realism, 79; mystical body of Christ, 239, 241, 248; preexistent from eternity, 15; and revelation, 98–99; world created for the sake of, 246n22
Church Fathers. *See* Fathers of the Church
classical philosophy, 12n20, 14, 29, 39, 143, 148. *See also* ancient thinkers
classification, medieval and modern systems of, 144–47
Clavius, Christopher, 95
common human experience, 13, 28–32, 37, 49, 55–56, 105, 139, 142, 177; of Aristotle's four causes, 35–36; as basis for proofs for the existence of God, 39; as basis for science, 37, 55, 78, 82, 121; of final causality, 126; learning from, 28–32; of movement, 107; of nature, 19–39, 58–59, 181; opposed to scientism, 27–28, 201, 307; and philosophy, 29, 110; of self-evident principles, 13n21, 39, 47. *See also* experience
Confirmation, 244
consciousness, 6–7, 13, 141
contemplation, 31, 200, 232, 276
Copernicanism, 2–3, 92–94, 181
Copernicus, 2, 3, 90, 92; *De Revolutionibus*, 92
cosmological worldview, ix–x, 9, 191–218, 295–97. *See also* hierarchy of being
cosmos: and the Church, 243–44; intelligence

as organizing principle, 122, 192; and the liturgy, 262–89. *See also* creation; universe
creation: account in Genesis, 3, 88, 212, 271–78; and deification, x, xn2, 218, 248; divine plan of, x, 218; doctrine of, 193–202; for education, 311; end in God, 198; liturgical, 14n22, 246–47, 311–12; modeled after the Church, 248; from nothing, 193; reflects divine nature, 193–94; for worship, 246n21
creationism, 15
Crick, Francis, 54
crucifixion, 240
culture, 161–66, 169–70; product of intellect, 73, 169–70; sexes as the basis for, 297

Damascene, Hiermonk, *Christ the Eternal Tao*, 294n1
Daniélou, Jean, 209, 218
Darwin, Charles, 2, 53–55, 183; *Origin of the Species*, 191
deacon, role of, 254–55
deification, x, 208, 225–41, 286n99; of Adam, 223, 230–31, 276; and the Eucharist, 259; and the Incarnation, 220, 229, 235–39; and the liturgy, 248; participation in divine life, 224, 226, 229–30, 234, 260–61; purgation, illumination, union, 248–52, 287
Dennett, Daniel, *Darwin's Dangerous Idea*, 306
deposit of faith, 98
Descartes, René, 76–77
development: of human society, 168–71; of life, 154–65; of nuclear family, 169; primary, secondary, tertiary, 128–31; stages of, 128–34, 140
Diamond, Jared, 170–71; *Guns, Germs, and Steel*, 170
Dionysius the Areopagite, x, 12n20, 249, 313; angelic hierarchy, 266–67; "Celestial Hierarchy," 247n23, 262n1
diversity: within the hierarchy of being, 133–34, 136, 175, 194; of organisms in modern science, 142, 147; reflects divine nature, 194
divine attributes, 98
divinization. *See* deification
DNA, 43–44, 53–55, 160–61, 164
Dobzhansky, Theodosius, 305
Draper, John Henry, 84, 90
dualism, 76–77

Easterbrook, Greg, "Forgotten Benefactor of Humanity," 4
Edelman, Gerald, 6
Eden, Garden of, 271–78; archetype of the kingdom of God, 277; beginning of the Church, 275; existence of, 274
effects proportionate to causes, 50–51, 66
efficient causality, 35–36, 52, 53, 138
Einstein, Albert, 113, 141
Eliot, George, *Daniel Deronda*, 314
emergence of species, 141. *See also* evolution
Enlightenment, 2–3, 14; difference between pre- and post-Enlightenment thought, 11, 19, 30, 39, 60–61; hostility toward religion, 96; and the intellect, 82; shift in thinking, 11, 31n19
environmentalism, 27
Ephraim the Syrian, 12n20, 275, 279
essence, 68, 70–73; of God, 184–85, 209, 218, 255, 261, 312
Eucharist, 208, 244–46, 250, 252, 256–61; and the Incarnation, 256; manna a type of, 275; transubstantiation, 256–258
eukaryotes, 152, 156–57, 161, 296, 299
evil, 281–83
evolution, 2, 3, 134, 140; in the hierarchy of being, 163–65; of humans, 165–73, 272n31; role in scientism, 306; simple to complex, 154–65, 300; of the universe, 151–54. *See also* emergence of species

facts, 7, 27–28, 55–56, 263, 294–95, 303, 309
faith: and nature, 8–9; and reason, history of, 86–101; reasonable, 11, 97; relationship to theology, 85
Fall of Adam. *See* original sin
family: basic unit of human life, 301; and deification, 233; development of, 169, 297; and devotion to God, 207; and the Trinity, 277n56
Fathers of the Church, 14, 75, 101, 213, 220, 229, 233n36, 249, 276, 285–86
final causality, 35–36, 52, 53, 126–128, 138, 141

Finocchiaro, Maurice, 83
formal causality, 35–36, 52–53, 70–74, 164; exists in intellect, 72, 119; and moderate realism, 79–81; soul as form of the body, 74–75
Foscarini, Paolo, *Letter on the Copernican Revolution*, 92
freedom: of Adam, 285; completion of necessity, 301; of God, 213–14; ontological freedom, 214
Frost, Robert, "Stopping by Woods on a Snow Evening," 107

Galileo, 50, 85, 92–96, 120; *Dialogue on the Two Great World Systems*, 94; *Discourse on the Two New Sciences*, 94; *Letter to the Grand Duchess Christina*, 92
Garrigou-Lagrange, Reginald, *God: His Existence and Nature*, 4
genetics, 8, 54; Adam and Eve, 262n31; and the hierarchy of being, 159–162; memes, 161n89
geometry, 41–43, 70
Giustiniani, Paul, 311
Gnosticism, 27
God: adoration of, 312; creator, 96–97, 193–202, 218; essence same as existence, 109, 177, 184–86, 209; the Father, 212–14; freedom of, 213–14; his own cause, 109, 186; the Holy Spirit, 216–17; idea of God in the brain, 81; immaterial, 73; infinite intellect, 98, 154, 177n1, 182–86, 309; love, 210–20; materialist questions about, 184–86; natural knowledge leads to, 90; neither male nor female, 212; personal, 60, 198, 294; the Son, 212-15; source of all truth, 87; transcends all being, 199; ultimate cause, 60; vision of, 226, 261. *See also* divine attributes; Trinity
Golitzin, Alexander, 249n34
goodness, 22–23, 30–32, 315; common good, 133–34; desire for the good called love, 62; and evil, 232, 241, 275, 279–81; freely chosen, 300; of God, 193–96, 199, 210, 263, 265, 288, 310; and hierarchy of being, 266–67, 282–84; of the human body, 75; transcendental, 36, 99
Gospel of John, 227–29, 236; and the hypostatic union, 237
grace, 99, 190, 222–23, 230–31, 238, 240, 261, 313; of Adam, 238, 273–74, 276; of angels, 286; does not destroy nature but perfects it, 99; of Christ, 241; grants vision of God, 261; of Mary, 287–288; order of, 243; sources of, 253–54. *See also* deification
Gregory, Brad, *Unintended Reformation*, 3, 3n2, 4
Gregory of Nyssa, 216, 285n91; *Life of Moses*, 250
Guillerand, Augustin, 313

Hahn, Scott, 246n17, 279
Hart, David Bentley, *Doors of the Sea*, 281n76
Heisenberg, Werner, 72, 148–49, 307–8
Herrnstein, Richard J., 172
hierarchy, 127–28, 138–42, 247n26; according to Dionysius, 247n23, 262n1; of angels, 264–71; of the Church, 253–56; of development, 131–32; diversity in, 132–34; and grace, 286–87; higher beings include lower, 122; in human society, 168–71; of living things, 111–20; for our education, 311; of perfections in nature, 135, 154n46; and the possibility of evil, 281–82; two vantage points, perfect and imperfect, 138. *See also* hierarchy of being
Hierarchy of Being, ix, 109, 118, 308–9; ambiguities in, 146; and Aristotle's four causes, 296; classification based on movement, 145; and economics, 171; erroneous conception of, 127; explanation of diversification, 158, 296–97; and exterior, interior change, 296–97, 308; integrative capacity, 174–75; and the liturgy, 252, 262–89; and modern science, 143–47, 173, 297; and physics, 147–51; and the principle of continuity, 162; and providence, 195–99; and psychology, 171–72; vestige of Eden, 208–9. *See also* hierarchy
holy orders, 244, 254
hope, 243
Hugh of St. Victor, 89–90; *Didascalion*, 89
human beings, 77; and anaphysics, 302–3; a bridge between material and immate-

rial, 120, 140, 198, 263; completion of the universe, 74, 134, 268, 301; composed of formal and material cause, 74–75; composed of soul and body, 74–75, 81; differ from other living things, 107–8, 111; end in the Trinity, 190n25, 218; essential part of the universe, 134; evolution of, 165–73; in the hierarchy of living things, 111–20, 134, 268–71; intelligence of, 63, 108; liturgical, 269; microcosm of creation, 120; purpose of, 218, 225, 301–2, 312; stages of development, 128–34; symbolic capacity of, 67–68, 168; transcend the material, 68
human nature: and grace, 99, 230; and sin, 232–35; of the Son, 236–40; transformed by the Eucharist, 258
Hume, David, 34
humility, 31, 59
Huxley, Thomas Henry, 84

illumination, 248; and angels, 265–66. *See also* perfection; purgation
imagination, 7–8, 28, 31
immanence, 108–10, 143, 147, 155n57, 174, 177. *See also* interiorization
immateriality, x, 6, 30; compatible with science, 305; of human intellect, 11, 13, 39, 57–82, 64n18, 64n19, 72, 119, 121, 142, 146; of human thought, 119, 121; material beings raised to immateriality through human knowing, 82; not opposite of material, 122; rational knowledge of, 11; and self-evident principles, 39
Incarnation, 98, 219–23; and deification, 235–39, 260; and the Eucharist, 258–59; fittingness of, 268–69; reasons for, 219–22; and the Trinity, 221–23. *See also* Jesus Christ
Inchofer, Melchoir, 94
Indiana, reflections on, 1–2, 20–24, 57–59, 106–7, 124–26, 205–8
individuality, 77, 179; in deification, 208; freedom from, 301; immateriality transcends, 72; intellect transcends, 66, 82
individuals, 44, 66, 85, 116; and animal knowing, 116–17, 145, 156, 200; as a causal locus, 33n22; in Christ, 239, 259–60; and human knowing, 71–73, 119, 270; of humans, 74–79; and the intellect, 82, 141, 189; from the material cause, 77; and moderate realism, 79–81; and original sin, 279–80; and society, 130–37, 168; symbolization exceeds, 67–70
inflationary theory, 149–50
intellect, 77; abstracts form from matter, 72, 75; allows us to participate in nature, God, 311; and anaphysics, 294, 303; of angels, 187–90; completion of all material actions, 140; as culmination of hierarchy of being, 122, 141, 169; elevates beings, 73, 141; end in Christ, 248; grasps being, 62; grasps causes, 4; and human culture, 169–70; immaterial, 11, 13, 57–82, 63–66, 68, 105, 119; integrates disciplines; knowledge of ends, 141, 196, 175; knows through senses, 79, 98, 119, 178; and the law of assimilation, 121; and love, 61–63; materialist view of, 118; and moderate realism, 79–81; moved internally, 140; personal nature of, 63, 109; in the *Philokalia*, 63n16; role in providence, 196–99; and self-knowledge, 119–20; and understanding, 61, 109, 187; understands essences, 70, 73, 303; unites with object in act of knowing, 61, 72, 82, 120-21. *See also* intelligence
intelligence, 61–70, 120; ancient and medieval definition, 61; apex of material reality, 141, 158, 169, 296–97; cause of order in nature, 126–28, 141; discursive and sequential, 181; interiority of, 155n57 181; modern definition, 61; organizing principle of the cosmos, 122, 153–54; and the soul, 74–77; symbolization a sign of, 67. *See also* intellect
intelligent design, 15
interiorization: in animals, 117, 168; in development of life, 155–65, 167–68, 177, 181, 296, 298; in plants, 114; trend toward, 173, 296
Irenaeus of Lyons, x, 262n2

Jesus Christ, 10, 98, 100, 208, 236–39; head of the Church, 245; his sacrifice, 239–41; hypostatic union, 237–38;

Jesus Christ (*cont.*)
last Adam, 233, 239; minister of the sacraments, 244; reveals the life of the Trinity, 222, 228, 256, 294; undergoes purgation, 263n2. *See also* Incarnation

John Chrysostom, 15n23, 285; liturgy of, 253, 287

John of the Cross, x, 207–9, 221–22, 233, 261, 309; on the Incarnation, 236; and intellectual union, 260; *Romance 2: On Communication among the Three Persons*, 207

John Damascene, 12n20, 285n91; "Orthodox Faith," 247n24

John Paul II, Pope, *Fides et Ratio*, 9; *Radiation of Fatherhood*, 314

Kant, Immanuel, 302

Kepler, Johannes, 50, 85, 91–92; *Harmony of the World*, 91

knowledge: through abstracting form from matter, 72; according to a materialist, 72; in animals, 117–18, 299–300; apophatic, 211, 230; begins with wonder, 314; cannot contradict faith, 96–97; of causes, 34, 119; desire for, 73, 270; elevates beings, 73, 141; of immaterial reality, 11, 61; leads to freedom, 301; leads to praise of God, 314; limits to, 98; natural, 83, 90, 97, 100, 176; natural and revealed, 97–98; of reality is possible, 49, 72; scientific, 6, 13, 55, 105; self-evident, 55–56; and self-gift, 301; three types, 97–100; two conceptions of, 177–80; and union with an object, 73, 300, 309

Koch, Christof, 7, 7n9, 10–11, 82; *Consciousness: Confessions of a Romantic Reductionist*, 2–3; on the soul, 76–79

Kohak, Erazim, 13n21, 24–25, 30n17, 31n19, 127, 304–5; *Embers and the Stars*, 24, 57

Krauss, Lawrence, 150–51; *Universe from Nothing*, 150, 184

Lao Tsu, *Tao Te Ching*, 294

law of assimilation, 120–21, 259

Lawrence of Brindisi, 223

laws of motion, 112–13

Leonardo da Vinci, 138–39, 141, 195, 248

Leo XIII, Pope, *Providentissimus Deus*, 93

Levering, Matthew, xn2

Lewontin, Richard, 179–80

liberal arts, 88, 89

life, 105–22; conditions for formation, 152; development from simple to complex, 154–66; higher forms more perfect, 110–11; and interiorization, 155–65, 167–68, 173, 177, 181, 296, 298; more than survival, 122, 155, 302; movement a criteria for, 108n3, 109n5, 107–8, 110, 177; object of science, 143; on other planets, 63n14; perfection in God, 109, 226–27, 245; tends toward intelligence, 122–23, 156–57, 309; three types of material life, 111

liturgical structure of Church, 14n22, 15, 208, 245–52; blueprint for creation, 15, 247; helps us perceive rational order of reality, 15

liturgical worldview, ix, 242–61

liturgy, 15, 242–61; participation in heavenly liturgy, 245–46, 312; purgation, illumination, union, 248–53, 262

love, 62; between persons of the Trinity, 207, 209; ends in union, 62–63, 261, 301; *eros, philia, agape*, 62; and freedom, 210; God's love, 210–20; and heavenly hierarchy, 255; the Holy Spirit, 216–17; and the idea of the self, 119; not an emotion, 63; origin in God, 261; related to the intellect, 61–63, 119

Marcus Aurelius, 32

marriage, sacrament of, 244, 274

Mary, Mother of Jesus, 237, 287–89; icon of the Church, 289; Mother of Signs, 287–88; Theotokos, 287

Maspero, Giulio, 294, 298n3

Mass. *See* Eucharist; liturgy

material causality, 35–36, 52, 53, 70–74, 138, 149, 164

materialism: causes faith to seem irrational, 12; challenged by common human experience, 105; denial of final causes, 126–28; empties reality of meaning, 173; errors of, 306–8; makes true knowledge impossible, 72; perspective on disorder, 284; questions about God, 184–86; and scientism, 19, 39, 179–80; sees religion and science in conflict, 84, 96–97; view of the intellect,

118, 308. *See also* materialistic worldview; scientism
materialistic worldview, 12–13, 83–84, 177; and evolution, 164. *See also* materialism; scientism
material reality, x; altered after the fall, 280–81; connected to immaterial by human beings, 120; elevated through human knowing, 82; intellect as culmination of, 122, 155; known by a combination of intellect and senses, 71; liturgical character of, 268–71; and Mary, Mother of God, 288–89; perfection does not exist in, 65; return to Creator, 82
matter, 71–72, 76, 77, 140, 148–49
Maximos the Confessor, 12n20, 213, 249–50, 313; purgation, illumination, union, 250n36; *Mystagogy*, 249
meaning: of content of faith, 85; crisis in the modern world, 11, 309–10; and the experience of reality, 32; given by God, 305; human capacity for, 67–68; and intelligibility, 24–25; known in the intellect, 68; in nature, 22–24, 27, 58, 181; objective, 31; in time, 25–29. *See also* purpose
medieval thinkers, 12n20; and Aristotle's four causes, 35, 75; definition of intelligence, 61; dismissal by modern thinkers, 14, 28; and the intellect, 73; open to evolution, 140n37, 141, 164–65; perfect and imperfect vantage points of hierarchy, 138–39, 263–64; and philosophy, 28, 40, 85; reflection on the sciences, 40–41; relevance of, 14; understanding of matter, 71; understanding of perfection, 130–31; understanding of reality as a hierarchy, 14, 144–47; understanding of the universe, 152–53
Mendel, Gregor, 54, 85
metaphor, 69, 79
metaphysics, 41, 243
miracles, 196
moderate realism, 79–81
monk, role of, 255
morality: and the natural world, 32, 269; objective basis of, 32; and the principle of non contradiction, 38
motion. *See* movement
movement, 107–11; Aquinas's teaching on motion, 112–13, 118–19; and classification in the hierarchy of beings, 145; Newton's laws of motion, 112; of nonliving things, 109, 111–14, 147–48, 308; self-movement criterion for life, 108n3, 109n5, 110, 177; of the will, 120
multiverses, 149–51

natural knowledge, 83; prepares us to accept revelation, 100, 247
natural science. *See* science
natural selection, 53, 154, 163, 191
natural theology, 41
natura rerum, 34
nature: causal powers of, 33–34; respect for, 58–59; cause of, 4; compatibility with Scripture, 95–96; composed of form and matter, 72; consequences of misunderstanding, 100; disorder and danger in, 280–84; as a divine book, 90; humans a part of, 27; leads to knowledge of God, 8–9, 247, 310–15; meaning hidden in, 11n17, 19, 22–24; possesses an end, 128; rhythms of, 20–24; three perfections in, 134–38
Nellas, Panayiotis, *Deification in Christ*, 233n36
New Testament, 75, 76, 147; and Greek philosophy, 75–76
Newton, Isaac, 49–51, 50n15, 53, 90, 111–13, 183; laws of motion, 112; *Principia Mathematica*, 50
Nicaea, Council of, 236–37
Nicene Creed, 215, 250
Nichols, Aidan, xn1, 262n2
nonliving things: change by external actions, 308; in the hierarchy of being, 111–20; liturgical, 250; movement of, 109, 111–14, 147–48, 308

Ockham, William of, 180–81
Ockham's razor, 180–81
order, 132–34; imperfect, 138, 153; in nature, 134–38; perfect, 138, 248; presupposes a cause, 137–38; presupposes intelligence, 127. *See also* hierarchy

Origen of Alexandria, 86, 87, 251
Original Justice, 231–32, 274, 276, 279
original sin, 14, 190, 219, 223, 232–33, 273–81; consequences of, 279–81, 286n93

pantheism, 11n14
perfection, 65–66; ancient and medieval understanding of, 130–31; and final causality, 138; modern understanding of, 130; in nature, 134–38; perfect and imperfect, orders of, 192; primary, secondary, and tertiary, types of, 132–33, 192, 192n32; purgation, illumination, union, 248–50, 270n27, 28; of stages of human development, 131–329
personal, 59–60; God as, 60, 198, 294; reality as personal, 59, 248; union, 260
personhood. *See* human beings
Philokalia, 63n16, 240n82
philosophy, 84–85; analytical, 110; handmaid of revelation, 85; natural, 89; and theology, 95, 175; the science of sciences, 40, 175; task of, 29
physics, 114; and the hierarchy of being, 147–51; philosophical physics, 143
Picarretta, Luisa, 227n6, 276n55
Pius XII, Pope, 272n31
plants, 111–20, 268–71, 298–99; ability to sense, 116n35, 117; interiorization, 114; and the law of assimilation, 121
Plato, 12n20, 74, 76, 85, 89, 176, 314
Plotinus, 12n20
potency of matter, 71–72, 148–49
prayer, 228n8; of Adam, 276–78
priest, role of, 254
principle: of continuity, 162, 187; of identity, 37–38, 48, 55, 307; of non-contradiction, 37–38, 47, 55, 307; of self-movement, 108, 177; stated by Augustine, 87, 93; tenet of Catholic theology, 95; a whole is greater than the sum of its parts, 37–38, 194n44
prokaryotes, 155–57, 296
proofs for the existence of God, 30n17, 39
Protestant Reformation, 90
providence, divine, 195–99
psyche. *See* soul
psychology, 171 –72
purgation, 248, 262n2, 271n28; and angels, 266. *See also* purgation, illumination, and union
purgation, illumination, and union, 248–52, 262n2, 287; according to Maximos the Confessor, 250n36; and angels, 264–71; and Eden, 275; and holy orders, 254; in the liturgy, 262, 289; of material universe, 248n32, 268–71; and perfect and imperfect orders, 263–64
purgatory, 210
purpose, 22–24, 124–26, 127, 136, 180–82, 208; of existence, 32; of human life, 225, 242, 302; of time, 25. *See also* meaning

quantum mechanics, 65, 298; does not contradict the hierarchy of being, 148–49; theory of, 113
quantum physics, 51–53

rationes seminales, 164–65
realism: moderate, 79–81; radical, 79
reality, 9–13; of Aristotle's four causes, 36–37; bifurcation into religious and nonreligious, 83, 177; Christian view of, 177–78, 208; elevated by human knowing, 73; goodness and beauty of, 30–31; as a hierarchy of beings, 14, 37; as ordered, 55; perceived through liturgical structure of church, 15; personal, 59, 248; received with humility, 31; of the transcendentals, 36; united to God through Christ, 244–45. *See also* hierarchy of being
reason, 11, 55, 97; complements faith, 96–101; and faith, history of, 86–96; and philosophy, 85; and revelation, 98, 190–91, 310–11
relationship, 82, 109; gives meaning to reality, 73; modeled after the Trinity, 301
relativism, 171
relativity, theory of, 113
religion, 7, 10, 83–85, 171; distinct from theology, 84. *See also* science and religion
Renaissance, 34
reproduction, 114, 118, 145, 160, 166–69, 200, 212; in the act of knowing, 119–20; asexual, 299; before the fall, 285n91; in humans, 269–70; life is more than, 122, 134; in plants, 117, 270; sexual, 115n30, 167, 296

revelation, 97–100; and reason, 98, 190–91, 310–11; two forms of, 98–99
Russell, Bertrand, 90

sacramental worldview, 243–45. *See also* Eucharist; liturgy
sacraments, 98, 244, 254, 274. *See also* Eucharist
Scheeben, Matthias, x, 209n5, 219n60, 240n77, 272n31
science, 4–9, 40; captivates our imagination, 7–8; classification of, 41–45; and common human experience, 13, 37, 55, 78, 82, 105, 121; compatible with immaterial reality, 55, 305; limits of, 8, 41–45, 61, 142, 305; medieval understanding of, 40, 89; nonlinear, 54; origins in antiquity, 32; search for unification, 183–84. *See also* science, empirical; science, modern
science, empirical, 40–56; cannot grasp natures, 42; distinct from mathematics, 42; goal of, 40; rests on self-evident principles, 41, 45–49, 53, 54, 55; great precision but low certainty, 43–44; measurement of individuals, 44–45, 178n2; observational versus experimental, 48; presupposes Aristotelian causality, 47; and the principle of identity, 48; and the principle of non-contradiction, 47
science, modern: advantages, 4; ambiguities in classification system 146; compatible with the hierarchy of being, 143, 174, 293; denial of final causes, 126–128
science and philosophy, 55
science and religion, 1–3, 84, 96, 179–180, 271; during the Galileo affair, 92–96; warfare between, 90–92, 96
scientific revolution, 90–91
scientism, 19, 27–28, 39, 72, 143, 271, 303; and Aristotle, 307; denial of final causes, 126–28, 179, 191; does not distinguish between religion and theology, 84; errors of, 306–8; inadequacy of, 75–79; reductive of humans, 118, 303; view of evolution, 154, 163; view of knowledge, 178, views life from primitive functions, 118
scientists: belief in God, 3, 28; religious motivations, 91
Scott, Alwyn, 54
Scripture, 88, 98, 176; compatibility with nature, 95–96; on the Incarnation, 220–21; interpretation of, 88, 95; and the liturgy, 251–52; reveals the Trinity, 215
Second Vatican Council, 310
secular worldview. *See* materialistic worldview
self, image of as knower, 119–20
self-evident principles, 37–39, 47, 55–56; as part of common experience of reality, 39, 55; as basis for empirical sciences, 41, 53, 54; truth, 306–7
self-evident truths, 306–7
self-movement. *See* movement
senses: known indirectly by intellect, 70 development in organisms, 154–65; required for activity of the intellect, 79, 98;
Sheen, Fulton, 13n21, 55–56, 81, 82; *Philosophy of Science*, 55–56
sin, 14; consequences of, 281–82. *See also* original sin
Skinner, B. F., 172
society, 130–37, 168–71, 199–200; organization of, 134–36
soul: versus the brain, 159; confusion of Platonic and Christian ideas of, 75–79; and deification, 240; different understandings of, 75–76; does not exist apart from matter, 75, 76, 81; and the Eucharist, 260; formal cause of human being, 74–75, 77n40; how and memory, 77–78; seat of the intellect, 100
Spinoza, Baruch, 11n14
Staniloae, Dimitru, 217
Stein, Edith, 310–11
Stern, Otto, 51–53
Stoics, 85
subatomic particles, 51–53, 71–72
symbolic communication, 69–70, 168
symbolization, 67

Tattersall, Ian, 66–70; *Masters of the Planet*, 66, 272n31
technology, 26–27, 197
Tertullian, 86

theology, 84–85, 175; apophatic, 211, 230; as "faith seeking understanding," 84, 100; relationship to philosophy, 175
theory/*theoria*, 31, 35
Thomas Aquinas, x, 12n20, 55, 68, 69, 79, 98, 108, 111, 117, 150, 176, 274, 308; Adam's knowledge of Christ, 274; and angels, 187–90, 266–67; ascent of the intellect to God, 248n32; on the cause of the universe, 152–54; *Commentary on Aristotle's Physics,* 165; *Commentary on Aristotle's Sense and Sensibles*, 171–72; *Commentary on the Divine Names*, 162; and the development of human society, 171; on evolution, 140n37; on the family, 207; good as the desire for being, 23n3; and the hierarchy of being, 118–20, 122, 262n1, 267n15; on immanence, 110n10; on the immateriality of the intellect, 64n19; and the Incarnation, 223; on knowledge of God, 211; *Literal Exposition on Job*, 99; and microevolution, 165; on movement as a criteria for life, 108n3, 109n5; on providence and governance of the universe, 199n73, 199n74; sexual reproduction before the Fall, 285n91; *Summa contra Gentiles*, 79, 96–97, 110, 183–84, 201–202; teaching on motion, 112–13; and transcendentals, 32n21; *Trinity and the Unicity of the Intellect*, 99
time, 24–29
transcendentals, 32, 36, 99, 305
Trinity, x, 10, 92, 98, 110, 205–24, 252, 294; archetype of human relationships, 301–2; cannot be known by reason, 198n72, 210; and the Eucharist, 258–59; Father, 212–14, 216; Holy Spirit 216–17, 261; human soul reflects, 120n50; Incarnation, 221–23; and Mary, 288; and purgation, illumination, union, 252n44; Son, 213–16; union with, 226. *See also* God
truth, 38, 49, 88, 95–96, 99, 306–7
understanding, 79, 109, 186–87
union: and angels, 265; with Creator, 73, 82; hypostatic, 237–38; of intellect and object, 61–62, 73, 82, 309; and the law of assimilation, 121; of persons, 109, 260; with the Trinity, 226; of two things produces a third thing, 115, 294
universe, x, 4, 114, 150–54; disorder and danger in, 281–84; after the Fall, 280–81; final cause or end of, 74, 141; formation of, 71–72, 114, 149–50; Greek idea of, 182–83; and human beings, 74, 120; love for, 194n44; and meaning, 180–82; perfections of, 192; personal, 59–60; two conceptions of, 177–80, 223–24. *See also* cosmos
Unmoved Mover, 182–83
Urban VIII, Pope, 93–94

Virgil, *Georgics*, 34
virtue, 8n10, 128, 131, 169, 229
Von Frisch, Karl, 69–70

Watson, James, 54
White, Andrew Dickson, 84, 90
Wilkins, Maurice, 54
will, 12, 120, 186, 310; and anaphysics, 303; in deification, 230, 241; emergence of, 300–301; free will, 194–96, 281–82, 301; God's will, 90, 214, 214n31, 227, 227n6, 261, 268n15, 294; in Jesus, 237–38; weakened by sin, 241
Wilson, Edward O., 134, 168; *Social Conquest of the Earth*, 134; *Sociobiology*, 134
wonder, 6, 314

Zizioulas, John, 214

DANIEL TOMA is a faculty member of the Department of Biological Sciences at Minnesota State University, Mankato. He earned a PhD in behavioral genetics from the University of Illinois at Urbana-Champaign.